PELICAN BOOKS

THE NEW INDUSTRIAL STATE

John Kenneth Galbraith, who was American Ambassador to India from 1961–3, is Paul M. Warburg Professor of Economics at Harvard University. He was born in 1908 in Canada, on a farm at Iona Station, Ontario. After graduating in agriculture at Toronto and taking a Ph.D. at the University of California, he became Social Science Research Council Fellow at Cambridge, Mass., and has taught at the Universities of California and Princeton.

During the war, at the American Office of Price Administration, he headed the wartime price control activities, and later was a director of the U.S. Strategic Bombing Survey and of the Office of Security Policy, receiving the Medal of Freedom and the President's Certificate of Merit for his work. Since the war he has been closely identified with the Democratic Party.

Professor Galbraith is well known as a contributor to leading American journals and reviews, and edits the 100-volume *Harvard Economic Studies*. His books include: *A Theory of Price Control*, *American Capitalism*, *The Affluent Society* (which held its place on the best-seller lists for some thirty weeks), *The Great Crash 1929*, *The Liberal Hour*, *The Non-potable Scotch*, and the present best-seller, *The New Industrial State*. He is also the author of a book of satirical sketches, *The McLandress Dimension*, the best-selling novel, *The Triumph*, and (with M. S. Randhawa) a study of Indian painting. He delivered the Reith Lectures in 1966.

The author, who is an enthusiastic skier, is married and has three sons. Much of his writing has been done in Switzerland and on an old farm in Vermont.

JOHN KENNETH GALBRAITH

The New Industrial State

PENGUIN BOOKS
IN ASSOCIATION WITH
HAMISH HAMILTON

Penguin Books Ltd, Harmondsworth, Middlesex, England
Penguin Books Australia Ltd, Ringwood, Victoria, Australia

—

First published in the U.S.A. 1967
Published in Great Britain by Hamish Hamilton 1967
Published in Pelican Books 1969

—

Copyright © John Kenneth Galbraith, 1967

—

Made and printed in Great Britain by
Hazell Watson & Viney Ltd,
Aylesbury, Bucks
Set in Linotype Times

FOR
ANDREA WILLIAMS

CONTENTS

	Foreword	9
1.	Change and the Industrial System	13
2.	The Imperatives of Technology	22
3.	The Nature of Industrial Planning	32
4.	Planning and the Supply of Capital	44
5.	Capital and Power	55
6.	The Technostructure	69
7.	The Corporation	81
8.	The Entrepreneur and the Technostructure	94
9.	A Digression on Socialism	106
10.	The Approved Contradiction	117
11.	The General Theory of Motivation	135
12.	Motivation in Perspective	146
13.	Motivation and the Technostructure	155
14.	The Principle of Consistency	165
15.	The Goals of the Industrial System	172
16.	Prices in the Industrial System	184
17.	Prices in the Industrial System (continued)	194
18.	The Management of Specific Demand	203
19.	The Revised Sequence	216
20.	The Regulation of Aggregate Demand	224
21.	The Nature of Employment and Unemployment	238
22.	The Control of the Wage-Price Spiral	251
23.	The Industrial System and the Union I	266
24.	The Industrial System and the Union II: The Ministerial Union	278
25.	The Educational and Scientific Estate	286
26.	The Industrial System and the State I	300
27.	The Industrial System and the State II	311
28.	A Further Summary	321

Contents

29. The Industrial System and the Cold War   328
30. The Further Dimensions   346
31. The Planning Lacunae   357
32. Of Toil   365
33. Education and Emancipation   372
34. The Political Lead   380
35. The Future of the Industrial System   389

An Addendum on Economic Method and the
    Nature of Social Argument   401

Index   413

FOREWORD

I STARTED this book nearly ten years ago and, in a sense, it started itself. What was to become *The Affluent Society* was nearing completion; principally missing, I imagine, was the note of spontaneity which comes into my writing in the fourth or fifth draft. Presently another and larger world began obtruding itself on my thoughts. This was a world of great corporations in which people increasingly served the convenience of these organizations which were meant to serve *them*. It was a world in which the motives of organization members seemed not to fit the standard textbook mould. Nor did the relationship between business and state. Nor did markets. Especially markets. So far from being the controlling power in the economy, markets were more and more accommodated to the needs and convenience of business organizations. Numerous writers had dealt with parts of this reality but without assuming larger change. I became persuaded, reluctantly, that these parts belonged, indeed, to a much greater and very closely articulated process of change.

I resisted these thoughts. The book on which I was working was too obviously one part of this movement. And, however unscientifically, one must accommodate task to talent. To tackle the larger task might mean never finishing the book in hand. Friends of mine, through a long life, have gained high academic credit for the perception and scope of their unpublished works and the vividness with which they describe them. But this is a special talent. I went ahead and published *The Affluent Society* and then settled down to try to see what I had only glimpsed.

I began also to accumulate some very great obligations. One was to the then Dean of the Harvard Faculty of Arts and Sciences, McGeorge Bundy, for allowing me to be absent for the greater part of two years while I studied organizations here and abroad and then, in Switzerland, sought to assemble the resulting ideas into a consistent whole. The Carnegie Corporation of New York helped with money (as did *The Affluent Society* which the Corporation had previously financed) and also with warm encouragement. Blessed by such leaders as John Gardner, now Secretary of Health, Education and Welfare, and James Perkins, now President of Cornell University, this has been the most imaginative and flexible of educational foundations. I pray that in the world to come these men have the shortest and least hideous punishment consistent with their past occupation. My Harvard colleagues are, I judge, reconciled to my habit of recommending highly responsible social conduct in my writing and evading my just responsibilities at the University. If they are not, I am even more grateful for they have been too agreeable to say.

At least until late middle age, all American authors of serious social purpose are required to thank their families for their forbearance and thus, more than incidentally, show that they have a wholesome family life. I am delighted to conform. I may report that my wife, Catherine, and my three sons have survived the strain of my labours quite remarkably and again seem well and happy.

I had nearly finished a preliminary draft of this book when President Kennedy asked me to go to India as his ambassador in 1961. With some misgiving I put the manuscript away in the vault of the bank. Only men of considerable vanity write books; consistently therewith, I worried lest the world were exchanging an irreplaceable author for a more easily purchasable diplomat. The danger was not as great as I imagined. I returned from India with some new thoughts and, in the end, a better view of the problem. I largely discarded the earlier manuscript. Had it not been for the diplomatic interlude, I might have published the more primitive version. Let every writer, if he cannot arrange a tour as ambassador before publishing, at least take a long reflective holiday.

I must again remind the reader that this book had its origins alongside *The Affluent Society*. It stands in relation to that book as a house to a window. This is the structure; the earlier book allowed the first glimpse inside. Anything that I covered in the earlier book and did not need for the present argument I have omitted or dismissed with brief mention. Thus with the evolution of economic ideas and associated goals, the problem of the balance between the public and private sectors of the economy, the notion of divorce of income from output, and the special problem of the poor in an industrial society. But a few of the ideas in the earlier book, notably the accommodation of consumer and public behaviour to the needs of producer organization, are indispensable and on a few other matters I have improved my view. In these cases I have thought it permissible to retrace some steps. The alternative is to send the reader back to the earlier book and such instructions, one senses, are poorly obeyed.

Two features of the exposition, one unavoidable and one deliberate, deserve a word. The first ten or so chapters lay the foundation for what follows. They are, unavoidably, somewhat more demanding than those that come after. I hope they will be found to have repaid the effort. The argument, it will be seen, proceeds for the first thirty chapters in progressive fashion. Much must be kept in mind. I have thought it useful, at intervals, to remind the reader of what has gone before. This is deliberate. The reader who finds these reminders redundant can take pleasure in reflecting that this is the price of exceptional memory and acuity.

Both the first manuscript and this one were under the skilled management of my indispensable ally in all literary matters, Andrea Williams. My debt to this informed, enthusiastic and loyal friend is simply immense. She has reduced by months the task of manuscript preparation and, for better or worse, added years to my life. Thus the grateful dedication. For skilful typing and retyping, along with a warm but agreeably irreverent interest in the subject, I am most grateful to Grace Johnson.

Like nearly everything else I have ever written, the manuscript of this book has been read by Arthur M. Schlesinger, Jr.

And with no small commitment to the need, he has advised and corrected me on many matters. I am very grateful. I have discussed numerous of the ideas herein with Professor Carl Kaysen and happily credit him with any number of the more meritorious. Carl Kaysen, now the head of the Institute for Advanced Study at Princeton, is one of those excellent men who have a genius for being published by other people. We who write more would have difficulty doing without them. At various points in the book I acknowledge help, direct or by way of their books, from my colleagues, Professors John Dunlop, Robert Dorfman and John Meyer. As with all who have worked on this range of matters at Harvard, I am in deep and continuing debt to Professor Edward S. Mason who also read the manuscript.

When he wrote his classic, *The General Theory of Employment Interest and Money*, John Maynard Keynes used the work of his great Cambridge colleague, Professor A. C. Pigou, as a point of departure for disagreement. He did so because it was the most distinguished exposition of the point of view. Without wishing to make too pretentious a comparison I have similarly on occasion used, and certainly for the same reason of distinction, the works of my colleague, Professor Robert Dorfman, and my old friend, Professor Paul Samuelson.

The background literature on the organization and structure of the American economy and the methods by which it is regulated is exceedingly voluminous and rich. It has occurred to me that the less experienced reader might wish to have the names of two books which I have myself found valuable and which give by far and away the best general view of the landscape. One is the brilliant small volume of my colleague, Professor Richard Caves, *American Industry: Structure, Conduct, Performance*. The other is the comprehensive and highly competent text of Professor Clair Wilcox of Swarthmore College, *Public Policies Toward Business*.

Chapter 1

CHANGE AND THE INDUSTRIAL SYSTEM

A CURIOSITY of modern economic life is the role of change. It is imagined to be very great; to list its forms or emphasize its extent is to show a reassuring grasp of the commonplace. Yet not much is supposed to change. The economic system of the United States is praised on all occasions of public ceremony as a largely perfect structure. This is so elsewhere also. It is not easy to perfect what has been perfected. There is massive change but, except as the output of goods increases, all remains as before.

As to the change there is no doubt. The innovations and alterations in economic life in the last seventy years, and more especially since the beginning of World War II, have, by any calculation, been great. The most visible has been the application of increasingly intricate and sophisticated technology to the production of things. Machines have replaced crude manpower. And increasingly, as they are used to instruct other machines, they replace the cruder forms of human intelligence.

Seventy years ago the corporation was still confined to those industries – railroading, steamboating, steel-making, petroleum recovery and refining, some mining – where, it seemed, production had to be on a large scale. Now it also sells groceries, mills grain, publishes newspapers and provides public entertainment, all activities that were once the province of the individual proprietor or the insignificant firm. The largest firms deploy billions of dollars' worth of equipment and hundreds of thousands of men in scores of locations to produce hundreds of products. The five hundred largest corporations produce close to half of all the goods and services that are available annually in the United States.

Seventy years ago the corporation was the instrument of its

owners and a projection of their personalities. The names of these principals – Carnegie, Rockefeller, Harriman, Mellon, Guggenheim, Ford – were known across the land. They are still known, but for the art galleries and philanthropic foundations they established and their descendants who are in politics. The men who now head the great corporations are unknown. Not for a generation have people outside Detroit and the automobile industry known the name of the current head of General Motors. In the manner of all men, he must produce identification when paying by cheque. So with Ford, Standard Oil and General Dynamics. The men who now run the large corporations own no appreciable share of the enterprise. They are selected not by the stockholders but, in the common case, by a Board of Directors which narcissistically they selected themselves.

Equally it is a commonplace that the relation of the state to the economy has changed. The services of Federal, state and local governments now account for between a fifth and a quarter of all economic activity. In 1929 it was about eight per cent. This far exceeds the government share in such an avowedly socialist state as India, considerably exceeds that in the anciently social democratic kingdoms of Sweden and Norway, and is not wholly incommensurate with the share in Poland, a communist country which, however, is heavily agricultural and which has left its agriculture in private ownership. A very large part (between one-third and one-half) of public activity is concerned with national defence and the exploration of space. This is not regarded even by conservatives as socialism. Elsewhere the nomenclature is less certain.

Additionally, in the wake of what is now called the Keynesian Revolution, the state undertakes to regulate the total income available for the purchase of goods and services in the economy. It seeks to ensure sufficient purchasing power to buy whatever the current labour force can produce. And, more tentatively and with considerably less sanction in public attitudes, it seeks, given the resulting high employment, to keep wages from shoving up prices and prices from forcing up wages in a persistent upward spiral. Perhaps as a result of these arrangements, and perhaps only to test man's capacity for feckless optimism, the production of goods in modern times has been notably high and remarkably reliable.

Previously, from the earliest appearance of capitalism until the beginning of Hitler's war, expansion and recession had followed each other, at irregular intervals, but in steady procession. The business cycle had become a separate subject of economic study; the forecasting of its course and the explanation of its irregularities had become a modest profession in which reason, divination, incantation and elements of witchcraft had been combined in a manner not elsewhere seen save in the primitive religions. In the two decades following World War II, there was no serious depression; from 1947 until this writing (1966) there has been only one year in which real income in the United States has failed to rise.

Three further changes are less intimately a part of the established litany of accomplishment. First, there has been a further massive growth in the apparatus of persuasion and exhortation that is associated with the sale of goods. In its cost and in the talent it commands, this activity is coming increasingly to rival the efforts devoted to the production of goods. Measurement of the exposure, and susceptibility, of human beings to this persuasion is itself a flourishing science.

Second, there has been the beginning of the decline of the trade union. Union membership in the United States reached a peak in 1956. Since then employment has continued to grow; union membership in the main has gone down. Friends of the labour movement, and those who depend on it for a livelihood, picture this downturn as temporary or cyclical. Quite a few others have not noticed it. There is a strong presumption that it is deeply rooted in related and deeper change.

Finally, there has been a large expansion in enrolment for higher education together with a somewhat more modest increase in the means for providing it. This has been attributed to a new and penetrating concern for popular enlightenment. As with the fall in union membership, it has deeper roots. Had the economic system need only for millions of unlettered proletarians, these, very plausibly, are what would be provided.

II

These changes or most of them have been much discussed. But to view them in isolation from each other, the usual practice, is greatly to minimize their effect. They are related to each other as cause to consequence. All are part of a yet larger matrix of change. In its effect on economic society this matrix has been more than the sum of its parts.

Thus mention has been made of machines and sophisticated technology. These require, in turn, heavy investment of capital. They are designed and guided by technically sophisticated men. They involve, also, a greatly increased elapse of time between any decision to produce and the emergence of a saleable product.

From these changes come the need and the opportunity for the large business organization. It alone can deploy the requisite capital; it alone can mobilize the requisite skills. It can also do more. The large commitment of capital and organization well in advance of result requires that there be foresight and also that all feasible steps be taken to ensure that what is foreseen will transpire. It can hardly be doubted that General Motors will be better able to influence the world around it – the prices and wages at which it buys and the prices at which it sells – than a man in suits and cloaks.

Nor is this all. The high production and income which are the fruits of advanced technology and expansive organization remove a very large part of the population from the compulsions and pressures of physical want. In consequence their economic behaviour becomes in some measure malleable. No hungry man who is also sober can be persuaded to use his last dollar for anything but food. But a well-fed, well-clad, well-sheltered and otherwise well-tended person can be persuaded as between an electric razor and an electric toothbrush. Along with prices and costs, consumer demand becomes subject to management. This adds an important further element of control over environment.

When investment in technological development is very high, a wrong technical judgement or a failure in persuading consumers to buy the product can be extremely expensive. The cost and associated risk can be greatly reduced if the state pays for more exalted technical development or guarantees a market for the technically advanced product. Suitable justification – national defence, the needs of national prestige, support to indispensable industries such as supersonic travel – can readily be found. Modern technology thus defines a growing function of the modern state.

And technology and associated requirements in capital and time lead even more directly to the regulation of demand by the state. A corporation, contemplating an automobile of revised aspect, must be able to persuade people to buy it. It is equally important that people be able to do so. This is vital where heavy advance commitments of time and money must be made and where the product could as easily come to market in a time of depression as of prosperity. So there must be stabilization of overall demand.

Affluence adds to the need for such stabilization of aggregate demand. A man who lives close to the margin of subsistence must spend to exist and what he spends is spent. A man with ample income can save, and there is no assurance that what he saves will be offset by the spending or investment of others. Moreover, a rich society owes its productivity and income, at least in part, to large-scale organization – to the corporation. Corporations also have the option of retaining or saving from earnings – and can exercise it with the unique sense of righteousness of men who are imposing thrift on others. There is no guarantee that this corporate saving will be offset by spending. In consequence, in a community of high well-being, spending and hence demand are less reliable than in a poor one. They lose their reliability precisely when high costs and the long period of gestation imposed by modern technology require greater certainty of markets. The Keynesian Revolution occurred at the moment in history when other change had made it indispensable. Like the other changes with which this chapter began, it is intimately a cause and consequence of yet other change.

III

In economics, unlike fiction and the theatre, there is no harm in a premature disclosure of the plot: it is to see the changes just mentioned and others as an interlocked whole. I venture to think that modern economic life is seen much more clearly when, as here, there is effort to see it whole.

I am also concerned to show how, in this larger context of change, the forces inducing human effort have changed. This assaults the most majestic of all economic assumptions, namely that man in his economic activities is subject to the authority of the market. Instead, we have an economic system which, whatever its formal ideological billing, is in substantial part a planned economy. The initiative in deciding what is to be produced comes not from the sovereign consumer who, through the market, issues the instructions that bend the productive mechanism to his ultimate will. Rather it comes from the great producing organization which reaches forward to control the markets that it is presumed to serve and, beyond, to bend the customer to its needs. And, in so doing, it deeply influences his values and beliefs – including not a few that will be mobilized in resistance to the present argument. One of the conclusions that follows from this analysis is that there is a broad convergence between industrial systems. The imperatives of technology and organization, not the images of ideology, are what determine the shape of economic society. This, on the whole, is fortunate although it will not necessarily be welcomed by those whose intellectual capital and moral fervour are invested in the present images of the market economy as the antithesis of social planning. Nor will it be welcomed by their disciples who, with lesser intellectual investment, carry the banners of free markets and free enterprise and therewith, by definition, of the free nations into political, military or diplomatic battle.

Nor will it be welcomed by those who identify planning exclusively with socialism. These are not, alas, the ideas of the consensus.

Nor is the good fortune unqualified. The subordination of belief to industrial necessity and convenience is not in accordance with the greatest vision of man. Nor is it entirely safe. On the nature of this subjugation, and its consequences, I also dwell at some length.

IV

The boundaries of a subject matter are conventional and artificial; none should use them as an excuse for excluding the important. Nor can one be indifferent to practical consequences of an effort such as this – whatever the tendency to celebrate such indifference as a manifestation of scientific detachment.

Accordingly, in the later chapters I turn to the effect of economic change on social and political behaviour, and to remedy and reform. As noted, I am led to the conclusion, which I trust others will find persuasive, that we are becoming the servants in thought, as in action, of the machine we have created to serve us. This is, in many ways, a comfortable servitude; some will look with wonder, and perhaps even indignation, on anyone who proposes escape. Some people are never content. I am concerned to suggest the general lines of emancipation. Otherwise we will allow economic goals to have an undue monopoly of our lives at the expense of other and more valuable concerns. What counts is not the quantity of our goods but the quality of life.

Our present method of underwriting advanced technology is exceedingly dangerous. It could cost us our existence. Here I suggest alternatives. There is also danger that our educational system will be too strongly in the service of economic goals. Here I suggest safeguards. The analysis leads to conclusions on the relation of the individual to his toil and the community to its planning. These are also discussed. And I deal with the unrealized political opportunities that are inherent in the dependence of the modern economy on trained and educated manpower. This all comes in the later chapters. The man who wants a political platform must obviously work his way up the stairs.

v

A year or two ago, the United States Department of Commerce, invading an activity hitherto reserved, at least in Democratic administrations, to private enterprise, published a small pamphlet setting forth the blessings of capitalism.[1] It illustrated these by describing the operations of a lemonade stand conducted by two children under the trees. This was in keeping with well-established practice in economic education which regularly holds that capitalism can best be understood by examining enterprises with little or no capital, guided by one person, without the complications of corporate structure and where there is no union. Economic life began with small firms, with small capital, each under the guiding hand of a single master. A systematic and internally consistent theory, that of the competitive firm in the market economy, is available for the explanation of such an economy. This lends itself well to pedagogy.

But this view of the economy is not sanctioned by reality. Nor is it sanctioned – a nostalgic and romantic minority apart – by economists. The changes mentioned earlier in this chapter have not spread themselves evenly over the economy. Agriculture, truck mines, painting, musical composition, much writing, the professions, some vice, handicrafts, some retail trade and a large number of repairing, cleaning, refurbishing, cosmetic and other household and personal services are still in the province of the individual proprietor. Capital, advanced technology, complex organization, and the other hallmarks of what we have come, not accidentally, to consider modern enterprise are limited or absent.

1. *Do You Know Your Economic A B C's? Profits in the American Economy*, United States Department of Commerce, 1965.

Change and the Industrial System

But this is not the heartland of the modern economy. Nor is it the theatre of the changes just mentioned. Nor is it, accordingly, the part of the economy which combines advanced technology with massive use of capital and of which the most conspicuous manifestation is the modern large corporation. Nearly all communications, nearly all production and distribution of electric power, much transportation, most manufacturing and mining, a substantial share of retail trade, and a considerable amount of entertainment are conducted or provided by large firms. The numbers are not great; we may think without error of most work being done by five or six hundred firms.

This is the part of the economy which, automatically, we identify with the modern industrial society. To understand it is to understand that part which is most subject to change and which, accordingly, is most changing our lives. No exercise of intelligence is to be deplored. But to understand the rest of the economy is to understand only that part which is diminishing in relative extent and which is most nearly static. It is to understand very little.

The two parts of the economy – the world of the few hundred technically dynamic, massively capitalized and highly organized corporations on the one hand and of the thousands of small and traditional proprietors on the other – are very different. It is not a difference of degree but a difference which invades every aspect of economic organization and behaviour, including the motivation to effort itself. It will be convenient, even in advance of more exact formulation, to have a name for the part of the economy which is characterized by the large corporations. One is readily at hand; I shall refer to it as the Industrial System. The industrial system, in turn, is the dominant feature of the New Industrial State. The latter, the larger frame – the house as well as its contents – provides the title for this book.

Chapter 2

THE IMPERATIVES OF TECHNOLOGY

ON 16 June 1903, after some months of preparation which included negotiation of contracts for various components, the Ford Motor Company was formed for the manufacture of automobiles. Production was to be whatever number could be sold. The first car reached the market that October. The firm had an authorized capital of $150,000. However, only $100,000 worth of stock was issued, and only $28,500 of this was for cash. Although it does not bear on the present discussion, the company made a handsome profit that year and did not fail to do so for many years thereafter. Employment in 1903 averaged 125 men.[1]

In the spring of 1964, the Ford Motor Company introduced what is now called a new automobile. In accordance with current fashion in automobile nomenclature, it was called, one trusts inappropriately, a Mustang. The public was well prepared for the new vehicle. Plans carefully specified prospective output and sales; they erred, as plans do, and in this case by being too modest. These preparations required three and a half years. From late in the autumn of 1962, when the design was settled, until the spring of 1964, there was a fairly firm commitment to the particular car that eventually emerged. Engineering and 'styling' costs were nine million dollars; the cost of tooling up for the production of the Mustang was fifty million dollars.[2] In 1964 employment in the Ford Motor Com-

1. Allan Nevins, *Ford, The Times, The Man, The Company* (New York: Scribner, 1954), pp. 220 et seq., and appendix.
2. I am grateful to Mr Walter T. Murphy of the Ford Motor Company for providing these details. In this and subsequent chapters, I have also drawn on earlier help of Robert McNamara which he gave when he was still an executive of Ford. I wish here, at the outset, not only to concede but to emphasize that one may have planning without precision of result and that there will also be occasional failures. Accordingly, to cite a

pany averaged 317,000. Assets were approximately six billion dollars.[3]

Virtually all of the effects of increased use of technology are revealed by these comparisons. We may pass them in preliminary review.

II

Technology means the systematic application of scientific or other organized knowledge to practical tasks. Its most important consequence, at least for purposes of economics, is in forcing the division and subdivision of any such task into its component parts. Thus, and only thus, can organized knowledge be brought to bear on performance.

Specifically, there is no way that organized knowledge can be brought to bear on the production of an automobile as a whole or even on the manufacture of a body or chassis. It can only be applied if the task is so subdivided that it begins to be coterminous with some established area of scientific or engineering knowledge. Though metallurgical knowledge cannot be applied to the manufacture of the whole vehicle, it can be used in the design of the cooling system or the engine block. While knowledge of mechanical engineering cannot be brought to bear on the manufacture of the vehicle, it can be applied to the machining of the crankshaft. While chemistry cannot be applied to the composition of the car as a whole, it can be used to decide on the composition of the finish or trim.

Nor do matters stop here. Metallurgical knowledge is brought to bear not on steel but on the characteristics of special steels for particular functions, and chemistry not on paints or plastics but on particular molecular structures and their rearrangement as required.[4]

---

failure – another Ford creation, the Edsel, comes automatically to the mind of the more impulsive critics – is not to disprove this argument.

3. 'The 500 Largest U.S. Industrial Corporations', *The Fortune Directory*, August 1964.

4. The notion of division of labour, an old one in economics, is a rudimentary and partial application of the ideas here outlined. As one

Nearly all of the consequences of technology, and much of the shape of modern industry, derive from this need to divide and subdivide tasks and from the further need to bring knowledge to bear on these fractions and from the final need to combine the finished elements of the task into the finished product as a whole. Six consequences are of immediate importance.

First. An increasing span of time separates the beginning from the completion of any task. Knowledge is brought to bear on the ultimate microfraction of the task; then on that in combination with some other fraction; then on some further combination and thus on to final completion. The process stretches back in time as the root system of a plant goes down into the ground. The longest of the filaments determines the total time required in production. The more thoroughgoing the application of technology – in common or at least frequent language, the more sophisticated the production process – the farther back the application of knowledge will be carried. The longer, accordingly, will be the time between the initiation and completion of the task.

The manufacture of the first Ford was not an exacting process. Metallurgy was an academic concept. Ordinary steels were used that could be obtained from the warehouse in the morning and shaped that afternoon. In consequence, the span of time between initiation and completion of a car was very slight.

The provision of steel for the modern vehicle, in contrast, reaches back to specifications prepared by the designers or the

---

breaks down a mechanical operation, such as the manufacture of Adam Smith's immortal pins, it resolves itself into simpler and simpler movements as in putting the head or the point on the pin. This is the same as saying that the problem is susceptible to increasingly homogeneous mechanical knowledge.

However, the subdivision of tasks to accord with area of organized knowledge is not confined to, nor has it any special relevance to, mechanical processes. It occurs in medicine, business management, building design, child and dog rearing and every other problem that involves an agglomerate of scientific knowledge.

laboratory, and proceeds through orders to the steel mill, parallel provision for the appropriate metal-working machinery, delivery, testing, and use.

Second. There is an increase in the capital that is committed to production aside from that occasioned by increased output. The increased time, and therewith the increased investment in goods in process, costs money. So does the knowledge which is applied to the various elements of the task. The application of knowledge to an element of a manufacturing problem will also typically involve the development of a machine for performing the function. (The word technology brings to mind machines; this is not surprising for machinery is one of its most visible manifestations.) This too involves investment as does equipment for integrating the various elements of the task into the final product.

The investment in making the original Ford was larger than the $28,500 paid in, for some of it was in the plant, inventory and machinery of those who, like the Dodge Brothers, supplied the components. But investment in the factory itself was infinitesimal. Materials and parts were there only briefly; no expensive specialists gave them attention; only elementary machinery was used to assemble them into the car. It helped that the frame of the car could be lifted by two men.

Third. With increasing technology the commitment of time and money tends to be made ever more inflexibly to the performance of a particular task. That task must be precisely defined before it is divided and subdivided into its component parts. Knowledge and equipment are then brought to bear on these fractions and they are useful only for the task as it was initially defined. If that task is changed, new knowledge and new equipment will have to be brought to bear.

Little thought needed to be given to the Dodge Brothers' machine shop, which made the engine and chassis of the original Ford, as an instrument for automobile manufacture. It was unspecialized as to task. It could have worked as well on bicycles, steam engines or carriage gear and, indeed, had been so employed. Had Ford and his associates decided, at any point, to shift from gasoline to steam power, the machine shop could have accommodated itself to the change in a few hours.

By contrast all parts of the Mustang, the tools and equipment that worked on these parts, and the steel and other materials going into these parts were designed to serve efficiently their ultimate function. They could serve only that function. Were the car appreciably altered, were it instead of a Mustang a Barracuda or possibly a Serpent, Scorpion or Roach, as one day with decent imagination there will be, much of this work would have had to be redone. Thus the firm commitment to this particular vehicle for some eighteen months prior to its appearance.

Fourth. Technology requires specialized manpower. This will be evident. Organized knowledge can be brought to bear, not surprisingly, only by those who possess it. However, technology does not make the only claim on manpower; planning, to be mentioned in a moment, also requires a comparatively high level of specialized talent. To foresee the future in all its dimensions and to design the appropriate action does not necessarily require high scientific qualification. It does require ability to organize and employ information, or capacity to react intuitively to relevant experience.

These requirements do not necessarily reflect, on some absolute scale, a higher order of talent than was required in a less technically advanced era. The makers of the original Ford were men of talent. The Dodge Brothers had previously invented a bicycle and a steam launch. Their machine shop made a wide variety of products, and Detroit legend also celebrated their imaginative exuberance when drunk. Alexander Malcolmson, who was Ford's immediate partner in getting the business under way, was a successful coal merchant. James Couzens, who may well have had more to do with the success of the enterprise than Henry Ford,[5] had a background in railroading and the coal business and went on from Ford to be Police Commissioner and Mayor of Detroit, Republican Senator from

5. A case I have argued elsewhere. Cf. 'Was Ford a Fraud?' in *The Liberal Hour* (Boston: Houghton, 1960), pp. 141 et seq.

Michigan and an undeviating supporter of Franklin D. Roosevelt. Not all of the present Ford organization would claim as much reach. But its members do have a considerably deeper knowledge of the more specialized matters for which they are severally responsible.

Fifth. The inevitable counterpart of specialization is organization. This is what brings the work of specialists to a coherent result. If there are many specialists, this coordination will be a major task. So complex, indeed, will be the job of organizing specialists that there will be specialists on organization. More even than machinery, massive and complex business organizations are the tangible manifestations of advanced technology.

Sixth. From the time and capital that must be committed, the inflexibility of this commitment, the needs of large organization and the problems of market performance under conditions of advanced technology, comes the necessity for planning. Tasks must be performed so that they are right not for the present but for that time in the future when, companion and related work having also been done, the whole job is completed. And the amount of capital that, meanwhile, will have been committed adds urgency to this need to be right. So conditions at the time of completion of the whole task must be foreseen as must developments along the way. And steps must be taken to prevent, offset or otherwise neutralize the effect of adverse developments, and to ensure that what is ultimately foreseen eventuates in fact.

In the early days of Ford, the future was very near at hand. Only days elapsed between the commitment of machinery and materials to production and their appearance as a car. If the future is near at hand, it can be assumed that it will be very much like the present. If the car did not meet the approval of the customers, it could quickly be changed. The briefness of the time in process allowed this; so did the unspecialized character of manpower, materials and machinery.

Changes were needed. The earliest cars, as they came on the market, did not meet with complete customer approval: there were complaints that the cooling system did not cool, the brakes did not brake, the carburettor did not feed fuel to the engine, and a Los Angeles dealer reported the disconcerting discovery that, when steered, 'Front wheels turn wrong.'[6] These defects were promptly remedied. They did the reputation of the car no lasting harm.

Such shortcomings in the Mustang would have been unpleasant. And they would have been subject to no such quick, simple and inexpensive remedy. The machinery, materials, manpower and components of the original Ford, being all unspecialized, could be quickly procured on the open market. Accordingly, there was no need to anticipate possible shortage of these requirements and take steps to prevent them. For the more highly specialized requirements of the Mustang, foresight and associated action were indispensable. In Detroit, when the first Ford was projected, anything on wheels that was connected with a motor was assured of acceptance. Acceptance of the Mustang could not be so assumed. The prospect had to be carefully appraised. And customers had to be carefully conditioned to want this blessing. Thus the need for planning.

III

The more sophisticated the technology, the greater, in general, will be all of the foregoing requirements. This will be true of simple products as they come to be produced by more refined processes or as they develop imaginative containers or unopenable packaging. With very intricate technology, such as that associated with modern weapons and weaponry, there will be a quantum change in these requirements. This will be especially so if, as under modern peacetime conditions, cost and time are not decisive considerations.

Thus when Philip II settled on the redemption of England at the end of March 1587, he was not unduly troubled by the seemingly serious circumstance that Spain had no navy. Some men-of-war were available from newly conquered Portugal but,

6. Nevins, op. cit., p. 248.

in the main, merchant ships would suffice.[7] A navy, in other words, could then be bought in the market. Nor was the destruction of a large number of the available ships by Drake at Cadiz three weeks later a fatal blow. Despite what historians have usually described as unconscionable inefficiency, the Armada sailed in a strength of 130 ships a little over a year later on 18 May 1588. The cost, though considerable, was well within the resources of the Empire. Matters did not change greatly in the next three hundred years. The *Victory*, from which Nelson called Englishmen to their duty at Trafalgar, though an excellent fighting ship, was a full forty years old at the time. The exiguous flying machines of World War I, built only to carry a man or two and a weapon, were designed and put in combat in a matter of months.

To create a modern fleet of the numerical size of the Armada, with aircraft carriers, and appropriate complement of aircraft, nuclear submarines and missiles, auxiliary and supporting craft and bases and communications, would take a first-rate industrial power a minimum of twenty years. Though modern Spain is rich beyond the dreams of its monarchs in its most expansive age, it could not for a moment contemplate such an enterprise. In World War II, no combat plane that had not been substantially designed before the outbreak of hostilities saw major service. Since then the lead time for comparable *matériel* has become yet greater. In general, individuals in late middle age stand in little danger of weapons now being designed; they are a menace only to the unborn and the uncontemplated.

IV

It is a commonplace of modern technology that there is a high measure of certainty that problems have solutions before there is knowledge of how they are to be solved. As this is written in 1966, it is reasonably certain that a man can be landed on

7. Instructions issued from the Escorial on 31 March. Cf. Garrett Mattingly, *The Armada* (Boston: Houghton, 1959), p. 80. Philip had, of course, been contemplating the enterprise for some years.

the moon within the next five years. However, many of the details of the procedure for doing so are not yet worked out. It is certain that air and water pollution can be more effectively controlled for those who, for better or worse, must remain on this planet. Uncertainty continues as to the best methods of doing so. It is probable that commuters can be moved in safety and some comfort into American cities. How this will be accomplished is still to be determined.

If methods of performing the specified task have been fully resolved, it follows that the need for bringing organized intelligence to bear will be less than if the methods are still uncertain. And this uncertainty will also lead to increased time and cost; the increase can be very great. Uncertainty as to the properties of the metal to be used for the skin of a supersonic transport; uncertainty therefore as to the proper way of handling and working the metal; uncertainty therefore as to the character and design of the equipment required to work it can add extravagantly to the time and cost of obtaining such a vehicle. This problem-solving, with its high costs in time and money, is a recognized feature of modern technology. It graces all modern economic discussion under the cachet of *Research and Development*.

The need for planning, it has been said, arises from the long period of time that elapses during the production process, the high investment that is involved and the inflexible commitment of that investment to the particular task. In the case of advanced military equipment, time, cost and inflexibility of commitment are all very great. Time and outlay will be even greater where, a common characteristic of weaponry, design is uncertain and where, accordingly, there must be added expenditure for research and development. In these circumstances, planning is both essential and difficult. It is essential because of the time that is involved, the money that is at risk, the number of things that can go wrong and the magnitude of the possible ensuing disaster. It is difficult because of the number and size of the eventualities that must be controlled.

One answer is to have the state absorb the major risks. It can provide or guarantee a market for the product. And it can underwrite the costs of development so that if they increase beyond expectation the firm will not have to carry them. Or it can pay for and make available the necessary technical knowledge. The drift of this argument will be evident. Technology, under all circumstances, leads to planning; in its higher manifestations it may put the problems of planning beyond the reach of the industrial firm. Technological compulsions, and not ideology or political wile, will require the firm to seek the help and protection of the state. This is a consequence of advanced technology of no small interest, and to which we shall return.

In examining the intricate complex of economic change, technology, having an initiative of its own, is the logical point at which to break in. But technology not only causes change, it is a response to change. Though it forces specialization it is also the result of specialization. Though it requires extensive organization it is also the result of organization. The changes stimulated by technology, slightly reordered for purposes of exposition, are nonetheless the themes of the ensuing chapters. First we shall look more closely at the effect of requirements of time and capital on industrial planning. Thereafter we shall look at the source and role of the capital which it employs in such large amounts. And then we shall examine the role of specialized manpower and its organization. Nor will this be the end. These themes, planning, specialization and organization, like the military symbolism of marching and combat in Protestant hymns and college sports, will recur throughout the book.

Chapter 3

THE NATURE OF INDUSTRIAL PLANNING

UNTIL the end of World War II, or shortly thereafter, planning was a moderately evocative word in the United States. It implied a sensible concern for what might happen in the future and a disposition, by forehanded action, to forestall avoidable misfortune. As persons won credit for competent planning of their lives, so communities won credit for effective planning of their environment. It was thought good to live in a well-planned city. The United States government had a National Resources Planning Board. During the war, postwar planning acquired the status of a modest industry in both the United States and the United Kingdom; it was felt that it would reassure those who were fighting as to their eventual utility as civilians.

With the Cold War, however, the word planning acquired ideological overtones. The communist countries not only socialized property, which seemed not a strong likelihood in the United States, but they planned, which somehow seemed more of a danger. Since liberty was there circumscribed, it followed that planning was something that the libertarian society should avoid. Modern liberalism carefully emphasizes tact rather than clarity of speech. Accordingly it avoided the term and conservatives made it one of opprobrium. For a public official to be called an economic planner was less serious than to be charged with communism or imaginative perversion, but it reflected adversely nonetheless. One accepted and cherished whatever eventuated from the untrammelled operation of the market. Not only concern for liberty but a reputation for economic hardihood counselled such a course.

For understanding the economy and policy of the United States and other advanced industrial countries, this reaction against the word planning could hardly have been worse timed.

It occurred when the increased use of technology and the accompanying commitment of time and capital were forcing extensive planning on all industrial communities. This has now been sensed. And, in many quarters, the word planning is again acquiring a measure of respectability.

Still what is not supposed to exist is often imagined not to exist. In consequence, the role of planning in the modern industrial society remains only slightly appreciated. Additionally, it is the sound instinct of conservatives that economic planning involves, inevitably, the control of individual behaviour. The denial that we do any planning has helped to conceal the fact of such control even from those who are controlled.

II

In the market economy the price that is offered is counted upon to produce the result that is sought. Nothing more need be done. The consumer, by his offer to pay, obtains the necessary responding action by the firm that supplies his needs. By offering to pay yet more he gets more. And the firm, in its turn, by similar offers gets the labour, materials and equipment that it requires for production.

Planning exists because this process has ceased to be reliable. Technology, with its companion commitment of time and capital, means that the needs of the consumer must be anticipated – by months or years. When the distant day arrives the consumer's willingness to buy may well be lacking. By the same token, while common labour and carbon steel will be forthcoming in response to a promise to pay, the specialized skills and arcane materials required by advanced technology cannot similarly be counted upon. The needed action in both instances is evident: in addition to deciding what the consumer will want and will pay, the firm must take every feasible step to see that what it decides to produce is wanted by the consumer at a remunerative price. And it must see that the labour, materials and equipment that it needs will be available at a cost consistent with the price it will receive. It must exercise control over what is sold. It must exercise control over what is supplied. It must replace the market with planning.

That, as more time elapses and more capital is committed, it will be increasingly risky to rely on the untutored responses of the consumer needs no elaboration. And this will be increasingly so the more technically sophisticated the product. There is a certain likelihood that even two or three years hence there will be a fairly reliable consumer demand for strawberries, milk and fresh eggs. There is no similar assurance that people will want, so spontaneously, an automobile of particular colour, or contour, or a transistor of particular size or design.

The effect of technology, and related change, in reducing the reliability of the market for labour or equipment and in making imperative the planning of their procurement, is equally clear and can be seen in the simplest case.[1] If men use picks and shovels to build a road, they can be called out on the same morning that the decision is taken to do the job. The picks and shovels serve a variety of purposes; accordingly, the market stocks them in readily available quantities. It will help in getting manpower if, as Marx thought necessary, there is an industrial reserve army of the unemployed. But an equally prompt beginning is possible by raiding the work force of another employer of unskilled labour with the simple market promise of more pay.

When specifications are raised to modern superhighway standards and heavy machinery is introduced, the market no longer works as well. Engineers, draftsmen, drainage experts and those who arrange the elimination of trees, grass, parkland, streams and the other environmental amenities may not be readily available even in response to a substantial advance in pay. Bulldozers and heavy earth-moving equipment cannot be

1. In technical terms the supply price of highly specialized materials, components and labour is inelastic. So is the demand for highly technical products. In the first instance large (and punishing) increases in prices will bring no added supply. In the second case large (and equally punishing) decreases will bring no added customers.

bought with the same facility as picks and shovels. In all of these cases anticipatory steps must be taken to ensure that the necessary supply is available at an appropriate wage or price. Market behaviour must be modified by some measure of planning.[2]

For inertial systems engineers, digital circuit design specialists, superconductivity research specialists, aeroelasticity investigators and radio test and evaluation engineers as also for titanium alloys in comparison with steel, and space vehicles as compared with motor-cycles, the market is greatly less dependable. Need must be elaborately anticipated and arranged. The language of both industry and government reflects the modern fact. Civil War quartermasters went into the market for their needs. So, in turn, did the contractors who filled these orders. The equivalent procurement would now be programmed.

As viewed by the industrial firm, planning consists in foreseeing the actions required between the initiation of production and its completion and preparing for the accomplishment of these actions. And it consists also of foreseeing, and having a design for meeting, any unscheduled developments, favourable or otherwise, that may occur along the way.[3] As planning is viewed by the economist, political scientist or pundit, it consists of replacing prices and the market as the mechanism for determining what will be produced, with an authoritative determination of what will be produced and consumed and at what price. It will be thought that the word planning is being used in two different senses.

2. That planning is necessary does not mean that it is well done. At any given time on any particular construction site, as everyone has observed, nothing much is happening. Planning, to anticipate and arrange material, machinery, manpower and subcontractor requirements, is necessary. But, in context, it is done with great imprecision or incompetence. Accordingly, something is normally being awaited.

3. 'In practice [business management] ... aims to minimize uncertainty, minimize the consequences of uncertainty, or both.' Robin Marris, *The Economic Theory of 'Managerial' Capitalism* (New York: The Free Press of Glencoe, 1964), p. 232.

In practice, however, the two kinds of planning, if such they may be called, are inextricably associated. A firm cannot usefully foresee and schedule future action or prepare for contingencies if it does not know what its prices will be, what its sales will be, what its costs including labour and capital costs will be and what will be available at these costs. If the market is unreliable, it will not know these things. Hence it cannot plan. If, with advancing technology and associated specialization, the market becomes increasingly unreliable, industrial planning will become increasingly impossible unless the market also gives way to planning. Much of what the firm regards as planning consists in minimizing or getting rid of market influences.

III

A variety of strategies are available for dealing with the increasing unreliability of markets. Not all, in fact, require their replacement. If the item is unimportant, market uncertainty can be ignored. For General Electric it is a matter of considerable interest to know the price at which it will be able to buy high alloy steel or sell large generators, and the quantities that will be forthcoming or which can be sold. No similar urgency attaches to knowledge of the price at which flatware will be available for the plant cafeterias. And size is a solvent for uncertainty that cannot otherwise be eliminated. In the late nineteen-fifties and early nineteen-sixties, the Convair Division of General Dynamics Corporation lost $425 million on the manufacture of jet transports. Part of this was the result of uncertainties associated with research and development; its 880 and 990 passenger jets cost more to bring into being than expected. But a major factor was the failure of the market – or more precisely default on or failure to obtain the contracts that were meant to reduce market uncertainty. The company did not fail (although it was a near thing) because it had annual revenues of around $2 billion from – in addition to aircraft – such diverse artifacts as missiles, building materials, submarines and telephones.[4] None of these was affected by the misfortunes of Convair. For a smaller company, with one product, a $425 million loss would have been uncomfortable. We have here an important explanation of one of the more notable corporate developments of recent times, the growth of the so-called polyglot corporation. It combines great size with highly diverse lines of manufacture. Thus it can absorb the adverse consequences of uncertainty that cannot otherwise be eliminated. Uncontrolled aversion of customers to one product, such as aircraft, is unlikely to affect telephones or building materials. The effects of market uncertainty are thus contained in what will often be a relatively small part of the total planning unit.

But the more common strategies require that the market be replaced by an authoritative determination of price and the amounts to be sold or bought at these prices. There are three ways of doing this:

(1) The market can be superseded.
(2) It can be controlled by sellers or buyers.
(3) It can be suspended for definite or indefinite periods by contract between the parties to sale and purchase.

All of these strategies are familiar features of the industrial system.

IV

The market is superseded by what is commonly called vertical integration. The planning unit takes over the source of supply or the outlet; a transaction that is subject to bargaining over prices and amounts is thus replaced with a transfer within the planning unit. Where a firm is especially dependent on an important material or product – as an oil company on crude petroleum, a steel firm on ore,[5] an aluminium company on bauxite or Sears, Roebuck on appliances – there is always

4. Richard Austin Smith, *Corporations in Crisis* (New York: Doubleday, 1963), pp. 91 et seq. The company's misfortunes in the sale of aircraft were intimately bound up with the contemporary difficulties of Howard Hughes at TWA.

5. This problem has been of importance in the difficulties experienced in recent years by Wheeling Steel, a non-integrated producer. 'Thus under

danger that the requisite supplies will be available only at inconvenient prices. To have control of supply – to rely not on the market but on its own sources of supply – is an elementary safeguard. This does not eliminate market uncertainty; rather, the large and unmanageable uncertainty as to the price of ore or crude is replaced by the smaller, more diffuse and more manageable uncertainties as to the costs of labour, drilling, ore transport and yet more remote raw materials. But this is a highly beneficial exchange. For Socony-Vacuum or Sohio, a change in the cost of crude is a serious matter, a change in the cost of drilling equipment a detail.

As viewed by the firm, elimination of a market converts an external negotiation and hence a partially or wholly uncontrollable decision to a matter for purely internal decision. Nothing, we shall see, better explains modern industrial policy in regard to capital and labour than the desire to make these highly strategic cost factors subject to purely internal decision.

Markets can also be controlled. This consists in reducing or eliminating the independence of action of those to whom the planning unit sells or from whom it buys. Their behaviour being subject to control, uncertainty as to that behaviour is reduced. At the same time the outward form of the market, including the process of buying and selling, remains formally intact.

This control of markets is the counterpart of large size and large size in relation to the particular market. A Wisconsin dairy farm cannot influence the price that it pays for fertilizer or machinery. Being small, its decision to purchase or not to purchase is of no appreciable significance to the supplier. The same is true of its sales. Having no control over its suppliers or its customers it pays and receives the going prices.

Not so with General Motors. Its decision to buy or not to

_____

its contracts Wheeling in the late 1950s and early 1960s found itself powerless to trim ore supplies as sales fluctuated. ... Moreover by the early 1960s the operating efficiencies of using beneficiated ores ... were fully apparent, but Wheeling, tied to outmoded sources of supply, lagged behind many in the industry in using such ores.' *Fortune*, June 1965.

buy will usually be very important to its suppliers; it may be a matter of survival. This induces a highly cooperative posture. So with any large firm.[6] Should it be necessary to press matters, General Motors, unlike the dairyman, has always the possibility of supplying a material or component to itself. The option of eliminating a market is an important source of power for controlling it.[7]

Similarly, size allows General Motors as a seller to set prices for automobiles, diesels, trucks, refrigerators and the rest of its offering and be secure in the knowledge that no individual buyer, by withdrawing its custom, can force a change. The fact that G.M. is one of a few sellers adds to its control. Each seller shares the common interest in secure and certain prices;

6. Economists, in the past, have been at pains to disassociate large absolute size from large size in relation to the particular market. 'Concentration [i.e. small numbers and hence large size in relation to the market] has nothing to do with size of firms, no matter by what resounding name it is called – big business, colossal corporation, financial giantism, etc. ... most of my fellow economists would agree that "absolute size is absolutely irrelevant".' M. A. Adelman, Hearings before the Subcommittee on Antitrust and Monopoly of the Committee on the Judiciary, United States Senate, Eighty-Eighth Congress, Second Session, Pursuant to S. Res. 262, Part I. *Economic Concentration. Overall and Conglomerate Aspects* (1964), p. 228. This contention, although wrong, is deeply grounded in contemporary economic attitudes.

Market power is associated by economists not with planning but with monopoly. Market concentration or monopoly in the conventional view is inimical to efficient employment of resources by the market and has strong overtones of illegality. If big business and monopoly power tend to be identical, then all big business is inefficient and presumptively illegal. This, however, given the evident role of large firms in the modern economy, is absurd. So disassociation of absolute from relative size is important if traditional antipathy to monopoly is to seem sensible and big business is to be legitimate. In fact, large absolute size and large size relative to the market do go together. Great firms – General Motors, Standard Oil, Ford, United States Steel – are invariably large in relation to their principal markets. On this see the sensible remarks of Carl Kaysen. 'The Corporation: How Much Power? What Scope?' in *The Corporation in Modern Society*, Edward S. Mason, ed. (Cambridge: Harvard University Press, 1959), p. 89.

7. There are similar, although more complex, possibilities for control of the labour market to which I will return.

it is to the advantage of none to disrupt this mutual security system. Competitors of General Motors are especially unlikely to initiate price reductions that might provoke further and retributive price-cutting. No formal communication is necessary to prevent such actions; this is considered naïve and arouses the professional wrath of company counsel. Everyone knows that the survivor of such a contest would be not the aggressor but General Motors. Thus do size and small numbers of competitors lead to market regulation.

Control of prices is only a part of market control; if uncertainty is to be eliminated there must also be control of the amount sold. But size also makes this possible. It allows advertising, a well-nurtured sales organization and careful management of product design which can help to ensure the needed customer response. And since General Motors produces some half of all the automobiles, its designs do not reflect the current mode, but are the current mode. The proper shape of an automobile, for most people, will be what the automobile majors decree the current shape to be. The control of demand, as we shall see later, is not perfect. But what is imperfect is not unimportant for reducing market uncertainty.

Finally, in an economy where units are large, firms can eliminate market uncertainty for each other. This they do by entering into contracts specifying prices and amounts to be provided or bought for substantial periods of time. A long-term contract by a Wisconsin dairy farmer to buy fertilizer or sell milk accords no great certainty to the fertilizer dealer or the dairy receiving the milk. It is subject to the capacity of the farmer to fulfil it; death, accident, drought, high feed costs and contagious abortion can all supervene. But a contract with the United States Steel Corporation to supply sheet steel or to take electric power is extremely reliable. In a world of large firms, it follows, there can be a matrix of contracts by which each firm eliminates market uncertainty for other firms and, in turn, gives to them some of its own.

Outside of the industrial system, most notably in agriculture, the government also intervenes extensively to set prices and ensure demand and thus to suspend the operation of the market and eliminate market uncertainty. This it does because the participating units – the individual farms – are not large enough to control prices. Technology and the associated commitment of capital and time require nonetheless that there be stable prices and assured demand.[8] But within the industrial system, similar action is also required where exacting technology, with extensive research and development, mean a very long production period and a very large commitment of capital. Such is the case in the development and supply of modern weapons, in the exploration of space and in the development of a growing range of modern civilian products or services including transport planes, high-speed ground transport and various applied uses of nuclear energy. Here the state guarantees a price sufficient, with suitable margin, to cover costs. And it undertakes to buy what is produced or to compensate fully in the case of contract cancellation. Thus, effectively, it suspends the market with all associated uncertainty. One consequence, as we shall see, is that in areas of most exacting and advanced technology the market is most completely replaced and planning is therefore most secure. As a further consequence this has become for the participants a very attractive part of the industrial system. The fully planned economy, so far from being unpopular, is warmly regarded by those who know it best.

V

Two things of some interest are evident from this analysis. It is clear, first of all, that industrial planning is in unabashed alliance with size. The large organization can tolerate market uncertainty as a smaller firm cannot. It can contract out of it as the smaller firm cannot. Vertical integration, the control of prices and consumer demand and reciprocal absorption of market uncertainty by contracts between firms all favour the large enterprise. And while smaller firms can appeal to the state to fix prices and ensure demand, this security is also provided

8. See below, Chapters 16 and 17.

by the state to the big industrial firm when it is most needed. Those circumstances – the exacting technology, large commitments of time and capital – make it fairly certain that most of this government work will be done by large organizations.[9]

By all but the pathologically romantic, it is now recognized that this is not the age of the small man. But there is still a lingering presumption among economists that his retreat is not before the efficiency of the great corporation, or even its technological proficiency, but before its monopoly power. It has superior capacity to extract profits. Therein lies its advantage. 'Big business will undertake only such innovations as promise to enhance its profits and power, or protect its market position . . . free competitive men have always been the true innovators. Under the stern discipline of competition they must innovate to prosper and to survive.'[10]

This, by the uncouth, would be called drivel. Size is the general servant of technology, not the special servant of profits. The small firm cannot be restored by breaking the power of

9. In 1960, 384 firms with 5,000 employees or more accounted for an estimated 85 per cent of all industrial research-and-development expenditure. Firms employing fewer than 1,000 people, though numbering 260,000, accounted for only 7 per cent of such expenditure. An estimated 65 per cent of these funds were supplied by the Federal Government. (M. A. Adelman, Hearings before the Subcommittee on Antitrust and Monopoly of the Committee on the Judiciary, United States Senate, Eighty-Ninth Congress, First Session, Pursuant to S. Res. 70, Part III. *Economic Concentration. Concentration, Invention and Innovation* [1965], pp. 1137, 1140.) In recent years the high degree of market security in the use of Federal funds – a secure coverage of all costs and a secure market for the product – has allowed a considerable number of small firms to enter the manufacture of highly technical products. These firms line highways adjacent to major educational centres, most notably in Massachusetts and California, and have encouraged the belief that the small firm has a major foothold in the manufacture of highly technical products and components particularly for defence and space exploration. Their share of the total is, in fact, negligible.

10. Horace M. Gray, Hearings before the Subcommittee on Antitrust and Monopoly of the Committee on the Judiciary, United States Senate, Eighty-Ninth Congress, First Session, Pursuant to S. Res. 70, Part III. *Economic Concentration. Concentration, Invention and Innovation* (1965), p. 1164.

the larger ones. It would require, rather, the rejection of the technology which since earliest consciousness we are taught to applaud. It would require that we have simple products made with simple equipment from readily available materials by unspecialized labour. Then the period of production would be short; the market would reliably provide the labour, equipment and materials required for production; there would be neither possibility nor need for managing the market for the finished product. If the market thus reigned there would be, and could be, no planning. No elaborate organization would be required. The small firm would then, at last, do very well. All that is necessary is to undo nearly everything that, at whatever violence to meaning, has been called progress in the last half century. There must be no thought of supersonic travel, or exploring the moon, and there will not be many automobiles.

We come thus to the second conclusion which is that the enemy of the market is not ideology but the engineer. In the Soviet Union and the Soviet-type economies, prices are extensively managed by the state. Production is not in response to market demand but given by the overall plan. In the western economies, markets are dominated by great firms. These establish prices and seek to ensure a demand for what they have to sell. The enemies of the market are thus to be seen, although rarely in social matters has there been such a case of mistaken identity. It is not socialists. It is advanced technology and the specialization of men and process that this requires and the resulting commitment of time and capital. These make the market work badly when the need is for greatly enhanced reliability – when planning is essential. The modern large corporation and the modern apparatus of socialist planning are variant accommodations to the same need. It is open to every free-born man to dislike this accommodation. But he must direct his attack to the cause. He must not ask that jet aircraft, nuclear power plants or even the modern automobile in its modern volume be produced by firms that are subject to unfixed prices and unmanaged demand. He must ask instead that they not be produced.

Chapter 4

PLANNING AND THE SUPPLY
OF CAPITAL

THE physical manifestation of the industrial system is the large amount of capital equipment it deploys – the mills, machinery, factories, shops, warehouses, stores, service stations, office buildings with which it covers the landscape. In the manner of all capital goods, and unlike the bread, meat and whisky that are consumed today, these yield their use only over time. And in the manner of all capital goods they have their source in savings – in the economic resources that individuals and corporations devote not to current consumption but to acquiring or building the equipment that allows of greater or different consumption in the future. All of this has the reassuring ring of the commonplace.

Technology and the associated commitment of time are coupled, we have seen, with large requirements for capital. This is matched in the modern economy by an equal and, on occasion, even greater capacity to provide it. This is also a planned supply; those who make large use of capital have successfully minimized their dependence on the market for what they use.

It is a feature of all planning that, unlike the market, it incorporates within itself no mechanism by which demand is accommodated to supply and the reverse. This is true of the supply of savings for capital formation. The recurrent tendency is for such savings to be excessive. Further planning, this by the state, is necessary in consequence to ensure that what is saved is invested. This tendency for savings to be unduly abundant has a further important bearing on the relation of capital to land and to the labour force and to the bargaining position of capital in relation to those who guide or provide technical knowledge to the industrial enterprise. This is a matter for later examination. The present chapter considers the planning that lies back of the capital supply, the resulting tendency to abundance and, in a preliminary way, the resulting need for ensuring that these savings are used.

II

The first feature of the industrial system which is favourable to a large supply of savings for capital formation is the scale of its production. In 1965, in the United States, $108 billion was saved by individuals and corporations from current product for investment at home and abroad. This would have been difficult to accomplish from a prewar Gross National Product which in equivalent prices was about $250 billion. It was easier from a 1965 Product of $676 billion.[1]

The most obvious effect of large production is that individuals can save more easily from the large personal incomes which this production returns. Consumption has the first claim on income even for the most austere when the alternative is hunger, chill or some other form of physical pain. But when a certain level of well-being is achieved people can choose to defer consumption in order to cover the needs of old age, or a rainy day or that they may risk the demoralization of unearned income. Poor societies in the past have had a considerable capacity to save as their surviving monuments attest. But the tourist who gazes on the Great Pyramids, Baalbek, St Peter's, Chartres, Versailles or Cuzco is not looking at the fruits of the voluntary savings of the masses. He is viewing the results of the highly involuntary deprivations of slaves, of the largely lost art of getting tax blood from very dry stones, and of insurance taken out against the danger of eternal damnation under conditions of grave discomfort. Or he sees the results of the savings of the minority who were very rich. Only in very recent times has the average man been a source of savings.

1. *Economic Report of the President*, 1966. The 1965 figures are subject to minor revision.

And he remains a minor source. The approved folk myths of economics have the individual or the household measuring the urgencies and enjoyments of immediate consumption against the foreseen and unforeseeable needs of the future. Allied with this is the calculation that if consumption is deferred and the proceeds are invested with prudence, or possibly courage, the reward will be interest, dividends or capital gains. From this highly rational and admirably individualistic choice comes the decision to save and therewith the supply of capital and the growth of the economy. Were it so, the supply of capital would be very small and the growth very slight.

In 1965 personal savings by individuals were $25 billion. Savings by business firms, primarily corporations, were $83 billion, or more than three times as great. Compared with the early fifties, personal savings had increased by about fifty per cent; business savings had nearly tripled. And most of the personal saving was by the affluent and rich. In 1950 households in the lower two-thirds of the income range, as measured by after-tax incomes, did no saving at all. On the contrary, they consumed substantially in excess of their income. More than half of all personal savings were supplied by those in the upper five per cent income bracket.[2] There is no reason to suppose that saving has become appreciably more democratic since that time.

III

The small volume of saving by the average man, and its absence among the lower-income masses, reflect faithfully the role of the individual in the industrial system and the accepted view of his function. The individual serves the industrial system not by supplying it with savings and the resulting capital; he serves it by consuming its products. On no other matter, religious, political or moral, is he so elaborately and skilfully and expensively instructed.

2. Irwin Friend and Stanley Schor, 'Who Saves?' *The Review of Economics and Statistics*, Vol. XLI, No. 2, Part 2 (May 1959).

Specifically, along with the production of goods go energetic and no less important efforts to ensure their use. These emphasize the health, beauty, social acceptability and sexual success – in sum, the happiness – that will result from the possession and use of a particular product. This communication combined each day with the effort on behalf of countless other products becomes, in the aggregate, an unremitting argument for the advantage of consumption. In turn, inevitably, this affects social values. A family's standard of living becomes an index of its achievement.[3] It helps ensure that the production and, *pari passu*, the consumption of goods will be the prime measure of social accomplishment. The reminder, so beloved by guardians of established social faith, that 'no economic system has ever in history provided such a high standard of living' takes for granted that the level of consumption is the proper measure of social merit. It would be highly inconsistent for a society which so values consumption, and so relentlessly presses its claims, to rely on consumers, through their savings, for its capital. It would be even more incongruous if the need for capital were large. In a society which so emphasizes consumption and so needs capital, the decision to save should obviously be removed from the consumer and exercised by other authority. All industrial societies do so. In the formally planned economies of the Soviet Union and Eastern Europe, income is withheld for investment by the industrial enterprise and especially by the state. In the United States and the western-type economies this withholding is performed by the corporation. The corporation serves here, as elsewhere, as the planning instrument.

IV

Control of the supply of savings is strategic for industrial planning. Capital use is large. No form of market uncertainty is so serious as that involving the terms and conditions on which

3. On this see also James S. Duesenberry, *Income, Saving and the Theory of Consumer Behavior* (Cambridge: Harvard University Press, 1949), pp. 28 et seq.

capital is obtained. Apart from the normal disadvantages of an uncertain price, there is danger that under some circumstances no supply will be forthcoming at an acceptable price. This will be at the precise moment when misfortune or miscalculation has made the need most urgent. And unlike suppliers of raw material or even labour, the supplier of funds is traditionally conceded some degree of power. Money carries with it the special right to know, and even to suggest, how it is used.[4] This dilutes the authority of the planning unit.

All of these dangers and difficulties are avoided if the firm has a secure source of capital from its own earnings. It no longer faces the risks of the market. It concedes no authority to outsiders. It has full control over its own rate of expansion, over the nature of that expansion and over decisions between products, plants and processes. The last chapter showed that one of the strategies for eliminating market uncertainty is to eliminate the market. This strategy is much used where, as in the case of crude petroleum, iron ore or bauxite, the firm is heavily dependent on a particular raw material and where, as a result, adverse market movements could be very costly. But for all production, capital is an indispensable and costly ingredient. To minimize dependence on this market is therefore a universal planning strategy.

There is a further advantage in bringing capital supply within the ambit of industrial planning. Capital and labour are partly substitutes for each other. If capital is subject to internal decision, it can be used as a partial substitute for labour which, in the normal case, is more subject to the external authority of the union. This is a matter for later attention.

4. '. . . creditors are likely to take a keen, and indeed a rather insistent, interest in company policies and may well interfere in certain aspects of management. . . . Retained earnings place the capital entirely at management's disposal without any promises or guarantees.' Wilbert E. Moore, *The Conduct of the Corporation* (New York: Random House Inc., 1962), p. 227.

Planning and the Supply of Capital

V

In the formally planned economies, although there is some slight reliance on voluntary savings by individuals, the basic decision on how much is to be saved is taken by the state. The decision is then made effective by taxation. Or industrial enterprises are encouraged to earn profits for reinvestment and, by suitable management of prices and costs, they are enabled to do so. In both cases it is the planners' and not the individual's decision that determines the volume of saving. Were it otherwise, consumption would be higher, savings would be smaller and the rate of capital formation and economic growth smaller than the planners believe necessary. However, the power of the planners to substitute their view of the desirable rate of saving for that of the individual is not unlimited. In Poland, Hungary and elsewhere in Eastern Europe, until the mid-fifties, planners sought a higher rate of savings than those who saved found tolerable. This was an important source of the unrest that ended the Stalinist era. Since then rates of saving have been, it would appear, much smaller.

In the western economies, industrial saving has been, by comparison, much more nearly painless. A plea for larger dividend payments is a staple item at stockholders' meetings. But it is heard respectfully and ignored. And the individual stockholder always has the option of selling his stock and spending his capital gains. Unions cite the level of earnings, including retained earnings, as a part of their case for wage increases. It is a bargaining point and not a grievance.

The nature of such saving must not, however, be misunderstood. The decisions which provide three-quarters of the community's supply of savings are made not by individuals but by authority, in the main by the managements of a few hundred corporations. And from these savings comes the major wherewithal for the growth of the economy.[5]

5. Where the reality does not accord with wish, our practice, as frequently noted, is to devise a myth which then serves as a bridge between evidence that cannot be escaped and the belief that is sought. However,

The parallel with the planned economies will be evident. No more than they does the industrial system entrust savings and growth to individual decision. Both entrust it to authority. In social argument one must never press a strong case too far. To do so accords the compulsive critic and the man who prefers error to inconvenient truth the handhold for which they yearn. There are great differences between the systems in the degree of centralization with which savings are planned as well as in the techniques by which they are extracted. But in the supply of capital, as elsewhere, the imperatives of industrialization bring, by whatever differences in path, a powerful convergence.

VI

The most celebrated feature of the market is that it equates supply with demand at a price. If there is an incipient surplus, a falling price encourages buyers, restrains sellers and thus eliminates it; if there is a momentary shortage, a rising price attracts suppliers, repels buyers and thus eliminates it. Planning has within itself, as noted, no similar equilibrating mechanism.

---

no acceptable myth relates the decisions of the management of the modern corporation on retention or paying out of earnings to the preferences of individuals as to savings and expenditure. It has been suggested that the Board of Directors, as the chosen representatives of the stockholders, sets the dividend and thus reflects the will of the stockholders. This hardly answers where, as in the common case, the Board is selected by, or is otherwise the instrument of, the management. Nor does it serve much better in the cases where the Board or some members have a measure of independence resulting from stock ownership. For even then the directors normally accept the lead of management on retention and investment of earnings. No one familiar with the constitution of the modern large corporation would suggest that the individual stockholder has a serious voice on this matter.

The stockholder, as noted, can contract out of the saving to which he is subject by selling his stock and spending capital gains. This does not alter the power exercised by the management over savings by the firm. It does of course reduce total saving by the community. One could imagine in theory, although not easily in practice, ways in which this could set an upper limit on corporate savings.

The planner must deliberately ensure that planned supply equals planned use. If he fails there will be surpluses or deficits. If the market mechanism is still not used – if prices are not lowered or raised – there will be a disagreeable problem of storing or destroying the surplus or an unseemly scramble for the insufficient supply. These are common results of planning, commonly accompanied by a drastic slump in the reputation of the planner concerned.

The decisions on what will be saved are made in the main by a few hundred large corporations. The decisions as to what will be invested are made by a similar number of large firms to which are added those of a much larger number of individuals who are buying dwellings, automobiles and household appliances. No mechanism of the market relates the decisions to save to the decisions to invest. If one of the motives for developing internal sources of savings is to free the firm from the uncertainties of the interest rate, it is evident that the decision on this saving will not be affected by the rate of interest. Having contracted out of the money market it will not be affected by the money market. If, as we shall see presently, investment is determined also by influences independent of the market – if it too is planned – the rate of interest does nothing to equate supply to demand. Both are independent of its influence, at least in this part of the economy. And the interest rate is the price that the market would presumably rely on to accommodate the supply of savings to requirements.[6]

If savings go unused, that is to say are unspent, demand for goods in the economy is by this much reduced. Sales of goods then fall below expected or planned levels and employment falls. Outside of the industrial system prices and employment also fall. This will lead to reduction in investment outside the

6. This is a brief view of the matter. There are influences both in the firm and in the economy as a whole which cause investment to increase when savings increase and vice versa. See below, p. 226. But the large role of industrial saving and investment in the total disposes of the theoretical possibility that such balancing might take place outside the industrial system. Few economists do, in fact, argue that savings and investment are responsive (and in the right way) to the interest rate.

industrial system and, with some delay, to a curtailment of planned investment within. In other words a failure to use all that corporations and individuals seek to save sets in motion the processes of recession and depression. These will continue until *they* reduce savings to the point where all are being absorbed by the smaller volume of investment.[7] If, in the opposite case, the economy is functioning at or near the capacity of its plant or labour force, or both, and corporations seek to invest in the aggregate more than the equivalent of the current supply of savings, there will be more spending for investment and consumption than the economy can accommodate. The result will be a bidding up of prices, especially of the market prices outside of the industrial system. This is inflation. The lurking threat of these discomforts thus requires that on the one hand the industrial system have machinery for ensuring that savings are used and on the other for ensuring that use is limited to the savings that are available.

Such machinery has come into use in all industrial countries in modern times. The state uses its power over taxation and expenditure to provide the balance between savings and their use that the industrial system cannot provide for itself. It supplies the missing element in the planning of savings. This is an integral necessity of modern industrial planning.

VII

In common view the problem of management of savings and their use – of what is called Keynesian fiscal policy – is symmetrical: there is a danger that savings will be greater than use and there is danger that investment (and other use) will exceed supply. There is, accordingly, equal need for measures that will increase use and limit use. In practice the problem changes radically with increasing wealth. In poor countries – India,

7. More precisely, intended savings. In Keynesian parlance savings are always offset. The fall in income reduces savings more than it reduces investment, including that in inventories, and equilibrium is found at a lower level of output, income and employment.

Pakistan, most of Latin America – the supply of savings, domestic and imported, is exceedingly meagre. There the problem is not to ensure use of savings but to limit investment and other claims to what is available, to ensure wise use of savings and to increase the available supply. In the United States, Western Europe and the older British Commonwealth, periods of war and extreme international tension apart, such a preoccupation would seem eccentric. Here the men responsible for economic policy anxiously contemplate estimates of intended industrial investment to see whether these, together with the probable government deficit, will absorb net savings. Failure to do so means recession or depression. For most of the thirty years since Keynes published *The General Theory*[8] the greatest concern has been with offsetting savings and thus preventing recession and unemployment.

In the two decades since World War II, as this is written, serious recession has been prevented. The further consequence of this has been to make the supply of savings even more ample.

That is because steady expansion of output and incomes is favourable to both corporate and individual saving; depression and recession, by contrast, bring a Malthusian reduction in both. Business saving fell from $11·5 billion in 1929 to $2·6 billion in 1933 and did not regain its pre-depression level until 1941. In 1932 and 1933 savings by individuals were negative, which is to say that individuals, in the aggregate, increased their indebtedness. In the other depression years individual savings were small or negligible. A serious recession any time in the last two decades would have had a similar effect. Even the lessened rate of expansion in 1959–60 brought a reduction in individual and business savings.[9] Here is the paradox of savings: the steps which ensure that they will be used serve also to increase their supply. The more effectively they are offset by investment the higher will be the income and the more savings there will be.

8. John Maynard Keynes, *The General Theory of Employment Interest and Money* (New York: Harcourt, 1936).

9. *Economic Report of the President*, 1965.

Most communities in the past were limited in their progress by the savings they could extract from their meagre product to invest in better methods of production. The same is true of poor nations today. The rich nations must also have savings to expand. But what is called economic progress here depends less on the supply of savings than on the effectiveness with which employment of a more than ample supply is ensured. Not a shortage of savings but a recession resulting from the failure to use all available savings is the spectre that haunts all policy makers. For investment to exceed savings, at least in peacetime, is thought exceptional. This tendency of savings and thus of capital to abundance, abundant use notwithstanding, is a matter of penetrating historical and social consequence to which I now turn.

Chapter 5

CAPITAL AND POWER

No subject has been more faithfully explored by economists than the relation between what anciently have been called the factors of production – land, labour, capital and the entrepreneurial talent which brings these together and manages their employment. Until recently, the problem of efficiency in production – that of getting the most from the available productive resources – was envisaged, almost entirely, as one of winning the best combination of these agents. The elucidation by means of diagrams of the arcane problems inherent in factor combination remains one of the prime pedagogical rites of economics.[1] Economists have been equally concerned with the way in which the prices of the factors of production – rents, wages, interest and profits – are determined. Indeed, in the classical tradition, the subject was thought of as falling in two

---

1. Changing technology, it is conceded, alters progressively and radically what can be obtained from any given supply of factors. But there is no way by which this intelligence can be developed at length in a textbook. So economic instruction concedes the important and then discusses the unimportant. Thus Professor Samuelson, rightly the most noted of contemporary economists, who more than anyone else has instructed adult Americans in the subject, observes that the output that can be obtained from a given stock of factors 'depends on the state of technology.' He then adds: *'But at any time, there will be a maximum obtainable amount of product for any given amounts of factor inputs.'* Paul A. Samuelson, *Economics*, Sixth Edition (New York: McGraw, 1964), p. 516. (Emphasis his.) The problem of factor allocation is the subject on which there is an available doctrine. So having given it such importance as italics provide, this is the subject he discusses. Were this all, he would not be especially open to criticism. Much economic instruction, and notably so in such fields as advanced theory, foreign trade and monetary policy, depends not on the relevance of the subject matter but on the existence of an intellectually preoccupying theory. In this case, however, there is a conflict between the technological development, to which Professor Samuelson properly accords the primary role in in-

parts: the problem of value having to do with the determination of the prices of goods, and the problem of distribution or how the resulting income was divided between landlords, workers, capitalists and entrepreneurs.

One aspect of the relationships between the factors of production has, however, been less examined. That is why power is associated with some factors and not with others. Why did ownership of land once convey plenary power over the dominant form of productive enterprise and, therewith, in the community at large? Why under other circumstances has it been assumed that such authority, both over the enterprise and in the society at large, should lie with the owner of capital? Under what circumstances might such power pass to labour?

It is a puzzling neglect. On coming on any form of organized activity – a church, platoon, government bureau, congressional committee, a house of casual pleasure – our first instinct is to inquire who is in charge. Then we inquire as to the qualifications or credentials which accord such command. Organization almost invariably invites two questions: Who is the head? How did he get there?

II

One reason the question was slighted was that for a long time, in formal economic inquiry, no one associated with economic activity was thought to have any worthwhile exercise of power. In the classical economic tradition – that of Adam Smith, David Ricardo, Thomas Malthus, J. S. Mill and Alfred Marshall – and increasingly as concepts were better defined, the business enterprise (like the Wisconsin dairy farm today) was assumed to be small in relation to the market supplied. The price it received was impersonally and competitively determined by the market. So were the prices paid to suppliers. Wages were also

---

creasing productivity, and the factor allocation which provides his pedagogical exercise. Technological development involves, as we have seen, heavy commitment of capital and time which is safeguarded by planning and companion control over costs, prices and demand. But the approved pedagogical exercise leads to the conclusion that optimal allocation of factors is obtained by the minimum of such interference with the market.

set by the market. So was the interest on borrowed funds. Profits reduced themselves to a competitive level. Technology was assumed to be stable. Under these circumstances the ideal volume of production for the firm was externally established by the relation of costs to the market price at various levels of output. If the man in charge of the firm has no power to influence prices, costs, wages or interest, and if even his best output is externally determined and his profits are subject to the levelling effect of competition, one can rightly be unconcerned about his power. He has none. Until well into the present century the economics of the textbooks assumed a world of such small and competitive firms. The counterpart neglect of the problem of power was both plausible and inevitable. Other traditions of thought, however, were less handicapped.

In particular there was Marx. In the middle of the last century he brought the subject of power into economic discussion with a vehemence which the world has not yet quite ceased to deplore. The notion of a system of competitive and hence passive business firms he dismissed as an exercise in vulgar apologetics. Production is dominated by those who control and supply capital – by a 'constantly diminishing number of the magnates of capital who usurp and monopolize all advantages of this process of transformation . . .'[2] Their authority in the enterprise is complete. Prices and wages are set in their collective interest. They dominate the society and set its moral tone. They also control the state which becomes an executive committee serving the will and interest of the capitalist class. There is no question of power being associated with any other factor of production. At this stage in historical development it belongs unequivocally and totally with capital.

In the classical tradition there was eventually a measure of agreement with Marx. The notion of the competitive market receded; it survives today in the textbooks as an exceptional case. The business enterprise is routinely assumed to have con-

2. Karl Marx, *Capital* (New York: The Modern Library), Chapter XXXII, p. 836.

trol over its prices and output – to have the power that is associated with one seller or monopoly, a few sellers or oligopoly, or with some unique feature of its products or service which accords it protection from competition. Only professional defenders of the free enterprise system, members of a lowly and poorly paid craft, still argue for the rule of competition, this being the test their clients are best calculated to fail.[3] There is general agreement that 'market power which large absolute and relative size gives to the giant corporation is the basis not only of economic power but also of considerable political and social power...'[4]

And the companion point of Marx is assumed. Such power as may be available naturally and inevitably belongs to capital. Its exercise is the prerogative of ownership. The claims of the other factors of production are inherently subordinate. In the assumption that power belongs as a matter of course to capital, all economists are Marxians.

Beyond this, the problem of power is still not much discussed. Prices and wages are fixed, investment determined, dividends declared, production decided by the owners of capital within the margin of discretion allowed by the market. Influence by business on the state is deemed irregular and illegitimate; such as is nonetheless exercised is by or in the interest of the owners of the enterprise. Alternatives as to the exercise of power by capital are not seriously considered.

In the last three decades there has been steady accumulation of evidence on the shift of power from owners to managers

3. 'To the extent that a price is reached by means that are *not* impersonal – to the extent that either the buyer or the seller can dictate or influence the setting of the price – to that extent our system of controlling the use of resources is not working properly.' *Do You Know Your Economic ABC's? Profits in the American Economy*, United States Department of Commerce, 1965, p. 13. This pamphlet was commissioned by John T. Connor, while Secretary of Commerce, to promote understanding of (and indicate sympathy for) American business. By the test of the pamphlet all large business would fail.

4. Carl Kaysen in *The Corporation in Modern Society*, Edward S. Mason, ed. (Cambridge: Harvard University Press, 1959), p. 99.

within the modern large corporation. The power of the stock-holders, as noted, has seemed increasingly tenuous. A small proportion of the stock is represented at stockholders' meetings for a ceremony in which banality is varied chiefly by irrelevance. The rest is voted by proxy for the directors who have been selected by the management. The latter, though their ownership is normally negligible, are solidly in control of the enterprise. By all visible evidence the power is theirs. Yet there has been great reluctance to admit of a significant and enduring shift of power from the owners of capital. Some observers have sought to maintain the myth of stockholder power. As in foreign policy it is hoped that incantation may save what the reality denies.[5] Others, including all Marxians, argue that the change is superficial, that capital retains a deeper and more functional control. Only the naïve react to the obvious. Some have conceded a change but have deferred judgement as to its significance.[6] Yet others have seen a possibly dangerous usurpation of the legitimate power of capital that should, if possible, be reversed.[7] Comparatively few have questioned the credentials of capital, where direction of the enterprise is concerned, or suggested that it might be durably in eclipse.

5. 'When, for example, John purchased a new issue of stock from the Keim Corporation last year ... [it gave] him a voice in the decision of "his" firm's management when he meets with other stockholders at annual meetings.' *Profits in the American Economy*, U.S. Department of Commerce, op. cit., pp. 17–18.

6. Cf. Edward S. Mason, 'The Apologetics of Managerialism,' *Journal of Business of the University of Chicago*, Vol. XXXI, No. 1 (January 1958). And 'Comment' in *A Survey of Contemporary Economics*, Bernard F. Haley, ed., Vol. II (Homewood, Illinois: Richard D. Irwin, Inc., 1952), pp. 221–2. It is Professor Mason's view that, while the capitalist entrepreneur has lost his power in the modern large corporation, there is no serviceable view of what has taken his place. Accordingly, one can still do best by assuming the entrepreneur and the traditional motivations. '[I] must confess a lack of confidence in the marked superiority *for purposes of economic analysis*, of this newer concept of the firm, over the older conception of the entrepreneur.' Ibid.

7. Cf. Adolf A. Berle, Jr, *Power Without Property* (New York: Harcourt, 1959), pp. 98 et seq.

III

Yet, over a longer range of time, power over the productive enterprise – and by derivation in the society at large – has shifted radically between the factors of production. The eminence of capital is a relatively recent matter; until about two centuries ago no perceptive man would have doubted that power was decisively associated with land. The comparative wealth, esteem, military position and the sanguinary authority over the lives of the populace that went with land ownership assured its possessor of a position of eminence in his community and power in the state. These perquisites of land ownership also gave a strong and even controlling direction to history. For two centuries, until about two hundred years before the discovery of America, it helped inspire the recurrent military campaigns to the East which are called the Crusades. Succour for Byzantium, which was beset by the infidels, and redemption of Jerusalem, which had been lost to them, served, without doubt, as a stimulant to ardour. But not exclusively. Relations between the eastern and western Christians were marked by profound mistrust. Jerusalem had been under Islam for 450 years; its redemption had not previously been considered of breathtaking urgency. The younger sons of the Frankish nobility, like the hungry peasants who followed Peter the Hermit, wanted land. Beneath the mantled cross beat hearts soundly attuned to the value of real estate. Baldwin, younger brother of Godfrey of Bouillon, found himself faced on the way to the Holy City with the taxing decision as to whether to continue with the redeeming armies or take up an attractive piece of property at Edessa. He unhesitatingly opted for the latter and, only on the death of his brother, did he leave his fief to become the first King of Jerusalem.[8]

For three and a half centuries after discovery of America,

8. 'The opportunity of combining Christian duty with the acquisition of land in a southern climate was very attractive.' Steven Runciman, *A History of the Crusades*, Vol. 1. *The First Crusade* (Cambridge, England: The University Press, 1954), p. 92.

appreciation of the strategic role of land gave it an even greater role in history. The Americas were populated as also the Steppes and the habitable parts of the Antipodes. Once again, religion went hand in hand with real property conveyancing, somewhat disguising the role of the latter. Spaniards considered themselves commissioned by God to win the souls of Indians; Puritans believed themselves primarily under obligation to find a favourable environment for their own. For Catholics and Cavaliers the Lord was believed to favour rather large acreages with the opportunity these accorded for the spiritual custody of aborigines and, as these gave out, of Africans. For Puritans and Protestants spiritual merit lay with the homestead and family farm. But these were details. In the New World, as in the Old, it was assumed that power belonged, as a right, to men who owned land. Democracy, in its modern meaning, began as a system which gave the suffrage to those who had proved their worth by acquiring real property and to no others.

This eminence of land, and the incentive to acquire it, were firmly grounded in economics. Until comparatively modern times, agricultural production – the provision of food and fibre – accounted for a large share of all production as it still accounts for seventy to eighty per cent of all output in such economically poor countries as modern India. Ownership or control of land thus accorded one a position in the dominant form of economic activity; to be landless was to be crowded into what was left.

Meanwhile other factors of production had a much less strategic role. Agricultural technology was stable and uncomplicated; accordingly, slaves apart, it offered small scope for capital and, as a broad rule, slaves could only be used in conjunction with land. Non-agricultural activity being relatively unimportant, its demand for capital was small and limited further by simple and stable technology. So – a somewhat neglected point – until two hundred years ago a meagre supply of capital was matched by an equally meagre opportunity for its use. If a man had land in England or Western Europe he could get the modest supply of capital he needed to till it.

Possession of this capital was no guarantee that he could get the land.

Nor was labour difficult to come by. Its well-established tendency was to keep itself in a state of great abundance. David Ricardo, having regard for experience to that time, could hold in 1817 that 'no point is better established than that the supply of labourers will always ultimately be in proportion to the means of supporting them.'[9] That was to say that, given a little time, an unlimited supply would be forthcoming at, or about, a subsistence wage. Enough labour would be used so that, through diminishing returns, the contribution of the marginal worker would be about equal to his subsistence. If he gave up this narrow contest with privation he could easily be replaced. If a man adds little and can easily be replaced, he has small power and small bargaining power.

But no one could doubt the advantage of laying one's hands on an acre, or a hundred acres, or a thousand acres of fertile land. Nor could one doubt the deadly consequences of losing like amounts. This meant that possession of land was strategic and not even the philosophers whose ideas ushered in the Industrial Revolution could quite envisage a society where this was otherwise. Adam Smith, though he was at odds on most points with his Physiocratic precursors in France who had made land the ultimate source of all wealth, attributed a special bounty to real property which was returned, as a special mark of grace, to those who owned it.[10] Forty years later, following the Napoleonic Wars, Ricardo and Malthus made ownership of land even more crucial. Population would grow in accordance with a biological dynamic of its own. This would make an ever more urgent claim on a much more slowly increasing food supply. In consequence the relative price of food and the

9. David Ricardo, *Works and Correspondence of David Ricardo*, Piero Sraffa, ed., Vol. I (Cambridge, England: The University Press, 1951), p. 292.

10. Adam Smith, 'Of the Rent of Land,' *Wealth of Nations*, Book I (London: Methuen, 1930), Chapter XI. Cf. Alexander Gray, *The Development of Economic Doctrine* (London: Longmans, 1931), p. 137.

share of income going to landlords would increase insouciantly and without limit. The decisive factor was the scarcity of land. 'The labour of nature is paid, not because she does much, but because she does little. In proportion as she becomes niggardly in her gifts, she exacts a greater price for her work. Where she is munificently beneficent, she always works gratis.' [11] Not surprisingly, those who owned this rare resource would exercise full authority in the dominant agricultural economy and be men of prestige and power in the community at large.

IV

Ricardo wrote at a moment in history when land was being dethroned. That was partly because the scarcity to which he attributed such importance had set in motion a phenomenal search for a new supply. And the two Americas, South Africa and Australia were all found to have large, unused and highly usable amounts. New land could be obtained or lost land could be replaced by going to the frontier. The need now was for capital to pay the passage for seed, livestock and equipment and to tide a man over until the first harvest. And if a varlet could, on occasion, get more acreage in the New World than the most majestic aristocrat owned in the Old, land was no longer a secure source of distinction.

Meanwhile, mechanical inventions and the growth of metallurgical and engineering knowledge were prodigiously expanding opportunities for the employment of capital. From this greater use of capital in more advanced technology came greater production. From that production came greater income and more saving. It is not clear that in the last century the demand for capital grew more rapidly than the supply. In the new countries, including the United States, capital was usually scarce and the cost was high. But in England, over most of the

11. Ricardo, op. cit., p. 76. Ricardo is here taking issue with Adam Smith's suggestion that the return to land was payment for nature's bounty. The point is of no importance here. For both, nature, by way of land, played a large part in determining incomes.

century, rates of return were low and Englishmen were under strong compulsion to find more profitable employments for their savings in distant lands. But there coal, iron and steel, railways, locomotives, ships, textile machinery, buildings and bridges were commanding an increasing share of the national product. For producing these, capital was what counted. Agriculture, with its peculiar dependence on land, contributed a diminishing share of total product. The man who owned or controlled capital could now command the needed labour and land. Control of labour or land accorded no reciprocal power to command capital.

So power over the enterprise passed to capital. And so did prestige in the community and authority in the state. At the beginning of the nineteenth century the British Parliament was still dominated by the great landed families. By the middle of the century they were acceding to industrial pressure to lower the price of food, and therewith the level of factory wages, at the expense of their rents. By the end of the century the premier figure in British politics was the great Birmingham industrialist and pioneer screw manufacturer, Joseph Chamberlain. At the beginning of the century, the United States Government was dominated by landed and slave-owning gentlemen of Virginia; by the end of the century by common agreement power had passed, depending on point of view, to the men of enterprise or the malefactors of great wealth. The Senate had become a club of rich businessmen.

The change, a point of much importance for what follows, did not seem natural. George Washington, Thomas Jefferson and James Madison seemed far more appropriate to positions of public power than Collis P. Huntington, J. P. Morgan or Andrew Mellon. They were credited with capacity for action apart from their own interests as the capitalists were not. And action in their own interest – the defence, for example, of slavery – seemed more gentlemanly, reasonable and legitimate than action by the capitalists in their own behalf. This contrasting impression still survives in public attitudes and the elementary history books. We may lay it down as a rule that the older the exercise of any power the more benign it will appear and the more recent its assumption the more unnatural and even dangerous it will seem.

V

It will now be clear what accords power to a factor of production or to those who own or control it. Power goes to the factor which is hardest to obtain or hardest to replace. In precise language it adheres to the one that has the greatest inelasticity of supply at the margin. This inelasticity may be the result of a natural shortage, or an effective control over supply by şome human agency, or both.[12]

In its age, if one had land then labour and capital (in the meagre amounts required) could be readily obtained. But to have labour and operating capital did not so readily ensure that a man could get land. There was an admixture, here, of cause and effect. Because land provided special access to economic and larger power, steps were taken, as through the laws of entail, to confine possession to the privileged or noble caste. And this, in turn, limited the opportunities for acquiring it and further increased the economic power and social authority which, from one generation to the next, land conferred on its owner.

In the age of capital, land was readily available in the minor amounts required for industrial enterprise and increasingly so for agriculture. Labour continued to be plentiful. Now possession of land and labour did not allow one to command capital; but with capital, land and labour could easily be obtained. Capital now accorded power in the enterprise and in consequence in the society.

12. Thus a union, which accords considerable power to labour in relation to such specific decisions as those affecting wages and working conditions, involves full control of supply. (In a successful strike the supply price of labour on the plant side of the picket line is infinitely high.) The union power is increased if the supply of labour is not too abundant.

Should it happen that capital were to become abundant, or redundant, and thus be readily increased or replaced, the power it confers, both in the enterprise and in the society, would be expected to suffer. This would seem especially probable if, at the same time, some other factor of production should prove increasingly difficult to add or replace.

VI

The last chapter made clear that in the industrial system, while capital is used in large amounts, it is, at least in peacetime, even more abundantly supplied. The tendency to an excess of savings, and the need for an offsetting strategy by the state, is an established and well-recognized feature of the Keynesian economy. And savings, we have seen, are supplied by the industrial enterprise to itself as part of its planning. There is high certainty as to their availability, for this is the purpose of the planning.

At the same time the requirements of technology and planning have greatly increased the need of the industrial enterprise for specialized talent and for its organization. The industrial system must rely, in the main, on external sources for this talent. Unlike capital it is not something that the firm can supply to itself. To be effective this talent must also be brought into effective association with itself. It must be in an organization. Given a competent business organization, capital is now ordinarily available. But the mere possession of capital is now no guarantee that the requisite talent can be obtained and organized. One should expect, from past experience, to find a new shift of power in the industrial enterprise, this one from capital to organized intelligence. And one would expect that this shift would be reflected in the deployment of power in the society at large.

This has, indeed, occurred. It is a shift of power as between the factors of production which matches that which occurred from land to capital in the advanced countries beginning two centuries ago. It is an occurrence of the last fifty years and is still going on. A dozen matters of commonplace observation – the loss of power by stockholders in the modern corporation, the impregnable position of the successful corporate management, the dwindling social magnetism of the banker, the air of quaintness that attaches to the suggestion that the United States is run from Wall Street, the increasingly energetic search for industrial talent, the new prestige of education and educators – all attest the point.

This shift of power has been disguised because, as was once true of land, the position of capital is imagined to be immutable. That power should be elsewhere seems unnatural and those who so argue seem to be in search of frivolous novelty. And it has been disguised because power has not gone to another of the established factors as they are celebrated in conventional economic pedagogy. It has not passed to labour. Labour has won limited authority over its pay and working conditions but none over the enterprise. And it still tends to abundance. If overly abundant savings are not used, the first effect is unemployment; if savings are used one consequence is a substitution of machine processes for unskilled labour and standard skills. Thus unskilled labour and workers with conventional skills suffer, along with the capitalist, from an abundance of capital.

Nor has power passed to the classical entrepreneur – the individual who once used his access to capital to bring it into combination with the other factors of production. He is a diminishing figure in the industrial system. Apart from access to capital, his principal qualifications were imagination, capacity for decision and courage in risking money including, not infrequently, his own. None of these qualifications are especially important for organizing intelligence or effective in competing with it.

Power has, in fact, passed to what anyone in search of novelty might be justified in calling a new factor of production. This is the association of men of diverse technical knowledge, experience or other talent which modern industrial technology and planning require. It extends from the leadership of the modern industrial enterprise down to just short of the labour force and embraces a large number of people and a large variety of talent. It is on the effectiveness of this organization, as most business doctrine now implicitly agrees, that the success of the modern business enterprise now depends. Were this organization dismembered or otherwise lost, there is no certainty that it could be put together again. To enlarge it to undertake new tasks is an expensive and sometimes uncertain undertaking. Here one now finds the problem of an uncertainly high supply price at the margin. And here one finds the accompanying power. Our next task is to examine in some depth this new locus of power in the business enterprise and in the society.

Chapter 6

THE TECHNOSTRUCTURE

> ... the prevalence of group, instead of individual, action is a striking characteristic of management organization in the large corporation. R. A. GORDON, *Business Leadership in the Large Corporation.*

THE individual has far more standing in our culture than the group. An individual has a presumption of accomplishment; a committee has a presumption of inaction.[1] We react sympathetically to the individual who seeks to safeguard his personality from engulfment by the mass. We call for proof, at least in principle, before curbing his aggressions against society. Individuals have souls; corporations are notably soulless. The entrepreneur – individualistic, restless, with vision, guile and courage – has been the economists' only hero. The great business organization arouses no similar admiration. Admission to heaven is individually and by families; the top management even of an enterprise with an excellent corporate image cannot yet go in as a group. To have, in pursuit of truth, to assert the superiority of the organization over the individual for important social tasks is a taxing prospect.

Yet it is a necessary task. It is not to individuals but to organizations that power in the business enterprise and power in the society has passed. And modern economic society can only be understood as an effort, wholly successful, to synthesize by organization a group personality far superior *for its purposes* to a natural person and with the added advantage of immortality.

1. 'Of the various mechanisms of management, none is more controversial than committees. ... Despite their alleged shortcomings, committees are an important device of administration.' Paul E. Holden, Lounsbury S. Fish and Hubert L. Smith, *Top Management Organization and Control* (New York: McGraw, 1951), p. 59.

The need for such a group personality begins with the circumstance that in modern industry a large number of decisions, and *all* that are important, draw on information possessed by more than one man. Typically they draw on the specialized scientific and technical knowledge, the accumulated information or experience and the artistic or intuitive sense of many persons. And this is guided by further information which is assembled, analysed and interpreted by professionals using highly technical equipment. The final decision will be informed only as it draws systematically on all those whose information is relevant. Nor, humans being what they are, can it take all of the information that is offered at face value. There must, additionally, be a mechanism for testing each person's contribution for its relevance and reliability as it is brought to bear on the decision.

II

The need to draw on, and appraise, the information of numerous individuals in modern industrial decision-making has three principal points of origin. It derives, first, from the technological requirements of modern industry. It is not that these are always inordinately sophisticated; a man of moderate genius could, quite conceivably, provide himself with the knowledge of the various branches of metallurgy and chemistry, and of engineering, procurement, production management, quality control, labour relations, styling and merchandising which are involved in the development of a modern motor car. But even moderate genius is in unpredictable supply, and to keep abreast of all these branches of science, engineering and art would be time-consuming even for a genius. The elementary solution, which allows of the use of far more common talent and with far greater predictability of result, is to have men who are appropriately qualified or experienced in each limited area of specialized knowledge or art. Their information is then combined for carrying out the design and production of the vehicle. It is a common public impression, not discouraged by scientists, engineers and industrialists, that modern scientific, engineering and industrial achievements are the work of a new and quite remarkable race of men. This is pure vanity; were it so, there would be few such achievements. The real accomplishment of modern science and technology consists in taking ordinary men, informing them narrowly and deeply and then, through appropriate organization, arranging to have their knowledge combined with that of other specialized but equally ordinary men. This dispenses with the need for genius. The resulting performance, though less inspiring, is far more predictable.

The second factor requiring the combination of specialized talent derives from advanced technology, the associated use of capital, and the resulting need for planning with its accompanying control of environment. The market is, in remarkable degree, an intellectually undemanding institution. The Wisconsin farmer, aforementioned, need not anticipate his requirements for fertilizers, pesticides or even machine parts; the market stocks and supplies them. The cost of these is substantially the same for the man of intelligence and for his neighbour who, under medical examination, shows daylight in either ear. And the farmer need have no price or selling strategy; the market takes all his milk at the ruling price. Much of the appeal of the market, to economists at least, has been from the way it seems to simplify life. Better orderly error than complex truth.

For complexity enters with planning and is endemic thereto. The manufacturer of missiles, space vehicles or modern aircraft must foresee the requirements for specialized plant, specialized manpower, exotic materials and intricate components and take steps to ensure their availability when they are needed. For procuring such things, we have seen, the market is either unreliable or unavailable. And there is no open market for the finished product. Everything here depends on the care and skill with which contracts are sought and nurtured in Washington or in Whitehall or Paris.

The same foresight and responding action are required, in lesser degree, from manufacturers of automobiles, processed foods and detergents. They too must foresee requirements and manage markets. Planning, in short, requires a great variety of information. It requires variously informed men and men who are suitably specialized in obtaining the requisite information. There must be men whose knowledge allows them to foresee need and to ensure a supply of labour, materials and other production requirements; those who have knowledge to plan price strategies and see that customers are suitably persuaded to buy at these prices; those who, at higher levels of technology, are so informed that they can work effectively with the state to see that it is suitably guided; and those who can organize the flow of information that the above tasks and many others require. Thus, to the requirements of technology for specialized technical and scientific talent are added the very large further requirements of the planning that technology makes necessary.

Finally, following from the need for this variety of specialized talent, is the need for its coordination. Talent must be brought to bear on the common purpose. More specifically, on large and small matters, information must be extracted from the various specialists, tested for its reliability and relevance, and made to yield a decision. This process, which is much misunderstood, requires a special word.

III

The modern business organization, or that part which has to do with guidance and direction, consists of numerous individuals who are engaged, at any given time, in obtaining, digesting or exchanging and testing information. A very large part of the exchange and testing of information is by word-of-mouth – a discussion in an office, at lunch or over the telephone. But the most typical procedure is through the committee and the committee meeting. One can do worse than think of a business organization as a hierarchy of committees. Coordination, in turn, consists in assigning the appropriate talent to committees, intervening on occasion to force a decision, and, as the case may be, announcing the decision or carrying it as information for a yet further decision by a yet higher committee.

Nor should it be supposed that this is an inefficient procedure. On the contrary it is, normally, the only efficient procedure. Association in a committee enables each member to come to know the intellectual resources and the reliability of his colleagues. Committee discussion enables members to pool information under circumstances which allow, also, of immediate probing to assess the relevance and reliability of the information offered. Uncertainty about one's information or error is revealed as in no other way. There is also, no doubt, considerable stimulus to mental effort from such association. One may enjoy the luxury of torpor in private but not so comfortably in public at least during working hours. Men who believe themselves deeply engaged in private thought are usually doing nothing. Committees are condemned by the cliché that individual effort is somehow superior to group effort; by those who guiltily suspect that since group effort is more congenial, it must be less productive; and by those who do not see that the process of extracting, and especially of testing, information has necessarily a somewhat undirected quality – briskly conducted meetings invariably decide matters previously decided; and by those who fail to realize that highly paid men, when sitting around a table as a committee, are not necessarily wasting more time than, in the aggregate, they would each waste in private by themselves.[2] Forthright and

2. Also committees are not, as commonly supposed, alike. Some are constituted not to pool and test information and offer a decision but to accord representation to diverse bureaucratic, pecuniary, political, ideological or other interests. And a particular committee may have some of both purposes. A committee with representational functions will proceed much less expeditiously, for its ability to reach a conclusion depends on the susceptibility of participants to compromise, attrition and cupidity. The representational committee, in its present form, is engaged in a zero sum game, which is to say what some win others lose. Pooling and testing information is nonzero sum – all participants end with a larger score.

determined administrators frequently react to belief in the superior capacity of individuals for decision by abolishing all committees. They then constitute working parties, task forces, assault teams or executive groups in order to avoid the one truly disastrous consequence of their action which would be that they should make the decisions themselves.

Thus decision in the modern business enterprise is the product not of individuals but of groups. The groups are numerous, as often informal as formal, and subject to constant change in composition. Each contains the men possessed of the information, or with access to the information, that bears on the particular decision together with those whose skill consists in extracting and testing this information and obtaining a conclusion. This is how men act successfully on matters where no single one, however exalted or intelligent, has more than a fraction of the necessary knowledge. It is what makes modern business possible, and in other contexts it is what makes modern government possible. It is fortunate that men of limited knowledge are so constituted that they can work together in this way. Were it otherwise, business and government, at any given moment, would be at a standstill awaiting the appearance of a man with the requisite breadth of knowledge to resolve the problem presently at hand. Some further characteristics of group decision-making must now be noticed.

IV

Group decision-making extends deeply into the business enterprise. Effective participation is not closely related to rank in the formal hierarchy of the organization. This takes an effort of mind to grasp. Everyone is influenced by the stereotyped organization chart of the business enterprise. At its top is the Board of Directors and the Board Chairman; next comes the President; next comes the Executive Vice-President; thereafter come the Department or Divisional Heads – those who preside over the Chevrolet division, the large-generators division, the computer division. Power is assumed to pass down from the pinnacle. Those at the top give orders; those below relay them on or respond.

This happens, but only in very simple organizations – the peacetime drill of the National Guard or a troop of Boy Scouts moving out on Saturday manoeuvres. Elsewhere the decision will require information. Some power will then pass to the person or persons who have this information. If this knowledge is highly particular to themselves then their power becomes very great. In Los Alamos, during the development of the atomic bomb, Enrico Fermi rode a bicycle up the hill to work; Major General Leslie R. Groves presided in grandeur over the entire Manhattan District. Fermi had the final word on numerous questions of feasibility and design.[3] In association with a handful of others he could, at various early stages, have brought the entire enterprise to an end. No such power resided with Groves. At any moment he could have been replaced without loss and with possible benefit.

When power is exercised by a group, not only does it pass into the organization but it passes irrevocably. If an individual has taken a decision he can be called before another individual, who is his superior in the hierarchy, his information can be examined and his decision reversed by the greater wisdom or experience of the superior. But if the decision required the combined information of a group, it cannot be safely reversed by an individual. He will have to get the judgement of other specialists. This returns the power once more to organization.

No one should insist, in these matters, on pure cases. There will often be instances when an individual has the knowledge to modify or change the finding of a group. But the broad rule holds: If a decision requires the specialized knowledge of a group of men, it is subject to safe review only by the similar

3. He was head of the Advanced Development Division of the Los Alamos Laboratory. His slightly earlier work was central to the conclusion that a self-sustaining chain-reaction was possible. Cf. Henry De Wolf Smyth, *Atomic Energy for Military Purposes* (Princeton: Princeton University Press, 1943), Chapter VI.

knowledge of a similar group. Group decision, unless acted upon by another group, tends to be absolute.[4]

V

Next, it must not be supposed that group decision is important only in such evident instances as nuclear technology or space mechanics. Simple products are made and packaged by sophisticated processes. And the most massive programmes of market control, together with the most specialized marketing talent, are used on behalf of soap, detergents, cigarettes, aspirin, packaged cereals and gasoline. These, beyond others, are the valued advertising accounts. The simplicity and uniformity of these products require the investment of compensatingly elaborate science and art to suppress market influences and make prices and amounts sold subject to the largest possible measure of control. For these products too, decision passes to a group which combines specialized and esoteric knowledge. Here too power goes deeply and more or less irrevocably into the organization.

For purposes of pedagogy, I have sometimes illustrated these tendencies by reference to a technically uncomplicated product, which, unaccountably, neither General Electric nor Westing-

4. I reached some of these conclusions during World War II when, in the early years, I was in charge of price control. Decisions on prices – to fix, raise, rearrange or, very rarely, to lower them – came to my office after an extensive exercise in group decision-making in which lawyers, economists, accountants, men knowledgeable of the product and industry, and specialists in public righteousness had all participated. Alone one was nearly helpless to alter such decisions; hours or days of investigation would be required and, in the meantime, a dozen other decisions would have been made. Given what is commonly called an 'adequate' staff, one could have exercised control. But an adequate staff would be one that largely duplicated the decision-making group with adverse effect on the good nature and sense of responsibility of the latter and the time required for decision. To have responsibility for all of the prices in the United States was awesome; to discover how slight was one's power in face of group decision-making was sobering. President Kennedy enjoyed responding to proposals for public action of one sort or another by saying: 'I agree but I don't know whether the government will agree.'

house has yet placed on the market. It is a toaster of standard performance, the pop-up kind, except that it etches on the surface of the toast, in darker carbon, one of a selection of standard messages or designs. For the elegant, an attractive monogram would be available or a coat of arms; for the devout, at breakfast there would be an appropriate devotional message from the Reverend Billy Graham; for the patriotic or worried, there would be an aphorism urging vigilance from Mr J. Edgar Hoover; for modern painters and economists, there would be a purely abstract design. A restaurant version would sell advertising or urge the peaceful integration of public eating places.

Conceivably this is a vision that could come from the head of General Electric. But the systematic proliferation of such ideas is the designated function of much more lowly men who are charged with product development. At an early stage in the development of the toaster the participation of specialists in engineering, production, styling and design and possibly philosophy, art and spelling would have to be sought. No one in position to authorize the product would do so without a judgement on how the problems of inscription were to be solved and at what cost. Nor, ordinarily, would an adverse finding on technical and economic feasibility be overridden. At some stage, further development would become contingent on the finding of market researchers and merchandise experts on whether the toaster could be sold and at what price. Nor would an adverse decision by this group be overruled. In the end there would be a comprehensive finding on the feasibility of the innovation. If unfavourable this would not be overruled. Nor, given the notoriety that attaches to lost opportunity, would be the more plausible contingency of a favourable recommendation. It will be evident that nearly all powers – initiation, character of development, rejection or acceptance – are exercised in the company. It is not the managers who decide. Effective power of decision is lodged deeply in the technical, planning and other specialized staff.

VI

We must notice next that this exercise of group power can be rendered unreliable or ineffective by external interference. Not only does power pass into the organization but the quality of decision can easily be impaired by efforts of an individual to retain control over the decision-making process.

Specifically the group reaches decision by receiving and evaluating the specialized information of its members. If it is to act responsibly, it must be accorded responsibility. It cannot be arbitrarily or capriciously overruled. If it is, it will develop the same tendencies to irresponsibility as an individual similarly treated.

But the tendency will be far more damaging. The efficiency of the group and the quality of its decisions depend on the quality of the information provided and the precision with which it is tested. The last increases greatly as men work together. It comes to be known that some are reliable and that some though useful are at a tacit discount. All information offered must be so weighed. The sudden intervention of a superior introduces information, often of dubious quality, that is not subject to this testing. His reliability, as a newcomer, is unknown; his information, since he is boss, may be automatically exempt from the proper discount; or his intervention may take the form of an instruction and thus be outside the process of group decision in a matter where only group decision incorporating the required specialized judgements is reliable. In all cases the intrusion is damaging.

It follows both from the tendency for decision-making to pass down into organization and the need to protect the autonomy of the group that those who hold high formal rank in an organization – the President of General Motors or General Electric – exercise only modest powers of substantive decision. This does not mean that they are without power. This power is certainly less than conventional obeisance, professional public relations or, on occasion, personal vanity insist. Decision and ratification are often confused. The first is important; the second is not. Routine decisions, if they involve a good deal of money, are also invariably thought important. The nominal head of a large corporation, though with slight power, and, perhaps, in the first stages of retirement, is visible, tangible and comprehensible. It is tempting and perhaps valuable for the corporate personality to attribute to him power of decision that, in fact, belongs to a dull and not easily comprehended collectivity.[5] Nor is it a valid explanation that the boss, though impotent on specific questions, acts on broad issues of policy. Such issues of policy, if genuine, are pre-eminently the ones that require the specialized information of the group.

Leadership does cast the membership of the groups that make the decisions and it constitutes and reconstitutes these groups in accordance with changing need. This is its most important function. In an economy where organized intelligence is the decisive factor of production this is not unimportant. On the contrary. But it cannot be supposed that it can replace or even second-guess organized intelligence on substantive decisions.

VII

In the past, leadership in business organization was identified with the entrepreneur – the individual who united ownership or control of capital with capacity for organizing the other factors of production and, in most contexts, with a further capacity for innovation.[6] With the rise of the modern corporation, the emergence of the organization required by modern technology and planning and the divorce of the owner of the capital from control of the enterprise, the entrepreneur no longer exists as an individual person in the mature industrial enter-

5. I return to these matters in the next chapter.
6. 'To act with confidence beyond the range of familiar beacons and to overcome that resistance requires aptitudes that are present in only a small fraction of the population and [they] define the entrepreneurial type as well as the entrepreneurial function.' Joseph A. Schumpeter, *Capitalism, Socialism and Democracy*, Second Edition (New York: Harper, 1947), p. 132.

prise.[7] Everyday discourse, except in the economics textbooks, recognizes this change. It replaces the entrepreneur, as the directing force of the enterprise, with management. This is a collective and imperfectly defined entity; in the large corporation it embraces chairman, president, those vice presidents with important staff or departmental responsibility, occupants of other major staff positions and, perhaps, division or department heads not included above. It includes, however, only a small proportion of those who, as participants, contribute information to group decisions. This latter group is very large; it extends from the most senior officials of the corporation to where it meets, at the outer perimeter, the white and blue collar workers whose function is to conform more or less mechanically to instruction or routine. It embraces all who bring specialized knowledge, talent or experience to group decision-making. This, not the management, is the guiding intelligence – the brain – of the enterprise. There is no name for all who participate in group decision-making or the organization which they form. I propose to call this organization the Technostructure.

7. He is still, of course, to be found in smaller firms and in larger ones that have yet to reach full maturity of organization. I deal with this evolution in the next chapters.

Chapter 7

THE CORPORATION

FEW subjects of earnest inquiry have been more unproductive than study of the modern large corporation. The reasons are clear. A vivid image of what *should* exist acts as a surrogate for reality. Pursuit of the image then prevents pursuit of the reality.

For purposes of scholarly inquiry, the corporation has a sharp legal image. Its purpose is to do business as an individual would but with the added ability to assemble and use the capital of several or numerous persons. In consequence, it can undertake tasks beyond the reach of any single person. And it protects those who supply capital by limiting their liability to the amount of their original investment, ensuring them a vote on the significant affairs of the enterprise, defining the powers and the responsibilities of directors and officers, and giving them access to the courts to redress grievance. Apart from its ability to mobilize capital and its lessened association with the active life of any individual, the corporation is not deemed to differ functionally from the individual proprietorship or partnership. Its purpose, like theirs, is to conduct business on equitable terms with other businesses and make money for the owners.

Such corporations do exist and in large numbers. But one wonders if the natural interest of the student of economics is the local paving firm or body repair shop. Or is it General Motors and Standard Oil of New Jersey and General Electric?

But these firms depart sharply from the legal image. In none of these firms is the capital pooled by original investors appreciable; in each it could be paid off by a few hours' or a few days' earnings. In none does the individual stockholder pretend to power. In all three cases, the corporation is far more influential in the markets in which it buys materials, components and labour and in which it sells its finished products than is commonly imagined to be the case with the individual proprietorship.

In consequence, nearly all study of the corporation has been concerned with its deviation from its legal or formal image. This image – that of 'an association of persons into an autonomous legal unit with a distinct legal personality that enables it to carry on business, own property and contract debts'[1] – is highly normative. It is what a corporation should be. When the modern corporation disenfranchises its stockholders, grows to gargantuan size, expands into wholly unrelated activities, is a monopsony where it buys and a monopoly where it sells, something is wrong.

That the largest and most famous corporations, those whose names are household words and whose heads are accorded the most distinguished honours by their fellow businessmen, should be considered abnormal must seem a little dubious.

Additionally, it must be evident that General Motors does not have much in common with the Massachusetts Institute of Technology professors who pool their personal funds and what they can borrow from the banks and their friends to supply some erudite item to the Department of Defense and thus, in their modest way, help to defend the country and participate in capital gains. Their enterprise, created, owned and directed by themselves and exploiting the advantages of the corporate form, approaches the established image. General Motors as clearly does not.

The answer is that there is no such thing as *a* corporation. Rather there are several kinds of corporations all deriving from a common but very loose framework. Some are subject to the market; others reflect varying degrees of adaptation to the requirements of planning and the needs of the technostructure. The person who sets out to study buildings on Manhattan on

1. Harry G. Guthmann and Herbert E. Dougall, *Corporation Financial Policy*, Second Edition (New York: Prentice-Hall, Inc., 1948), p. 9.

the assumption that all are alike will have difficulty in passing from the surviving brownstones to the skyscrapers. And he will handicap himself even more if he imagines that all buildings should be like brownstones and have load-carrying walls and that others are abnormal. So with corporations.

II

The most obvious requirement of effective planning is large size. This, we have seen, allows the firm to accept market uncertainty where it cannot be eliminated; to eliminate markets on which otherwise it would be excessively dependent; to control other markets in which it buys and sells; and it is very nearly indispensable for participation in that part of the economy, characterized by exacting technology and comprehensive planning, where the only buyer is the Federal Government.

That corporations accommodate well to this need for size has scarcely to be stressed. They can, and have, become very large. But because of the odour of abnormality, this adaptation is not stressed. The head of the largest corporation is automatically accorded precedence at all business conventions, meetings and other business rites and festivals. He is complimented for his intelligence, vision, courage, progressiveness and for the remarkable rate of growth of his firm under his direction. But the great size of his firm – the value of its assets or the number of its employees – is not praised although this is its most striking feature.

Nothing so characterizes the industrial system as the scale of the modern corporate enterprise. In 1962 the five largest industrial corporations in the United States, with combined assets in excess of $36 billion, possessed over 12 per cent of all assets used in manufacturing. The fifty largest corporations had over a third of all manufacturing assets. The 500 largest had well over two-thirds. Corporations with assets in excess of $10,000,000, some 2,000 in all, accounted for about 80 per cent of all the resources used in manufacturing in the United States.[2] In the mid nineteen-fifties, twenty-eight corporations provided approximately 10 per cent of all employment in manufacturing, mining and retail and wholesale trade. Twenty-three corporations provided 15 per cent of all the employment in manufacturing. In the first half of the decade (June 1950–June 1956) a hundred firms received two-thirds by value of all defence contracts; ten firms received one-third.[3] In 1960 four corporations accounted for an estimated 22 per cent of all industrial research and development expenditure. Three hundred and eighty-four corporations employing 5,000 or more workers accounted for 85 per cent of these expenditures; 260,000 firms employing fewer than 1,000 accounted for only 7 per cent.[4]

Planning is a function that is associated in most minds with the state. If the corporation is the basic planning unit, it is appropriate that the scale of operations of the largest should approximate those of government. This they do. In 1965, three industrial corporations, General Motors, Standard Oil of New Jersey and Ford Motor Company, had more gross income than all of the farms in the country. The income of General Motors,

2. Hearings before the Subcommittee on Antitrust and Monopoly of the Committee on the Judiciary, United States Senate, Eighty-Eighth Congress, Second Session, Pursuant to S. Res. 262, Part 1. *Economic Concentration. Overall and Conglomerate Aspects* (1964), p. 113. Data on the concentration of industrial activity in the hands of large firms, and especially any that seem to show an increase in concentration, sustain a controversy in the United States that, at times, reaches mildly pathological proportions. The reason is that much of the argument between those who see the market as a viable institution and those who feel that it is succumbing to monopolistic influences has long turned on these figures. These figures are thus defended or attacked according to predilection. However, the general orders of magnitude given here are not subject to serious question.

3. Cary Kaysen in *The Corporation in Modern Society*, Edward S. Mason, ed. (Cambridge: Harvard University Press, 1959), pp. 86–7.

4. M. A. Adelman, Hearings before the Subcommittee on Antitrust and Monopoly of the Committee on the Judiciary, United States Senate, Eighty-Ninth Congress, First Session, Pursuant to S. Res. 70, Part III. *Economic Concentration, Concentration, Invention and Innovation* (1965), pp. 1139–40.

of $20·7 billion, about equalled that of the three million smallest farms in the country – around ninety per cent of all farms. The gross revenues of each of the three corporations just mentioned far exceed those of any single state. The revenues of General Motors in 1963 were fifty times those of Nevada, eight times those of New York and slightly less than one-fifth those of the Federal Government.[5]

Economists have anciently quarrelled over the reasons for the great size of the modern corporation. Is it because size is essential in order to reap the economies of modern large scale production?[6] Is it, more insidiously, because the big firm wishes to exercise monopoly power in its markets? The present analysis allows both parties to the dispute to be partly right. The firm must be large enough to carry the large capital commitments of modern technology. It must also be large enough to control its markets. But the present view also explains what the older explanations don't explain. That is, why General Motors is not only large enough to afford the best size of automobile plant but is large enough to afford a dozen or more of the best size; and why it is large enough to produce things as diverse as aircraft engines and refrigerators, which cannot be explained by the economies of scale; and why, though it is large enough to have the market power associated with monopoly, consumers do not seriously complain of exploitation. The size of General Motors is in the service not of monopoly or the economies of scale but of planning. And for this planning – control of supply, control of demand, provision of capital, minimization of risk – there is no clear upper limit to the desirable size. It could be that the bigger the better. The corporate form accommodates to this need. Quite clearly it allows the firm to be very, very large.

5. Data from *Fortune*, U.S. Department of Agriculture and *Statistical Abstract of the United States*.
6. Cf. Joe S. Bain, 'Economics of Scale, Concentration and the Condition of Entry in Twenty Manufacturing Industries,' *The American Economic Review*, Vol. XLIV, No. 1 (March 1954).

III

The corporation also accommodates itself admirably to the needs of the technostructure. This, we have seen, is an apparatus for group decision – for pooling and testing the information provided by numerous individuals to reach decisions that are beyond the knowledge of any one. It requires, we have also seen, a high measure of autonomy. It is vulnerable to any intervention by external authority for, given the nature of the group decision-making and the problems being solved, such external authority will always be incompletely informed and hence arbitrary. If problems were susceptible to decision by individuals, no group would be involved.

One possible source of such intervention is the state. The corporate charter, however, accords the corporation a large area of independent action in the conduct of its affairs. And this freedom is defended as a sacred right. Nothing in American business attitudes is so iniquitous as government interference in the *internal* affairs of the corporation. The safeguards here, both in law and custom, are great. There is equally vehement resistance to any invasion by trade unions of the prerogatives of management.

There is also, however, the danger of intervention by the owners – by the stockholders. Their exclusion is not secured by law or sanctified by custom. On the contrary, either directly or through the agency of the Board of Directors, their power is guaranteed. But being legal does not make it benign. Exercise of such power on substantive questions requiring group decision would be as damaging as any other. So the stockholder too must be excluded.

In part this has been accomplished by the simple attrition of the stockholder's power as death and the distribution of estates, the diversifying instincts of trusts and foundations, the distributional effects of property settlements and alimony, and the artistic, philanthropic and social enjoyments of non-functional heirs all distribute the stock of any corporation to more and more hands. This process works rapidly and the distribution need by no means be complete to separate the stockholder from all effective power. In the mid nineteen-twenties, in the first case to draw wide public attention to this tendency, it became known that Colonel Robert W. Stewart, the Chairman of the Board of Directors of the Standard Oil Company of Indiana, had, in concert with some of the men who later won immortality as the architects of the Teapot Dome and Elk Hills transactions, organized a highly specialized enterprise in Canada called the Continental Trading Company. This company had the sole function of buying crude oil from Colonel E. A. Humphreys, owner of the rich Mexica field in east central Texas, and reselling it to companies controlled by the same individuals, including Standard Oil of Indiana, at a mark-up of twenty-five cents a barrel. It was an excellent business. No costs were involved, other than a small percentage to the Canadian lawyer who served as a figurehead and went hunting in Africa whenever wanted for questioning, and for mailing back the proceeds after they had been converted into Liberty Bonds. (If some of these had not been used, carelessly, to bribe Secretary of the Interior Albert B. Fall and others to pay the deficit of the Republican National Committee, Continental might have forever remained unknown as was un-questionably intended.) It was Colonel Stewart's later conten-tion that he had always intended to turn over the profit to Standard Oil of Indiana. But, absent-mindedly, he had allowed the bonds to remain in his own possession for many years and had cashed some of the coupons. In 1929 Standard of Indiana was only eighteen years distant from the decree which had broken up the Standard Oil empire of John D. Rockefeller of which it had been an important part. The Rockefellers still owned 14·9 per cent of the voting stock of the Indiana Company and were deemed to have the controlling interest. They reacted sternly to the outrage; the elder Rockefeller had, on notable occasions, imposed a somewhat similar levy on his competitors, but never on his own company. With the aid of the publicity generated by the Teapot Dome scandal, his own high standing in the financial community, his brother-in-law Winthrop W.

Aldrich, who solicited proxies, and a very large expenditure of money, John D. Rockefeller, Jr, was able to oust the Colonel, although not by a wide margin.[7] (The latter had the full support of his Board of Directors.) In the absence of the scandal and his ample resources, Rockefeller, it was realized with some shock, would have had little hope.

In most other large corporations, the chance for exerting such power would have been less and it has become increasingly less with the passage of time. Professor Gordon's prewar study of the 176 largest corporations showed that at least half of their stock was held in blocks of less than one per cent of the total outstanding. In less than a third of the companies was there a stockholder interest large enough to allow of potential control, i.e., the election of a Board of Directors, and 'the number of companies in which any large degree of *active* leadership is associated with considerable ownership is certainly even smaller.'[8] That was a quarter of a century ago; the dispersion of stock ownership, which was then much greater for the older railroad corporations than for newer industrial corporations, has almost certainly continued.[9] It means that to change control more stockholders must be persuaded, against the advice of management, to vote their stock for someone whom, in the

7. Cf. Adolf A. Berle, Jr, and Gardiner C. Means, *The Modern Corporation and Private Property* (New York: Macmillan, 1934), pp. 82–3. Of the 8,465,299 shares represented, Rockefeller got the votes of 5,510,313. Stewart retired on a pension of $75,000 a year. M. R. Werner and John Starr, *Teapot Dome* (New York: The Viking Press, Inc., 1959), pp. 274–5.

8. R. A. Gordon, *Business Leadership in the Large Corporation* (Washington: Brookings, 1945), Chapter II. The median holdings of management were 2·1 per cent of the stock. In 56 per cent of the companies, management owned less than one per cent; in only 16 of the companies did it own as much as 20 per cent of the stock outstanding. A more recent study by Mabel Newcomer, *The Big Business Executive* (New York: Columbia University Press, 1955), showed that by 1952 there had been a further reduction in management holdings.

9. This is explicitly confirmed by a study by R. J. Larner, 'The 200 Largest Nonfinancial Corporations,' *The American Economic Review,* Vol. LVI, No. 4, Part 1 (September 1966), pp. 777–87, which appeared just as this book was going to press.

nature of the case, they do not know and will not be disposed to trust. The effort must also contend with the tendency of the indifferent to give proxies to management. It is also in face of the requirement that the loser of a proxy battle, if he is an outsider, must pay the cost. And it must contend finally with the alternative, always available to the dissatisfied stockholder, of simply selling his stock. Corporate size, the passage of time and the dispersion of stock ownership do not disenfranchise the stockholder. Rather, he can vote but his vote is valueless.

IV

To be secure in its autonomy, the technostructure also needs to have a source of new capital to which it can turn without having, as a *quid pro quo*, to surrender any authority over its own decisions. Here capital abundance enters as a factor. A bank, insurance company or investment banker cannot make control of decision, actual or potential, a condition of a loan or security underwriting if funds are readily available from another and more permissive source and if there is vigorous competition for the business.

The complexity of modern technological and planning decisions also protects the technostructure from outside interference. The country banker, out of his experience and knowledge of the business, can readily interpose his judgement, as against that of a farmer, on the prospects for feeder cattle – and does. Not even the most self-confident financier would wish to question the judgement of General Electric engineers, product planners, stylists, market researchers and sales executives on the culturally advanced toaster taken up in the last chapter. By taking decisions away from individuals and locating them deeply within the technostructure, technology and planning thus remove them from the influence of outsiders.

But the corporation accords a much more specific protection to the technostructure. That is by providing it with a source of capital, derived from its own earnings, that is wholly under its own control. No banker can attach conditions as to how retained earnings are to be used. Nor can any other outsider. No one, the normally innocuous stockholder apart, has the right to ask about an investment from retained earnings that turns out badly. It is hard to overestimate the importance of the shift in power that is associated with availability of such a source of capital. Few other developments can have more fundamentally altered the character of capitalism. It is hardly surprising that retained earnings of corporations have become such an overwhelmingly important source of capital.

v

There remains one final source of danger to the autonomy of the technostructure. That arises with a failure of earnings. Then there are no retained earnings. If new plant is needed or working capital must be replenished, there will have to be appeal to bankers or other outsiders. This will be under circumstances, i.e., the fact that the firm is showing losses, when the right of such outsiders to inquire and to intervene will have to be conceded. They cannot be told to mind their own business. Thus does a shortage of capital, though limited in time and place, promptly revive the power of the capitalist. And it is in times of such failure of earnings, and then only, that the stockholder of the large corporation can be aroused. In large corporations, battles for control have been rare in recent times. And in all notable cases involving large corporations – the New York Central, Loew's, TWA, the New England railroads, Wheeling Steel, Curtis Publishing – the firm in contention was doing badly at the time. If revenues are above some minimum – they need not be at their maximum for none will know what that is – creditors cannot intervene and stockholders cannot be aroused.

Here too the corporation, and the industrial system generally, have adapted effectively to the needs of the technostructure, though, surprisingly, the nature of the adaptation has been little noticed. The adaptation is, simply, that big corporations do not lose money. In 1957, a year of mild recession in the United

States, not one of the one hundred largest industrial corporations failed to return a profit. Only one of the largest two hundred finished the year in the red. Seven years later in 1964, a prosperous year by general agreement, all of the first hundred again made money; only two among the first two hundred had losses and only seven among the first five hundred. None of the fifty largest merchandising firms – Sears, Roebuck, A & P, Safeway *et al*. – failed to return a profit. Nor, predictably, did any of the fifty largest utilities. And among the fifty largest transportation companies only three railroads, and the momentarily unfortunate Eastern Airlines, failed to make money.[10]

The American business liturgy has long intoned that this is a profit and loss economy. 'The American competitive enterprise system is an acknowledged profit and loss system, the hope of profits being the incentive and the fear of loss being the spur.'[11] This may be so. But it is not true of that organized part of the economy in which a developed technostructure is able to protect its profits by planning. Nor is it true of the United States Steel Corporation, author of the sentence just cited, which has not had losses for a quarter of a century.

VI

As always, no strong case is improved by overstatement. Among the two hundred largest corporations in the United States – those that form the heart of the industrial system – there are few in which owners exercise any important influence on decisions. And this influence decreases year by year. But there are exceptions. Some owners – the du Pont, and in lesser measure the Firestone and Ford, families are examples – participate, or have participated, actively in management. Thus they earn influence by being part of the technostructure and their influence is unquestionably increased by their ownership. Others, through position on the Board of Directors, have power in the selection of management – in deciding on those who

10. *The Fortune Directory*, August 1958, August 1965.
11. United States Steel Corporation. *Annual Report, 1958*.

make decisions. And yet others may inform themselves and intervene substantively on individual decisions – a merger, a plant acquisition or the launching of a new line.

In the last case, however, there must always be question as to how much the individual is deciding and how much has been decided for him by the group which has provided the relevant information; the danger of confusing ratification with decision must again be emphasized. And in all circumstances it is important to realize that corporate ceremony more or less deliberately disguises the reality. This deserves a final word.

Corporate liturgy strongly emphasizes the power of the Board of Directors and ultimately, thus, of the stockholders they are assumed to represent. The rites which attest this point are conducted with much solemnity; no one allows himself to be cynical as to their substance. Heavy dockets, replete with data, are submitted to the Board. Time is allowed for study. Recommendations are appended. Given the extent and group character of the preparation, rejection would be unthinkable. The Board, nonetheless, is left with the impression that it has made a decision.

Corporate procedure also allows the Board to act on financial transactions – changes in capital structure, declaration of dividends, authorization of lines of credit. These, given the control by the technostructure of its sources of savings and capital supply, are frequently the most routine and derivative of decisions. But as elsewhere noted, any association with large sums of money conveys an impression of power. It brings it to mind for the same traditional reasons as does a detachment of soldiers.

With even greater unction although with less plausibility, corporate ceremony seeks also to give the stockholders an impression of power. When stockholders are (or were) in control of a company, stockholders' meetings are an occasion of scant ceremony. The majority is voted in and the minority is voted out, with such concessions as may seem strategic, and all understand the process involved. As stockholders cease to have influence, however, efforts are made to disguise this nullity. Their convenience is considered in selecting the place of meeting.

They are presented with handsomely printed reports, the preparation of which is now a specialized business. Products and even plants are inspected. During the proceedings, as in the report, there are repetitive references to *your* company. Officers listen, with every evidence of attention, to highly irrelevant suggestions of wholly uninformed participants and assure them that these will be considered with the greatest care. Votes of thanks from women stockholders in print dresses owning ten shares 'for the excellent skill with which you run *our* company' are received by the management with well-simulated gratitude. All present show stern disapproval of critics. No important stockholders are present. No decisions are taken. The annual meeting of the large American corporation is, perhaps, our most elaborate exercise in popular illusion.

In 1956 upwards of 100,000 stockholders of Bethlehem Steel returned proxies to a management committee. These were voted routinely for a slate of directors selected by management exclusively from among its own members. The following colloquy occurred in Washington the following year:

Senator Kefauver: The exhibit shows that the members of the Board of Directors paid themselves $6,499,000 in 1956.

Mr Homer (President of Bethlehem Steel Corporation): I wish to interpose there, Senator, we did not pay ourselves. I wish that term would not be used.

Senator Kefauver: Very well, approved by the stockholders.

Mr Homer: That is better.[12]

12. U.S. Congress, Hearings on Administered Prices, Part II. *Steel*, p. 562.

Chapter 8

THE ENTREPRENEUR AND THE
TECHNOSTRUCTURE

THE corporation allows the adaptation of organization to need. As the need is different for different purposes, so is the resulting adaptation. The modern large corporation is adapted to the needs of advanced technology and the large amounts of capital and comprehensive planning which this requires. It reflects the need of its technostructure for freedom from outside interference. It wins this freedom in various ways including the provision to itself of its own supply of capital.

But if technology is simple, the capital supply need not be large. Since markets then function more reliably, there is less opportunity and less need for planning. And for these reasons there is less need for specialized intelligence and associated organization. As a result, the firm can be small. The manufacture of jet engines or the construction of nuclear reactors is open only to the large firm. But the selling of gasoline at retail or the growing of apples remains available to the relatively small concern.

This firm, as noted, is subject to the market. It cannot influence the prices at which it buys or the quantities that are available at those prices. It cannot much influence the prices at which it sells or the amounts that it sells at those prices. Nothing so effectively economizes effort and intelligence, as distinct from anxiety, as the knowledge that nothing can be done. Decisions concerning production being also simple, the whole process is well within the intellectual competence of a dominant stockholder. Others who have contributed capital can, for the same reason, inform themselves on their investment and the same remains true if the business is conducted by a hired manager. The firm being small and the number of stockholders being also small, the voting power of the stock remains important. Thus to the comprehensibility of the small corporation is added the power to make this knowledge effective. Given the risks to which the market exposes it, the owners also have need to keep watch on their property. This they can also do. Thus the corporation adapts itself well to the needs of the small enterprise. This adaptation, it will be observed, conforms (as the large corporation does not) to the design that is adumbrated in corporation law and celebrated in the well-regarded textbooks.

With growing size and complexity of operation, smaller or more passive owners tend to lose their power of decision. The number of stockholders usually increases; the share of voting power of each owner thus declines. More important, perhaps, is the failure of knowledge. Those who are not active in the management of the enterprise have less and less knowledge of what is happening, and less opportunity of informing themselves, at a time when the increasing size and complexity of the enterprise mean that more and more knowledge is required for intelligent decision. The individual or individuals who are immediately in authority, by contrast, retain the knowledge that goes automatically with such association. This knowledge often accords an individual full authority over the enterprise in the absence of voting control. Others have no alternative but to accept his lead. The one thing worse than the loss of power by the small or passive stockholder would be its uninformed exercise. So the corporation again adapts itself to need – the need at a certain stage in growth to concentrate power in some part of the ownership. This power is concentrated in someone who combines a command of capital with capacity to exercise command over the enterprise. Thus appears, in classical form, the figure of the entrepreneur.

The entrepreneur can survive a substantial degree of industrial development. Running a large mine may as well be within his reach as a small one. In the early and elementary stages of steel-making he could exercise as much authority over several Bessemer converters as over one. The vital requirement is that both technology and planning remain relatively simple – or limited.

The decline in power of the minority – or possibly even of a sufficiently dispersed majority – also provides the entrepreneur with the opportunity for growth by combination. The possession of a controlling interest gives him access to capital both from within and outside the firm. With this capital other controlling interests in other firms can be bought. Only some fraction of the total value of the enterprise must be paid for in cash. Such consolidation, led by an entrepreneur more highly capitalized or more highly motivated than his fellows, has been a feature of virtually every American industry. The process has been invariably regarded with uneasiness by all except those immediately responsible, and only the eventual results have been viewed with approval. Petroleum, steel, tobacco, copper, shipping, meat packing, processed foods, dairy products, electric and gas utilities, communications, grocery stores, drugstores, even hotels, motels, drive-in theatres and other places of rest, recreation and assignation have had their era of consolidation or currently are having one. Those whose names are linked to such consolidation – Rockefeller, Morgan, Duke, Harriman, Guggenheim, Durant, du Pont, Chrysler, Hartford, Hilton – all united control of capital with unquestioned authority in the enterprise.[1] In light of the preceding and following argument, it is worth noting that no one of equal notoriety ever followed these pioneers. The names of the successors in office are lost to history or were never known.

II

The great entrepreneur must, in fact, be compared in life with the male *Apis mellifera*. He accomplishes his act of conception at the price of his own extinction. The older entrepreneurs combined firms that were not yet technologically complex. As in the case of steel at the turn of the century when U.S. Steel was formed, a small corps of managers and supervisors directed a large and comparatively untrained and homogeneous work-

1. This was not necessarily exercised directly. As in the case of J. P. Morgan through Elbert Gary, it could be exercised through agents.

ing mass. With consolidation came control of markets – the forerunner of modern planning. But this – the setting of prices for petroleum, steel, tobacco and other products – called for very little subtlety. The feelings of customers were not much consulted. Competitors were told in idiomatic English to conform or suffer the consequences. None of this required specialized talent.

But the act of combination added new plants and products and therewith the need for specialization by function and knowledge. Sooner or later came more complex tasks of planning and control. Technology, with its own dynamic, later added its demands for capital and for specialized talent with need for yet more comprehensive planning.[2] Thus what the entrepreneur created passed inexorably beyond the scope of his authority. He could build. And he could exert influence for a time. But his creation, were it to serve the purposes for which it was brought into being, required his replacement. What the entrepreneur created, only a group of men sharing specialized information could ultimately operate.[3]

2. Before the end of the century the Standard Oil Company of New Jersey already owed much of the excellence of its technical performance not to its principal founder but to what would now be called a management team consisting of H. M. Flagler, John D. Archbold, H. H. Rogers, Charles Pratt, Oliver H. Payne and others. Cf. Allan Nevins, *Study in Power. John D. Rockefeller.* Vol. II (New York: Scribner, 1953), Chapter XXII. As early as 1882 John D. Rockefeller had the following report from a subordinate recently at headquarters. 'While in New York I was brought in contact a good deal with the Manufacturing Committee [this was a committee subordinate to the Executive Committee], and privately discussed a good many questions now before them and coming up in the near future. There is some clashing of opinion and a great deal of individuality in the committee . . . that may be detrimental to correct conclusions . . .' Ibid., Vol. II, p. 21.

3. Professor Ben B. Seligman, an astute observer of these matters, has made this point in more general terms. '. . . finance capitalism was surprisingly shortlived, for the new managerial class discovered that with an adequate supply of funds stemming from accumulated profits they could get along quite well without Wall Street tutelage. . . . Today, it is the paid professional who governs the corporation.' 'The American Corporation: Ideology and Reality,' *Dissent*, Summer 1964, p. 323.

On a few occasions entrepreneurs dramatized the point by resisting their loss of authority and thus taking issue with the inevitable. Through the twenties, thirties and into the forties, Henry Ford, ageing and autocratic, became increasingly resentful of the organization without which his company could not be run. He reacted by shunning employees of specialized technical knowledge – for many years college graduates were not only not sought but not hired at River Rouge. And he systematically fired all who, by rising in the hierarchy, seemed to be arrogating responsibility. Many of the most illustrious names in the automobile industry – Couzens, Wills, Hawkins, Rockelman, Knudsen (who helped to build General Motors), the Lelands (who founded Cadillac and Lincoln), Klingensmith and Kanzler – were extruded or axed. For a long time the executioner was Charles E. Sorenson; then Ford executed Sorenson. In the early forties, he was left with only one significant senior executive, Harry Bennett, who, with assorted pugilists, baccalaureates of the Michigan penal system, an unfrocked football coach and other colleagues of similar calibre, spent much of his time ensuring that no one threatened the authority that Ford was determined to monopolize.[4]

The result for the company was near disaster. Cars were either obsolescent or technically eccentric. Planning, particularly market control, was highly exiguous. Ford once prohibited advertising for several years and, in the classic manifestation of his attitude toward modern merchandising, said that the customer could have any colour of car provided it was black. In the thirties, the company lost money in large amounts. In the war years, its performance was so deficient that its seizure by the government was discussed as also the uniquely insulting proposal that it be managed by the Studebaker Company.[5] Withal it is doubtful if Ford replaced group decision. Rather

4. I have dealt with the Ford history in *The Liberal Hour* (Boston: Houghton, 1960), pp. 141 et seq. Peter Drucker has come to similar conclusions in his *The Practice of Management* (New York: Harper, 1954), pp. 111–20.

5. Drucker, op. cit., pp. 113–14.

he pressed it down to ever more obscure participants and thus merely impaired it.[6] He was defeated despite his complete ownership of the company. On his death, the technostructure was reconstituted by Ernest Breech. The company promptly retrieved lost ground.

At Montgomery Ward in the thirties and forties, Sewell Avery waged a similar struggle. Though he had only a minority stock interest, his legal control was not challenged for many years. '... executives who reached the top levels at Montgomery Ward knew that their chances of surviving long were meagre.'[7] On seeming to assume power that Avery believed to belong to him they were turned out and others turned in as through a revolving door. Some fifty senior officers were fired during his tenure. The company which once had parity of position with Sears, Roebuck fell far behind. And in the end Avery, like Ford, was defeated. The costs of the effort could no longer be sustained; the stockholders finally coalesced and ousted him, by now an old and senile man. Power was then lodged firmly with the technostructure.

It will be suggested that Henry Ford and Sewell Avery were men of marked eccentricity in whom the desire for power increased with age. Accordingly, they were singularly unqualified for one-man rule of a great corporation. This is true. But men of lesser eccentricity and greater judgement would not have tried. In most cases control passes smoothly from the entrepreneur to the technostructure. The exceptions show only that the transition must be accomplished.[8]

6. Ford executives of secondary rank sometimes came almost surreptitiously to Washington during the war to discuss prices. Ford did not concede the right of the government to fix prices. So it was necessary to participate in these negotiations without his knowledge or, at least, without his being fully aware of what was transpiring.

7. *The Executive Life*. By the Editors of *Fortune* (New York: Doubleday, 1956), p. 192.

8. The airlines, growing rapidly in size and technical complexity, have provided two recent examples of the transition, neither a completely peaceful passage. Howard Hughes, operating from a strong ownership position, long resisted the passage of control of TWA to the techno-

In the pages that follow it will be necessary to distinguish between corporations in which age, size and simplicity of operation still accord power to an individual who has control of capital and those where the technostructure has taken over. I will refer to the first as the Entrepreneurial Corporation and the second as the Mature Corporation.

III

Until recent times, senior officials of the mature corporation were inclined to assume the public mantle of the entrepreneur. They pictured themselves as self-reliant men, individualistic, with a trace of justifiable arrogance, fiercely competitive and with a desire to live dangerously. Individualism is the note that 'sounds through the business creed like the pitch in a Byzantine Choir.'[9] 'They're bred to race. It's the same with people. It's something that's born into you.'[10] 'Business is tough – it's no kissing game.'[11] These characteristics are not readily reconciled with the requirements of the technostructure. Not indifference but sensitivity to others, not individualism but accommodation to organization, not competition but intimate and continuing cooperation are the prime requirements for group action.

Nor is any reconciliation possible. The assertion of the competitive individualism of the corporate executive, to the extent that it continues, is ceremonial, traditional and, on occasion, a manifestation of personal vanity. In World War II, commanders of armoured units, functioning from well to the

---

structure. And Eddie Rickenbacker fought a similar devolution of power at Eastern Airlines. Both companies suffered during this period. Both recovered promptly when the technostructure took over.

9. Francis X. Sutton, Seymour E. Harris, Carl Kaysen and James Tobin, *The American Business Creed* (Cambridge : Harvard University Press, 1956), p. 251.

10. Charles 'Tex' Thornton, President of Litton Industries, describing the qualities of a senior executive. Osborn Elliott, *Men at the Top* (New York: Harper, 1959), p. 21.

11. J. Peter Grace, President of W. R. Grace and Co. Ibid., p. 69.

rear and worrying about gasoline, spare parts, reinforcements and their influence with Eisenhower, identified themselves, nonetheless, with Lord Cardigan and the Light Brigade.

In romance the past greatly improves on the present. In the history of almost every industry, there has been a famous and sometimes flamboyant entrepreneur. Like the tank commander, the head of the modern enterprise, in which all important actions are studiously considered by committees, all contingencies carefully anticipated and all adverse ones either prevented or negated, seeks to see himself in an earlier and more heroic image. Doubtless this does no harm. Additionally his function is to lend dignity and an aspect of power to stockholders' and directors' meetings and other business ceremonials; to salute customers and clients of equal or greater dignity; to give the equivalent of the royal assent to agreements, contracts and indentures; to represent the enterprise in its more honorific relations with government; to act as an emissary to liberal learning; and to affirm, on appropriate public occasions, faith in free enterprise, the social responsibility of business and the continuing relevance of ancestral virtues. For all these rites the mantle of Carnegie, Rockefeller or Henry Ford is more than a little helpful.[12]

And this reaching for the mantle of the classical entrepreneur is, almost certainly, a passing phase. A younger generation of executives accepts the fact of organization and its bearing on behaviour. 'To a surprising degree, American businessmen and writers about business have [stopped] interpreting our cooperative society as individualistic and [have stopped] concealing our quest for security in phrases like competition . . .'[13] Interdependence is recognized. As in all organization, there is

12. We have here the reason generals, admirals and diplomats, after a lifetime in public service, frequently spend their last years as heads of business corporations, and serve with success in a role for which they are manifestly unqualified. It is because they are well qualified for ceremonial functions, and this (including honorific appearance in Washington) is what the position almost exclusively requires.

13. Earl F. Cheit in *The Business Establishment*, Earl F. Cheit, ed. (New York: Wiley, 1964), p. 155.

protective compassion for the man who, because of misfortune, temperament, personal inadequacy, or alcohol, falls by the wayside.[14] Executive life, so far from being competitive and dangerous, is highly secure. Of some eight hundred senior executives – the recipients of the highest salaries in each of approximately three hundred industrial, railroad and utility corporations – who were in office in 1952, three-quarters had been with their particular company for more than twenty years.[15] A few years ago the subsequent careers of 308 senior executives – board chairmen and presidents of the largest corporations – who were in office in 1925 were traced to their end. Of these 265 continued with the same firm until death or retirement. Only thirteen resigned before retirement and this included those who resigned to take better jobs. Sixteen lost their jobs because of changes in the control of the company but this included some who left because they had sold their own interest. Only five lost their jobs because the company failed or because they were fired. These men enjoyed a marked increase in their security of tenure as compared with 313 executives in office in 1900 of whom only 157 eventually achieved death or honourable retirement.[16] A study of more recent classes would almost certainly show, along with some increased mobility between corporations, a yet further increase in security of executive employment in general.

IV

It is noteworthy that the financial markets have long since accepted the reality of the technostructure as distinct from the entrepreneur. Were the latter in command of the large corporation – if he exercised important power – anything affecting his tenure in office would have an important effect on its pros-

14. Cf. 'The Alcoholic Executive,' *Fortune*, January 1960, pp. 99 et seq.

15. *The Executive Life*, p. 30. The responses being not quite complete, the number works out to fewer than three to a company.

16. Mabel Newcomer, *The Big Business Executive* (New York: Columbia University Press, 1955), pp. 93 et seq.

pective earnings, growth and capital gains. The stock market would then be vitally concerned. Were he taken ill, financial reporters would seek hard news at the hospital. The ticker would carry electrocardiograms. Holders of stock on margin would have doctor's bulletins relayed to them in Nassau. The market would rise and fall with his temperature, blood pressure and cholesterol count.

Similarly the months preceding his scheduled retirement would be a nervous time. News would be sought on whether a successor had been trained or a replacement found. The new man would be handicapped like a horse – his special talents would be appraised and his experience, temperament, family situation, working hours and drinking habits assessed. Stock in firms headed by an able man who was a heavy cigarette smoker would sell at a slight discount.

None of this happens for it is known that retirement, death and replacement, however important for the individual involved, have not the slightest effect on General Motors or Continental Can.[17] Power, it is implicitly recognized, has passed to the technostructure. So its exercise is unaffected by the age or morbidity of any man. Though men accord the head of the great corporation the deference his position calls for, no one allows this to affect his financial judgement.

V

Because individuals have more standing in the culture than organizations, they regularly get credit for achievement that belongs, in fact, to organization. It is not Procter and Gamble that has been winning new worlds in detergents; it is Procter and Gamble under the inspired leadership of Neil H. McElroy. To this tendency, principals, on occasion, contribute. 'At every turn the chief executive must be prepared to persuade people that his point of view must prevail.'[18]

17. The stock of a smaller or newer company dominated by one man, in contrast, does move on news of personnel changes.

18. John T. Connor, then President of Merck & Company, in *Men at the Top*, p. 10.

Clearly some individuals do add lustre to organization. The accomplishments of the great physician are his own, not those of the hospital where he serves. The achievements of the poet are his own, not those of the institution where he is currently the artist in residence. Similarly the opera singer or actor and, though not always, the great scientist.

Men are, in fact, either sustained by organization or they sustain organization. They are either esteemed because of organization or the organization is esteemed because of them. The individual is himself rarely a sound judge of these matters. Those who are esteemed because of organization almost invariably attribute the acclaim to their own personality.

But there is an infallible test. That is to observe what happens to the individual when he leaves the organization or retires. The great physician is not greatly diminished by being separated from his hospital. Nor, except as regards regular salary, is the poet when he leaves the university. Nor is the competent newspaperman when he moves on. Nor the great scientist nor the entertainer. They sustained, and were not sustained by, the organization to which they belonged.

By contrast the politician when he is defeated, the ambassador when he retires, the university president when he becomes emeritus and the peacetime general who fails to become a corporation president face total obscurity. They were sustained by organization; on losing its support they pass permanently into the shadows. To some who have naturally assumed that their eminence was their own the shock is very severe. Others sense their situation. Nothing so explains the primordial vigour with which politicians fight for office and seek to retain it to senility and beyond. Between being in and out of political office the difference is not slight. It is total.

But for none is the transition more drastic than for the great business executive. Even the scrupulously inadequate governor or the tediously time-serving senator can count, after well-merited retirement, on some of the graces of public position. He will be a delegate to national conventions, be introduced at fund-raising dinners as 'that great statesman' and always be addressed by his former title. For the corporation president, by contrast, there is only Stygian darkness. Following the final flight in the company jet, there will be only an honorific association with the Board of Directors and sometimes not that. His memoirs will not be in demand; the United Fund will want a man more affirmatively identified with affairs; his only continuing public responsibilities will be in his own church; his name will not again appear in the papers until the day following his death. The great entrepreneur lived out his last days disposing of his wealth or resisting those who sought to have him do so. The modern executive does not have enough money so to occupy himself. Such is his recessional. The conclusion requires no undue emphasis: Pre-eminently the organization man is sustained by organization.

Chapter 9

A DIGRESSION ON SOCIALISM

From the standpoint of the employee, it is coming to make less and less practical difference to him what his country's official ideology is and whether he happens to be employed by a government or commercial corporation ... ARNOLD J. TOYNBEE, *Harvard Business Review*, September–October 1958.

IN the industrial enterprise, power rests with those who make decisions. In the mature enterprise, this power has passed, inevitably and irrevocably, from the individual to the group. That is because only the group has the information that decision requires. Though the constitution of the corporation places power in the hands of the owners, the imperatives of technology and planning remove it to the technostructure.

Since technology and planning are what accord power to the technostructure, the latter will have power wherever these are a feature of the productive process. Its power will not be peculiar to what, in the cadenzas of ideology, is called the free enterprise or capitalist system. If the intervention of private authority, in the form of owners, must be prevented in the private firm, so must the intervention of public authority in the public firm. Otherwise, it will be damaging as the intervention of Ford and Avery was damaging.

As a further consequence, puzzlement over capitalism without control by the capitalist will be matched by puzzlement over socialism without control by the society. A final consequence is a drastic revision of the prospects for socialism in the form, at least, in which most socialists think it worth having. Three cases of the technostructure under socialism throw light on these matters.

II

Following World War II Great Britain committed herself to limited socialism under parliamentary auspices. The British, who have a superior instinct for administration, recognized the need for autonomy for the nationalized industries. A key issue, seemingly small but in fact decisive, was that of parliamentary questions. Were these allowed on the decisions of the technostructure, ministers would have to be informed of such decision in advance. Otherwise they would confess neglect of duty. But the decisions, or the important ones, which Parliament would be most likely to question would depend on complex and technical information. If the minister were to exercise informed judgement he would need the help of a staff. Responsibility would thus be removed from the firm to the ministry. The cost in time would also be high. Only if such parliamentary intervention were excluded could the firm, and therein the technostructure, act responsibly and promptly on decisions requiring specialized information. Coal, electricity, gas, transport, the airlines and other publicly owned industries have, in consequence, all been accorded such autonomy.

This autonomy is necessary both for small decisions and what appear to be large questions of policy. Whether to rely on atomic energy for power has the aspect of a question of policy. But the comparative advantages of atomic and molecular reactions for the generation of electricity are decided only by a variety of scientific, technical, economic and planning judgements. Only a committee, or more precisely a complex of committees, can combine the knowledge, training and experience that must be brought to bear. So also with the question of whether the North Atlantic should be flown by American or British aircraft. So, in only slightly less measure, the question of how wage scales are to be revised or the railways rationalized. Everywhere the group has the monopoly of competent knowledge. In consequence in Britain '. . . the public corporation has not up to the present been in any real sense accountable to Parliament whose function has been limited to

107

fitful, fragmentary, and largely ineffective *ex post facto* criticism.' [1]

For most socialists the purpose of socialism is the control of productive enterprises by the society. For democratic socialists this means the legislature. None, or not many, seek socialism so that power can be exercised by an autonomous authority. Yet this is where power must reside. And, to repeat, this is true not only of small decisions where delegation might be expected but of great ones where Parliament might reasonably be expected to have a voice. It does not matter that the capitalist, the ancient enemy of the socialist, himself suffers from the same exclusion. Most socialists set great store by traditional belief as distinct from reality. They do not see, or admit, that the capitalist is similarly excluded from power. Capitalism is still capitalism. But there is considerable distress over how little difference nationalization of an industry means. 'If an intelligent observer from Mars or Venus could come and examine all large contemporary industrial concerns – public or private – as *working enterprises*, he would notice, I suspect, only their overwhelming sameness.' [2] The technostructure in the cases of both public and private ownership assumes similar powers and uses the same group methods for arriving at decisions. That it looks very much alike is not surprising.

The late Aneurin Bevan reacted to the gravitational descent of power into the technostructure of the public enterprise by asking for much stronger parliamentary control. This, of course, would have collided with the vulnerability of the technostructure to outside interference. Control would then be at the expense of competence. This has occurred; I will examine some cases in a moment. A much larger number of socialists have come to feel that public corporations are, by their nature,

1. C. A. R. Crosland in *The Corporation in Modern Society*, Edward S. Mason, ed. (Cambridge: Harvard University Press, 1959), p. 268. Mr Crosland is an economist, a senior figure in the British Labour Party and, at this writing, Minister of Education.

2. A. M. F. Palmer, 'On Public Accountability,' *Socialist Commentary*, January 1960, p. 13.

'remote, irresponsible bodies, immune from public scrutiny or democratic control.'[3] They have given up the fight for public ownership or accord it only lip service. Socialism has come to mean government by socialists who have learned that socialism, as anciently understood, is impractical.

III

In a number of new countries the effort to exercise social control, forsworn in the British experiment, has been tried. It has been, perhaps, the most uniformly dismal experiment of countries seeking economic development.

At Oxford, the London School of Economics and the Sorbonne, the British and French trained the elites of their erstwhile empires to a deep faith in socialism. To this was later added a practical case. Much of the capital for development in new countries comes from abroad as publicly organized aid. Or it is raised locally not from voluntary savings of individuals and corporations but from domestic taxation or other public sources.[4] It has seemed plausible that the state should invest publicly raised funds in publicly owned firms. And private entrepreneurs of requisite competence and responsibility have not always been abundant.

In India and Ceylon, as also in some of the African countries, public enterprises have not, as in Britain, been accorded autonomy. Here the socialist faith has been thought to require parliamentary control – the right to examine budgets and expenditures, review policies and, in particular, to question management through the responsible minister on any and all actions of the corporation. Here, as elsewhere, if the minister is to be questioned, he must have knowledge. He cannot plead that he is uninformed without admitting to being a nonentity – a condition, common enough in politics, that cannot however

3. Crosland, op. cit., p. 268.

4. Notably by buying resources away from private individuals and firms, and thus imposing a form of saving on the private sector of the economy by inflation.

be confessed. Technical personnel are less experienced than in the older countries. Organization is less mature. These lead to error, and suggest to parliamentarians and civil servants the need for careful review of decisions by higher and presumably more competent authority.[5] Poverty makes nepotism and favouritism in letting contracts both more tempting and more culpable than in the rich country where jobs are plentiful and business is easier to come by.[6] This calls for further review. And rigid personnel and civil service rules, the established British answer to primitive administrative capacity, extend into the public firm and prevent the easy constitution and reconstitution of groups, with information relevant to changing problems. This, we have seen, is the essence of effective action by the technostructure.[7]

The effect of this denial of autonomy and the ability of the technostructure to accommodate itself to changing tasks has been visibly deficient operations. Delay occasioned by checking decisions has added its special dimensions of cost. In business operations a wrong decision can often be reversed at little cost when the error becomes evident. But the cost of a delayed decision – of the men and capital that stand idle awaiting the decision – cannot be retrieved.

As a further consequence of this interference, social control bears most strongly on the two decisions which are of the greatest popular interest – on the prices charged the public and the wages paid to workers. This has the effect of keeping prices

5. India, in particular, as a legacy of its colonial past has an illusion of official omnipotence which extends to highly technical decisions.

6. 'Employment policies are especially likely to be subject to external pressure; decisions on how many people are hired or – more important – fired and who they are, invite political intervention where employment is rife and highly particularistic loyalties persist.' Elliot J. Berg, 'Socialism and Economic Development in Tropical Africa,' *The Quarterly Journal of Economics*, Vol. LXXVIII, No. 4 (November 1964), p. 570.

7. I have discussed these matters, in the context of India, in *Economic Development* (Boston: Houghton, 1964), Chapter VIII. Also *Economic Planning in India: Five Comments* (Calcutta: Indian Statistical Institute, 1956), and with regard to Ceylon in *Papers by Visiting Economists* (Colombo: Planning Secretariat, 1959).

lower and wages higher than the more autocratic technostructure would permit. It eliminates net earnings and therewith this source of savings. The poor country, which most needs capital, is thus denied the source on which the rich countries most rely. In India and Ceylon nearly all publicly owned corporations operate at a loss.[8]

The experience with public enterprises, where autonomy is denied, thus accords fully – and tragically – with expectation.

IV

When the case of democratic socialism began to emerge in the closing decades of the last century, the capitalist entrepreneur was still in authority. The firm was small enough and the state of technology simple enough so that he could wield substantial power of decision. The belief that his power could be exercised instead by a parliament or by a directly responsible agent was not an idle dream. Certainly a public body could supersede his power to set prices and wages and therewith his power to exploit the consumer and the wage-earner.

The misfortune of democratic socialism has been the misfortune of the capitalist. When the latter could no longer control, democratic socialism was no longer an alternative. The technical complexity and planning and associated scale of operations, that took power from the capitalist entrepreneur and lodged it with the technostructure, removed it also from the reach of social control.

In nearly all of the non-communist world, socialism, meaning public ownership of industrial enterprises, is a spent slogan.

8. The exceptions in India in recent years have been Air India and the Hindustan Machine Tool Company, both of which have a substantial measure of autonomy and thus affirm the point, and the railroads which have an ancient tradition of substantial independence. It is interesting that governments, which are reluctant to grant autonomy to other enterprises, regularly accord it to their airline and often with very good results. It seems possible that public officials, who are among the important patrons, sense the unique dangers of denying autonomy in this industry.

Like promises to enforce the antitrust laws in the United States, it is no longer a political programme but an overture to nostalgia. The choice being between success without social control and social control without success, democratic socialism no longer seems worth the struggle. There have been few more important consequences of the take-over by the technostructure.

It is possible that there is, in fact, more to the case for the autonomous public corporation than the modern socialist now sees. The problem of the technostructure, as we shall presently observe, is whether it can be accommodated to social goals or whether society will have to be accommodated instead to its needs. The nature of the legal ownership has an undoubted bearing on the amenability of the technostructure to social goals. I shall come back to this in later chapters.

V

If autonomy is necessary for the effective performance by the technostructure, it should be needed by the firm in the Soviet-type economies. The requirement begins with the need to combine the specialized information of different men. There is nothing about this requirement that is peculiar to any economic system or which can be dispensed with by any ideology.

The need for autonomy in the Soviet firm could, however, be somewhat less, for its functions are far fewer than those of an American enterprise of comparable size in a similar industry. That is because much planning that is done by the American or Western European firm is, in the Soviet-type economy, done by the state. The large American corporation sets its minimum prices, organizes the demand for its products, establishes or negotiates prices for its raw materials and components and takes steps to ensure supply. It also establishes or negotiates rates for various categories of trained and specialized talent, as well as of labour, and here again takes steps to ensure supply. In the U.S.S.R. these functions are all performed, well or less well, by the state planning apparatus.[9] Production and investment targets, which are established by the American firm for itself, are given to the Soviet firm, though with some flexibility in application, by the state. The firm is the basic planning unit in the western economies. In the Soviet system it is still the state.

In consequence, the organization of the Soviet firm is far simpler than that of its American counterpart. There are no comparable sales, merchandising, dealer relations, product planning, procurement or like departments. Most of the top positions in the Soviet firm are held by engineers. This is in keeping with its much greater preoccupation with technical and managerial as distinct from planning functions.[10]

It would appear, nonetheless, that considerable and increasing store is set by the autonomy of this, by American standards, very simple organization. There are two[11] major sources of outside interference – the state planning apparatus and the Communist Party.[12] Soviet economic literature recurrently warns against bureaucratic interference by either with the operations of the firm.

The Russians have learnt by experience that you cannot have responsible and efficient action at the level of the firm with continuous intervention and instruction from numerous outside authorities. Conflicting instructions from outside give the manager innumerable excuses for failure, and waste and inefficiency may result from a

9. Although the public supply of materials and components is far from reliable, the firm is prohibited, under penalty of law, from hiring 'expediters' or otherwise intervening in the procurement process.

10. 'In the United States and other Western countries the problems of management include planning and innovation. ... These decisions are taken in the U.S.S.R. above the level of the enterprise manager.' Report of the IIE Seminar on Industrial Technology in the Soviet Union, 24–5 March 1960, Institute of International Education, New York.

11. A third, the trade union, is clearly of lesser importance. I advert to it in Chapters 23 and 24.

12. I draw here not only on the literature of Soviet Planning but on fairly extensive first-hand observation in the spring of 1959 and very briefly in the summer of 1964. I am extensively grateful to Soviet economists and plant managers for help and hospitality.

serious attempt to run the firm from a distance. Every argument for delegation, decentralization, and devolution used in discussions about business administration in the west is echoed, although in a different jargon, in Russia. And the case for such devolution has been pressed with increasing emphasis as Russian industry has grown and become more complex.[13]

Plant managers do not hesitate to stress to visitors both their need for autonomy and their past difficulties. On occasion they defend the need to ignore or violate orders from outside.[14] On the other side, managements, especially those of large firms, are frequently condemned for breaking off diplomatic relations with higher authority and behaving as 'feudal lords' above the law. In the Soviet Union the most important medium of social comment, poetry apart, is the novel; one of the half-dozen most discussed works since World War II has been Dudintsev's defence of the small and independent inventor and his condemnation of the mindless bureaucracy of the great metal *combinat*.[15]

The position of the Party secretary is also predictably difficult. He enters the plant hierarchy horizontally as a member of the staff or working force and is subject to the external authority of the Party. If he participates as a member of the decision-making group, he naturally becomes responsible for

13. Ely Devons, 'The Enigma of the Russian Economic System,' *Listener*, Vol. LVIII, No. 1483, London (29 August 1957).

14. On this see David Granick's *The Red Executive* (New York: Doubleday, 1960), pp. 162 et seq. And his earlier volume *Management of the Industrial Firm in the U.S.S.R.* (New York: Columbia University Press, 1954), especially pp. 127 et seq. The following reference to feudal lords is from page 128 of the latter.

15. Vladimir Dudintsev, *Not by Bread Alone* (New York: Dutton, 1957). The author's affections are in close harmony with the American who, in the tradition of Brandeis, argues for the genius of the small entrepreneur as against the stolid, unimaginative behaviour of the great corporation. Both have more support from humane instinct than reality. Neither sees that modern technology makes essential the machinery for mobilizing specialized knowledge. Dudintsev's inventor, however attractive, could have made no useful contribution, as a lone individual, to getting the cosmonauts into space.

the decisions. He is no longer an independent agent of the Party. If he does not participate, he no longer knows what is going on. If he is too good a source of information, 'he may be raised in [Party] rank but . . . then he will not be able to find out what is going on in the plant. Nobody will have any confidence in him . . .'[16] Professor Granick concludes that the relationship is 'an uneasy compromise'[17] Given the imperatives of group decision and the need of the group to protect itself from outside intervention, this would seem to be the only possible result.

In sum, it seems likely that the Soviet resolution of the problem of authority in the industrial enterprise is not unlike that in the West – although no one can be precisely sure. Full social authority over the large enterprise is proclaimed. Like that of the stockholder and the Board of Directors in the United States, it is celebrated in all public ritual. The people and Party are paramount. But in practice large and increasing autonomy is accorded to the enterprise.

This is further suggested by the trend to decentralization, so-called, in the Soviet and other Eastern European countries. This has accorded greater authority over prices, individual wage rates, production targets, investment and other employment of earnings, to the firm. In the West, especially among professional ideologists and volunteer propagandists, this has been widely hailed as a step towards control by the market. It isn't. There is no tendency for the large Soviet firm to become subordinate and subject to uncontrolled markets for its products, production needs or labour supply, and thus for its production decisions. Given the level of technology, the related commitment of time and capital and the effect of techno-

16. Joseph S. Berliner, *Factory and Manager in the U.S.S.R.* (Cambridge: Harvard University Press, 1957), p. 265. This study is based on information from individuals familiar with Soviet industrial life who have come to the West. This speaker was an engineer and a former high official of a large machine-building plant. The obsolescence rate of such observations must be kept in mind – along with the danger of attaching undue importance to any single view.

17. Granick, op. cit.

logy on the functioning of markets, this would no more be possible in the U.S.S.R. than in the United States.

Decentralization in the Soviet-type economies involves not a return to the market but a shift of some planning functions from the state to the firm. This reflects, in turn, the need of the technostructure of the Soviet firm to have more of the instruments for successful operation under its own authority. It thus contributes to its autonomy. There is no tendency for the Soviet and the Western systems to convergence by the return of the former to the market. Both have outgrown that. There is measurable convergence to the same form of planning.

The next question, important for both socialist and non-socialist societies, is what the technostructure seeks to do with the autonomy it requires. What are its goals? Do these accord with those of society? What is the interaction between the two? To these questions, after a preparatory look at existing belief, I now turn.

Chapter 10

THE APPROVED CONTRADICTION

The beauty of the economic man was that we knew exactly
what he was after. ALFRED NORTH WHITEHEAD

THE market has only one message for the business firm. That
is the promise of more money. If the firm has no influence on
its prices, as the Wisconsin dairy farm has no influence on the
price of milk, it has no options as to the goals that it pursues.
It must try to make money and, as a practical matter, it must
try to make as much as possible. Others do. To fail to conform
is to invite loss, failure and extrusion. Certainly a decision to
subordinate interest in earnings to an interest in a more con-
tented life for workers, cows or consumers would, in the absence of exceptional supplementary income, mean financial
disaster. Given this need to maximize revenue, the firm is thus
fully subject to the authority of the market.

When the firm has influence on market prices – when it has
the power commonly associated with monopoly – it has also
long been assumed that it will seek as large a profit as possible.
It could settle for less than the maximum but it is assumed that
it seeks monopoly power in order to be free of the limitations
set by competition on its return. Why should it seek monopoly
power and then settle for less than its full advantages? When
demand is strong, the monopolistic firm can extract more
revenue from the market; when demand slackens, it can get
less. But so long as it tries to get as much as possible it will
still be subject to control by the market and ultimately, as
sustained by the compulsions of avarice, by the preferences of
consumers, as expressed by their purchases. Were the mono-
polist regularly to settle for something less than a maximum
return, the causes of this restraint would have to be explained
by forces apart from the market. Along with the state of
demand these forces would be a factor determining prices,

production and profit. Belief in the market as the transcendent regulator of economic behaviour requires, therefore, a parallel belief that participating firms will always seek to maximize their earnings. If this is assumed there is, by exclusion, no need to search for other motives.

When planning replaces the market this admirably simple explanation of economic behaviour collapses. Technology and the companion commitments of capital and time have forced the firm to emancipate itself from the uncertainties of the market. And specialized technology has rendered the market increasingly unreliable. So the firm controls the prices at which it buys materials, components and talent and takes steps to ensure the necessary supply at these prices. And it controls the prices at which it sells and takes steps to ensure that the public, other producers or the state take the planned quantities at these prices. So far from being controlled by the market, the firm, to the best of its ability, has made the market subordinate to the goals of its planning. Prices, costs, production and resulting revenues are established not by the market but, within broad limits later to be examined, by the planning decisions of the firm.

The goal of these planning decisions could still be the greatest possible profit. We have already seen that a high and reliable flow of earnings is important for the success of the technostructure. But the market is no longer specifying and enforcing that goal. Accordingly profit maximization – the only goal that is consistent with the rule of the market – is no longer necessary. The competitive firm had no choice of goals. The monopoly could take less than the maximum; but this would be inconsistent with its purpose in being a monopoly. But planning is the result not of the desire to exploit market opportunity but the result, among other factors, of the unreliability of markets. Subordination to the market, and to the instruction that it conveys, has disappeared. So there is no longer, *a priori*, reason to believe that profit maximization will be the goal of the technostructure. It could be, but this must be shown. And it will be difficult to show if other things are more important than profit for the success of the technostructure. It will also be difficult to show if the technostructure does not get the profit.

If the technostructure has goals other than profit maximization, this is a matter of considerable interest and importance. At any given time the public aims, professed, unrevealed or concealed, of the President of the United States and of cabinet officials, legislators and jurists and generals, nourish a large volume of scholarship, punditry, reportorial enterprise and fantasy. Similarly, in lesser measure, the governments of states, cities and school districts. But much of our life, and nearly all of it that involves the procurement and use of income, is subject to the decisions of the technostructure. It sets our prices, persuades us on our purchases and distributes the resulting income to those who participate in production. The planning of the technostructure also extends, we have seen, to the management of the demand for those products that are purchased by the state. Thus to know how and to what ends we are governed it is necessary to know the goals of the technostructure. These are no longer confined to profit maximization; there is a choice. Depending on this choice prices, production and income will be different. In none of these matters does the corporation have plenary power; but neither do politicians have absolute power, and interest in their intentions does not for that reason diminish. The simple will seek only to know how they are governed from Washington, Albany, Sacramento and City Hall. Others will ask also for an understanding of the goals of industrial planning.

However, these issues, it will be evident, only come up for consideration when it is agreed that the market is not in full control. And this point is still contested with some vigour. The nature of this resistance must now be examined.

II

That the firms that comprise the industrial system have extensive power over their prices is common ground among economists. Supporters of the market take up their position on a second line of defence. The firm is controlled by the market not in the total subservience of the dairy farmer, but as the classical monopoly is controlled.

The defence has two parts. The firm is not assumed to exercise any significant influence over purchase by the consumer or the state. That these remain sovereign is not argued; it is an article of faith. And it is further assumed that, although it could do otherwise, the firm compulsively maximizes profits. Therefore as consumer choice varies or the requirements of the state change, the prices and levels of output at which profits are maximized also change. To these changes the firm responds. Thus its behaviour remains subject to control by the market and, ultimately, by the consumer. This will be so, however large and powerful the firm may be, as long as it subordinates all discretionary power to the desire to make as much money as possible.

It follows that conservatives should be expected to insist on the assumption of profit maximization. The power of the market, which is the fulcrum of traditional attitudes, depends on the validity of this assumption. It is a far, far better thing to admit to monopoly profits, even at extortionate levels, than to concede that the market is impotent. And acute conservatives do their duty. Profit maximization is held to be 'the strongest, the most universal, and the most persistent of the forces governing entrepreneurial behaviour.'[1] 'Few trends could so thoroughly undermine the very foundation of our free society as the acceptance by corporate officials of a social responsibility other than to make as much money for their stockholders as possible.'[2]

But profit maximization is also defended by liberals. One

1. George J. Stigler, *The Theory of Price*, Revised Edition (New York: Macmillan, 1952), p. 149.
2. Milton Friedman, *Capitalism and Freedom* (Chicago: The University of Chicago Press, 1962), p. 133. Also quoted by Earl F. Cheit in *The Business Establishment* (New York: Wiley, 1964), p. 163. Professors Stigler and Friedman are, by wide agreement, the two ablest exponents of conservative economic attitudes in the United States.

branch of the liberal faith for which monopoly is the ancient *bête noire* rejects as special pleading any suggestion that the great corporation does not exact its pound of flesh. To suggest this is to apologize for monopoly. And another group, while agreeing that the firm may not maximize its revenues, argues that it should, for this is the only legitimate exercise of business power. If it takes less than the maximum – if it pursues any goal other than profit – it is assuming public responsibilities which are no part of its task. 'The function of business is to produce sustained high-level profits. The essence of free enterprise is to go after profit in any way that is consistent with its own survival. . . . It should let government take care of the general welfare. . . .'[3] 'If we are to have rulers . . . let us join in choosing our rulers – and ruling them.'[4]

That the consumer and that state are not sovereign in their demand – that they are subject to the management of the firms that supply them with goods and services – is sufficiently argued elsewhere in this book. And the methods used in this management, for example advertising in managing the consumer, are not of a kind that can be practised in secret. The reader is not without resources for personal verification. The case for (and against) maximization of revenue must however be examined in detail. This is necessary even though the self-contradictions involved will seem rather evident to most readers. The way is not open for the examination of the goals of the technostructure until profit maximization is expelled from its presumptively pre-emptive role. For the instinct of traditionalists in defending it is strategically sound. Once the assumption of profit maximization is abandoned the way is open for a flood of new, inconvenient and sometimes disturbing ideas. It is then

3. Theodore Levitt, 'The Dangers of Social Responsibility,' *Harvard Business Review*, Vol. 36, No. 5 (September–October 1958), pp. 44–9.
4. Ben W. Lewis, 'Economics by Admonition,' *The American Economic Review*, Supplement, 49 (1959), p. 395. Quoted by Eugene V. Rostow in *The Corporation in Modern Society*, Edward F. Mason, ed. (Cambridge: Harvard University Press, 1959), p. 68. The same point is urged by Professor Rostow.

evident how shrewd was the instinct of the traditionally-minded in holding to the formula that kept them out.

Nor is exposure of the contradiction in the case for profit maximization, although it requires a measure of patience, without its further rewards. In our culture few things give more pleasure than the sight of men caught in embarrassments of their own manufacture. Such is the pleasure when a liberal explains why his house deed has a restrictive covenant. Such is the joy when a segregationist mayor is found in a Negro brothel. Such has always been the joy when an advocate of fiscal rectitude is caught with his hand in the cash register. In the thirties, Mr Richard Whitney, recently the President of the New York Stock Exchange, was convicted of stealing some millions of dollars held by him in trust for others. There was, regrettably, much public pleasure. This was not because people are cruel or relish seeing a fellow citizen or even a Harvard man enter Sing Sing. It was because Mr Whitney had previously been famous for his insistence that both he and all other members of the money market were touched by a fiscal divinity which excluded any possible wrongdoing. Economists have long been uncompromising in their insistence that no human motive can rival in power the pursuit of personal profit. There is charm in discovering that their case for profit maximization must be combined with the assumption that the men who are said to maximize profits do not maximize their profits.

III

The assumption that men seek to maximize their own return – to make as much money for themselves as possible – has an attractively unsentimental quality. It is the behaviour that capitalists have always felt obliged to defend and which socialists have always thought deplorable but also insistently human. It would be good were man so constituted that he would labour on behalf of others. Taking him as he is, this is not really to be expected and certainly not in modern business.

The Approved Contradiction

Yet it is also agreed that the modern large corporation is, quite typically, controlled by its management. The managerial revolution as distinct from that of the technostructure is accepted. So long as earnings are above a certain minimum it would also be widely agreed that the management has little to fear from the stockholders. Yet it is for these stockholders, remote, powerless and unknown, that management seeks to maximize profits. Management does not go out ruthlessly to reward itself – a sound management is expected to exercise restraint. Already at this stage, in the accepted view of the corporation, profit maximization involves a substantial contradiction. Those in charge forgo personal reward to enhance it for others.

The contradiction becomes much sharper as one recognizes the role of the technostructure. If power is regarded as resting with a few senior officers, then their pecuniary interest could be imagined at least to be parallel to that of the owners. The higher the earnings the higher the salaries they can justify, the greater the return on any stock they may themselves hold, and the better the prospect for any stock options they may have issued to themselves. Even these contentions stand only limited examination. There are few corporations in which it would be suggested that executive salaries are at a maximum. As a not uncritical observer has recently observed, '. . . [the] average level of salaries of managers even in leading corporations is not exceptionally high.'[5] Astronomical figures, though not exceptional, are usually confined to the very top. Stock holdings by management are small and often non-existent.[6] Stock op-

5. Wilbert E. Moore, *The Conduct of the Corporation* (New York: Random House, Inc., 1962), p. 13.

6. As noted in Chapter 7, in 176 of the largest corporations studied by R. A. Gordon in 1939, the median ownership of officers and directors was 2·11 per cent. That of officers was very much less and it was much lower among older railroad than younger industrial corporations. Gordon's list included some firms, such as Ford, which were still wholly owned by the controlling interest. As the study of Miss Newcomer shows, there has been a further large decline in management holdings in the quarter-century since Gordon's study was made.

tions, the right to buy stock at predetermined prices if it goes up in value, though common, are by no means universal and are more widely valued as a tax dodge than as an incentive.[7] So even the case for maximization of personal return by a top management is not strong.

But with the rise of the technostructure, the notion, however tenuous, that a few managers might maximize their own return by maximizing that of the stockholders, dissolves entirely. Power passes down into the organization. Even the small stock interest of the top officers is no longer the rule. Salaries, whether modest or generous, are according to scale; they do not vary with profits. And with the power of decision goes opportunity for making money which all good employees are expected to eschew. Members of the technostructure have advance knowledge of products and process, price changes, impending government contracts and, in the fashionable jargon of our time, technical breakthroughs. Advantage could be taken of this information. Were everyone to seek to do so – by operations in the stock of the company, or in that of suppliers, in commodity markets, by taking themselves and their knowledge into the employ of another firm for a price – the corporation would be a chaos of competitive avarice. But these are not the sort of thing that a good company man does; a remarkably effective code bans such behaviour. Group decision-making ensures, moreover, that almost everyone's actions and even thoughts are known to others. This acts to enforce the code and, more than incidentally, a high standard of personal honesty as well. The technostructure does not permit of the privacy that misfeasance and malfeasance require.

So the technostructure, as a matter of necessity, bans personal profit-making. And, as a practical matter, what is banned for the ordinary scientist, engineer, contract negotiator or sales executive must also be banned for senior officers. Resistance to pecuniary temptation cannot be enforced at the lower levels if

7. 'They are, of course, really tax-avoiding schemes . . . as the profit from sale of stocks is taxed as capital gains at a maximum of 25 per cent. . . .' Moore, op. cit., pp. 13–14.

it is known that the opportunity to turn a personal penny remains the prerogative of the high brass.

The members of the technostructure do not get the profits that they maximize. They must eschew personal profit-making. Accordingly, if the traditional commitment to profit maximization is to be upheld, they must be willing to do for others, specifically the stockholders, what they are forbidden to do for themselves. It is on such grounds that the doctrine of maximization in the mature corporation now rests. It holds that the will to make profits is, like the will to sexual expression, a fundamental urge. But it holds that this urge operates not in the first person but the third. It is detached from self and manifested on behalf of unknown, anonymous and powerless persons who do not have the slightest notion of whether their profits are, in fact, being maximized. In further analogy to sex, one must imagine that a man of vigorous, lusty and reassuringly heterosexual inclination eschews the lovely, available and even naked women by whom he is intimately surrounded in order to maximize the opportunities of other men whose existence he knows of only by hearsay. Such are the foundations of the maximization doctrine when there is full separation of power from reward.

IV

In earlier stages of the development of the corporation, and notably in the decade of the thirties, it was feared that those in control would make their firm an instrument of their own personal enrichment. And this would, it was also feared, destroy corporate enterprises as a whole.

The portents seemed impressive and grave. When the great utility empires of the Insulls and Associated Gas and Electric collapsed, it became evident that the pecuniary interests of the individual stockholder had been callously subordinated to the wealth and ambition of those in command. Similarly with other great power, transportation and industrial enterprises that fell during this period. In all of these enterprises the financial interest of those in control was small or negligible in relation to total assets – O. P. and M. J. Van Sweringen, the eccentric Cleveland railroad collectors, controlled their two-billion-dollar railroad system on an investment of some twenty million dollars. Albert H. Wiggin of the Chase National Bank was heavily short in the stock of the bank he headed at the time of the stock market crash in 1929. As a result, he made a small fortune on the decline of the stock and, a resourceful man in debate, he later argued that not owning stock, which is the nature of a short position, gave an officer a real interest in the enterprise. After Ivar Kreuger had said farewell to his trusting financial friends in Paris on 12 March 1932, and had shot himself to death with a newly purchased pistol, it was learned that he had used his control of corporations in a dozen countries to separate their owners from hundreds of millions of dollars. This was personal profit maximization on a truly massive scale. Scholars concluded that those in control of the great corporation, as they became able to do so, would combine such maximization with personal aggrandizement. The result would be larceny of unprecedented magnitude. Professor William Z. Ripley of Harvard, the leading authority on the corporation in the twenties, warned President Coolidge that 'prestidigitation, double-shuffling, honey-fugling, hornswoggling and skulduggery'[8] were threatening the entire economic system. Adolf A. Berle, Ripley's successor as the prime authority on the corporation, concluded that the mature corporation accorded no effective rights to the owners of the enterprise. There could, in consequence, be only one of two results. Managers would become trustees, properly supervised, on behalf of the 'inactive and irresponsible'[9] owners, which would have an unhappy effect on initiative. Or they would 'operate in their own interests and ... divert a portion of the asset fund to their own uses.'[10]

8. Quoted in William Allen White, *A Puritan in Babylon* (New York: Macmillan, 1939), p. 337.

9. Adolf A. Berle, Jr, and Gardiner C. Means, *The Modern Corporation and Private Property* (New York: Macmillan, 1948), p. 354.

10. Ibid.

There would develop 'a corporate oligarchy coupled with the probability of an era of corporate plundering.'[11] Neither of these results being agreeable, Professor Berle concluded that the state would have to take over from the managers.[12]

The danger did not develop. This, without doubt, was partly because some of the more promising avenues of enrichment were closed by law. The Federal Securities Act of 1933 and its subsequent amendments required management to disclose its own compensation and pension rights. It also required disclosure of the value of any property or services sold to the corporation – for these, when overvalued, serve admirably to siphon corporate funds into a privy purse. And it required disclosure of trading, and prohibited short selling, by the insiders. The Public Utility Holding Company Act of 1935 limited pyramiding through the use of holding companies as a device for excluding owners from control. And the Securities and Exchange Commission was created to administer this legislation. The authors of this legislation believed firmly that profit maximization by those in control of corporations, as distinct from the owners, was deeply inimical to the profit system. It may be added that, in their efforts to restrict it and thus protect the system, they earned an unparalleled reputation for radicalism.

But the legislation principally affected those who, like murderers and thieves in less exalted areas, find it difficult to live in accordance with the accepted canons of behaviour. In most corporations, even in the twenties, there was no abuse, as personal profit maximization by insiders was even then called. And the legislation closed only a few of the avenues for enrichment. The management of every mature and profitable corporation has numerous lawful and unexploited opportunities for increasing its personal revenue at the expense of the stockholder. Most of the devices – more pay, more deferred compen-

11. Ibid., p. 355.
12. This formidable conclusion, which was expressed in guarded terms, came towards the end of a long book. It seems to have been overlooked. Had his numerous critics been more diligent, Professor Berle's early commitment to socialism would, one imagines, have been more celebrated during his long and highly distinguished public career.

sation or pension rights, more stock options or stock purchase plans, more profit-sharing – would require only the routine blessing of counsel.

The danger of abuse, through personal profit maximization, disappeared as power passed into the technostructure. In all of the corporations that aroused alarm in the nineteen-twenties and thirties, there was still a dominant entrepreneurial figure. His investment was often small but his control rested on financial position and not on managerial or technical competence. With the rise of the technostructure with its new attitudes and its widely diffused power acting as a safeguard against individual avarice (or larceny), the danger disappeared. Although in the twenties and thirties there was widespread doubt that the corporation could survive the personal profit-maximizing tendencies of those who might seize financial control, in the sixties the issue had become academic.[13]

Some will already have sensed a relation between this discussion and the earlier examination of the changing association of power and the factors of production. When capital was decisive and the capitalist was in control of the corporation, he maximized that which he provided, namely money. He specifically did so when his investment was small, when in consequence he had little to gain from improved earnings but when he could enrich himself greatly by looting the assets of the firm. The technostructure does not supply capital, but specialized talent and organization. There is, *a priori*, no reason to believe that it will maximize the return to capital. More plausibly it will maximize its success as an organization. Before pursuing this lead, however, it is necessary to say some final words to the defenders of maximization.

13. In the early nineteen-sixties it became known that senior officers of the Chrysler Corporation were providing themselves with notable rewards by virtue of their interest in enterprises selling products or services to the company. But the great attention that this case aroused, together with the prompt correction, is an indication of its exceptional character. It is also significant that it coincided with generally poor managerial performance. Personal profit maximization at the top had led to a predictable poor performance by the technostructure.

v

Quite a few economists avoid reflection on the conflict between profit maximization and what is universally considered sound management behaviour by the convenient, although not wholly reassuring, device of simply ignoring the contemporary reality. In teaching and theoretical model-building, the modern large corporation is ignored. An entrepreneur is assumed. To 'most economists, even today, the "entrepreneur" still means only the owner-manager, usually by implication, of a small manufacturing business'.[14]

The caste structure of university departments of economics, an interesting matter, supports this simplification. Economic theory is the most prestigious subject of instruction and study. Agricultural economics, labour economics and marketing are lower caste fields of study. So are industrial organization and corporation finance. With students of the corporation, the divorce of ownership from control in the large enterprise is an old story. But coming from an inferior intellectual tradition, it can be ignored by the theorist. His higher caste allows him to make such assumptions as he prefers. Accordingly, he assumes that the direction of the enterprise continues to involve extensive participation in revenues. This being so there is no

14. R. A. Gordon, *Business Leadership in the Large Corporation* (Washington: Brookings, 1945), p. 11. This was written some twenty-five years ago, but few sciences have ever shown such stability, at least in error. Almost exactly the same observation was made in 1964 by Robin Marris in his very interesting book, *The Economic Theory of 'Managerial' Capitalism* (New York: The Free Press of Glencoe, 1964), p. 5. Professor Gordon added that, 'Developments in mathematical economics and general equilibrium theory have reinforced the mechanistic approach to entrepreneurial activity.' Op. cit., p. 18. The assumption that ownership is united with management is more convenient for such theoretical and mathematical exercise. To accommodate assumptions not to reality but to the requirements of technique will be thought a rather dubious scientific procedure. It is one of the curiosities of economics that it is often employed by the men who most pride themselves on their scientific and technical virtuosity and who even volunteer on occasion to serve as censors of scientific morality.

reason to question the assumption that revenues will be maximized.[15] And there is, further, no reason to consider other goals. This will not, to everyone, seem an ideal arrangement; many will react uneasily to the exclusion of General Motors, General Electric and Standard Oil of New Jersey and their companions in scale and organization from modern economic analysis. But, to an astonishing degree, this is accomplished and serves in turn to exclude goals other than profit maximization and thus to preserve the authority of the market.

However, numerous modern theorists do accept General Motors. They agree that the modern corporation is run by the managers. They accept its market power. And they cautiously agree that it does not maximize its return. They imply, however, that this does not greatly change things. 'As soon as the firm becomes of any considerable size and begins to enjoy some control over price, it can often afford to relax a little in its maximizing activities.'[16] '... there is little room for such waywardness [i.e. not maximizing return] and ... where significant distortion is present, the fault lies in market power ...'[17] '... the profit-maximizing hypothesis works better when applied to industries composed of a large number of firms than when applied to monopolies or to industries with only a few members'.[18]

15. Many theorists are, in fact, more circumspect. My very distinguished colleague, Professor Robert Dorfman, makes the following more cautious assumption: 'On balance, the maximization hypothesis is not as firmly grounded in the facts of life as a fundamental scientific hypothesis should be. But substantial and prolonged divergences from the behavior it implies are rare, particularly in industries with many participants. It therefore *can still be entertained* as a sound working hypothesis.' *The Price System* (New York: Prentice-Hall, Inc., 1964), p. 42. Italics added. However in confining maximization to industries with 'many participants' he is, as I note presently, excluding the industrial system as here specified and, therewith, the largest and most modern part of the economy.

16. Paul A. Samuelson, *Economics*, Sixth Edition (New York: McGraw, 1964), p. 488.

17. Shorey Peterson, 'Corporate Control and Capitalism', *The Quarterly Journal of Economics*, Vol. LXXIX. No. 1 (February 1965), p. 14. This article by Professor Peterson is a lucid and skilful defence of the orthodox case here under scrutiny.   18. Dorfman, op. cit., p. 42.

The Approved Contradiction

But on closer scrutiny, these statements turn out to make no minor concession. They exclude large firms or those with market power from maximization. To say that large firms do not maximize returns, or to suggest that there is room for other goals whenever there is market power, is to agree that maximization does not occur in the part of the economy with which we are here concerned. It does not occur in automobiles, aluminium, rubber, synthetic fabrics, transportation, tin cans, chewing gum, chocolates, glass, soap, breakfast foods, cigarettes, most electrical goods, aircraft, tractors, computers, typewriters, most chemicals, all communications and a host of other industries where firms are large in relation to the market and their power over the market is not only considerable but very great.[19] The defenders of maximization are seen to be perpetrating, no doubt innocently, a rather subtle trick. Profit maximization may be assumed. But as a concession to reality the industrial system – the largest, most typical and most modern part of the economy – is excluded. The captious would be critical of any description of the social geography of the United States which, by assuming away New York, Chicago, Los Angeles and all other communities larger than Cedar Rapids, was then able to describe the country as, essentially, a small-town, front-porch community. Only an assumption very important to economics, as it is conventionally taught, would justify such a questionable defence.

Other economists have implicitly abandoned the commitment to maximization whenever the corporation is under pressure of public responsibility or concern for public policy. Thus price increases in the industrial system characteristically follow

19. The foregoing list, apart from transportation and communications, is selected at random from sixty industries in which the largest eight firms were estimated to account for 75 per cent of all shipments by value in 1958. Hearings before the Subcommittee on Antitrust and Monopoly of the Committee on the Judiciary, United States Senate, Eighty-Eighth Congress, Second Session, Pursuant to S. Res. 262, Part I. *Economic Concentration. Overall and Conglomerate Aspects* (1964), p. 89. However this by no means exhausts the list of industries where firms exercise market power. It does not include steel, for example.

the negotiation of a collective bargaining contract. But if revenues can be increased by raising prices after a wage increase they could have been increased before. Some consideration, other than the goal of maximized return, must have occasioned this restraint.

Modern economic policy cultivates this restraint. It seeks to hold wage increases within what can be afforded by lowered costs – lowered costs that reflect, in particular, the increased productivity resulting from technological advance. Cost of production thus being constant, firms are persuaded to continue to keep prices stable. None denies that the corporations involved could make higher returns by raising prices; the policy rests firmly on the fact that they do not maximize returns. Accordingly economists who urge this policy have abandoned, however tacitly, their commitment to maximization. I later argue that this policy is an indispensable feature of economic management of the industrial system.

Finally, a small group of scholars, Robin Marris of Cambridge,[20] William Baumol of Princeton, Jack Downie of London and, somewhat more circumspectly, my brilliant former colleague, Carl Kaysen of the Institute for Advanced Study, have accepted the separation of ownership from control in the mature corporation and its implications for profit maximization. They have gone on to devise explanations of managerial behaviour that are, or seem to be, consistent with this separation. These efforts are still subject to the mystique of the market; were they to accept the full significance of the abandonment of profit maximization they would go on, as here, to examine the modern corporation as an instrument of planning that transcends the market. Yet, nonetheless, they light a part of the way and I make full use of them in what follows.[21, 22, 23]

20. *The Economics of 'Managerial' Capitalism.*
21. William J. Baumol, *Business Behavior, Value and Growth* (New York: Macmillan, 1959).
22. Jack Downie, *The Competitive Process* (London: Duckworth, 1958).
23. Among other papers, Carl Kaysen, 'The Social Significance of the

VI

As now sufficiently emphasized, profit maximization excludes other goals. That is why its affirmation is so necessary for holding discussion of corporate behaviour within the ambit of the economist. That is why it is so urgently defended.

In recent years, in addition to the few economists who have defected, quite a number of business leaders and spokesmen have abandoned the commitment to maximization. Not all of this is to be taken seriously: in the past, many notably avaricious men have thought it well to protest their fealty to a higher morality than making money. Only the excessively gullible have been fooled. Faith in profit maximization is still sustained by the fear of seeming gullible again. But some have sensed quite honestly that the mature corporation exercises plenary power apart from profit-making. This has an effect on the community. They have sought, in accordance with their own lights and preferences, to specify the rules for its use.

The result has been a cacophony of voices proclaiming the purposes of the corporation. These have ranged from the suggestion of Mr Frank Abrams, former Board Chairman of the Standard Oil Company of New Jersey, that the primary goal is a just distribution of income, i.e., 'to maintain an equitable and working balance among the claims of various directly interested groups – stockholders, employees, customers, and the public at large'[24] – to pronouncements of a primary concern for improving higher education, increasing economic literacy, resisting subversion, supporting American foreign policy, upbuilding the community, strengthening the two-party system, upholding the Constitution, amending the Constitution to preserve its original intent, and defending freedom and free enterprise. Many years ago Bruce Barton, the advertising man and

Modern Corporation,' *The American Economic Review*, Vol. XLVII, No. 2 (May 1957); also in *The Corporation in Modern Society* and 'Another View of Corporate Capitalism,' *The Quarterly Journal of Economics*, Vol. LXXIX, No. 1 (February 1965).

24. Quoted by Rostow in *The Corporation in Modern Society*, p. 60.

legislator, concluded that Jesus, were he alive today, would be a businessman rather than a member of the building trades. On occasion so fulsome have been the professions of higher corporate purpose that observers have been led to wonder if the Barton dream had come to pass. 'Today pronouncements about social responsibility issue forth so abundantly from the corporations that it is hard for one to get a decent play in the press. Everybody is in on the act, and nearly all of them actually mean what they say! Dedication reverberates throughout the upper reaches of corporate officialdom.'[25]

It would be wrong to dismiss these assertions of social purpose by corporate spokesmen exclusively as an exercise in competitive banality. They also reflect the underlying reality which is that the modern corporation has power to shape society. And this power does not disappear when the businessmen, following the advice of economic traditionalists, proclaim that their only purpose is profits. It can be used to pursue profits. But this is an exercise of power. There is also power to pursue other goals. Power is not something that can be assumed or discarded at will like underwear.

However, the real purpose of this power is not proclaimed in the corporate press releases and speeches. What is dispensed, as many have rightly suspected, is mostly hot air. Power is used, as might be expected, to serve the deeper interests or goals of the technostructure, for this possesses the power. These goals are not proclaimed. Rather, like most human aspirations, they are taken profoundly for granted. Our task now is to identify these goals and the means by which society is accommodated to their service.

25. Levitt, op. cit., p. 42.

Chapter 11

THE GENERAL THEORY
OF MOTIVATION

OUR need is to know the real goals of the technostructure and how they are pursued. Thus we will know to what purposes and by what means we are governed in that large part of our life which is influenced by the industrial system. Men have long thought it important to know how governments determine their taxes. It is rather more important to know the governing processes by which their incomes are determined, their prices set and their purchasing habits shaped.

The problem of goals begins with the relation of the individual to organization, in this case to the technostructure. What an organization will seek from society will be a reflection of what members seek from the organization. If soldiers serve only for pay, the army is not likely to concern itself deeply in politics – at least so long as the pay is forthcoming. But if, as with Cromwell's men, they serve with a view to the salvation of their souls, they are unlikely long to be politically neutral, at least in a wicked country. Legislatures will do well to keep their doors locked. If, as in Latin America, men join the army less from an excess of martial valour than from a minimum of political ambition, the danger will be even greater. If men principally want money from a corporation, the corporation will be primarily concerned with extracting money from the society. If they are interested in economic security or personal prestige, the corporation can hardly fail to reflect this in the kind of business it conducts.

What the society can ask from organization will depend, similarly, on the relation of the organization to the individual. When soldiers serve for pay, the state must pay the army that it summons to its call. The southern planter could be summoned by the impressment along with his slaves for his slaves had no choice but to come. Volunteer armies need not be paid but they must have a cause. A laboratory run by the California Institute of Technology can be asked to work long hours to follow a space probe. Those who man it are united with the organization by scientific interest. A textile mill or an auto plant would not be capable of a similar response; its operatives or employees work for pay.

These matters have not been much studied by economists. Men, it is assumed, act in economic matters only in response to pecuniary compensation or to force. Force in the modern society is largely, although by no means completely, obsolete. So only pecuniary compensation remains of importance. The more of this, broadly speaking, the individual receives, the better and more sustained his efforts. Only as to the very poor and those in menial occupations such as domestic service is there occasional concern that excessive pay may prove damaging to effort.

Pecuniary compensation as a motivation, in its turn, supports profit maximization as the preclusive goal of the firm. Profit maximization gets the greatest return from the market; this enables the firm to buy the optimum effort from its members.

Though all this notably simplifies the economist's life, it is, unfortunately, at odds with the reality. In addition to pecuniary compensation, two other forces, out of a possible four, powerfully relate the individual to organization. These further motives are inconsistent with a commitment by the firm to profit maximization. This is no logical misfortune. Profit maximization, we have just seen, is inconsistent with the behaviour of the technostructure in the mature corporation. The other motives repair this inconsistency. What is more, they are essential to a satisfactory explanation of the behaviour of the technostructure. As always, reality is in harmony within itself.

II

The most famous definition of an organization holds it to be a 'system of consciously coordinated activities or forces of two or more persons'.[1] The most important word here is coordination. It means that the participating individuals are persuaded to set aside their individual purposes or goals and pursue those of the organization. All having done so, all work to the common goals. They are coordinated. Motivation is the means or inducements by which such coordination is effected – the means or inducements by which individuals are led to abandon their own goals and, with greater or less vigour, to pursue those of the organization.

The essentials of the matter are evident when a group of men dig a ditch. Ditch-digging is an unlikely passion for the average person. A useful completed excavation is a plausible goal of a group or organization. The problem is to win the surrender of individual preference in favour of the disciplined wielding of a spade. This can be brought about in the following ways:

(1) The group may compel the acceptance of its goals. Behind the man with the spade is another with a club. Failure to accept the goals of the group brings the negative reward of punishment. Without extravagant novelty, this motivation may be called *compulsion*.

(2) The acceptance of the common goal may be purchased – at the end of the trench is a man with money. Acceptance of the goals of the organization brings not a negative but an affirmative reward. In return for this inducement, the individual 'offers the organization . . . undifferentiated time and effort'.[2] Such is pecuniary motivation.

(3) The individual, on becoming associated with the group, may conclude that its goals are superior to his own. In the case

1. Chester I. Barnard, *The Functions of the Executive* (Cambridge: Harvard University Press, 1958), p. 73.

2. Herbert A. Simon, *Administrative Behavior*, Second Edition (New York: Macmillan, 1957), p. 115.

of ditch-digging the likelihood is less than in a chamber music group, a political conspiracy or the Marine Corps. Yet it exists. If the ditch drains a particularly nauseous and malarial swamp, the individual on associating himself with the excavators may then become aware of the utility of their enterprise. This is to say that he finds the goals of the group superior to his own previous purposes and so he joins. 'Humans, in contrast to machines, evaluate their own positions in relation to the value of others and come to accept others' goals as their own.'[3] Such an exchange is not compelled. Neither is it purchased, although it is not inconsistent with compensation. Following Professor Herbert Simon, this motivating influence may be called identification.[4]

(4) Finally, the individual may serve the organization not because he considers its goals superior to his own, but because he hopes to make them accord more closely with his own. By being a member of the ditch-digging organization, he can hope for a ditch that, in capacity, depth or direction, conforms more closely to his ideal.

But once again the ditch-digger is not the most powerful case. The cabinet officer who serves, and on occasion concurs, in action that he finds repugnant in order to advance measures of which he approves, is a better one. So is the politician who

3. James G. March and Herbert A. Simon, *Organizations* (New York: Wiley, 1958), p. 65.

4. This term which has overtones of suburban psychology is not entirely satisfactory. When first working out these ideas, I used the word *conformance* – and this will appear in past, and presumably long unread, lecture notes of my students. Its tone implies, however, that the individual is somehow pressed or forced to conform and this is not the meaning sought. Identification has no connotation of compulsion and has the claim of prior use. I should like to acknowledge my debt to Professor Simon and his associates. The literature dealing with organization and organization theory is of singular aridity. By far the most distinguished of the exceptions is the work of Herbert A. Simon and his past and present colleagues at the Carnegie Institute of Technology. The two key volumes are *Administrative Behavior* and *Organizations*. Everyone professionally concerned with organization should become acquainted with these difficult but rewarding books.

would rather influence modestly the policies of a great party than be in full command of a one-man movement. And so is the corporation executive who strings along with much that he thinks routine and unenterprising in the hope of winning support for a few new ideas of his own.

The pursuit of the goals of organization because of the prospect or in the hope of accommodating these goals more closely to the participant's preference is an important motivation. But unlike compulsion, pecuniary compensation or even identification, it has also much less standing in the theory of organization. A name for it must be coined and I propose to call it *adaptation*. Adaptation, it will be evident, has much to do with the urge for power in a world of organization.

Compulsion, pecuniary compensation, identification and adaptation can motivate an individual either separately or in combination. Their collective influence I shall refer to as the motivating system. The strength of any given motivation or of the motivating system will be measured by the effectiveness with which it aligns the individual with the goals of the organization. The motivating system varies greatly in power depending on the motivations that are combined. Some motivations clash and so neutralize each other. Some combine passively. Some strongly reinforce each other. What is called an effective organization is one which, in substantial measure, has a motivational system that is internally reinforcing. The goals of the organization are thus pursued with the greatest possible effect. I turn now to the relation between the several motivating forces.

III

Compulsion and pecuniary compensation exist in varying degrees of association with each other. Those who are compelled to accept the goals of organization by fear of punishment – of negative reward – always have some affirmative compensation for such acceptance. The slave got the whip when he did not work; he got food and shelter of a sort when he did. As we shall see presently, varying amounts of compulsion are associated with pecuniary compensation.

Compulsion is inconsistent with either identification or adaptation. If a person is compelled to accept the goals of an organization, he is unlikely, at least so long as he is under the sense of compulsion, to find them superior to his own. The conflict is not quite absolute. Household slaves – in contrast with field-hands – were believed to accept the goals of their masters. In consequence, they were thought unreliable material for insurrections. The reluctant draftee may come, in time, to relish the barracks and parade ground. But the broad rule holds: What is compelled cannot be a matter of choice. Alienation, not identification, will be the normal result. Bondsmen and serfs have regularly been held to love their masters – to have identified themselves deeply with their masters' goals. This has rarely prevented them, when the opportunity arose, from asserting their own very different goals, frequently after burning the master's house, together with its occupants, or showing some similar manifestation of distaste.

Nor is compulsion consistent with adaptation. If the individual is obliged to accept the goals of organization, he will not embrace them in the hope of accommodating them more closely to his own. When his acceptance is forced he will understand that he has no power over the goals to which he is compelled. The serf, slave or prison occupant takes the goals of the organization with which he is associated as given and, eccentric cases apart, is alienated from them all. He does only what avoids punishment. Similarly, the oldest rule of the reluctant soldier is to take life as it comes and never volunteer.

Pecuniary motivation may be associated in greater or less measure with compulsion. This will depend on the level of the compensation and the nature of the individual's alternatives. If the element of compulsion is high, it follows that pecuniary motivation will then be inconsistent with identification and adaptation. If it is low, they are readily reconciled. The difference here is of great importance for understanding modern economic behaviour.

The worker in a Calcutta jute mill who loses his job – like his American counterpart during the Great Depression – has no high prospect of ever finding another. He has no savings. Nor does he have unemployment insurance. The alternative to his present employment, accordingly, is slow but definitive starvation. The fate of a defecting southern slave before the Civil War or a serf before Alexander II was not appreciably more painful. The choice between hunger and flogging may well be a matter of taste. The aversion to the organization that compels the acceptance of its goals will be much the same in each instance. This aversion excludes identification. To repeat, the fact that the worker serves because he is compelled sufficiently reveals to him his powerlessness vis-à-vis the organization and its goals. Adaptation is thus also excluded.

The modern industrial employee who loses or abandons his job has, by contrast, every expectation of finding another. In the meantime he has unemployment compensation and perhaps some personal resources and, if the worst comes to the worst, he can obtain welfare support. The danger of physical discomfort has been much reduced and therewith, in general, the element of compulsion. In higher income brackets, as a rule, it will be yet lower. As compulsion as an aspect of pecuniary compensation diminishes or disappears, so do the barriers to identification and adaptation.

IV

The diminishing role of compulsion in pecuniary compensation has been a force of no small historical importance. Among other things it goes far to explain the disappearance of slavery. Until two centuries ago the motivation of the wage labourer in most parts of the world was not radically different from that of the bondsman. Both got little; both toiled in fear of the alternative.

The slave, accordingly, had no reason to regard the free wage worker with much envy. He did not press aggressively to change his position. Nor did society on his behalf. But as the wage worker improved his material position, the element of compulsion to which he was subject diminished. Then the contrast between free man and slave deepened and slavery became untenable. In the absence of the Civil War, slavery in the United States could have lasted only a few more years. For, in a relatively short time, industrialization and rising living standards in the North together with improving communications would have made it increasingly difficult to keep the slaves in the fields. And the cost of patrols and the machinery for redeeming fugitives, together with the capital loss from those who made good their escape into northern employments, would have been intolerable. Planters would have been forced to pay inducements, i.e. wages, to hold their men. As in other countries, at a roughly similar stage in economic development, slavery would have been given up. The reform would have been attributed to the innate humanity of man to man. By 1880 or 1890 at the latest, the more respected philosophers would have been congratulating the nation on having accomplished peacefully what men once feared could only have been done by war.

As it is wrong to deny the role of conscience in human affairs, it is also an error to minimize that of economics. Speaking to the same subject, when bondsmen were still valuable property, Adam Smith observed: 'The late resolution of the Quakers in Pennsylvania to set at liberty their negro slaves, may satisfy us that their number cannot be very great.'[5]

V

As compulsion and pecuniary compensation are associated in varying mix, so also are identification and adaptation. The two are highly complementary. An individual, on becoming associated with an organization, will be more likely to adopt its goals in place of his own if he has hope of changing those he finds unsatisfactory or repugnant. And if he is strongly identi-

5. Adam Smith, *Wealth of Nations*, Book III (New York: The Modern Library, 1937), Chapter II, p. 366.

fied with the goals of an organization, he will be moved all the more strongly to try to improve it – to alter (i.e. adapt) any unsatisfactory goals so that they accord with his own. A member will identify himself more enthusiastically with a political party if he feels that he has some power to influence its platform; he will work more diligently to influence the platform if he is generally in accord with the party's goals.

The relation of identification to adaptation is partly a matter of temperament; the disposition of some on associating themselves with an organization is to accept its goals and of others to improve them. Some college presidents and diplomats, by disposition, accept the goals of their respective institutions; others seek to advance the purposes of education or peace. Adaptation is also partly a matter of position. It more strongly motivates a President of the United States than a postman making his rounds, more strongly the general manager than the receptionist, the pastor than the sexton.

VI

Pecuniary motivation cannot be combined with identification and adaptation when the element of compulsion is large. It can be when the element of compulsion is small. This means that the motivational system will be different in the poor country as compared with the rich, and different for the poor man as compared with the well-to-do. And what begins as a difference in degree widens, ultimately, into a difference in kind.

In the poor country, and among the poorly paid, labour relations will, in general, be harsh and angry. The compulsion associated with low compensation alienates the worker from the employer. This being so, the employer does not seek to cultivate his employee's loyalty – to encourage his identification with the firm – for this he knows to be impossible. There being nothing to lose, nothing is lost by arrogant or offensive behaviour. The worker, not being identified with the employer, will be receptive to the goals of the union. He will also be vulnerable to threats from the employer that he will be fired if he joins for this is precisely the hardship he fears and which compels his effort. The stage is thus set for disagreeable behaviour on both sides. Those concerned have rarely failed to conform to expectation.

In the richer country, and among the well-to-do, everything is more benign. Compulsion will have receded. In consequence, there is little or no alienation; the way is open for the worker to accept the goals of the organization. The worker will have less inducement to join a union but much less to fear in doing so. The employer will seek to encourage the identification of the worker with the firm; the worker having less to fear, the employer will find it less useful to play on his fears. The worker being more identified with the firm, the union has less enmity to arouse. On both sides the motivational system both allows and rewards more agreeable behaviour. This mellowing of industrial relations, the result of wealth, will, however, be attributed to more humane instincts, greater employer enlightenment, more responsible unions and the spread of industrial statesmanship.[6]

The paradox of pecuniary motivation is that, in general, the higher the amount the less its importance in relation to other motivations. This is not because of the declining marginal utility of money although, along with progressive income taxation, this may reduce its capacity to buy effort. Rather it is because with higher incomes there is, under most circumstances, a lessened dependence on a particular employment. So there is a lessened element of compulsion and this paves the way for identification and adaptation. These supplement and may transcend pecuniary compensation in their importance in the motivational system.

It will be clear that we have here a solution, or in any case a clue, to the contradictions encountered in the last chapter. Pecuniary compensation need not be the main motivation of members of the technostructure. Identification and adaptation may be driving forces. Above a certain level these may operate independently of income. Maximization of income for the

6. I return to these matters in Chapters 23 and 24 below.

technostructure is neither needed nor sought. The question of what goals members of the technostructure identify themselves with, and to what personal goals they seek adaptation, remains. But it will be clear that there is no necessary conflict with the stockholders as there would be if both were seeking to maximize pecuniary return.

VII

One test of sound social analysis is that it explains small matters as well as great. One of the most puzzling pleas of the American business executive, regularly echoed in public rituals, is for lower taxes to encourage initiative and effort. The puzzle lies in the fact that few executives would ever admit to putting forth less than their best effort for their present income after taxes. To suggest such malingering would be considered a gross insult.[7]

An explanation is now at hand. The reference to incentives is traditional, a hangover from a more primitive association of income and effort. It accords seeming respectability and social utility to the desire for lower taxes or the natural wish to shift more of the existing burden to the poor. But the reality is that the executive's present level of income allows for identification and adaptation. These are the operative motivations. They are also the only personally reputable ones: the executive cannot afford to have it thought that his commitment to the goals of the corporation is less than complete or that he is at all indifferent to his opportunity to shape these goals. To suggest that he subordinates these latter motives to his response to pay would be to confess that he is an inferior executive.

7. A very recent study under the auspices of the Brookings Institution, Washington, fully affirms the point: *The Economic Behavior of the Affluent* by Robin Barlow, Harvey E. Brazer and James N. Morgan, 1966.

Chapter 12

MOTIVATION IN PERSPECTIVE

POWER in economic life has over time passed from its ancient association with land to association with capital and then on, in recent times, to the composite of knowledge and skills which comprises the technostructure. Reflecting the symmetry that so conveniently characterizes reality, there have been associated shifts in the motivations to which men respond. Compulsion had an ancient association with land. Pecuniary motivation had a similar association with capital. Identification and adaptation are associated with the technostructure.

Land, as the strategic factor of production, made highly advantageous the use of compulsion. Agriculture, by its nature, scatters men over a wide space. Thus they required protection. The feudal lord who commanded their effort as cultivators also organized them into elementary military units for their mutual defence. As a further manifestation of the consistency that characterizes these matters, the relation of the lord to his temporal ruler was similar. As the price of peaceful possession of his land, he provided his ruler with armed men for the common defence or aggression. Dispersion also protected serfs and helots from the heresies and discontents which would have been brewed in mass association with each other in the towns and cities. On occasion it minimized the chance that they would come together for the ceremonial immolation of their masters.

Urbanization and compulsion go poorly together; the city, all but inevitably, has accorded the individual opportunities to escape his bond. And it has nurtured the ideas that give this escape moral sanction. Nor has slavery been easily adapted to the factory. In the early stages of the factory system, wage labour compelled by the fear of hunger was also, almost certainly, cheaper than slave labour compelled by the fear of physical violence. So, with the emergence of capital as the strategic factor of production, pecuniary compensation became the primary motivation. Ownership of capital accorded power in the industrial enterprise. Nothing could seem more natural than that money – the physical manifestation of capital – should buy effort. As the feudal lord had access to force and used force to align others with his goals, so the capitalist had capital and used capital to align others with his goals. No one celebrated the change so vividly as Marx. Capital, through the agency of the bourgeoisie, has 'pitilessly torn asunder the motley feudal ties which bound man to his "natural superiors," and has left no other nexus between man and man than naked self-interest, than callous "cash payments".'[1] So cash payments, callous and otherwise, came in time to be considered the only motivation worthy of serious attention in the economic system.

Specialized knowledge and its coordination have now, as we have seen, become the decisive factor in economic success. This requires that men work in groups. And power passes to these groups. The participants are well-compensated; few regard their compensation with disinterest. But on associating with the group the individual finds himself attracted or compelled by its goals. He substitutes these goals for his own. He sees also the advantage – the access of power and influence – from exchanging a major pursuit of his own goals to a much smaller influence on the much greater power of the organization. Thus, from organization, comes a further system of motivation. As with pecuniary compensation and capital and land and compulsion, it is appropriate to its context. Pecuniary compensation, as an explanation of effort, has now a relatively much diminished role.

This is not a conclusion which will come easily to economists or perhaps even to others. There is again the muscular vigour of the assumption that people are primarily motivated by money and the reassurance that resides in the knowledge that one is relying on the seemingly cruder manifestations of human nature. That one need never look beyond the love of money

1. *The Communist Manifesto.*

for explanation of human behaviour is one of the most jealously guarded simplifications of our culture.

It is worth recalling, however, that the commitment to force was once equally strong. The classical economists, writing in the late eighteenth and early nineteenth centuries, felt it necessary to enlarge at length on the advantages of free over slave labour. It was not what the sound and practical citizen could yet be expected to believe or what the colonial plantation owner could even contemplate.[2] There was long an atavistic conviction that superior social attitudes were associated with land ownership. More remarkably, there is still an atavistic conviction that force has a unique motivational value. In consequence those who, because of deficient conscience or lack of respect for civilized values, are able to employ it are believed to have great advantage. Where its use is still allowed to civilized communities it is, for the same reason, greatly admired. The point is worth a moment's notice.

II

During World War II it was widely believed that the ruthlessly exercised power of the German dictatorship was a major source of strength and one manifestation was its ability to command more than seven million foreign workers[3] from all the races of Europe. Here was the awesome power with which the opposition had to contend. Closer examination revealed no advantage. The slaves were brought, not in preference to wage workers, but as an expedient to replace them. And it is

2. Adam Smith resorted to egregious exaggeration in making the point. 'The experience of all ages and nations, I believe, demonstrates that the work done by slaves, though it appears to cost only their maintenance, is in the end the dearest of any.' *Wealth of Nations*, Book III (New York: The Modern Library, 1937), Chapter II, p. 365. This is wholly untrue. In their time and for their mainly agricultural tasks they were more economical than any alternative supply of free labour.

3. Of which 1·8 million were prisoners of war and of which some portion came voluntarily. *The Effects of Strategic Bombing on the German War Economy*, United States Strategic Bombing Survey, 1945, p. 34.

not evident that it was the best expedient. The most responsible
and intelligent German leaders felt that more production could
have been obtained by leaving French and other Western
European workers to work for wages in their own factories
than by bringing them as slaves to Germany. Or they favoured
greater reliance on voluntary recruiting of wage workers.[4] Or
they urged greater employment of women and domestic workers as in Great Britain and the United States. A careful postwar
study of the German experience concludes that the slave
workers in Germany were an indifferent substitute for the
women and domestic workers whom Britain brought into her
labour force. 'Civilian employment was maintained in Britain
by internal mobilization, in Germany by the importation of
labour.'[5] But the atavism which dominated so many of the
attitudes of, and towards, the Third Reich set high store by
compulsion. Compulsion was believed to be a manifestation of
strength.

Similarly it has been widely assumed that the Soviet Union,
in the past, has gained great advantages from its power to
compel effort.

Thus, in the West by free consent, and in the Soviet Union largely
by compulsion, two different conceptions of the ends and means of

4. This was a major point of controversy between Fritz Sauckel,
minister in charge of labour recruitment, and Albert Speer, the highly
intelligent arms minister. At one time during the war Speer arranged
that designated industrial establishments in France would be given orders
for munitions and their workers would be exempt from recruitment for
forced labour in the Reich. Sauckel's men promptly descended on these
factories and carried off the workers to forced employment in the Reich.
Since there was no chance that others would expose themselves to the
dangers of recruitment by making themselves so conveniently available,
he effectively put an end to the experiment. The quarrel between Sauckel
and Speer was still raging when they fell into Allied custody – I was one
of the custodians – at the end of the war. Each intimated that hanging
would not be inadvisable for the other. Sauckel was hanged. Speer, to
Sauckel's unquestioned distress, received twenty years from the Nurem-
berg Tribunal.

5. Burton H. Klein, *Germany's Economic Preparation for War* (Cambridge: Harvard University Press, 1959), pp. 136 et seq.

social life have [been devised] ... for the economic development of their societies. ... . The liberal Western way of development is economically more difficult and morally more demanding than the totalitarian or authoritarian way. But its material and spiritual rewards are correspondingly greater.[6]

But again, on closer examination, the gains from compulsion dissolve. Presumably these were at their greatest in the labour camps of the Stalinist era. The dissolution of these by Khrushchev was widely thought to be a concession to more civilized procedures rather than efficiency. Yet few, if any, of these camps seem ever to have provided labour for modern industry. They were in remote areas and devoted to land-clearing, forestry, mining or construction, where labour productivity was almost certainly low. The closing of the camps made possible the employment of the inhabitants, together with their guards and keepers, in more productive enterprises. The gains must have been appreciable.

Elsewhere in the Soviet Union men work for wages and are at liberty to change their places of employment. Much store is set in Soviet industry by both identification and adaptation. The bulletin boards of the factories are papered with the pictures of the more committed proletarians. The latter are heavily decorated with medals and conspicuously featured in public ceremonials. All are given the impression that their suggestions for improved performance are gratefully received and closely considered. A sense of compulsion would be inconsistent with this emphasis on identification and adaptation; it would weaken, not strengthen, the motivational system. It is characteristic of many who speak most of individual freedom in such matters that they do not think well enough of it to imagine that it might also be efficient.

6. *The Political Economy of American Foreign Policy*, Report of a Study Group Sponsored by the Woodrow Wilson Foundation and the National Planning Association (New York: Holt, 1955), p. 179. The ten authors of the book, including William Y. Elliott, Harry D. Gideonse, H. van B. Cleveland, were all distinguished exponents of the approved view of American foreign policy in the postwar years.

III

A strong commitment to compulsion still survives in the United States in the case of military service. On examination this too turns out to be atavistic. Once military service was painful and hazardous. Nations by modern standards were poor and their tax systems even weaker; and their predominantly rural populations were not easily attracted to other employments. Men would not have responded in sufficient numbers to a promise of higher pay. Had they done so, it might have been prohibitively expensive. Taxes would have been insufferable and war itself economically unsound.

None of these conditions now holds for peacetime service in the United States. There has been a radical change even since World War II. In hours of work, variety of experience, travel, intellectual challenge and discipline, military service now compares favourably in attractiveness with a wide range of civilian employments. In peacetime the danger of death or dismemberment is negligible and the standard of medical care is far superior to that of the average civilian. The physical hazards of minor wars may be appreciably greater than the hazards of civilian life. The danger in the event of major conflict is not. The cost of a military establishment of the size the United States has come to think necessary could easily be afforded even were it necessary to keep rates of pay above civilian levels for comparable work. Efficiency would be greatly enhanced. There would be time, during the longer enlistments, to train men adequately in the sophisticated technology and procedures that comprise the modern military art. The Navy, Air Force and Marine Corps have long encouraged volunteers for they recognize that compulsion is destructive of identification – of *esprit de corps*, as identification with the goals of a military organization is described.

Nonetheless, the commitment to compulsion survives. It is deemed to be morally beneficial for those it strikes. And it is imagined that it transfers some of the cost of military service from the well-to-do taxpayer to the draftee who serves at less than market rates.

The strength of the surviving commitment to compulsion measures our task as we move on from pecuniary motivation to win even a supplementary role for identification and adaptation in the mature corporation. There is a unique sanctity about what has long been believed. Moreover identification and adaptation do not lend themselves to quantification and comparison, as does the amount paid to different men. And for this reason they are not easily adapted to the simplifications of mathematics and symbolic logic. Scientific truth in economics is not always what exists; often it is what can be handled by seemingly scientific methods. There is a further problem concerning what is taught. This depends on the textbook, and here truth must be tempered by what is marketable. The latter, not unnaturally, is what is commonly believed or what is commonly believed to be believed. This, needless to say, is that pecuniary compensation is the only 'hard' motivating force of analytical importance. Those who, for any reason, find the present ideas unpalatable should not be unduly disturbed. They will not have an easy passage. I venture to refer the reader to the addendum to this volume on the nature of social argument and its resistance to change.

Yet these ideas are consistent with everyday attitudes. A President of the United States is measured, as a matter of course, by the extent to which he is motivated by identification and adaptation – by the depth of his commitment to the goals, commonly called the welfare, of the nation, and by his willingness to use his office to advance the goals which he thinks desirable, which, in common phrase, is to exercise leadership. A candidate for President who was thought too subject to pecuniary motivation – whose career had been too palpably devoted to making money out of oil, real estate, lumber, television or the stock market – would be under serious handicap.

Once in office, a President must, of course, eschew all pecuniary interests.

The same is true, in deteriorated form, for other politicians. Identification with the goals of the nation, state or community and adaptation expressed as a desire 'to make something of the office' are the only acceptable motives. To suggest to a candidate that he is running for Congress or similar office because of the pay is to invite indignant denial.

The motivation of lawyers, physicians, artists and scientists is assumed to be similar. A good man is committed to the common professional, artistic and scientific goals; he seeks to alter these in accordance with his instinct, taste or knowledge. These alone are respectable motives. To be preoccupied with pecuniary return is to be substandard. Even the economist, who most takes for granted the primacy of pecuniary motivation, looks askance at the colleague who is too avid for consulting fees from corporations or textbook revenues or travel at the expense of the Ford Foundation. Academic courtesy may require that he refrain from first-person comment, but duty dictates that he be vigorously critical when the transgressor is absent.

To reject adaptation and identification is to commit oneself to some difficult distinctions. In recent years, leadership in the exploration of distant space has been assumed by the Jet Propulsion Laboratory. This is operated on behalf of the National Space Agency by the California Institute of Technology. It is a nonprofit enterprise. It is taken for granted that the scientists, engineers and technicians associated with this enterprise are strongly identified with its goals and deeply proud of their contribution (i.e. their adaptive role) in this enterprise. It would seem silly, as well as insulting, to suggest that pecuniary compensation is the sole or even the dominant motive. A few miles away similar scientists, engineers and technicians are employed on tasks of similar character and complexity at Lockheed and Hughes Aircraft. These are private corporations. Their men, it is assumed, are more or less exclusively motivated by the money they earn. Obviously such distinctions make no sense.

A decent respect for reality requires that we recognize that men serve organizations in response to a complex system of motivations. The mixture will be different in different cases. In the entrepreneurial corporation, in which those in charge have a primary concern for income, pecuniary motivation may be strong throughout the enterprise. In the mature corporation, identification and adaptation may be much more important and this is especially probable if it has a strong scientific and technical orientation. And in the mature corporation the motivation will be very different for different levels or kinds of participants. To these differences I now turn.

Chapter 13

MOTIVATION AND THE TECHNOSTRUCTURE

THE mature corporation is a large and complex organization, and individuals align themselves with its goals in response to diverse motives. This motivational system can best be understood if we abandon the conventional image of the corporate structure. This image is of a geometric hierarchy. Authority passes down from the top. At the summit, in a rectangular box, are the stockholders, the repository of ultimate power. Next come their representatives, the Board of Directors; then the executive officers or top management. Off to the sides are counsel, auditors, public relations and other staff. From the top executives, the line of authority continues down through departments, divisions, plants, units and other subdivisions. It ends, untactfully, at the bottom with the proletarian.

In the mature corporation, however, the stockholders are without power; the Board of Directors is normally the passive instrument of the management; decisions, since complexity is usually associated with importance, are effectively the work of groups. When taken the resulting advice moves up through the organization. It follows that the conventional image of organization – the customary organization chart – is aggressively misleading. So, accordingly, will be any analysis which uses it as a guide in relating individuals and groups to the corporation. The notion of a formal structure of command must be abandoned.

It is more useful to think of the mature corporation as a series of concentric circles. The band within each pair of circles represents a group of participants with a different motivational system. In the more spacious bands at the outer reaches are the most numerous groups. Such in general is their motivational system that they are the most loosely attached. At the centre is what is now called the top management. Theirs is the firmest attachment. Between are the others. With this image in mind the motivational system of the various participants in the corporation can be much more intelligently considered.

II

In the outermost circle in the mature corporation are the ordinary stockholders. This for all practical purposes is a purely pecuniary association. The typical stockholder does not identify himself with the goals of the enterprise; he does not expect to influence these goals. He has a share in the ownership; normally his only concern is that it return him as much money as possible. If he can get more income or capital gain with equal security elsewhere, he sells and invests there. No sense of loyalty – no identification with the goals of the enterprise – normally prevents his doing so.

This is the general case. That of the sizable stockholder who sits or is represented on the Board is different. So is that of the owner who, in the past manner of the du Pont family, participates in management. But these cases diminish in significance as the corporation matures. At the time of his death the largest stockholder in American Telephone and Telegraph was, reputedly, the late Billy Rose. It seems unlikely that this distinguished songwriter and theatrical entrepreneur identified himself closely with the telecommunications industry or regarded himself as a force therein. The relation to the corporation of the largest stockholders of General Motors, United States Steel, Standard Oil and like enterprises, with few exceptions, is equally impersonal. Certainly it is so of the ordinary stockholders.

As earlier noted, corporate folk rites seek to have the stockholders think possessively of their company. Few are fooled. The relation of the ordinary stockholder to the corporation is the purest case of pecuniary motivation.

III

The next inward circle is occupied by the production workers. Here, already, motivation becomes mixed. Clearly, pecuniary compensation is important; one test is the effect of a reduction in pay at the margin – say a cut from double to straight time for overtime work. In most enterprises it would bring a prompt reduction in hours worked and effort expended. Some part of this effort is tedious or monotonous. Whatever the goals it serves, they are not those of the worker. These he would expect to pursue with a fishing rod, a television screen or a blend of whisky and grain neutral spirits. He has no illusion that he can adapt the goals of the organization to his own.

Yet, in fact, motives are more complex. The worker, unlike the stockholder, lives in immediate daily association with the organization. This is itself an inducement to identification; an individual comes to think of himself as an IBM man, a Corning Glass man or a Sears man. The element of compulsion in the association has receded and, therewith, this barrier to identification. The entrepreneurial corporation sought to maximize the return to the owners. The maximization of the pecuniary return of distant and presumably well-to-do persons was not a goal with which the ordinary worker, human nature what it is, would be likely to identify himself. The more ambiguous and less visibly egotistical goals of the technostructure[1] are less sharply in conflict with identification by the worker. Comparative security of tenure and the physically untaxing and, on occasion, interesting character of modern technological processes also lower the barriers to identification.

In fact the motivation of the production worker is a mixture of pecuniary compensation and identification. The particular combination will vary greatly with the circumstances of the industry and firm. If the pay is high, the work interesting and the security of tenure great and the firm seems plausibly concerned with some goal other than making the most money for stockholders or management, identification will be significant.

1. Chapter 15.

Given the routine and tedious assembly line work that is subject to recurrent lay-offs and a seeming commitment to simple money-making, the likelihood of identification will be less.

These differences bear strongly on the strategy of the firm in its labour policy. If identification is strong and can be strengthened, it will narrow the opportunities for the union. The latter has a chance only when commitment to the goals of the corporation is sufficiently slight so that it can win commitment to its own. (In everyday language loyalty to the company must not conflict unduly with loyalty to the union.) And identification can be increased by substituting automated for manual processes. This, at one step, reduces the number of workers susceptible to union goals and, by adding to the pay, interest and physical ease of those remaining, increases the tendency to identification. With such identification, and associated elimination of union power, industrial planning becomes more secure. Wage costs are predictable; there is no danger of the withdrawal of the labour force in a strike. It follows that even though automated processes are more expensive, the resulting identification and support to planning may make them worthwhile. These, obviously, are matters of first importance for judging the prospects for labour relations in the industrial system. I return to them below.[2]

IV

Next, as one moves inward, are foremen and supervisory personnel and the clerical, sales and other routine white collar personnel. These merge at their inner perimeter with technicians, engineers, sales executives, scientists, designers and other specialists who comprise the technostructure. Beyond these at the centre are the executives or management. As one moves through these inner circles, identification and adaptation become increasingly important.

The barriers to identification disappear. There is no sense of compulsion and thus no bar to voluntary adoption of the

2. Chapters 23 and 24.

goals of the employing organization. In the entrepreneurial corporation men at all levels work, in principle at least, for the enrichment of someone else. This, as noted, is not an easy goal for men of average meanness to adopt. In the mature corporation, power has passed to the technostructure. Whatever its goals they cannot be, and as we shall see are not, hostile to those of its own members. Identification is thus facilitated. That the technostructure has power assures that, within limits, it has power to adapt the goals of the enterprise to its own. Adaptation is thus facilitated. Thus, as one moves to the centre of the technostructure, identification and adaptation become increasingly plausible motivations.

Regarding identification others have agreed. Professors Simon and March suggest that identification will be strong if members see, or sense, that the goals of the organization are shared by participants. This restates the tendency just described. They list, in addition, four other circumstances inducing identification as follows:

(1) If the prestige of the group or organization attracting identification is high and widely perceived.
(2) If there is frequent interaction between the individuals who comprise the organization.
(3) If a large number of the needs of the individual are satisfied within the organization.
(4) If competition between members of the organization is minimized.[3]

All of these requirements are met in the mature corporation, and increasingly so in the inner circles of the technostructure. Although, as later chapters will suggest, the prestige of business organization is declining, the large corporation continues to be a symbol of success and achievement in the culture.[4] It

3. James G. March and Herbert A. Simon, *Organizations* (New York: Wiley, 1958), pp. 65–6. The foregoing is a paraphrase of their specifications.
4. Ibid., p. 67.

endows its members with this prestige; it is obviously better to be a General Motors or Western Electric man than an ordinary unattached citizen. The question automatically asked when two men meet on a plane or in Florida is, 'Who are you with?' Until this is known, the individual is a cipher. He cannot be placed in the scheme of things; no one knows how much attention, let alone respect, he deserves or whether he is worthy of any notice at all. If he is with a well-known corporation – a good outfit – he obviously counts. The organization man has been a subject of much sorrow. But all who weep should recall that he surrenders to organization because organization does more for him than he can do for himself. For the moment it is sufficient for the mature corporation has the prestige which induces and encourages the individual to accept its goals in place of his own.

The requirement of frequent interaction between partici-pants is also met. The technostructure, we have seen, is a mechanism for group decision-making. Such decisions are the result of intense interaction between individuals.[5] So, by its very nature, the technostructure provides this inducement to identification.

The technostructure, and especially in the inner circles, also meets a large share of the needs of the individual. In very recent times, it has become fashionable, although not yet obligatory, for the corporation executive to have some non-business interests apart from therapeutic recreation and com-munity service. The collection of abstract art, Indian pottery, old campaign posters or antique harmonicas; or patronage of the ballet or birth control; or cultivation of eccentric office designs are all manifestations of this trend. But it is still norm-

---

5. On the basis of interviews supplemented by questionnaires with 221 executives and managers of various rank, William H. Whyte, Jr, con-cluded that: 'the average executive spends roughly six of his eight office hours talking with other executives in meetings and conferences, and he would be considered an odd bird indeed if he went out to lunch by him-self. . . .' *The Executive Life*, by the Editors of *Fortune* (New York: Doubleday, 1956), p. 64.

ally a matter of pride that the corporation absorbs nearly all his waking energy. All else including family, politics, sometimes even alcohol and sex, are secondary. 'To the executive there is between work and other aspects of one's life a unity he can never fully explain. . . . How can you overwork, executives ask, if your work is your life?'[6] This is to say that the organization satisfies his needs with marked repleteness – that this inducement to identification is also fully satisfied.

Finally, although there is rivalry within the technostructure, the competition is not that of a zero sum game. Even though only one man gets promoted to the top job, all can get promoted. This also is consistent with identification. The small-town automobile dealer pursuing a customer or the small-city contractor pursuing a particular paving contract is, by contrast, in a zero sum game. (Significantly the participants themselves call it a cutthroat game.) When he wins a sale or contract, his competitor loses it and vice versa. The inducement is to individually asserted goals and not to a cooperative acceptance of common ones.

Within the technostructure, we may concede, the factors making for identification have a clear run.

v

The technostructure, to repeat once more, lodges the power of decision with groups. And these involve the participation of a large number of individuals of widely varying rank and position. Thus, a large number of people have access, or the illusion of access, to power. The goals of the entrepreneurial

---

6. Ibid., p. 69. Whyte quotes a steel executive in the following idyll of his business and family life:

'Instead of relaxing at night with a mystery story, you keep at it until eleven o'clock and finally you say to yourself, "The devil with it, I'm going to have a highball or two and go to bed." But I sit there stewing until twelve-thirty or one. As a result I'm very uncompanionable at breakfast. My wife says I just sit there and dream, and maybe she's right. But I get a kick out of keeping well informed about business.'

corporation were rigidly identified with the pecuniary interest of the entrepreneur. As this goal discouraged identification, so the rigidity of the commitment discouraged adaptation. In the mature corporation there is already indication that the goals are less rigidly prescribed. And they are within the ambit of the technostructure. The scope for adaptation is thus markedly enhanced.

Adaptation, as a motive, will be stronger as one approaches the inner circles of the technostructure. Here both the illusion and fact of power are greatest. The individual will have increasing reason to feel that, by serving the organization, he can align it more closely with his own goals. The decisions of the groups in which he participates will be wider in scope. And his higher position in the hierarchy will contribute to his impression of power.

Adaptation, in the mature corporation, is also reinforced by the nearly invariable tendency for individuals to narrow the universe so that it is coterminous with their own horizons. This is most important. The schoolteacher's world is the school. The world of the preacher is bounded by the spiritually more marginal members of his congregation; the souls of those beyond are housed, not in theory but in practical attitude, in second-class citizens. The world of the bureaucrat is his unit, section, branch or bureau; for the prerogatives and performance of this he feels an intense responsibility and for the rest of the government a certain indifference, resentment or even contempt. Nothing is so important for the university professor as the department in which he serves. The university is a thin penumbra beyond. Only the exceptionally ambitious seek influence in the distant world of the Modern Language Association. It is in these circumscribed worlds, not the world at large, that each man observes the struggle, chicanery, duplicity, favouritism and political alliances which, as he sees them, really count. And it is this sub-universe that he seeks to accommodate to his own goals. To the desire of the individual to mould the world to his goals, a thoughtful Providence has added the illusion of a great ability to do so. This is accomplished by reducing each individual's world to manageable size. Adaptation, as a motive, is much strengthened as a result.[7, 8]

These sub-universes in the mature corporation are numerous and come, for their members, to be similarly large in life. For those concerned with hiring, nothing is so important as personnel policy; for those concerned with information and data control, all other activities are secondary; for those teamed for the development of a new product, nothing is so central. For the lawyers, the general counsel's office is the brain of the enterprise. For the accountants, it is accounting. For the sales staff, it is sales. All this enhances the role of adaptation.

VI

So it can reasonably be concluded that identification – the voluntary exchange of one's goals for the preferable ones of organization – and adaptation – the association with organization in the hope of influencing its goals to accord more closely with one's own – are strong motivating forces in the techno-

7. The ancient and well-recognized pleasure in talking shop stems from this preoccupation with one's immediate community. Those who belong share the feeling that theirs is the only world that counts. Only to outsiders does their conversation seem parochial or uninteresting.

8. This tendency is of great importance in government where small administrative subdivisions regularly acquire a larger than life reality to those associated with them and thus enlist diligent, devoted and ingenious service as well as fierce bureaucratic loyalties. After World War II, when Ph.D. thesis requirements in economics at Harvard were being extensively satisfied by war memoirs, I received a document of several hundred pages on the operations of the unit of the Office of Price Administration which had been concerned with price control for leather and synthetic shoe soles and heels. Price control for these products, I learned from this account, had been administered with energy, intelligence and ingenuity – heels were even tested on the shoes of Washington mail carriers and priced according to durability as so demonstrated. The thesis came close to associating success or failure in wartime administration with the success or failure of this unit of the price control organization. Though in charge of price control, I had not previously known of the unit or of its accomplishments. Nor did the thesis mention my office except as a distant and largely regrettable point of clearance.

structure and become increasingly so in the inner circles. This is obscured because, as one moves to the inner circle – to what is called top management – pecuniary compensation becomes generous. For the senior executives of the large corporation it is, on occasion, spectacular. Those who respond best to the visible associate motivation with this high compensation.

But, as we have previously seen, few things are so certain as the absence of any close relationship between compensation and effort in the inner circles of the mature corporation.[9] At the centre of the corporation compensation is only a part of a larger motivational system which allows also for the full manifestation of identification and adaptation. To the specific goals these serve, after a word of summary, we now turn.

9. Cf. R. A. Gordon, *Business Leadership in the Large Corporation* (Washington: Brookings, 1945), pp. 312 et seq. and Mabel Newcomer, *The Big Business Executive* (New York: Columbia University Press, 1955), pp. 121 et seq. Both authors conclude, in effect, that above a given level of compensation and subject to inevitable exceptions, pecuniary motivation is of secondary importance. This is to say that increases or decreases in compensation would not affect effort. In the course of interviews with executives Whyte found that while complaints of high taxes were common, most conceded that they had no effect on their effort. This was at a maximum in any case. *The Executive Life*, p. 66.

Chapter 14

THE PRINCIPLE OF CONSISTENCY

IT is now necessary to summarize and to reaffirm a rule. The relationship between society at large and an organization must be consistent with the relation of the organization to the individual. There must be consistency in the goals of the society, the organization and the individual. And there must be consistency in the motives which induce organizations and individuals to pursue these goals.

As always, in social matters, we have here a deeply interconnected matrix. And it follows that if we know the goals of the society we will have guidance to the goals of the organizations that serve it and the individuals that comprise these organizations. And the reverse will also hold. Similarly, if we know how individuals are motivated, we will know how organizations are motivated and also the reverse.

Unfortunately, to lay down a principle is neither to win understanding nor establish proof. Some elaboration is necessary.

II

In simple cases, consistency in the motivation of organization and individuals, and in the goals they pursue, is taken for granted. When, to recur to a previous illustration, the feudal lord was summoned to his military duty, he summoned, in turn, the liege men who were bound to accompany him. Compulsion disguised or reinforced by tradition motivated both. And compulsion, by its nature, required lord and subject to accept the same goals. Were the lord required to make a maximum display of martial ardour, this objective would have also to be imposed upon his followers. Otherwise his goal would be defeated, as has not infrequently happened in history, by a jarring contrast between the sanguinary courage of a leader and the prudence of the led.

The lord could not be called to duty with his men unless the power by which he was commanded was available to him, in turn, to command his followers. Since he was unpaid, it would have been impossible, or in any case fiscally unattractive, for him long to induce service by hiring men at going rates. And if he were himself rewarded for his service, he would have had, sooner or later, to negotiate some mercenary arrangement with his men, perhaps a profit-sharing arrangement on plunder. No one would be likely to supply him with power to enforce service for which they had already paid and not many would be likely to serve well without pay for the profit of another. Thus do circumstances compel symmetry in the motivation and goals of organizations and the individuals comprising them.

These rules hold equally in the market economy. The accepted goal of such a society was to maximize its wealth and income. This measured its success. It is consistent with this social goal that business firms should seek to maximize their income. And it is consistent with this goal of the firm that individuals should seek to maximize their personal return. The society frowned on those who settled for less than the best they might earn or on firms which did not maximize their income (those which were poorly run) or which maximized return in such fashion – as by monopoly or fraud – as to prevent the society from doing so. As force motivated both the lord and his liege, so pecuniary return motivated both the business firm and its members.

The mature corporation, as we have seen, is not compelled to maximize its profits and does not do so. This allows it to pursue other goals and this accords similar alternatives to the members of the technostructure. The need for consistency, nonetheless, still holds. The goals of the corporation, though so freed, must be consistent with those of the society and consistent, in turn, with those of the individuals who comprise it. So also must be the motivations.

III

More specifically, the goals of the mature corporation will be a reflection of the goals of the members of the technostructure. And the goals of the society will tend to be those of the corporation. If, as we have seen to be the case, the members of the technostructure set high store by autonomy, and the assured minimum level of earnings by which this is secured, this will be a prime objective of the corporation. The need for such autonomy and the income that sustains it will be conceded or stressed by the society.

So with other goals, and so matters work also in reverse. If the society sets high store by technological virtuosity and measures its success by its capacity for rapid technical advance, this will become a goal of the corporation and therewith of those who comprise it. It may, of course, be subordinate, as a goal, to the need to maintain a minimum level of income – the fact that the goals of the mature corporation are plural rather than singular does not mean that all have the same priority. Rather, a hierarchy of goals is quite plausible. And given the requisite consistency between social, corporate and individual goals there is no *a priori* reason for assuming that the priorities will be exactly the same for any two corporations.

The same consistency characterizes motivation – the stimuli that set individuals and organizations in pursuit of goals. Pecuniary compensation is an extremely important stimulus to individual members of the technostructure up to a point. If they are not paid this acceptable and expected salary, they will not work. But once this requirement is met, the offer of more money to an engineer, scientist or executive brings little or no more effort. Other motivation takes over. Similarly, until the minimum requirements of the corporation for earnings are reached, pecuniary motivation will be strong. For it too, above a certain level, additional income brings little or no additional effort. Other goals become more important.

Consistency is equally necessary in the case of identification. The individual will identify himself with the goals of the corporation only if the corporation is identified with, as the individual sees it, some significant social goal. The corporation that is engaged in developing a line of life-preserving drugs wins loyalty and effort from the social purpose its products serve or are presumed to serve. Those engaged in the design or manufacture of a space vehicle identify themselves with the goals of their organization because it, in turn, is identified with the scientific task of exploring space or the high political purpose of outdistancing the Russians. The manufacturer of an exotic missile fuel, or a better trigger for a nuclear warhead, attracts the loyalty of its members because their organization is seen to be serving importantly the cause of freedom. It is felt no doubt that human beings, whose elimination these weapons promise, have an inherent tendency to abuse freedom.

There is no similar identification if the firm is simply engaged in making money for an entrepreneur and has no other claimed social purpose. It is noteworthy that when a corporation is having its assets looted by those in control it simultaneously suffers a very sharp reduction in executive and employee morale. All concerned recognize that the corporation is no longer serving any social purpose of any kind.

IV

Consistency in the identification of individuals and organizations with social goals is possible because, running as a parallel thread from individual through organization to social attitudes, is the presence of adaptation as a motivating force. The individual serves organization, we have seen, because of the possibility of accommodating its goals more closely to his own. If his goals reflect a particular social attitude or vision, he will seek to have the corporation serve that attitude or vision. More important, he will normally think that the goals he seeks have social purpose. (Individuals have a well-remarked capacity to attach high social purpose to whatever – more scientific research, better zoning laws, manufacture of the lethal weapons just mentioned – serves their personal interest.) If he succeeds, the corporation in turn will advance or defend these goals as socially important. The corporation becomes, thus, an instrument for attributing social purpose to the goals of those who comprise it. Social purpose becomes by this process of adaptation what serves the goals of members of the technostructure.

This process is highly successful in our time. Much of what is believed to be socially important is, in fact, the adaptation of social attitudes to the goal system of the technostructure. What counts here is what is believed. These social goals, though in fact derived from the goals of the technostructure, are believed to have original social purpose. Accordingly, members of the corporation in general, and of the technostructure in particular, are able to identify themselves with the corporation on the assumption that it is serving social goals when, in fact, it is serving their own. Even the most acute social conscience is no inconvenience if it originates in one's own.

V

The process by which social goals become adapted to the goals of the corporation and ultimately the technostructure is not analytical or cerebral. Rather it reflects a triumph of unexamined but constantly reiterated assumption over exact thought. The technostructure is principally concerned with the manufacture of goods and with the companion management and development of the demand for these goods. It is obviously important that this be accorded high social purpose and that the greater the production of goods, the greater be the purpose served. This allows the largest possible number of people to identify themselves with social function.

From a detached point of view, expansion in the output of many goods is not easily accorded a social purpose. More cigarettes cause more cancer. More alcohol causes more cirrhosis. More automobiles cause more accidents, maiming and death; also more preemption of space for highways and parking; also more pollution of the air and the countryside. What is called a high standard of living consists, in considerable measure, in arrangements for avoiding muscular energy, increasing sensual pleasure and for enhancing caloric intake above any conceivable nutritional requirement. Nonetheless, the belief that increased production is a worthy social goal is very nearly absolute. It is imposed by assumption, and this assumption the ordinary individual encounters, in the ordinary course of business, a thousand times a year. Things are better because production is up. There is exceptional improvement because it is up more than ever before. That social progress is identical with a rising standard of living has the aspect of a faith. No society has ever before provided such a high standard of living as ours, hence none is as good. The occasional query, however logically grounded, is unheard.

There are other examples. Successful planning in areas of expensive and sophisticated technology requires that the state underwrite costs, including the costs of research and development, and that it ensure a market for the resulting products. It is important to the technostructure, therefore, that technological change of whatever kind be accorded a high social value. This too is agreed. In consequence, the underwriting of sophisticated technology by the state has become an approved social function. Few question the merit of state intervention for such social purpose as supersonic travel or improved applications of nuclear power. Even fewer protest when these are for military purposes. Social purpose is again the result of adaptation. This is a matter of obvious importance and one to which I will return.

None of this is to suggest that all social attitudes originate with the technostructure and its needs. Society also has goals, stemming from the needs which are unassociated with its major productive mechanism, and which it imposes on the mature corporation. As elsewhere I argue only for a two-way process. The mature corporation imposes social attitudes as it also responds to social attitudes. Truth is never strengthened by exaggeration. Nor is it less the truth by being more complex than the established propositions that assert the simple eminence of pecuniary goals and pecuniary motivation.

Happily this complexity diminishes appreciably as these general rules are put to practical use.

Chapter 15

THE GOALS OF THE INDUSTRIAL SYSTEM

THE individual member of the technostructure identifies himself with the goals of the mature corporation as, and because, the corporation identifies itself with goals which have, or appear to him to have, social purpose. And members seek to adapt the goals of the corporation to accord with their own with the result that the corporation accommodates social attitudes to its needs. What is deemed to be sound social purpose is a reflection of the goals of the corporation and the members of the technostructure. What remains now is to give concrete form to these relationships. We need to specify the social goals with which the corporation and the members of its technostructure identify themselves. And we need to specify the goals to which, in accordance with their needs, they ascribe social purpose.

These are, we may remind ourselves once more, problems of some novelty. As economic life is ordinarily regarded, they do not arise. The sovereign consumer has wants and desires original to himself or which, at most, arise by imitation from the consumption of his fellows. These wants and desires or the lack of them he manifests by his purchases or non-purchases in the market. This, with the like action of others, is the social edict. To it the corporation, and all other producers, respond and, because of their commitment to maximize return, they do so without latitude or choice. The firm is wholly subordinate to the social edict as prescribed by the consumer. So, accordingly, are the people who comprise the firm. They do not impose their imprint on the goals of society.

This is also a reassuring formula. The social will to which the business firm is subordinate is exercised in simple fashion from public master to corporate servant. The influence or power of the latter can cause no concern. If the reader senses that this may understate the social role of such evidently influential and conceivably omnipotent organizations as General Motors or Standard Oil, General Electric or General Dynamics, he will have correctly guessed the thrust of this book and he will be receptive to its argument. If he suspects that economics, as it is conventionally taught, is in part a system of belief designed less to reveal truth than to reassure its communicants about established social arrangements, he will also be right.

For it is so. Modern economic belief can be understood only as the servant, in substantial measure, of the society which nurtures it. And not the least of its services to that society is to render instruction to the young which, rather systematically, excludes speculation on the way the large economic organizations shape social attitudes to their ends. Nor is the service less important for being rendered, in the main, in innocence and in the name of scientific truth. On the contrary, were it arranged and paid for it would cease to be of much effect. The wiles of the prostitute can be far more professional and superficially compelling than those of her artless competition, but many more men succumb to the latter.

II

For any organization, as for any organism, the goal or objective that has a natural assumption of preeminence is the organization's own survival. This, plausibly, is true of the technostructure.

The first requisite for survival by the technostructure is that it preserve the autonomy on which its decision-making power depends. This means, we have seen,[1] that it must have a secure minimum of earnings. Power passes to the technostructure when technology and planning require specialized knowledge and group decision. The power remains securely with the technostructure as long as earnings are large enough to make accustomed payments to the stockholders and provide a supply

1. Chapter 6.

of savings for reinvestment. If earnings are less than this level, it will be necessary to appeal to outside suppliers of capital. These, in turn, can ask questions and impose conditions and thus abridge the autonomy of the technostructure. And if the accustomed dividends are not covered, stockholders cannot wholly be counted upon to remain quiescent; as we have seen, struggles for control in large corporations occur all but exclusively in those that are suffering losses or which have meagre and irregular earnings.[2]

The effects of low and high earnings on the technostructure are not symmetrical. With low earnings or losses it becomes vulnerable to outside influence and loses its autonomy. But above a certain level more earnings add little or nothing to its security therein. This autonomy has become nearly absolute. This casts light, in turn, on the assumption that the mature corporation will seek to maximize its profits. By the most elementary calculation of self-interest, the technostructure is compelled to put prevention of loss ahead of maximum return. Loss can destroy the technostructure; high revenues accrue to others.[3] If, as will often happen, the maximization of revenues invites increased risk of loss, then the technostructure, as a matter of elementary interest, should forgo it.[4]

2. There is a further and poignant reason for wanting to protect a minimum rate of return. While suppliers of capital tend to recognize at least implicitly that decision-making in the modern corporation requires autonomy – that they must not 'interfere' with management decision – investigation and study are legitimate and are invited by inadequate return. And the management consulting industry, which exists in response to this opportunity, is highly available for such tasks. It, in turn, brings the pay, position and performance of members of the technostructure under a scrutiny that most executives would wish to avoid.

3. 'They [executives of the large corporation] do not receive the profits which may result from taking a chance, while their position in the firm may be jeopardized in the event of serious loss.' R. A. Gordon, *Business Leadership in the Large Corporation* (Washington: Brookings, 1945), p. 324.

4. The importance of a minimum level of return is stressed, although not as strongly as here, by William J. Baumol, in *Business Behavior, Value and Growth* (New York: Macmillan, 1959), especially pp. 48–53. What he calls the 'security' of the managerial group is a major theme

The need for protecting a minimum level of return will have, in turn, an important effect on industrial planning. While it will be desirable to achieve planned results, it will be even more important to avoid unplanned disasters. The first is pleasing; the second can be mortal. Even more important than a good price is protection against a price collapse. Even more important than a strong demand for the product is protection against a wholesale rejection. I return to the effect of these needs on the management of prices and demand in the next three chapters. And we shall see, thereafter, that the relation of the mature corporation to the state – its support of steps to regulate aggregate demand and its strong encouragement of public underwriting of expensive technology – arises from the same effort to exclude any threat to minimum levels of earnings. Similar considerations will be seen to underlie modern labour policy.

III

If the principle of consistency holds, the autonomy of the technostructure should be a goal of social policy. And, as a moment's thought will suggest, it is.

The doctrine of the industrial system stresses powerfully its inherently and functionally independent character. It is the *private* enterprise system. A great gulf is deemed to divide the state from the business firm. Only in the rarest instances may there be any constraining action across this chasm. On nothing is the burden of proof so strong as on a measure – to provide standards of automobile safety, of drug advertising, of weights

---

of Mr Marris's analysis. (Robin Marris, *The Economic Theory of 'Managerial Capitalism* [New York: The Free Press of Glencoe, 1964].) Professor Kaysen states the same conclusion as follows: 'While the firm in the highly competitive market is constrained to seek after maximum profits, because the alternative is insufficient profit to insure survival, the firm in the less competitive market can choose whether to seek maximum profit or to be satisfied with some "acceptable" return and to seek other "goals".' In *The Corporation in Modern Society*, Edward F. Mason, ed. (Cambridge: Harvard University Press, 1959), p. 90.

of packages, of health claims on behalf of cigarettes – which involves the regulation of an industrial enterprise.

The grounds on which this separation is defended are palpably bogus. It is held that nothing must interfere with the independent operation of the market mechanism to which the firm is subject. The reality in the case of the mature corporation, as we have sufficiently seen, is that prices are substantially controlled by the firm and the latter goes on to exercise influence on the amounts that are purchased and sold at these prices. The imperatives of technology and capital use do not allow the firm to be subordinate to the market and the mature corporation so far from being separated organically from the state exists, as we shall presently see, only in intimate association with it.

Yet autonomy is necessary. The real reasons why it is needed not being clearly seen, the power of the market and the allegedly deep and inherent separation between private enterprise and government are advanced in their place. Both are articles of faith. It is a tribute to the power of adaptation that it can win social attitudes favourable to the autonomy of the technostructure that have such negligible relation to reality.

And the requisite social attitudes have been secured. The right of the technostructure to autonomy, and more than incidentally to the earnings that assure it, is wholly accepted. Not for years has any serious aspirant for public office run on a platform of tighter regulation of business. Nor does anyone question the sanctity of an adequate level of profits.

There remains, indeed, a compulsive worry by businessmen over government interference which is matched by a desire by public officials to reassure that none is intended. This is much misunderstood. To the entrepreneurial corporation the state was a threat to its income. It resisted public regulation for the purpose of protecting its profits. The modern observer, noticing that the mature corporation is making a good return, is surprised to find its executives alarmed about government intrusion or asking for comfort that none is intended. 'Why are they so worried?' he asks. 'Surely they are making plenty of money.' He fails to see that the technostructure is protecting something more important than its profits – something indeed which profits themselves protect. That is its autonomy.[5]

IV

Once the safety of the technostructure is ensured by a minimum level of earnings, there is then a measure of choice as to goals. Nothing is so compelling as the need to survive. However, there is little doubt as to how, overwhelmingly, this choice is exercised: It is to achieve the greatest possible rate of corporate growth as measured in sales.

This goal also commends itself strongly to the self-interest of the technostructure. Expansion of output means expansion of the technostructure itself. Such expansion, in turn, means more jobs with more responsibility and hence more promotion and more compensation. 'When a man takes decisions leading to successful expansion, he not only creates new openings but also recommends himself and his colleagues as particularly suitable candidates to fill them.'[6] The paradox of modern economic motivation is that profit maximization as a goal requires that the individual member of the technostructure subordinate his personal pecuniary interest to that of the remote and unknown stockholder. By contrast, growth, as a goal, is wholly consistent with the personal and pecuniary interest of those who participate in decisions and direct the enterprise. The reader will sense once more how important profit maximization must be for the defence of traditional economic theory and specifically the rule of the market. Its use survives in competition with

5. I have discussed somewhat related considerations in *American Capitalism: The Concept of Countervailing Power* (Boston: Houghton, 1956), Chapter VI.

6. Marris, op. cit., p. 102. Although reached by highly theoretical techniques, Mr Marris's conclusions as to the goals of the mature corporation are consistent with mine. So are Professor Baumol's, op cit., which are based partly on theoretical argument and partly on empirical observation.

goals which reflect the self-interest of those immediately involved.[7]

The growth of the firm serves another important purpose for the technostructure. It is the best protection against contraction. For the firm with a small contingent of managers and supervisors and a large undifferentiated mass of blue collar workers, a shrinkage in production presents no great difficulties. A notice is posted and the men go; when needed they are called back. Those who post the notice are not personally involved.

With the rise of the technostructure, any contraction of output becomes much more painful and damaging. Costs can no longer be reduced simply by laying off blue collar workers. A substantial share of total costs are now accounted for by the technostructure. If this remains intact, the firm will have a burdensome overhead in the form of a partially employed organization. In the technostructure men work in groups. Whole groups cannot be discharged. The discharge of individuals – or their voluntary withdrawal in response to their easily perceived unemployment – impairs the working efficiency of those that remain. Moreover, decisions for curtailment are made within the technostructure itself. They involve its own members. They do not have the agreeable impersonality which is associated with firing someone at a greater distance, or of a different social class.

All of these unpleasant contingencies are avoided by expansion. Their avoidance may even justify comparatively unremunerative expansion. This is the meaning of the frequently

7. Professor Peterson has argued ('Corporate Control and Capitalism', *The Quarterly Journal of Economics*, Vol. LXXIX, No. 1 [February 1965], p. 11) that the need for profits to finance growth means that there is little practical difference between growth as a goal and profit maximization as a goal. Growth may be the best long-run strategy for maximizing profits. This is not so. While, if one waits long enough, one may sooner or later find one strategy miscarrying and another serving its ends better, the proper test is *ex ante* not *ex post* behaviour. Price, sales, cost and other policies to maximize growth will differ within any given time horizon from those to maximize profits. Nor will profits be maximized if, as in the case of the technostructure, there is special reason to minimize risk.

heard statement that business is being taken, not for its profit, but 'to hold the organization together'. It can be a highly rational course.[8]

V

The growth of the firm as a goal of the technostructure is strongly supported by the principle of consistency. No other social goal is more strongly avowed than economic growth. No other test of social success has such nearly unanimous acceptance as the annual increase in the Gross National Product. And this is true of all countries developed or undeveloped; communist, socialist or capitalist. Japan has been deemed a successful society since World War II because of its very high rate of increase in Gross National Product. So also Germany and Israel and latterly, France. Britain with a much smaller increase has been perilously close to being a failure. The communist countries have been greater or less rivals of the non-communist states in accordance with their greater or less increase in output. There are differences of opinion between communist and non-communist scholars on the validity of the statistics and concepts which are employed in the two worlds to measure economic growth. But there is no disagreement on the validity of the goal itself. Similarly it is now agreed that ancient cultures – India, China and Persia – should measure their progress toward civilization by their percentage increase in G.N.P. Their own scholars are the most insistent of all.

Given the agreement on economic growth as a social goal, the goal of the technostructure has a strong social purpose. Members can identify themselves with it in the secure knowledge that they are serving a larger purpose than their own. They seek to further the growth of their firm. This furthers the growth of the economy. Identification, as a motivation, reinforces the self-interest that is associated with such expansion.

---

8. In another view, as the technostructure grows the proportion of the working force that must be treated as an overhead cost grows. But it is a special type of overhead. Unlike machinery or plant it disintegrates rapidly if not fully employed.

The question inevitably arises to what extent economic growth, as a social goal, reflects adaptation. Does it reflect original social need? Has it been imposed on society by the technostructure? This question cannot be answered categorically. No doubt the emphasis on economic growth is partly grounded in man's ancient and seemingly always inadequate supply of goods. And in modern times growth has been a principal therapy for unemployment.[9] Also economic growth eases many problems of allocation in the economy – it is much easier to find resources for education or the poor by taking these from increased output than by subtracting them from the existing standard of living. But, as always, we must be alert to a two-way influence. The acceptance of economic growth as a social goal coincides closely with the rise to power of the mature corporation and the technostructure. And the latter has had every reason to value it as a social goal. It does not argue the merits of this goal. As always it proceeds by massive assumption. What other goal *could* be socially so urgent? [10]

VI

Associated with growth, as a goal of the technostructure, is technological virtuosity. This also serves the needs of the members. Progressive technology means jobs and promotion for technologists. Capacity for expansion likewise depends very largely on capacity for innovation. It is by technical innovation, real or simulated, that the firm holds and recruits customers for its existing products and expands to produce new ones. Such capacity for innovation is obviously important for keeping or

9. Not infrequently in western countries the amount of unemployment is cited as a measure of the success or non-success of the system. But this, for nearly all scholars, is merely an indication of an insufficient output. Given a greater rate of increase in Gross National Product – a more successful economy by this standard – unemployment or most of it would disappear.

10. The reader in search of verification will have a remarkably easy way of satisfying himself on this point. He will need only to examine the dominant tone of the more orthodox reviews of this volume.

expanding the firm's share of weapons, space and other businesses with a high technological dynamic. But such innovation tends also to have standing in its own right. As in the scientific work of a university, prestige adheres to successful practitioners; it is a goal with which men readily identify themselves. Here again the principle of consistency leads us to look at social attitudes. And here again we find technological *advance*, as significantly it is called, solidly enshrined as a social good. It is progress. It is synonymous with social achievement. One would encounter less dispute, on the whole, by questioning the sanctity of the family or religion than the absolute merit of technical progress.

Technological virtuosity can be a goal of the technostructure only if it does not prejudice a minimum level of earnings. Given the costs and uncertainties associated with research and development, this can easily happen. Then this goal must be abandoned or the cost and attendant risk must be transferred to the state: that is to say, government support for the particular development, or the underlying research, must be sought. Given the high social purpose attributed to technological change, this socialization of development is strongly approved. Adaptation has paved the way. Nor need attention be paid to whether this investment of resources in technological and underlying scientific development is important in relation to alternatives. There is no need to measure the advantages of space achievements against help to the poor. In the nature of successful adaptation the absolute virtue of technological advance is again assumed.

VII

Now a concession must be made to seeming orthodoxy. A rate of earnings that allows, over and above investment needs, for a progressive rise in the dividend rate will also regularly be a goal of the technostructure. This return must not be achieved by prices which would prejudice growth. Nothing better suggests the primacy of growth as a goal than the vehemence with

181

which this would be dismissed as unsound business practice. The risks taken for such higher return, it is axiomatic, must not jeopardize the basic level of earnings. But tradition inherited from the entrepreneurial firm associates success with a rising level of realized earnings. And social attitudes, on the whole, take such an improvement in earnings over time as an indication of sound service to the community.

A secure level of earnings and a maximum rate of growth consistent with the provision of revenues for the requisite investment are the prime goals of the technostructure. Technological virtuosity and a rising dividend rate are secondary in the sense that they must not interfere with the two first-mentioned objectives. After these ends are achieved there is further opportunity for a variety of other and lesser goals. These are subject only to the limitation that they must not interfere with the two primary objectives. They are in no sense less rational or legitimate. But since these further goals will sometimes threaten minimum earnings and will not always contribute to the growth of the firm, their role will be closely circumscribed.

Building a better community; improved education; better understanding of the free enterprise system; an effective attack on heart ailments, emphysema, alcoholism, hard chancre or other crippling disease; participation in the political party of choice; and renewed emphasis on regular religious observances are all examples of such further goals. Some may also serve the primary and secondary goals – they contribute to what is called a sound corporate image and thus help recruiting and worker morale, avoid unwelcome taxes or cultivate a better public attitude towards products. But this is not necessary to justify the activity. It is sufficient that it serve goals that the technostructure (and the society) think good and that it be not in conflict with higher goals.

Nearly all economists, and a great many others, dismiss pursuit of such goals as irrelevant window-dressing. This is an error. So long as their subordinate role is clearly recognized, including the limitations imposed by cost, they are a perfectly plausible expression of the goals of the individual members of the technostructure and, thus, collectively of the mature corporation. What has been called the 'social corporation' is a logical manifestation of the mature corporation and the motivation of its members.

VIII

At any given time the symbols of business success will faithfully reflect success in pursuit of the currently accepted goals. In the latter half of the last century, the greatest folk hero of the economic system was the elder Rockefeller. This was the era of the entrepreneurial corporation; by its goals he was the greatest success for he had made more money than anyone else.

In our time no man of wealth enjoys comparable distinction. Nor is esteem associated with individuals; by the nature of the technostructure they are submerged in the group. Esteem is associated with corporations. And among these, the first requirement is a secure earnings record. Any firm that fails this requirement is a dog. Its management is regarded with condescension, even pity. Sooner or later even subordinate employees will sense their loss of public respect and match it with a loss of self-respect. In the fashion increasingly affected by the latter-day railway employee they will conduct themselves in a slovenly and offensive manner indicating their feeling that the world in general and their customers in particular are their enemy. Or they will go elsewhere.

Given a secure level of earnings the esteemed firms are those that are large – that have a record of achieved growth – or which are growing with particular speed. Increasingly, esteem is associated with the latter. And if a firm has a reputation for technological innovation, it is additionally known as a smart outfit. Thereafter the dividend record will be mentioned. One knows little of life unless he has a theoretical system by which to interpret it. But there is little in theory that cannot be tested in life.

Chapter 16

PRICES IN THE INDUSTRIAL SYSTEM

IT will be evident that the need to keep the modern corporation subordinate to the market causes grave problems for the otherwise estimable subject of economics. But nowhere are the contradictions so evident, and the problems of illogic so melancholy, as in the theory of price behaviour that results. And nowhere are the clarifying rewards of reality so great.

The way prices are set – what economists have always called value theory – was until very recent times the heart of the subject. For thousands of reluctant scholars, a few distantly remembered curves depicting the interaction of supply and demand to establish prices have for long been the only permanent return on an investment in economic education. Let me now state in more detail an argument earlier introduced.

There has also long been agreement on how, in an ideal world, prices should be set. The process would be impersonal. No individual or firm by its presence or absence in the market would have power durably to affect that market. If it could do so, it would influence prices in its own favour. Such power will be least when all participants are small in relation to the market in which they participate. It will be greatest where there are few sellers or buyers or only one. The latter situation, that of the monopolists, is the apogee of improper influence. In the English language only a few words – fraud, defalcation, subversion and sodomy – have a greater connotation of non-violent wickedness.

Yet in the characteristic market of the industrial system there are only a handful of sellers. The domestic automobile market is shared by four firms and dominated by three. Markets for primary aluminium, copper, rubber, cigarettes, soap and detergents, whisky, heavy electrical gear, structural steel, cans, computers, aircraft engines, sugar, biscuits, pig iron, iron, tin-plate, trucks and a host of other items are each dominated by four firms.[1] Nearly all are examples of the mature corporation with which we are here concerned. Such is the industrial system.

This market situation is recognized in all modern economic theory. Under the cognomen of oligopoly it is assumed in its price-making to have some of the powers of a monopoly and some of the restraints of competition. A variety of arrangements and conventions facilitate its approach to the monopoly goal. There may be, though rarely, some clandestine negotiation on prices to establish the one that is best for all. Or one firm – in steel until a decade or so ago it was the United States Steel Corporation – acts as price leader. It calculates the price that will best serve the interest of all, presumably with some special attention to its own needs. Others unfailingly follow. Or, on the basis of common knowledge of costs and demand, each firm calculates and proclaims the price that will serve the interests of the industry. Minor differences in the resulting published schedules are then composed. The uncertainty of these procedures keeps the oligopoly price from being as favourable to the participants as that of a monopoly. There is a tendency, also, to leave it unchanged for long periods since any substantial movement invites the risk that others will not follow.

Although price competition is inconsistent with the common concern to achieve the closest possible approach to a monopoly price and profit, and indeed is a source of grave alternative dangers, this does not mean that competition is exorcised. Competition is inherent in the animal spirits of the entrepreneur. In response thereto he advertises and merchandises his product with even greater energy and aggressiveness for not being allowed to cut prices. And for the same reasons he

1. In the case of all mentioned, the largest four firms in the mid fifties had two-thirds or more of the market. Ralph L. Nelson, *Concentration in the Manufacturing Industries of the United States* (New Haven: Yale University Press, 1963).

remodels, repackages and, on occasion, seeks to improve his product in order to entice customers from his rivals.[2]

Although the theory of price-making under oligopoly is subject to some further refinements, it is not an especially complicated area of economics. Dubious as the reader may be of anything so simple, the foregoing is the essence of what is now taught.

II

In this analysis the firm, however large, remains safely subject to control by the market. It wishes, in general, to maximize its profits. It does the best it can and though it fails, and though the failure makes its performance more tolerable than that of a monopoly, it does not make it less subject to the control of the market. So the genie of independent pursuit of alternative goals – of exercise of plenary power unrelated to market motivation – is kept safely in the bottle. Oligopoly is in safe descent from its competitive antecedents. But the price of this accomplishment is rather appalling. It is that oligopoly, the prevailing form of industrial market organization, is inefficient and shouldn't exist.

That is the ancient conclusion concerning monopoly. It extracts prices higher in relation to costs than does a competitive firm. It gets wealth which, otherwise, would remain with the buyer in the form of lower prices. And the counterpart of the higher prices is a smaller volume of sales and a smaller output of goods than if prices were those that a competitive firm would have to set. The labour and capital that are not employed because of these higher prices, and the consequent smaller production for smaller sales, must find less advantageous employment elsewhere. An oligopoly is not as iniquitous

---

2. 'We have already remarked the firm determination with which oligopolists eschew the use of prices in maintaining and advancing their market positions. In lieu of this [they rely on] competition through advertising and other merchandising efforts, and competition through style changes and product improvement.' Robert Dorfman, *The Price System* (New York: Prentice-Hall, Inc., 1964), p. 102.

as a monopoly. But that is not because of aspiration but ability. Oligopoly is an imperfect monopoly. Like the despotism of the Dual Monarchy, it is saved only by its incompetence.

These sombre implications are not evaded in contemporary economic discourse and instruction. It is accepted that oligopoly – and therewith the corporations that comprise the industrial system – are economically inefficient. This being agreed, the matter is then resolved by a further tacit and, indeed, sometimes acknowledged agreement that nothing of importance should be done about it. It is conceded, finally, that what is inefficient in each part is efficient in the aggregate. This will not seem very satisfactory, on purely logical grounds, but difficulty must be expected in reconciling an erroneous premise with reality. The standard literature readily reveals the contradiction.

Thus, recurring to the Department of Commerce's explanation of the economy, we find it laying down the requirements for efficient pricing as follows: 'To the extent that a price is reached by means that are *not* impersonal – to the extent that either the buyer or the seller can dictate or influence the setting of the price – to that extent our system of controlling the efficient use of resources is not working properly.'[3] Since all large firms can dictate or influence prices, this means that wherever they are present the economy will not work properly. The most distinguished textbooks affirm the same conclusion. 'On all the evidence, oligopoly is an unfortunate market form. It has many of the drawbacks of monopoly and, in addition, a rigidity and an incitement to wasteful forms of competition that are peculiarly its own. . . . How to live with oligopoly is one of the most challenging current problems of economic policy.'[4] 'The economic evils of [oligopoly and other market imperfections] transcend the mere matter of monopolistic profits . . . monopolistic and oligopolistic pricing . . . brings distortion of resource allocation even if the firms involved

3. *Do You Know Your Economic ABC's? Profits and the American Economy*, U.S. Department of Commerce, 1965, p. 13.
4. Dorfman, op. cit., p. 103.

have their excess profits taxed away.'[5] 'To reduce imperfections of competition, a nation must struggle perpetually and must ever maintain its vigilance.'[6]

The main point may again be stressed. Most industrial production comes from large firms which have extensive power in the market. They are oligopolies. So the textbook finding is that the modern economy is mainly exploitive in the prices that it charges, wasteful and inefficient in the way it employs resources and challenging in its need for reform. Then comes the conclusion from the same books that the modern economy is highly efficient. 'I, myself, have no firm conviction about whether the current fabulous growth in economic productivity will ever come to an end, though no end seems imminent.'[7] 'As to productivity, there is no indication that manhour efficiency and new techniques have begun to slacken off.' 'The United States . . . can hardly help but grow at the rate of three per cent or more, even if we do not rouse ourselves. . . .'[8] Detailed performance is bad but aggregate performance is excellent. To the person who insists on asking how this contradiction is resolved, the answer is that it is not. The theory of price-making under oligopoly leads to conclusions that cannot be reconciled with the results on which the theorists themselves agree.[9, 10]

5. Paul Samuelson, *Economics*, Sixth Edition (New York: McGraw, 1964), p. 508.

6. Ibid., p. 507.   7. Dorfman, op. cit., p. 144.

8. Samuelson, op. cit., pp. 359 and 792.

9. In much contemporary economic instruction, the conflict is again concealed by the division of labour. Market theory belongs to what is called microeconomics. Here oligopoly prevails and the problem of efficiency and performance is very grave. The growth of the economy as a whole is treated under the rubric of macroeconomics, which has to do with aggregate movements in income and output. Here the problems of market behaviour are not examined, oligopoly is not considered and productivity gains are very high.

10. As a purely technical safeguard, I must point out that the contradiction cannot be resolved by claiming that while market behaviour and consequent resource distribution under oligopoly is very inferior, this is offset by the high capital investment, effective organization and tech-

III

The public policy which derives from the present view of price-making in the industrial system involves the same contradictions as the theory and a roughly similar resolution. Monopoly is illegal. The market power associated with oligopoly or small numbers is not, in principle, presumed to yield different results. It is viewed with suspicion. But since in practice it serves quite well, nothing is done about it. This evasion is then disguised by a great deal of peripheral litigation and by the well-understood tendency for any learned discussion, if sufficiently voluminous, to obscure the issue.

Since 1890, in the United States, the wickedness of monopoly, anciently asserted in English common law, has been affirmed by statute. In that year the Sherman Act prohibited combinations in restraint of trade and made it a misdemeanour to 'monopolize or attempt to monopolize' any interstate or foreign commerce. The Clayton and Federal Trade Commission Acts of the early Wilson Administration extended the prohibition to particular steps – price discrimination, exclusive contracts, acquisition of stock in a competing corporation, undefined unfairness – which might lessen competition. And legislation following World War II – the Celler-Kefauver Antimerger Act – proscribed mergers between firms which might promote monopoly. This made effective an earlier ban on purchase by one firm of the stock of a competitor which, conveniently, had not prevented forthright purchase of its assets.

---

nological virtuosity of the oligopolist. Cf. Professor Dorfman's suggestion along these lines. Op. cit., p. 144. For apart from the fact that it is the usual claim against the oligopolist that he keeps prices too high and has an undercommitment of capital and labour, it is evident that he makes effective use of capital, organization and technology because he is big and because he is big he is also an oligopolist. No one can ask him to be an oligopolist for the purposes of capital investment, organization and technology and to be small and competitive for the purposes of prices and allocative efficiency. There is a unity in social phenomena which must be respected.

Almost everyone concerned with the enforcement of the antitrust laws would agree, in principle, that oligopoly is an imperfect form of monopoly. This has also a measure of acceptance in the court decisions. In 1946, the large cigarette companies were successfully prosecuted for tightly parallel action in setting cigarette prices, a commonplace aspect of oligopoly pricing.[11] And there would be agreement that oligopoly is not a special but a general case – it is the market structure of the industrial system. An antitrust policy that would go 'to the problems of the existence and significance of market power' would not be 'aimed at merely marginal or special phenomena, but at phenomena spread widely through the economy.'[12]

The solution has been, nonetheless, to ignore oligopoly. Monopoly is illegal. Oligopoly, which is agreed to have the same consequences but with diminished force, is not. In the parallel case in criminal law, a man who hits his neighbour heavily over the head with a sledge hammer is guilty of assault. A man who uses a somewhat lighter instrument or has a poorer aim, is innocent. The reason is that, the theory notwithstanding, it is impracticable to indict and prosecute – if possession of market power be the test – the whole industrial sector of the economy. It is also conceded that performance under oligopoly does not, in fact, accord with what the theory leads one to expect. 'We can . . . [not] predict market performance from market structure.'[13] It may not be bad at all.

The conflict between the legal condemnation of monopoly

11. *American Tobacco Company vs. United States.* 328 U.S. 781, 810.

12. Carl Kaysen and Donald F. Turner, *Antitrust Policy. An Economic and Legal Analysis* (Cambridge: Harvard University Press, 1959), p. 41. Mr Turner, as this is written, is Assistant Attorney General in Charge of the Antitrust Division, Department of Justice.

13. Ibid., p. 61. The authors elsewhere (pp. 44–5) go even farther to suggest that 'the primary goal of antitrust policy be the limitation of undue market power to the extent consistent with maintaining desirable levels of economic performance.' This, of course, implies that higher levels of market power are associated with higher levels of economic performance. Market power, in other words, is socially efficient.

and its *de facto* acceptance, in slightly imperfect form as oligopoly, is stark. In real life it is blurred, as noted, by the very exhaustiveness of the discussion surrounding the subject and also by a good deal of enforcement activity which deals not with the fact of oligopoly and market power but with actions which might promote it. This leads to further contradictions.

The law is very severe on any overt collusion in the setting of prices. Such collusion simplifies the task of the oligopolists in seeking to arrive at the most advantageous price for all. And the government scrutinizes closely mergers which might have the effect of increasing the market power of the individual oligopolist. The most important effect is to deny market power to those who do not have it or have difficulty in exercising it while according immunity to those who already have such power.

Thus, the three majors in the automobile industry, as the result of long and intimate study of each other's behaviour within the confines of one city, are able to establish prices which reflect the common interest. And they can do so with precision. No consultation is required. The procedure is legally secure. Not much would be changed were the companies allowed, in fact, to consult and agree on prices.

A group of smaller suppliers of parts or sub-assemblies to the automobile industry will not have the same capacity for estimating each other's needs and intentions. They may also be more numerous – that is to say they will have less market power. Should it become known that in response to their weaker (and more competitive) position they have come together to discuss prices, and thus to win some of the ability to control prices that the automobile majors possess as a matter of course, the law would be upon them like a tiger. It exempts the market power of the strong. And it partly disguises this exemption by attacking efforts by the weak to acquire like power.

Similarly, if a large and puissant corporation has forty or fifty per cent of the market for some steel, chemical, drug, vehicle or other product, and is expanding its share vigorously, it is regarded by the law with a benign eye. But if two smaller competitors unite and the resulting union has more than a mere fifteen per cent of the market, there is every likelihood that the law will be invoked. Again the law exempts those who possess the market power and concentrates on those who would try to possess it. The form is prosecuted; the substance is exempt. We discriminate against those who, as the result of numbers and weakness, must use crude or overt methods to control their markets and in favour of those who, because of achieved size and power, are under no such compulsion.

This, to be sure, is not the whole story of the antitrust laws. They also prevent unfair aggression, as the community regards it, by large firms against the small. And they curb, on occasion, the rapacity of individuals and firms who survive in the entrepreneurial mould and who unite to enrich themselves at the popular expense. Such accomplishments are not negligible. But in their bearing on the industrial system, and their need to exempt in practice the market power that they condemn in principle, the antitrust laws are sadly at odds with reality.

They have also an obscurantist role. In some rather special circumstances in their planning, members of the technostructure may risk running afoul of the antitrust laws. They are then, if caught, made to suffer considerable personal indignity and chagrin. Otherwise to the large firm the antitrust laws are harmless. And meanwhile, these laws add to the illusion of control by the market. What the theory asserts as to the paramountcy of the market, the law affirms. The fig leaf by which power is kept out of sight is held in place not only by economists but by the statutes of the United States and the decisions of its courts.

The antitrust laws still claim the full affection of lawyers – independently, in part, of the handsomely rewarded litigation that they nourish. In the last ten years or so their place in the economists' decalogue has diminished. Many would agree that they have little real nexus with the major sources of market power. And there would be a measure of agreement that present enforcement attacks the symbols of market power and leaves the substance.[14] But the question as to why market power does not have the inimical tendencies anciently associated with monopoly remains largely unanswered and ignored in modern economic theory. It will remain thus until prices are seen in their modern role as instruments of industrial planning in the service of the goals of that planning. To this I now turn.

14. For an interesting and important account of the declining faith in the antitrust laws and the reasons, which parallels much of the present argument, see Richard Hofstadter, 'What Happened to the Antitrust Movement' in Earl F. Cheit, *The Business Establishment* (New York: Wiley, 1964), pp. 113–51.

Chapter 17

PRICES IN THE INDUSTRIAL SYSTEM
(CONTINUED)

THE contradiction between a price theory that condemns the inefficiency of the system and a result that is applauded for its efficiency disappears when prices are viewed in the full context of industrial planning and in full service to the goals of the technostructure.

Specifically, industrial planning requires that prices be under control. Modern technology reduces, we have seen, the reliability of the market. And it increases the commitment of time and capital that are required in production. For this reason prices cannot be left to the vagaries of the unmanaged market.

But this control, naturally enough, is so exercised that it serves the goals of the technostructure. These, we have seen, are first, to minimize the risk of loss, and therewith of damage to the autonomy of the technostructure, and secondly, to maximize the growth of the firm. Prices are so managed as to serve these goals. Price competition with its attendant dangers must be prevented. Prices must be low enough to facilitate the recruitment of customers and the expansion of sales and at the same time high enough to provide earnings to finance growth and keep the stockholders content. These prices are readily reconciled with accepted social goals or what society has been persuaded to accept as goals. There is no barrier, as there would be given the unmitigated pursuit of monopoly profit, to identification by members with the technostructure.

This is why price control by the mature corporation is combined not with inefficient performance as the traditional theory prescribes but with the generally favourable performance that its exponents concede. And it is also why this control enjoys immunity under law. However socially inimical the control of prices is in principle, the results are not so viewed. The law is helpless in applying penalties to what is socially acceptable.

We may look first at the way price control is effected, and how protection against disastrous price failure is ensured, and then at the level that is set.

II

The industrial system provides the price control that it requires as an effortless consequence of its own development. Modern industrial planning requires and rewards great size. This means that a comparatively small number of large firms will share the typical market. Each will act with full consideration of its own needs and of the common need. Each must have control of its own prices and will recognize this to be the common requirement. Each will forswear any action, and notably any sanguinary price-cutting, which would be prejudicial to the common interest in price control. This control is not something that must be contrived. Nor, except in a few peculiarly complex cases, is it very difficult to sustain.

We are profoundly conditioned by the theology of the market. Consequently, nothing seems good or normal that does not accord with the requirements of the market. A price that is fixed by the seller to a singular degree does not seem good. Accordingly, it requires a major act of will to think of price-fixing as both normal and having economic function. In fact, it is normal in all advanced industrial societies.[1] The non-

1. Even modern agriculture, although it is outside the industrial system, cannot accommodate itself effectively to radical price changes and all countries with highly developed agriculture have moved towards planning in this industry to the extent of establishing systems of price control. This has been the direct result of advancing technology and increasingly heavy capital requirements. And the consequence (and most notably in the United States) of price security and associated ability to plan has been much increased investment by farmers in new capital and technology. The further result has been gains in productivity in recent years that have been considerably greater in agriculture than in industry. However, farmers being numerous, there is no chance for the non-governmental regulation of prices that characterizes the industrial system. It has had to

socialist economies of countries other than the United States employ it, usually in a less embarrassed and more overt fashion. Formal price-fixing by cartel or other agreements covering the members of the industry are commonplace. So is a good deal of straightforward communication between firms in setting prices. But even where tradition frowns on such agreements or communications, as in Canada and to some extent in Britain, there is the same tacit control as that of oligopoly in the United States. Were there something peculiarly efficient about the market and inefficient about formal price-fixing, the countries eschewing the first and using the second would have suffered drastically in their development. There is no indication that they have. The reason is that theirs is merely a more formal variant on American industrial price-control.

Socialist industry also works, as a matter of course, within a framework of controlled prices. In recent times the Soviet Union, following the earlier Yugoslav practice, has been according to firms and industries some of the flexibility in adjusting prices that the more informal evolution has accorded the American system. This has been widely hailed as a return, by these countries, to the market. That is a mirage. It does not mean, any more than in the American system, that the socialist firm is subject to control by market prices over which it exercises no influence. It means only that its control can be more flexibly exercised in response to change.

III

The first concern of the technostructure, as we have seen, is to protect the minimum level of return which secures its auto-

---

be done by the government. And so deep is the commitment to the illusion of control of the enterprise by the market that this price regulation – which cannot be concealed – is still not wholly accepted by economists, including those who otherwise applaud agricultural efficiency. The fixed prices, by distorting resource use, are thought to be a source of inefficiency. It is not observed that the same fixed prices make possible the advanced technology and higher capital inputs which greatly enhance productivity.

nomy and hence its survival. For this reason it must minimize the risk of any development that might threaten minimum return and thus its survival. A breakdown in prices, a possibility that is inherent in an uncontrolled market or which might result from an outbreak of competitive price-cutting, is pre-eminently such a danger. This danger the technostructure is at great pains to exclude. And, with rare exceptions, it is successful.

This is accomplished, in all ordinary circumstances, by a common response to a clearly recognized and common danger. Any large firm in a modern industry of few firms which used prices as a weapon of competitive aggression would force the others to respond in kind. All would suffer. Accordingly, no matter how great the rivalry between firms or how carefully cultivated are the institutional feuds and dislikes, such behaviour is exorcised by the strongest canons of corporate behaviour. It is a tribute to the social capacity of man that such mutually destructive behaviour is so successfully banned.

It does occur, however, in exceptional circumstances where there are technical difficulties in arriving at equal prices. This requires resort to illegal collusion and explains the occasional brush of the mature corporation with the antitrust laws.

Thus, in the early nineteen-sixties, General Electric, Westinghouse, Allis-Chalmers, Ingersoll-Rand and other manufacturers of electrical equipment were prosecuted for conspiring to fix the prices of heavy electrical apparatus. A number of senior executives in several of these companies were lodged briefly in the common gaol. It was then a matter of some wonder as to what sacrificial avarice could cause paid executives to risk such infamy on behalf of stockholders they would never know. The explanation however is clear. The price-fixing was for transformers and switch-gear which are built to specification and sold, in part, by sealed bids. Unlike standard electric motors, washing machines or refrigerators, these have no common price. There being no such price, taut adherence to a given price or price schedule was impossible. And the low bidder took all of the business. In the past in consequence there had been severe price-cutting; there was, at the time, a prospect of heavy losses.

It was this – the technical difficulty of tacit control and the prospect of losses – that caused the executives to come together. It is most unlikely that a simple desire to enhance profits would have led to the conspiracy. The error of the executives was not in fixing prices but in being engaged in a branch of a business where price-fixing involved such exceptional difficulty. Prices were equally regulated for electric motors or household appliances but there it could be done without collusion.

Recent suits against the steel companies have charged collusion in setting the prices for specialized steel products. These, evidently, involve a similar problem in setting prices. This collusion has been singled out for prosecution although not even the most devoted friend of the antitrust laws would argue that prices of ordinary steel are governed other than by a well-recognized industry-wide schedule to which all firms adhere as a matter of course.

IV

Once established, industrial prices tend to remain fixed for considerable periods of time. None supposes that prices of basic steel, aluminium, automobiles, machinery, chemicals, petroleum products, containers or like products of the industrial system will be sensitive to the changes in cost or demand which cause constant price readjustments for commodities, such as lesser agricultural products, where producers are still subject to control by the market. This stability of prices, in face of changing costs and demand, is further indication, it may be noted, that in the short run the mature corporation pursues goals other than profit maximization.

Stable prices reflect, in part, the need for security against price competition. Under modern industrial conditions a seller has rarely a single price. More often the firm has an infinitely complicated schedule for all of the models, grades, styles and specifications that comprise its offering. For several firms to change prices more or less simultaneously and without according some price advantages to part of the product line of any one firm and without discussion of the matter is a delicate procedure. And there is always a chance that a firm will be thought to be seeking a competitive advantage on some part of its product line. This, in turn, could invite the retributive price-cutting that so contravenes the canons of corporate behaviour with the danger that the whole price schedule will be broken down. Convenience as well as the security of the earnings of the firm thus counsel keeping prices unchanged for relatively long periods.

But price stability also serves the purposes of industrial planning. Prices being fixed, they are predictable over a substantial period of time. And since one firm's prices are another's costs so costs are also predictable. Thus on the one hand, stable prices facilitate control and minimize the risk of a price collapse that could jeopardize earnings and the autonomy of the technostructure. In this they serve a prime goal of the technostructure. At the same time they facilitate planning by the firm in question and by those to which it sells.

This structure of control is far more important than the precise price level at which it exists. In 1964 the major automobile firms had profits on sales ranging from five to over ten per cent. There was security against collapse of prices and earnings at either level. Planning was possible at either level of return. All firms could function. But none could have operated successfully had the prices of a standard model fluctuated, depending on whim and reaction to the current novelties, from $1,750 to $3,500 with steel, glass, plastics, paint, tyres, sub-assemblies and labour moving over a similar range.

v

However, the level of prices is not unimportant. And, from time to time in response to major changes in cost – often when the renegotiation of a wage contract provides a common signal to all firms in the industry – prices must be changed.

The prices so established will reflect the commitment of the technostructure to the goal of expansion or growth. They will involve a compromise between two conflicting requirements for such growth. The need to expand sales which are the *sine qua non* of growth will argue, generally, for low prices. At the same time, depending on the nature of cost behaviour, demand and the problems of demand management, the need for earnings to finance the growth will argue for higher prices. No rule can be laid down as to the result. It seems likely that prices will most often be set by an industry at a level that provides for an established payment to stockholders and covers the investment requirements (with some margin of safety) of the expansion that is possible at that price.[2] But this is at best only a probability. There is no *a priori* reason why the policy pursued by any two mature corporations will be the same, for there is no reason to assume that the goals or intensity of commitment to goals will be the same in any two cases. Further, where firms are large they will deal, increasingly, with other firms that are large. And size and associated power in one place make it necessary elsewhere. Prices under such circumstances will reflect not an independent judgement as to what is required but an accommodation between firms.[3] And, although the policy does not yet enjoy formal acceptance – we encounter here another radical departure of practice from principle – price-making in the industrial system is also subordinate to the social need for price stability and stable price-wage relationships.[4]

2. And there is danger in assigning one-way causation. Prices have anciently been assumed to be an adjustable instrument of economic policy as wages, for example, are not. But as control and stability become objects in themselves, then prices are not adjusted and other magnitudes adjust themselves to the level of prices. Prices may not be set at the level that produces the maximum growth that can be financed from investment. Rather, after satisfying stockholders, the volume of investment may be determined, at least in the short run, by the earnings yielded by the current level of prices. Cf. John R. Meyer and Edwin Kuh, *The Investment Decision*, Harvard Economic Studies. CII (Cambridge: Harvard University Press, 1957).

3. I have dealt with this phenomenon in detail in *American Capitalism: The Concept of Countervailing Power* (Boston: Houghton, 1956).

4. Chapter 22 below.

VI

When price control is seen to be directed towards ensuring the security of the technostructure, as serving also the goal of growth and, more than incidentally, also providing a stable numerator for planning decisions, there is no longer anything startling in its *de facto* exemption from the antitrust laws. It would be more startling were it attacked. There is considerable injustice in the immunity enjoyed by those who have achieved a strong market position as compared with those who, being much weaker, seek, by merger or collusion, to win a stronger position. No doubt in a just society such anomalies in law enforcement should not exist. But it might be an error to move prematurely to eliminate them. For when revision comes it must be in light of full recognition that the antitrust laws were placed on the statute books to preserve the power of the market against those who might subordinate it to the purpose of monopoly. Meanwhile something very different has happened. The mature corporation has taken control of the market – not alone the price, but also what is purchased – to serve not the goal of monopoly but the goals of its planning. Controlled prices are necessary for this planning. And the planning, itself, is inherent in the industrial system. It follows that the antitrust laws, in seeking to preserve the market, are an anachronism in the larger world of industrial planning. Reform of the antitrust laws must wait, however, until the action is illuminated by this far larger fact. The process by which it will come, it may be mentioned in passing, will follow a fairly predictable course. Devotees of the market and friends of the antitrust laws are not lacking in intellectual commitment and even passion. They will respond to suggestions that these laws are largely unrelated to the modern scene with vigour and, on occasion, with indignation. They will note that such questions have been raised before, sometimes by those with a frivolous view of the problem, sometimes by those with a special reason for wishing exemption from the laws. These men, on the whole, will dominate the argument. But circumstance will be on the other side. And that, as always, will prove a decisive handicap. After much discussion, the laws will one day be accommodated formally to the reality. In the meantime the convention by which they exist but are not enforced is by no means intolerable.

Chapter 18

THE MANAGEMENT OF SPECIFIC DEMAND

Bristol-Myers does not, in general, develop products in its labs and then determine how they might be marketed. It ordinarily *begins* with extensive consumer testing and other market research, proceeds from there to develop some concept of a marketing opportunity, including even some notions about advertising campaigns; and only then does it turn to the labs for products that might meet these specifications. *Fortune*, February 1967.

FOR all planning, that of the United States as well as of other industrial societies, the control of prices is strategic. These must be subject to the authority of the planning unit; otherwise there is risk of loss from uncontrolled price movements and there is no reliable number by which units of product and input can be multiplied to get projected income and outlay. If these estimates are not available in reliable form, there is a large random element in decisions as to what to produce, and with what and by what means, and there is total uncertainty as to the outcome – whether there will be profit or loss and in what dimension. Such error is the antithesis of effective planning. A moment's thought will suggest not only how nearly impossible it would make modern industrial performance but how remote, in practice, such uncontrolled prices are from real life.

The control of prices in the industrial system is not perfect, and the fact of this imperfection is important not only in itself but also for economic polemics. It is a well-established technique of argument, on encountering something which cannot easily be reconciled with preconception, to point to the exceptions. What does not invariably exist is held not to exist. Economics is committed by ancient faith to the control of the firm by the market. Some, accordingly, will be tempted to argue that since the control of prices by the mature corporation is not complete, it can be dismissed. This mode of argument need not detain us; once recognized as a polemical device, it becomes unpersuasive. It is worth noting that until comparatively recently trade unions were held by some to be relatively unimportant in wage-setting because their sway was incomplete or their powers circumscribed.[1] And even the large corporation was ignored because it had not completely replaced the proprietary firm. Though imperfect, control of prices in the industrial system is organic – it serves its most fundamental goals. And the fact of such control, fortunately for anyone who urges the reality, is admirably visible.

Control of prices is for a purpose – for the security of the technostructure and to allow it to plan. But price control does little to advance these goals unless there is also control over the amounts that are bought or sold at these prices. Security, growth and effective planning would be jeopardized by erratic or unpredictable price behaviour. But these would equally be frustrated by a decision by the public not to buy at the controlled prices. It would be quixotic for the mature corporation to seek control over its prices and then leave purchases at these prices to the random fate of taste and accident. Such fluctuations in the amounts taken would be no less damaging to planning and the goals that it serves than fluctuations in prices. Moreover, the fluctuations in amounts taken are accentuated by price control; a fall in prices (through elasticity of demand) no longer acts to arrest a fall in purchases and vice versa. So, intimately intertwined with the need to control prices is the need to control what is sold at those prices.

The control or management of demand is, in fact, a vast and rapidly growing industry in itself. It embraces a huge network

1. '[The] weak unions are probably more numerous than the strong ... statistical studies find little relationship between unionization and long-term wage movements.' George J. Stigler, *The Theory of Price*, Revised Edition (New York: Macmillan, 1952), pp. 256–7. Cf. also 'Addendum on Economic Method and the Nature of Social Argument' later in this volume.

of communications, a great array of merchandising and selling organizations, nearly the entire advertising industry, numerous ancillary research, training and other related services and much more. In everyday parlance this great machine, and the demanding and varied talents that it employs, are said to be engaged in selling goods. In less ambiguous language it means that it is engaged in the management of those who buy goods.

The key to the management of demand is effective management of the purchases of final consumers – of individuals and the state. If these are under effective control, there will then be a comparatively reliable demand for raw materials, parts, machinery and other items going into the ultimate product. If the demand for its automobiles is reliable, General Motors can accord its suppliers the security of long-term contracts. And, in the absence of such contracts, there will still be a reliable and predictable flow of orders which allows of planning. Although the techniques for managing government purchases are different from those employed for consumer demand they make the same contribution to planning by prime and sub-contractors.

The effective management of consumer behaviour does not embrace the whole task of controlling demand. An automobile company must ensure that consumers devote a dependable share of their outlays to automobiles in general and to its cars in particular. But its sales will still be highly irregular if, though they spend a constant share of their income on its vehicles, there is a radical fluctuation from year to year in what they have to spend. It follows that effective control of consumer demand requires management not only of how income is spent but also of the amount of income that is available for spending. There must be management of demand both for the specific product and for products in general. Measures to maintain a desired level of aggregate demand are part and parcel of the task of industrial planning.[2] We are here con-

2. A circumstance, as previously noted, which greatly diminishes the significance of one of the common distinctions in economics – that between microeconomics or the theory of prices and the market, and macroeconomics or the theory which concerns itself with national aggre-

cerned with the management of demand for the specific product.

II

As so often, change in the industrial system has made possible what change requires. The need to control consumer behaviour is a requirement of planning. Planning, in turn, is made necessary by extensive use of advanced technology and capital and by the related scale and complexity of organization. These produce goods efficiently; the result is a very large volume of production. As a further consequence, goods that are related only to elementary physical sensation – that merely prevent hunger, protect against cold, provide shelter, suppress pain – have come to comprise a small and diminishing part of all production. Most goods serve needs that are discovered to the individual not by the palpable discomfort that accompanies deprivation, but by some psychic response to their possession. They give him a sense of personal achievement, accord him a feeling of equality with his neighbours, divert his mind from thought, serve sexual aspiration, promise social acceptability, enhance his subjective feeling of health, well-being or orderly peristalsis, contribute by conventional canons to personal beauty, or are otherwise psychologically rewarding.

Thus it comes about that, as the industrial system develops to the point where it has need for planning and the management of the consumer that this requires, it is also serving wants which are psychological in origin and hence admirably subject to management by appeal to the psyche.

Hunger and other physical pain have an objective and compelling quality. No one whose stomach is totally empty can be persuaded that his need is not for food but for entertainment. A man who is very cold will have a high preference for what makes him warm. But psychic reactions have no such internal

gates. Both prices and aggregate demand are ultimately accommodated to the planning needs of the technostructure. I return to this problem in Chapter 20. Chapters 26 and 27 take up the special problems of managing the state as a consumer.

anchor; since they exist in the mind they are subject to what influences the mind. Though a hungry man cannot be persuaded as between bread and a circus, a well-nourished man can. And he can be persuaded as between different circuses and different foods. The further a man is removed from physical need the more open he is to persuasion – or management – as to what he buys. This is, perhaps, the most important consequence for economics of increasing affluence.[3]

III

Along with the opportunity for managing consumer demand, there must also be a mechanism for managing it. Authority is not well regarded here. By giving him a ration card or distributing to him the specific commodities he is to use, the individual can be required to consume in accordance with plan. But this is an onerous form of control, ill-adapted to differences in personality. Save under conditions of great stress as during war or for the very poor, it is not thought acceptable in advanced industrial societies. Even the formally planned economies – the Soviet Union and the Eastern European states – regard rationing as a manifestation of failure. It is easier and, if less precise, still sufficient to manage demand by persuasion rather than by fiat.

3. I have dealt with this tendency on two earlier occasions (*American Capitalism, The Concept of Countervailing Power* [Boston: Houghton, 1956], Chapter VIII; and *The Affluent Society* [Boston: Houghton, 1958], Chapter 11). Accordingly, I am confining myself here to the barest essentials. These notions, particularly the distinction between physical and psychologically based wants, together with a declining marginal utility of income, though they will seem eminently sensible to the reader, are not widely accepted by economists. There are certain methodological excuses but the reason has, alas, more to do with the instinct for professional self-preservation than with science. As elsewhere noted, a central problem of economics, and long *the* central problem, was the allocation of resources between uses, that is to say, between products. If this choice is not terribly important and becomes increasingly less important, with increasing income, the economic problem also diminishes in importance and so, unhappily, do the scholars who dwell on it.

Although advertising will be thought the central feature of this management, and is certainly important, much more is involved. Included among the managers are those who sell goods and design the strategies by which they are sold. And so are many who are thought of as engaged in the production of goods. The management of demand consists in devising a sales strategy for a particular product. It also consists in devising a product, or features of a product, around which a sales strategy can be built. Product design, model change, packaging and even performance reflect the need to provide what are called strong selling points. They are thus as much a part of the process of demand management as an advertising campaign.[4]

IV

The purpose of demand management is to ensure that people buy what is produced – that plans as to the amounts to be sold at the controlled prices are fulfilled in practice. Not all advertising and selling activity is directed to this end. This fact has polemical importance for it is readily possible to cite forms of advertising or sales effort which are unrelated to the purposes of demand management and industrial planning.

Thus a certain amount of advertising, that of the classified ads and the department store displays, has no great purpose beyond that of conveying information – of advising the public that a particular person or enterprise has a particular item for sale and at what price. Such advertising is seized upon to show that the function of advertising is merely to convey information although, as I have noted on other occasions, only a gravely retarded citizen can need to be told that the American Tobacco Company has cigarettes for sale.

4. In a culture which places high value on technological change, there will be a natural presumption that any 'new' product is inherently superior to an old one. This attitude will be exploited by those who devise sales strategy with the result that a great many changes in product and packaging will be merely for the sake of having something that can be called new. We have here the explanation of the repetitious claims in virtually all advertising that products are new.

The Management of Specific Demand

Economic theory, under the cachet of monopolistic competition, has also long featured the case of the seller, one among many, who seeks by advertising to associate particular qualities with his product and thus reduce the chances for substitution by another. He then has liberty to charge a higher price and, at least in the short run, reward himself with monopoly profits. This too is a possible case although its requirements as imposed by the textbooks – *numerous* sellers who have comparative ease of entry into the industry – make it of small practical importance. The accounts of the monopolistically competitive sellers are not those that are cherished by J. Walter Thompson, McCann-Erickson or Ogilvy, Benson and Mather.

Finally, conventional economic theory associates advertising and related arts with oligopoly. Here the characteristic firm of the industrial system eschews price competition as too dangerous and channels its rivalry into ever-changing strategies for winning customers away from another. 'In lieu of [price competition] oligopolists rely on ... competition through advertising and other merchandising efforts, and competition through style changes and product improvement. ... These large advertising budgets, like heavy armaments, largely cancel each other out. Not even the oligopolists benefit from them.'[5]

If it be assumed that the consumer is sovereign, save that he is in doubt as to whose product he will buy, this conclusion – that such advertising and by implication many other expenditures including that for model and design changes[6] are self-cancelling and functionless – is inescapable. Firms spend money to take business away from each other; all cannot succeed so the result is a stand-off. The only consequence is that prices are

5. Robert Dorfman, *The Price System* (New York: Prentice-Hall, Inc., 1964), p. 102. Samuelson agrees but in much more circumspect language. See Paul A. Samuelson, *Economics*, Sixth Edition (New York: McGraw, 1964), pp. 485, 500–501.

6. Franklin M. Fisher, Zvi Griliches and Carl Kaysen, 'The Costs of Automobile Model Changes Since 1949', *The Journal of Political Economy*, Vol. LXX, No. 5 (October 1962).

higher and profits are lower than if by some act of government or industrial statesmanship the struggle were curbed.

But such a notion of limited sovereignty is nonsense. If advertising affects the distribution of demand between sellers of a particular product it must also be supposed that it affects the distribution as between products. This is not functionless; rather it increases the flow of revenue to all who advertise. And in the context of planning it does much more. For, along with the other arts of demand management, it allows the firm a decisive influence over the revenue it receives. What seems to the traditional market economists a sense-deadening struggle between the detergent-makers leading only to stalemate serves a deeper and highly important purpose.

There will be comfort in this conclusion. The present disposition of conventional economic theory to write off annual outlays of tens of billions of dollars of advertising and similar sales costs by the industrial system as without purpose or consequence is, to say the least, drastic. No other legal economic activity is subject to similar rejection. The discovery that sales and advertising expenditures have an organic role in the system will not, accordingly, seem wholly implausible.

The general effect of sales effort, defined in the broadest terms, is to shift the locus of decision in the purchase of goods from the consumer where it is beyond control to the firm where it is subject to control. This transfer, like the control of prices, is by no means complete. But again what is imperfect is not unimportant. The 'general rule with fewer exceptions than we would like to think, is that if they make it we will buy it'.[7]

The specific strategy, though it varies somewhat between industries and over time, consists first in recruiting a loyal or automatic corps of customers. This is variously known as building customer loyalty or brand recognition. To the extent that it is successful, it means that the firm has a stable body of custom which is secure against the mass defection which might

7. Andrew Hacker, 'A Country Called Corporate America', *The New York Times Magazine*, 3 July 1966.

follow from freely exercised consumer choice. This is the initial contribution to the firm's planning.

A purely defensive strategy will not, however, suffice. Given the goals of the technostructure all firms will seek to expand sales. Each, accordingly, must seek to do so if it is not to lose out to others. Out of this effort, from firms that are fully able to play the game, comes a crude equilibrating process which accords to each participant a reasonably reliable share of the market. It works, very roughly, as follows.

When a firm is enjoying steady patronage by its existing customers and recruiting new ones, the existing sales strategy, broadly defined, will usually be considered satisfactory. The firm will not quarrel with success. If sales are stationary or slipping, a change in selling methods, advertising strategy, product design or even in the product itself is called for. Testing and experiment are possible. Sooner or later, a new formula that wins a suitable response is obtained. This brings a countering action by the firms that are then failing to make gains.

This process of action and response, which belongs to the field of knowledge known as game theory, leads to a rough equilibrium between the participating firms. Each may win for a time or lose for a time, but the game is played within a narrow range of such gain or loss. As in the case of Packard or Studebaker (as a producer of cars), firms that do not have the resources to play – particularly to stand the very large costs of product design and redesign – will lose out and disappear. And the firms that can play the game will, on occasion, find customers adamant in their resistance to a particular product; no response can be obtained at tolerable cost by any strategy that can be devised.[8] The size and product diversification of the mature corporation allow the firm to accept an occasional such failure without undue hazard. But it is the everyday

8. As in the case of the Edsel. I mention this again for, to a quite remarkable extent, this disaster is cited (by those who are made unhappy by these ideas) to prove that planning will not work. It proves what I unhesitatingly concede, which is that it doesn't work perfectly. Its notoriety owes much to its being exceptional.

assumption of the industrial system that, if sales are slipping, a new selling formula can be found that will correct the situation. By and large this assumption is justified, which is to say that means can almost always be found to keep exercise of consumer discretion within workable limits.

Were there but one manufacturer of automobiles in the United States, it would still be essential that it enter extensively on the management of its demand. Otherwise consumers, exercising the sovereignty that would be inconsistent with the company's planning, might resort to other forms of transportation and other ways of spending their income. (This is the answer to the orthodox contention that advertising is principally induced by market oligopoly.) And under present circumstances a slippage in automobile sales as a whole sets in motion by all the firms the sales strategies (including always the product redesign) by which it is offset. This, in turn, stabilizes the expenditures accruing to the industry.

V

Persuasion on the scale just outlined requires that there be comprehensive, repetitive and compelling communication by the managers of demand with the managed. It should be capable of holding the attention of the consumer for considerable periods of time and in a comparatively effortless manner. It should reach people in all spectrums of intelligence. None should be barred by illiteracy or unwillingness to read. Such a means of mass communication was not necessary when the wants of the masses were anchored primarily in physical need. The masses could not then be persuaded as to their spending – this went for basic foods and shelter. The wants of a well-to-do minority could be managed. But since this minority was generally literate, or sought to seem so, it could be reached selectively by newspapers and magazines, the circulation of which was confined to the literate community. With mass affluence, and therewith the possibility of mass management of demand, these media no longer served.

The Management of Specific Demand

Technology, once again, solved the problems that it created. Coincidentally with rising mass incomes came first radio and then television. These, in their capacity to hold effortless interest and their accessibility over the entire cultural spectrum, and their independence of any educational qualification, were admirably suited to mass persuasion. Radio and more especially television have, in consequence, become the prime instruments for the management of consumer demand. There is an insistent tendency among solemn social scientists to think of any institution which features rhymed and singing commercials, intense and lachrymose voices urging highly improbable enjoyments, caricatures of the human oesophagus in normal or impaired operation, and which hints implausibly at opportunities for antiseptic seduction, as inherently trivial. This is a great mistake. The industrial system is profoundly dependent on commercial television and could not exist in its present form without it. Economists who eschew discussion of its economic significance, or dismiss it as a wicked waste, are protecting their reputation and that of their subject for Calvinist austerity. But they are not adding to their reputation for relevance.

VI

The management of demand, as here to be seen, is in all respects an admirably subtle arrangement in social design. It works not on the individual but on the mass. Any individual of will and determination can contract out from its influence. This being so, no case for individual compulsion in the purchase of any product can be established. To all who object there is a natural answer: You are at liberty to leave! Yet there is slight danger that enough people will ever assert their individuality to impair the management of mass behaviour.

This management performs yet another service. For, along with bringing demand under substantial control, it provides, in the aggregate, a relentless propaganda on behalf of goods in general. From early morning until late at night, people are informed of the services rendered by goods – of their profound indispensability. Every feature and facet of every product having been studied for selling points, these are then described with talent, gravity and an aspect of profound concern as the source of health, happiness, social achievement, or improved community standing. Even minor qualities of unimportant commodities are enlarged upon with a solemnity which would not be unbecoming in an announcement of the combined return of Christ and all the apostles. More important services, such as the advantages of whiter laundry, are treated with proportionately greater gravity.

The consequence is that while goods become ever more abundant they do not seem to be any less important. On the contrary it requires an act of will to imagine that anything else is so important. Morally, we agree that the supply of goods is not a measure of human achievement; in fact, we take for granted that it will be so regarded.

Yet it might not have been. In the absence of the massive and artful persuasion that accompanies the management of demand, increasing abundance might well have reduced the interest of people in acquiring more goods. They would not have felt the need for multiplying the artifacts – autos, appliances, detergents, cosmetics – by which they were surrounded. No one would have pressed upon them the advantages of new packages, new forms of processed foods, newly devised dentifrices, new pain-killers or other new variants on older products. Being not pressed by the need for these things, they would have spent less reliably of their income and worked less reliably to get more. The consequence – a lower and less reliable propensity to consume – would have been awkward for the industrial system. That system requires that people will work without any limiting horizon to procure more goods. Were they to cease to work after acquiring a certain sufficiency, there would be limits on the expansion of the system. Growth could not then remain a goal. Advertising and its related arts thus help develop the kind of man the goals of the industrial system require – one that reliably spends his income and works reliably because he is always in need of more.

The Management of Specific Demand

This effort has the further effect of sustaining the prestige of the industrial system. Goods are what the industrial system supplies. Advertising by making goods important makes the industrial system important. And therewith it helps to sustain the social importance and prestige that attach to the technostructure. As the landowner and the capitalist lost prestige when land and capital ceased to be socially decisive, so the technostructure would soon sink into the background were the supply of industrial products to become routine in the manner of water from a waterworks in a year of adequate rainfall. This would have happened long since had not advertising, with its unremitting emphasis on the importance of goods, kept people persuaded to the contrary.

When viewed not in the absolute context but in the relevant context of industrial planning, it will be evident that advertising and its related arts have a large social function. This extends on from the management of demand, the necessary counterpart of the control of prices, to the conditioning of attitudes necessary for the operation and prestige of the industrial system. For advertising men it has long been a sore point that economists dismissed them as so much social waste. They have not quite known how to answer. Some have doubtless sensed that, in a society where wants are psychologically grounded, the instruments of access to the mind cannot be unimportant. They were right. The functions here identified may well be less exalted than the more demanding philosophers of the advertising industry might wish. But none can doubt their importance for the industrial system, given always the standards by which that system measures achievement and success.

Chapter 19

THE REVISED SEQUENCE

The consumer is, so to speak, the king ... each is a voter who uses his votes to get things done that he wants done. PAUL SAMUELSON, *Economics*.

The inescapable [fact] is that we're artificing a social machine for its own aggrandizement. PAUL GOODMAN, *People or Personnel*.

THE time has come for yet another word of summary. In virtually all economic analysis and instruction, the initiative is assumed to lie with the consumer. In response to wants that originate within himself, or which are given to him by his environment, he buys goods and services in the market. The opportunities that result for making more or less money are the message of the market to producing firms. They respond to this message of the market and thus, ultimately, to the instruction of the consumer. The flow of instruction is in one direction – from the individual to the market to the producer. All this is affirmed, not inappropriately, by terminology that implies that all power lies with the consumer. This is called consumer sovereignty. There 'is always a presumption of consumer sovereignty in the market economy'.[1] The unidirectional flow of instruction from consumer to market to producer may be denoted the Accepted Sequence.

We have seen that this sequence does not hold. And we have now isolated a formidable apparatus of method and motivation

1. Franklin M. Fisher, Zvi Griliches, and Carl Kaysen, 'The Costs of Automobile Model Changes Since 1949,' *The Journal of Political Economy*, Vol. LXX, No. 5 (October 1962), p. 434. These three men are rightly among the most highly regarded of the modern generation of economic theorists. Their statement of the matter is exceptional for, at least by implication, they detach themselves from full acceptance of the notion of consumer sovereignty. It is merely the frame in which they work.

causing its reversal. The mature corporation has readily at hand the means for controlling the prices at which it sells as well as those at which it buys. Similarly, it has means for managing what the consumer buys at the prices which it controls. This control and management is required by its planning. The planning proceeds from use of technology and capital, the commitment of time that these require and the diminished effectiveness of the market for specialized technical products and skills.

Supporting this changed sequence is the motivation of the technostructure. Members seek to adapt the goals of the corporation more closely to their own; by extension the corporation seeks to adapt social attitudes and goals to those of the members of its technostructure. So social belief originates at least in part with the producer. Thus the accommodation of the market behaviour of the individual, as well as of social attitudes in general, to the needs of producers and the goals of the technostructure is an inherent feature of the system. It becomes increasingly important with the growth of the industrial system.

It follows that the accepted sequence is no longer a description of the reality and is becoming ever less so. Instead the producing firm reaches forward to control its markets and on beyond to manage the market behaviour and shape the social attitudes of those, ostensibly, that it serves. For this we also need a name and it may appropriately be called The Revised Sequence.

II

Those who yearn for the defeat of their enemy are said to wish that he might write a book. Far better that he should resort to overstatement. I do not suggest that the revised sequence has replaced the accepted sequence. Outside the industrial system – beyond the limits of the large corporations – the accepted sequence still rules. Within the industrial system it is of diminished importance in relation to the revised sequence. Here too the consumer can still reject persuasion. And, in consequence, through the market he and his fellows can force accommodation by the producer. But consumers, and the prices at which they buy, can also be managed. And they are. The accepted and revised sequences exist side by side in the manner of a reversible chemical reaction. Doubtless it would be neater were it one way or the other. But, again, the reality is plausible but untidy.

In the form just presented, the revised sequence will not, I think, be challenged by many economists. There is a certain difficulty in escaping from the inescapable. There is more danger that the point will be conceded and its significance then ignored. To ensure against this – to provide text for all who ally themselves in the preventive therapy – it is well that the consequences of the revised sequence be briefly adumbrated.

III

The revised sequence sends to the museum of irrelevant ideas the notion of an equilibrium in consumer outlays which reflects the maximum of consumer satisfaction. According to this doctrine, beloved in economic instruction and still honoured in the economics textbooks, the individual or household arranges his or its purchases so there is approximately equal satisfaction from the last dollar spent for each of the several opportunities for consumption or use of goods.[2] Were it otherwise – were it so that a dollar spent on cosmetics returned more satisfaction than a dollar spent on gasoline – then spending on cosmetics would have been increased and that on

2. 'Each good – such as sugar – is consumed up to the point where the marginal utility per dollar (or penny) spent on it is exactly the same as the marginal utility of a dollar (or penny) spent on any other good – such as salt. If any one good gave more marginal utility per dollar, one would gain by taking money away from other goods and spending more on it.... If any good gave less marginal utility per dollar than the common level, one would buy less of it until the marginal utility of the last dollar spent on it had risen back to the common level.' Paul A. Samuelson, *Economics*, Sixth Edition (New York: McGraw, 1964), p. 429.

gasoline diminished. And the reverse being true of comparative satisfaction from cosmetics and gasoline, the reverse would have occurred. In other words, when the return to a small added outlay for different purposes is unequal, satisfaction can always be increased by diminishing the expenditure where the satisfaction is less, and enlarging it where the satisfaction is greater. So it follows that satisfaction is at a maximum when the return to a small increment of expenditure is the same for all objects of expenditure.

But it is also true that, since an individual's satisfaction from his various opportunities for expenditure is his own, there must be no interference with this equalizing process. Dictation from any second person on how to distribute income, however meritorious, will not reflect the peculiar enjoyment pattern of the person in question. Presumably it will reflect the preferences of the instructor.

Such is the established doctrine. And if the individual's wants are subject to management this is interference. The distribution of his income between objects of expenditure will reflect this management. There will be a different distribution of income – a different equilibrium – in accordance with the changing effectiveness of management by different producers.[3] It is to the nature and purposes of this management, not simply to the effort of the individual to maximize his satisfactions, that the scholar must look if he is to have any adequate view of consumer behaviour.

It is true that the consumer may still imagine that his actions respond to his own view of his satisfactions. But this is superficial and proximate, the result of illusions created in connexion with the management of his wants. Only those wishing to evade the reality will be satisfied with such a simplistic explanation. All others will notice that if an individual's satisfaction is less from an additional expenditure on automobiles than from one on housing, this can as well be corrected by a change in the selling strategy of General Motors as by an

3. What the lay reader will recognize, for example, to be the ordinary and expected result of the changing effectiveness of advertising campaigns.

increased expenditure on his house.[4] Similarly, a perfect state of equilibrium with marginal utilities everywhere equal can be upset not by a change in the individual's income or by a change in the goods available but by a change in the persuasion to which he is subject.

The problem of economics here, once again, is not one of original error but of obsolescence. The notion of the consumer so distributing his income as to maximize satisfactions that originate with himself and his environment was not inappropriate to an earlier stage of economic development. When goods were less abundant, when they served urgent physical need and their acquisition received close thought and attention, purchases were much less subject to management. And, on the other side, producers in that simpler and less technical world were not under compulsion to plan. Accordingly they did not need to persuade – to manage demand. The model of consumer behaviour, devised for these conditions, was not wrong. The error was in taking it over without change into the age of the industrial system. There, not surprisingly, it did not fit.[5]

IV

To jettison the accepted sequence has more than pedagogical consequences. Even the most jejune and precious social theory is likely to support some structure of social attitude and action. The accepted sequence, with the resulting doctrine of consumer maximization of satisfactions, sustains a great deal.

4. As a related technical point, indifference curves do not survive the revised sequence. The indifference map reflects, at any given time, the comparative effectiveness of the sales strategies behind the products in question. It will change as these change. The logic of the indifference curve requires that it be original with the individual whose preferences it describes.

5. Economists, all but invariably, have used a simple but revealing device to improve the fit. That is to illustrate the theory of consumer behaviour with commodities – bread, tea, oranges, salt, sugar – which are produced outside the industrial system or for which the management of demand is peculiarly difficult. Cf. Samuelson, op. cit.

Specifically it supports the conclusion that the individual is the ultimate source of power in the economic system. And it assures us that this exercise of power grows out of his own unaided tendency and ability to make the most out of his situation. It is highly reassuring that the individual should have, or be imagined to have, such power in association with such capacity to use it. It is, perhaps, especially reassuring in a culture which sets a high and even mystical store by the individual and which may suspect that, somehow, he is being threatened by organization.

The accepted sequence also raises barriers against a wide range of social action which, though in fact inconvenient to organization, specifically to the technostructure, is held by the theory to be inimical to this maximization of satisfaction by the individual. We have seen how jealously the technostructure seeks to safeguard its autonomy of decision. The management of demand requires, also, that it have the greatest possible freedom in the exercise of persuasion. Anything that limits or circumscribes the claims that it can make for a product interferes in some measure with the management of demand. The accepted sequence holds that the individual guides the economy while obtaining for himself the highest level of satisfaction from the income he receives. Any interference with his exercise of choice leads to a less satisfactory result from the viewpoint of the individual. In a society composed of, and guided by, individuals, it will presumably be socially less good. So public objection to lethal automobile design, disabling drugs, disfiguring beauty aids or highly caloric reducing compounds are interference with the individual's design for maximizing his satisfaction and with the resulting economic response. The doctrine thus outlaws a wide range of government interference and does so in the name of the individual. This accords powerful protection to the autonomy of the technostructure and great immunity to its techniques for managing demand. A doctrine that celebrates individuality provides the cloak for organization. And this depends wholly on the accepted sequence. Once it is agreed that the individual is subject to

management in any case – once the revised sequence is allowed
– the case for leaving him free from (say) government interference evaporates. It is not the individual's right to buy that is
being protected. Rather, it is the seller's right to manage the
individual.

The accepted sequence, with its emphasis on the assumed
power of the individual, serves in other ways to sanction organization. Men accept the disciplines of the great industrial enterprise in order to serve the ultimate interests of the individual
consumer. By bowing to rules, subordinating their personality
to organization, being good members of the team, they help to
enlarge the range of choice of individual consumers. It is
proper that they subordinate their lesser liberty to that greater
one. Or so it is held.

Much more can be so justified. Industrial squalor, air and
stream pollution, sacrifice of aesthetic values – even the rhymed
commercials and billboards which are part of the process of
consumer management – expand the quantity and variety of
product. So they increase the scope for exercise of the sovereign
power of the consumer. Again, it is held, lesser values are
subordinated to the greater liberty that is allied with the ultimate and controlling power of the individual in an economic
system with a maximum range of choice.

Again none of these contentions survive the revised sequence.
There is no case for subordinating the lesser liberty of the
organization man to the greater liberty of the consumer unless
that latter liberty exists. If that has already been subordinated
to organization, the argument lapses. So does the case for industrial squalor and industrial convenience.

The authority that is exercised in industrial production by the
industrial firm also acquires legitimacy from the larger freedom
that it accords the consumer. This is power only to serve; in the
last analysis the greatest corporation is but the humble servant
of the consumer. 'One way of shedding awkward responsibility
is to believe that the consumer is the real boss, that the businessman merely carries out his ... orders. ... It is not by chance
that consumer sovereignty is generally described in terms sug-

gesting the processes [i.e., balloting in the market place] of political democracy.'[6] If the consumer is not sovereign – if the ballots are cast partially at the behest of the producer – this argument does not merely disappear. Rather it remains to react sharply against the person who employs it for it draws attention to power that embraces also the management of the consumer.

V

It is possible that people need to believe that they are unmanaged if they are to be managed effectively. We have been taught to set store by our freedom of economic choice; were it recognized that this is subject to management, we might be at pains to assert our independence. Thus we would become less manageable. Were instruction in economics, supported by the formidable wisdom of the economics textbooks, to proclaim that people are partly in the service of those who supply them, this might cause those so educated to desert that service.

This is speculation; my preference is to keep the argument on firmer ground. It will be clearly evident that attitudes of the highest importance flow from the accepted sequence. And so do policies that are highly protective of the industrial system. Such is the very considerable service of myth. It would be optimistic to imagine that so serviceable a myth will be easily abandoned or even to expect universal gratitude for those who dispel it.

6. Francis X. Sutton, Seymour E. Harris, Carl Kaysen and James Tobin, *The American Business Creed* (Cambridge: Harvard University Press, 1956), p. 361.

Chapter 20

THE REGULATION OF
AGGREGATE DEMAND

THE industrial system requires that prices be under effective control. And it seeks the greatest possible influence over what buyers take at the established prices. And it seeks certainty in the supply and prices of the important requisites of production – as we shall see presently, it is adding steadily to the certainty of its manpower supply. All of this gives precision to its planning. And it serves admirably goals, those of security and growth in particular, of the technostructure. But there remains uncovered another exceedingly important risk. That is of severe fluctuation in the total demand available for all the products of the industrial system. We must look now at the larger dimensions of this problem and its solution.

From the viewpoint of the industrial firm, the regulation of total or aggregate demand is a matter of the highest urgency. Not only is it necessary that the public be persuaded to buy its automobiles, packaged cereals or household appliances in roughly predetermined volume but it is also necessary that people be able to do so. The best management of consumer behaviour will come to nothing if there is a sharp reduction in employment and therewith in incomes and if consumers, in consequence, are no longer able (or disposed) to buy as before. A man in imminent danger of being hanged is little worried about catching cold. There is no point in eliminating a minor source of uncertainty if a major one remains. Purchasing power must be reliably available in sufficient volume to absorb the current production of the industrial system at the established prices.

By the nature of its own development, the industrial system has made the regulation of purchasing power or demand ever more urgent. An economy pays out in the course of production the wages, salaries, interest and profits that comprise the wherewithal for buying what it produces. In a poor and simple society what is paid and spent tends to match in value what is produced. People of small income do not have the option of suddenly not spending that income, i.e., of suddenly increasing their savings. Spending is in the straitjacket of physical need. The consumption function is stable.

Also in such a society since savings are small, investment will be small. Most production will be for current consumption. Production for such current use is more stable than production in response to investment decisions with their changing estimate of an unknown future.

We have seen also that in an earlier and simpler stage of society in which savings are small, capital is scarce and of decisive importance for production. That is to say that, ordinarily, there are many claimants for the savings that are available. What the community spends for consumption is, quite obviously, spent. But under these more primitive circumstances what it saves from consumption is subject to the insistent need for investment and thus is also spent. So all income made in production goes for production. One of the familiar antiquities of economics is Say's Law of Markets. This holds that an economy always provides demand sufficient to buy its own output. A deficiency of purchasing power or demand is thus impossible. Say's Law no longer commands belief. But in the world of its author, nearly two centuries ago, it had much merit.

II

In the industrial system, by contrast, personal savings are no longer made at the cost of physical hardship. Most personal saving is by persons in the upper half of the income brackets; for many it is automatic. And far more important than such savings by individuals – which in 1965 amounted to $25 billion – are the retained earnings of business firms which were $83 billion in that same year. This saving is by decision of the technostructure. Consumers do not press to spend these funds. They are not accorded the option of doing so.

In general the technostructure will increase its investment as its retained earnings increase. Having taken care of its stockholders and creditors and therewith assured its own security, it then devotes funds to the next highest priority among its goals, which is growth. And if the funds so available are inadequate, the technostructure will increase its earnings or withhold more from the stockholders.[1]

Thus within the industrial system, savings and outlays for investment will tend to rise and fall together. But this does not mean that they will be equal – that investment will offset savings. Nor is there any mechanism in the organized economy by which savings decisions and investment decisions are made to equal each other.[2]

If the various decisions to increase savings are not offset by decisions to invest a like amount or if decisions to reduce capital outlays and other investments are not matched by a reduction in savings, then some of the current production of the industrial system will be without purchasing power and buyers. Output and employment will fall. In the world of Jean Baptiste Say, the prices of goods would fall; the increased savings would then be offset by the increased purchases of other people at the lower prices. But in the industrial system prices, we have seen, are controlled, so the initial effect will be on output and therewith on employment. This could, in turn, lead on to a further curtailment of investment, a further curtailment of production and employment, and thence to a self-generating downward spiral.

1. '[The] investment outlay on fixed and working capital seems, in the short run ... a residual ... between the total net flow of funds realized from current operations less the established or conventional dividend payments.' John R. Meyer and Edwin Kuh, *The Investment Decision*, Harvard Economic Studies, CII (Cambridge: Harvard University Press, 1957), p. 204.

2. Interest rates, the classical equilibrating mechanism, have not for many years been thought by economists to perform this function. Like other prices in the industrial system interest rates tend to be firmly stable. While changes in interest rates are assumed to have an effect on investment there is no agreement as to their effect, if any, on the total volume of savings.

In summary, the industrial system has built into itself very comprehensively the need to regulate aggregate demand. Its advanced technology and high use of capital require planning. From this planned use of resources comes an ample production that allows of a high level of savings. The technostructure has strong inducements to keep these savings at a high level. These savings, if not offset, can lead to a serious and cumulative reduction in aggregate demand. The same advanced technology and high capital use, which force the industrial firm to plan, make it vulnerable to a fall in aggregate demand. The technostructure is similarly vulnerable. So, effective regulation of such demand is imperative.

Nor is this quite all. As earlier noted, effective regulation of aggregate demand adds paradoxically to the need for such regulation. Such regulation prevents a cumulative downward spiral in income and saving. This, in the past, has borne the same relation to saving and capital accumulation as famines to the population of India. The Great Depression reduced personal savings from $4·2 billion in 1929 to a net dissaving of $600 million in 1932 and reduced the retained earnings of business firms from $16·2 billion to under a billion.[3] The mild recession of 1960 brought a $2 billion drop in personal savings as compared with a $3 billion increase the year before and held the retained earnings of business constant as compared with an increase of $7 billion the previous year. In the absence of recessions, savings continue high; so does capital investment and so does the purchasing power generated by such investment. And so, therefore, does the dependence of the economy on the measures by which savings are offset.

If savings are not offset, output and employment fall. If savings are more than offset when the economy is at or near full employment, output and employment cannot rise or cannot rise appreciably. Instead prices rise and, in the industrial system, while there is elaborate protection against price reduction, price increases, which are without similar danger to the

3. It is this reduction in saving that eventually brings them back into equilibrium with a smaller but less drastically reduced level of investment.

227

technostructure, occur far more easily. This, as we shall see presently, leads to the need for yet further government intervention. It requires also that the regulation of aggregate demand be reversible. There must be means for correcting both a shortage and an excess of demand.

The regulation of aggregate demand, it will be evident, is an organic requirement of the industrial system. In its absence there would be unpredictable and almost certainly large fluctuations in demand and therewith in sales and production. Planning would be gravely impaired; capital and technology would have to be used much more cautiously and far less effectively than now. And the position of the technostructure, since it is endangered by the failure of earnings, would be far less secure. The need for regulation of aggregate demand is now fully accepted. However, its integral relationship to modern economic development has never been fully appreciated. There is an impression, growing partly out of some curiosities in the history of this regulation and partly out of a continuing failure to look at the process of regulation as a whole, that the business firms that comprise the industrial system have been hostile to it. This on closer examination turns out to have been far from the case.

III

The regulation of demand became a recognized public policy during the thirties. The policy was decisively advocated by John Maynard (later Lord) Keynes[4] and was propagated in the United States by a comparatively small number of liberal economists – members of a community generally considered at the time to be antipathetic to large-scale business enterprise.[5]

4. In particular from *The General Theory of Employment Interest and Money* (New York: Harcourt, 1936), although it had been foreshadowed in numerous earlier proposals of Keynes as also of others.

5. Conservatives have long contended that the Keynesian revolution in the United States was the work of a handful of Keynes's disciples, advocates and interpreters, centring mostly on Harvard University and led principally by Professor Alvin Hansen with Professor Seymour Harris as the most articulate spokesman, and Professor Paul Samuelson of

The Regulation of Aggregate Demand

It was put into effect by the Roosevelt Administration which also had its quarrels with business. The policy was seen primarily (although not exclusively) as a remedy for unemployment – a colouration which it still retains – and thus appeared to be an action on behalf of the labour movement. It had the support of labour and at a time of bitter labour-management disputes. Not remarkably it was regarded by the public at large, as well as by businessmen, as a dubiously experimental welfare measure which could be expected to prove costly or damaging to business in some unspecified way.

More important, the regulation of aggregate demand has a very different impact on the entrepreneurial and the mature corporation. In the thirties, reflecting a common lag, business spokesmen were still giving voice to the interests of the entrepreneurial corporation under the impression that this reflected the common interest of all business.

The entrepreneurial corporation has much less need than the mature corporation for the regulation of aggregate demand. The mature corporation is an accommodation to advanced technology and heavy capital use. Planning is part of this accommodation. So is the technostructure. Regulation of aggregate demand is necessary to give certainty to this planning and to protect the technostructure. The entrepreneurial corporation with simpler technology and a smaller commitment of capital has less need to plan. And it has no (or a much smaller) technostructure. This means, in practical terms, that if demand falls, it can adjust to it by laying off workers. The mature

---

M.I.T. as the author of the first great Keynesian textbook. These men are held to have applied Keynes's ideas to the American scene and directly or through students sold Keynes's ideas to Washington and the public. The charge has been protested, and even denied, and it is somewhat difficult to see why, for it is essentially true. The Keynesian revolution was also an epochal contribution to the development of the industrial system and the preservation of what is commonly called capitalism. Architects of such a useful revolution should have pride in their work. I have dealt at some length with the history of the Keynesian revolution in an article in *The New York Times Book Review*, 15 May 1965.

corporation by contrast cannot lay off its capital. The technostructure is large and costly and to curtail it is to disintegrate the very brain of the enterprise.

The autonomy of the technostructure, we have also seen, is vulnerable to a failure in earnings and this is most likely to result from a curtailment of demand and accompanying depression. Control of the entrepreneurial corporation rests firmly on ownership. If it is not burdened by debt, it can ride out a temporary failure in earnings.

Further, it is possible that a few farsighted entrepreneurs in the thirties may have seen or sensed that the regulation of demand would require a drastic enlargement of the role of the state in the economy and that it would change the tax system from an instrument for raising revenue to one for regulating demand. This too would have a very different effect on the entrepreneurial as compared with the mature corporation.

The actual burden of both corporate and personal income taxes is, in substantial measure, on the entrepreneur. The corporation income tax does not directly affect the member of the technostructure. And the impact of the personal income tax, the size of the income considered, is likely to be lighter than on the entrepreneur. As between paying and not paying income taxes there is a difference.

Finally, a close look at the particular form of regulation that eventually came into use discloses the interesting fact that it did, indeed, have the very strong support of the mature corporations and their technostructure.

IV

In the thirties it was generally believed that aggregate demand might be regulated by increasing or decreasing government spending, the level of taxation remaining the same. The policy was not regarded as altering in any basic way the relation of the state to the economy. The latter would increase its outlays at some periods, reduce them at others, but, on the average, remain on about the same scale in relation to the economy as a whole.

This view of the policy was chimerical. Public expenditures can be increased although this requires time. Once increased, however, they are not readily reduced. Spending, all agree, must be for useful or seemingly useful purposes. Like private consumption, any new public service quickly becomes a part of the accustomed standard of living. Once given, support to schools or hospitals or parks or public transportation cannot be readily withdrawn. Non-recurrent expenditures, notably for public works, can be curtailed by the device of not starting new ones. But this takes time and such expenditures are also rather slow to take effect.[6] Demand, by contrast, can fall rather rapidly and with cumulative effect.

The alternative is to have a permanently high level of public expenditures. This in turn must be supported by taxes that increase as incomes increase, thus curtailing demand, and fall as incomes fall, thus releasing spending to support demand. This alternative has been adopted. Since World War II, government spending has been increased substantially in periods of recession or stagnation. But, overwhelmingly, reliance in regulating demand has been on a continuing high level of public outlays supported by such a self-adjusting level of taxation.[7]

6. Cf. J. K. Galbraith and G. G. Johnson, *The Economic Effects of the Federal Public Works Expenditures*, National Resources Planning Board, Washington, 1940. Some expenditures, most notably for unemployment compensation, increase automatically when demand falls and unemployment increases. But the volume of such compensatory spending is declining relatively with the decline in the importance of the blue-collar working force in the industrial system.

7. Between 1957, a year of comparatively high income, and 1958, which was one of mild recession, the Eisenhower Administration increased the government contribution to spending in the economy by $11·4 billion. This resulted from a $3·2 billion reduction in revenues and an $8·2 billion increase in expenditures. Between 1960 and 1961, a period of comparative stagnation, the Kennedy Administration added $8·0 billion to income. Revenues increased only by $1·6 billion between these years; spending was increased by $9·6 billion. Figures are for calendar years. *Economic Report of the President*, 1964, p. 277.

The taxes that render this service are the personal and corporate income taxes. Both are admirably designed to regulate demand; and since both antedate this function and were, in fact, originally designed to raise revenue and induce a greater measure of equality in income distribution, either a magnanimous Creator or much good luck must be assumed on occasion to manifest itself in the affairs of modern states. With higher income in the economy, individuals, inevitably, have higher income. They thus become subject to the personal income tax or, if already subject to it, to a higher surtax rate. Thus the personal income tax takes an increasing proportion of increased income and so acts progressively to curtail demand as income rises. In the opposite case of declining income, the yield of the tax reduces itself more than proportionately as people move off the tax rolls or to lower brackets. It thus releases an increasing share of income for spending. Although the corporation income tax is levied at approximately fixed percentage rates, its effect is similar for, with rising income, corporation earnings rise very rapidly – much more rapidly than any other class of income.[8] These earnings being subject to the corporation tax, an increased share of all income is subject to this tax. The reverse is again true when national income falters or falls.

But this regulation, however admirable, will work only if the magnitudes are great enough to count. Taxes must be appreciable in relation to income if they are to affect incomes and therewith demand. They will be large enough, it follows, only if the operations of the state are sufficiently large in relation to the economy as a whole. Government must also be large, if changes in its expenditures are to be used with effect. A $10 billion increase in public outlays can be easily and promptly made if it increases government outlays by only 10 per cent. It will be very time-consuming if it involves a doubling of public expenditures. So an adequate scale of government expenditure – a sufficient public sector – is the fulcrum for the regulation of aggregate demand. With it regulation of

8. Cf. *Economic Report of the President*, January 1965, p. 102.

demand is relatively easy; without it such regulation is impossible.

V

In 1929, Federal expenditures for all goods and services amounted to $3·5 billion; by 1939 they were $12·5 billion; in 1965 they were approximately $57 billion.[9] In relation to Gross National Product they increased from 1·7 per cent in 1929 to 8·4 per cent in 1965 and earlier in the same decade they had been substantially in excess of 10 per cent.

Although the cliché is to the contrary, this increase has been with the strong approval of the industrial system. There is also every reason to regard it, and the social attitudes and beliefs by which it is sustained, as reflecting substantial adaptation to the goals of the mature corporation and its technostructure. For the cliché has noticed only the ritual objection of business to government expenditure. Much of this objection comes from small businessmen outside the industrial system or it reflects entrepreneurial attitudes rather than those of the technostructure. And it is directed at only a small part of public expenditure.

All business objection to public expenditure automatically exempts expenditures for defence or those, as for space exploration, which are held to serve equivalent goals of international policy. It is these expenditures which account for by far the largest part of the increase in Federal expenditure over the past thirty-five years. Accordingly they account for most of the expansion in the role of the Federal Government in the economy. In the decade of the thirties, expenditures for national defence (excluding those for veterans and interest) amounted to between 10 and 15 per cent of the administrative budget. In the first half of the sixties they were between 55 and 60 per cent.[10] This reflected an increase in the annual outlay

9. *Economic Report of the President*, January 1966. Figures are in 1958 prices.

10. *Statistical Abstract of the United States*, 1964, p. 254. This does not include expenditures for space exploration.

from about three-quarters of a billion dollars at the beginning of the thirties and a little over a billion in 1939 to a little over $50 billion in 1965.[11]

If a large public sector of the economy, supported by personal and corporate income taxation, is the fulcrum for the regulation of demand, plainly military expenditures are the pivot on which the fulcrum rests. Additionally they provide underwriting for advanced technology and, therewith, security for the planning of the industrial system in areas that would otherwise be excluded by cost and risk. And, to repeat, these expenditures are strongly supported by businessmen. Not for many years has any important business executive condemned the prodigality of expenditures on defence. From all pleas for public economy, defence expenditures are meticulously excluded. These have a justification that transcends ordinary questions of economic policy or everyday fears of socialism and the state. Legislators who most conscientiously reflect the views of the business community regularly warn that insufficient funds are being spent on particular weapons. No more than any other social institution does the industrial system disapprove of what is important for its success. Those who have thought it suspicious of Keynesian fiscal policy have failed to see how precisely it has identified and supported what is essential for that policy.

However, it would be unjust to suggest that the modern industrial generation confines its approval of the regulation of aggregate demand to defence expenditures. Most members of the technostructure of mature corporations would also, it seems probable, approve other areas of government activity, including in particular those that support advanced technology. And many would accept the need for the associated system of taxation. Resistance now comes from entrepreneurs large and small. Or it is traditional and nostalgic.

11. This was before there had been any pronounced effect from the conflict in Vietnam. Thereafter there was a further and sharp increase.

VI

In much social comment, including that of numerous economists, there has been a tendency to minimize or ignore the role of military expenditures in the regulation of demand. There is much that is unsettling about dependence on such outlays. That weaponry in the higher megaton ranges of destructive power has an organic relation to the performance of the economic system leads to unpleasant introspection. It seems also a poor advertisement for the system and lends comfort to a frequent allegation of Marxists. So scholarly and textbook discussion slights the role of military spending in the regulation of demand and concentrates, instead, on refinements of tax policy or other more appetizing issues. The subject of military spending is dismissed by saying that were it not required by higher national policy, then the same effect could easily be obtained by shifting the outlays to civilian purposes or returning them to private use.[12]

This, it will be evident, is too simple. Income released to or taken from private expenditure will only serve effectively to regulate demand if the public sector is large and the resources released or absorbed are large enough to count. Military expenditures are what now make the public sector large. Without them the Federal Government would be rather less than half its present size. It is most unlikely that this would exercise the requisite leverage on the private economy.

Nor is it sufficient that other public outlays make up the quantitative total. For in addition to the problem of obtaining them in the necessary volume, there is also that of underwriting technology and therewith the planning of the industrial system. Spending for schools, parks and the poor would not do this. Substitute spending would need to have somewhat of the same relation to technology as the military spending it replaces. To this, in much greater detail, I presently return and with a view also to seeking solutions.

12. Cf. Paul A. Samuelson, *Economics*, Sixth Edition (New York: McGraw, 1964), p. 785. I once held the same view.

VII

The revised sequence, we have seen, accommodates the consumer to the goals of the technostructure and provides a climate of social belief that is favourable to this result. It would be odd, indeed, were this tendency to operate only in relation to the consumer – were the state, and the climate of belief in which it functions, to be wholly uninfluenced by those who sell it goods. But if the revised sequence operates in relation to public procurement then defence expenditures in their present magnitude are, in part, an accommodation to the needs of the industrial system and the technostructure.

That military expenditures serve the needs of the industrial system – and that the underlying climate of belief on national policy is favourable to their doing so – will seem reasonable to many, and perhaps most, readers. This does not mean that it will be readily accepted. Our practice in these matters is to be guided less by truth than by formulas. It is our further practice, visible also in considerable measure in our diplomacy, to rest responsibility with those who are untroubled by the use of such conventional formulas – who, as the need arises, can react with moral fervour on behalf of the absurd. That defence requirements are set purely by national interest, that they are independent of any needs of the industrial system, is a useful formula. It sanctifies expenditures that could not be defended for their support to the industrial system. It likewise lends credence to the belief, important for the autonomy of the technostructure, that a deep chasm separates state and private business. The first decides and commands; the second responds. Were the function of the state admitted to be an accommodation to the needs of the industrial system, it would no longer be possible to regard the latter as an independent entity.

But formulas are not the best guide for the concerned and intelligent in these matters. Important questions are involved including human safety, even survival. We should not risk less than the truth. Modern military and related procurement and policy are, in fact, extensively adapted to the needs of the industrial system. (It seems very probable that this is a tendency of all planning, communist, socialist or non-socialist, however denoted.) The reversible or two-way reactions of the revised sequence operate here as elsewhere. And the line dividing the state from what is called private enterprise, or at least from the highly organized part of it, is a traditional fiction. However, this problem must be allowed to rest at this point until the further regulation of prices and wages and the role of labour and unions in the industrial system are examined.

Chapter 21

THE NATURE OF EMPLOYMENT
AND UNEMPLOYMENT

There is no rate of pay at which a United States pick-and-shovel laborer can live which is low enough to compete with the work of a steam shovel as an excavator. NORBERT WIENER, *Control and Communication in the Animal and the Machine*, 1948.

ON few matters is the image of industrial civilization so sharp as on that of its labour force. This is a great mass – the word itself is ubiquitous – which streams in at the beginning of the shift and out at the end. It consists of comparatively unskilled operatives who guide or attend the machines and a smaller aristocracy who have skills beyond the scope of the machine. When the system is functioning well, all or nearly all are at work. When it is not, the notices appear on the board, the men remain at home and the rising percentage of unemployed in the labour force as a whole measures the extent of failure of the economic system. Similarly, when labour relations are tranquil, men pass peacefully through the gates. When they are not, a picket line appears and the plant either shuts down or functions in face of the threats of the milling crowd outside. There are others in the enterprise – managers, engineers, designers, clerks, auditors and salesmen – but they are part of a shadowed background. The labour force, that which counts, is the great homogeneous blue-collared proletariat.

The image is not yet at odds with the reality of the industrial system. But it is strongly at odds with its trend. Within the system the blue-collared proletarian is sharply in decline, both in relative numbers and in influence. And the notion of unemployment, as traditionally held, is coming year by year to have less meaning. More and more, the figures on unemployment enumerate those who are currently unemployable by

the industrial system. This incapacity coexists with acute shortages of talent. The view of the system in the preceding chapters makes these tendencies predictable; and the statistics,
which in this case are good, affirm the expectation or are
consistent with it.

II

The industrial system, we have seen, has a strong technological
orientation; indeed one of the subordinate goals of the technostructure is a showing of technical virtuosity. And the technostructure itself, among other things, is an apparatus that brings
into conjunction the various branches of specialized scientific
and engineering knowledge which bear on the solution of
particular problems.

We have seen, also, that advanced technology in combination with high capital requirements make planning imperative.
All planning seeks, so far as may be possible, to ensure that
what it assumes as regards the future will be what the future
brings. This accords, too, with the concern of the technostructure for its own security, for such control minimizes the like'i-
hood of developments which might jeopardize its earnings and
thus its tenure.

These considerations tell with considerable precision the
manpower requirements and labour policies of the industrial
system and forecast virtually all of its principal tendencies.

That it will have a large and growing requirement for qualified talent is evident. Technology, planning and the coord'nation of the resulting organization all require such talent. This
requirement, it is perhaps unnecessary to notice, is for
educationally qualified, as distinct from skilled, manpower.
Engineers, salesmen and sales managers, managers and management engineers, and the near infinity of other such specialists, though they are trained in their particular task, can only be
so trained if they have prior preparatory education. This is not
necessarily the case of the tool-and-die maker, carpenter, plas-
terer or other skilled craftsman. The engineer, sales manager,

or personnel director applies specialized mental qualifications to a particular task. He must have, before learning his particular speciality, the requisite intellectual or mental preparation. The skilled journeyman brings manual dexterity and experience to bear. For this there is no minimum educational level.

At the same time the industrial system reduces relatively, and, it seems probable, absolutely, its requirement for blue-collared workers, both skilled and unskilled.

This situation arises partly from the nature of technology. Machines do easily and well what is done by repetitive physical effort unguided by significant intelligence. Accordingly they compete most effectively with physical labour, including that of no small dexterity and skill.[1]

But to see mechanization and automation purely as a problem in comparative cost is greatly to minimize their role – and to pay further for the error of confining economic goals, and economic calculation, to profit maximization.[2] The techno-structure, as noted, seeks technical progressiveness for its own sake when this is not in conflict with other goals. More important, it seeks certainty in the supply and price of all the prime requisites of production. Labour is a prime requisite. And a large blue-collar labour force, especially if subject to the external authority of a union, introduces a major element

1. This is a generalization. There are numerous operations – the sensory-manipulative operations that are involved in handling a power shovel for example – which have no appreciable educational requirements but which do not lend themselves to automatic processes.

2. For such an argument see Charles E. Silberman, 'The Real News About Automation,' *Fortune*, January 1965. For an opposing and, I believe, more persuasive case see Ben B. Seligman, 'Automation and the Unions' in *Dissent*, Winter 1965. The word automation, narrowly construed, refers to an industrial process which provides data from its own operations and feeds this back usually through a computer to controls which fully govern the process. It thus dispenses with all direct manpower. But automatic machinery dispensing with much but not all human guidance is, of course, very important. And this too is called automation. Because of this ambiguity I have used the phrase automation sparingly and mostly where paraphrasing popular argument.

of uncertainty and danger. Who can tell what wages will have to be paid to get the men? Who can assess the likelihood, the costs and consequences of a strike?

In contrast mechanization adds to certainty. Machines do not go on strike. Their prices are subject to the stability which, we have seen, is inherent in the contractual relationships between large firms. The capital by which the machinery is provided comes from the internal savings of the firm. Both its supply and cost are thus fully under the control of the firm. More white-collar workers and more members of the technostructure will be required with mechanization. But white-collar workers with rare exceptions do not join unions; they tend to identify themselves with the goals of the technostructure with which they are fused.[3] To add to the technostructure is to increase its power in the enterprise. Such is the result of replacing twenty blue-collar workers with two men who are knowledgeable on computers.

Thus the technostructure has strong incentives, going far beyond considerations of cost (which may themselves be important), to replace blue-collar workers.

In the thirteen years from 1951 to 1964, although the labour force in the United States grew by about 10 million – from 60·9 millions to 70·6 millions – blue-collar employment did not increase at all, and during the earliest years of the period it declined. This includes blue-collar employment outside the industrial system, except for agriculture and the service industries. In basic steel, automobiles, petroleum, tobacco and much food processing – industries marked by a relatively small number of very large firms and thus strongly characteristic of the industrial system – blue-collar employment in 1964 remained well below (and in some instances far below) that of 1951[4] and continued so until more recently. In 1964, production of all goods was half again as great as in 1951. In 1960 the

3. I return to these matters in more detail in Chapters 23 and 24.

4. *Manpower Report of the President and A Report on Manpower Requirements, Resources, Utilization and Training,* United States Department of Labor, March 1966, pp. 164, 200.

automobile industry had 172,000 fewer production workers than in 1953 and produced a half-million more passenger cars and about the same number of trucks and buses.[5] During the whole period there was a very large increase in white-collar employment.[6] Recent studies suggest, in general, that these trends will continue. There will be a rapid increase in professional and white-collar requirements, only a modest increase in blue-collar employment.[7]

III

As the relative demand for blue-collar workers declines, the requirement for those with higher educational qualification increases. These are needed by the technostructure. And, though with more modest educational qualification, they are required for the white-collar tasks.

It follows, further, that if the educational system does not keep abreast of these requirements there will be a shortage of those with a higher educational qualification and a surplus of those with less. This is the present situation.

It is the vanity of educators that they shape the educational system to their preferred image. They may not be without influence but the decisive force is the economic system. What the educator believes is latitude is usually latitude to respond to economic need.

In the early stages of industrialization, the educational requirement for industrial manpower was in the shape of a very

5. 'The U.S. Labor Force, 1950–1960', *Population Bulletin*, Vol. XX, No. 3 (May 1964), pp. 73–4.

6. I return to this in Chapter 25.

7. National Commission on Technology, Automation and Economic Progress, *The Outlook for Technological Change and Employment*, Appendix Volume I (February 1966), p. I-10. Here is the Commission's estimate of change between 1964 and 1975.

'The greatest increase in requirements will be for professional and technical workers; more than $4\frac{1}{2}$ million additional personnel will be required, an increase of 54 per cent. The white-collar group as a whole is expected to expand by nearly two-fifths, and to constitute 48 per cent squat pyramid. A few men of varying qualifications – managers, engineers, bookkeepers, timekeepers and clerks – were needed in the office. The wide base reflected the large requirement for repetitive labour power for which even literacy was something of a luxury. To this pyramid the educational system conformed. Elementary education was provided for the masses at minimum cost. Those who wanted more had to pay for it or to forgo income while getting it. This ensured that it would be sought only by a minority. To this day the school systems of the older industrial communities in West Virginia, central and western Pennsylvania, northern New Jersey and upstate New York still manifest their ancient inferiority. It is assumed that an old mill town will have bad schools.[8]

By contrast, the manpower requirements of the industrial system are in the shape of a tall urn. It widens out below the top to reflect the need of the technostructure for administrative, coordinating and planning talent, for scientists and engineers, for sales executives, salesmen, those learned in the other arts of persuasion and for those who programme and command the computers. It widens further to reflect the need for white-collar talent. And it curves in sharply towards the base to reflect the more limited demand for those who are qualified only for muscular and repetitive tasks and who are readily replaced by machines.

This revision of educational requirements is progressive. The top of the urn continues to expand while the bottom remains the same or contracts. To this change the educational

---

of all manpower requirements in 1975. The blue-collar occupations are expected to expand at less than half this rate, and will constitute 34 per cent of all requirements. A rapid expansion in requirements for service workers [generally outside the industrial system] is anticipated – a 35 per cent increase in employment, bringing this group to about 14 per cent of the total.'

8. Outside the industrial system, the same is true of the rural areas of the South. Here, too, the need was for crude, illiterate labour power and provision, accordingly, was made for nothing more. Northern agriculture was more demanding and the rural schools better. However, differences in income were a cause as well as a result of the difference.

system responds. It does so with a lag which is partly in the nature of any social response. But also the newly demanded education has required a sharp break with the social attitudes of the entrepreneurs. These, as noted, held the state to be an incubus; they sought to confine it to the provision of law and order, the protection of property and the common defence. Now the mature corporation must acknowledge dependence on the state for a factor of production more critical for its success than capital. Such a revision of attitudes takes time and so accordingly does the public response to it.

IV

The effect of this delayed response is that when employment is comparatively high there will be numerous vacancies for those of higher qualification and most of the unemployed will be without educational qualification or without compensating work experience or seniority. This is the present situation – and as this is written in 1966, it has been so for a number of years. There are many openings for individuals with advanced educational qualification. The ardent recruitment efforts of the industrial system in universities and colleges and, even more, its newspaper advertising, attest the fact.[9] At the same time, since these vacancies are not yet fully recognized as the normal counterpart of unemployment, statistics thereon are meagre.

The figures on the educational qualifications of the unemployed are better. In the spring of 1962, when the official unemployment rate was 6·0 per cent of the labour force it was 10·4 per cent for those with four years of schooling and 8·5 per cent for those with five to seven years of schooling. Those who are unemployable eventually become discouraged (as other workers do not) and withdraw from the labour market. When those not actively looking for work were added to the

9. A Boston newspaper editor noted in 1966 that his revenues from advertising of job opportunities had come to exceed that from department stores, with many fewer troublesome suggestions.

labour force the national unemployment rate was estimated at 7·8 per cent. For those with four years of schooling or less it was 17·2 per cent. For those with five to seven years of schooling it was 12·2 per cent. Among those with sixteen years of schooling or more, unemployment was only 1·4 per cent. Of all those officially counted as unemployed at the time, 40 per cent had eight years of schooling or (in most cases) much less.[10] Unemployment of teen-agers, reflecting the combined handicap of limited work experience and, in many cases, limited schooling, was 11·8 per cent. Adding those not in the labour force it was 25·6 per cent.[11] Additionally, the individual with a limited number of years of schooling will, ordinarily, have had poorer schooling than the person who has had more. Two principal reasons why he discontinues school are because the schools are bad and because he is doing badly. These suggest that his few years have been less good than the average. There can be no doubt, accordingly, that the unemployed include the predicted concentration of the uneducated.[12]

10. Charles C. Killingsworth, 'Unemployment and the Tax Cut,' Address before Conference on Economic Security, Michigan State University (26 October 1963), Mimeographed.

By way of comparison, national unemployment was estimated at 25 per cent of the civilian labour force in 1933, the worst year of the Great Depression.

11. William G. Bowen, 'Unemployment in the United States: Quantitative Dimensions,' in *Unemployment in a Prosperous Economy*, William G. Bowen and Frederick Harbison, eds. A report of the Princeton Manpower Symposium, Princeton University, 1965, p. 36.

12. It must be kept in mind that the educational requirements and disqualifications discussed here are those of the industrial system while the educational characteristics of the unemployed are those of the labour force as a whole. And, without doubt, the opportunities for employment of those with minimal educational qualifications are better outside the industrial system. The service industries, construction and agriculture all have a substantial continuing requirement for common labour. In the case of migrant agricultural labour, one sees again how responsive the educational system is to context. No education is required for harvesting crops. And by more or less effectively denying education to the children of those who participate, further generations of such labour are assured.

v

Lack of education is not the only disability of those who are rejected by the industrial system. A large proportion are Negroes or members of other racial minorities and it has anciently been observed that the Negro worker is the last to be hired when employment is expanding and the first to be fired when it is contracting. Negroes do suffer a special handicap. But a great deal must be attributed to the low level of educational qualification among Negroes, reflecting not discrimination, *per se*, by the industrial system but prior disadvantage in schools and environment. A well-educated Negro is not so necessarily the first fired or the last hired.[13]

Some unemployment is also associated with industrial change – with the decline of anthracite coal-mining in central Pennsylvania, the mechanization and consolidation of mining in the bituminous region, the loss of industry by mill towns in New York, New England or elsewhere. Here again, however, much must be attributed to the exiguous educational system which served the industries of these regions where, characteristically, a boy went into the mine or mill at the earliest age at which he was capable of manual labour. A well-educated population would not have remained stranded or it would have drawn industry to itself. An aeronautical engineer, with the decline in demand for manned military aircraft, may have trouble finding employment in his speciality. But with a little training and some slight loss of dignity he becomes an excellent appliance salesman.

The point is of much importance. Unemployment in the industrial system includes those who cannot find work in their particular craft or skill. It also includes qualified workers who are in the wrong place and who are reluctant to move. The number who fall in these categories will increase as demand presses less strongly on the capacity of the labour force

13. Although earnings of educated Negroes remain well below those of white citizens of comparable qualifications. *Population Bulletin*, p. 78.

and unemployment rises in consequence. But the increasing educational requirements of the industrial system add to the mobility of the working force both as between occupations and regions. The skilled craftsman of modest education does not easily learn a new skill. And the risks of movement are his own. So if he establishes himself as a tool-and-die-maker in Detroit there is a fair chance that he will remain there. The engineer or sales executive, though he is strongly specialized as to task, can acquire another perhaps less demanding qualification if he must. He is but little tied to his surroundings. If there is greater need for his speciality on the other side of the country he moves in response to a promise of employment, or is moved by his new employer as a matter of routine.

In recent years economists have debated whether unemployment in the modern economy is primarily structural, which is to say the result of a poor adaptation of the worker's qualification and skills to need, or whether it is the result of a general shortage of demand. Some blood has been spilled, for the argument has an important bearing on remedy. If unemployment is structural, the remedy is to retrain those who are out of work. But if the problem is merely a shortage of demand, then general action to increase spending or reduce taxes will suffice. The use of tax reduction as a remedy for insufficient demand has added a point to the debate. For it has been felt by advocates of structural causes and remedies that this may limit the spending on education, training and retraining which is the remedy for unemployment.

We now see the answer. Unemployment is both structural and the result of inadequate demand but also something more. It will appear with slackening of aggregate demand and it will be among those who are most inflexibly tied to particular occupations and locations. At the same time there will be vacancies in positions requiring high and specialized qualification. Employment would be higher both with stronger demand and with a better accommodation of qualification to need.

But unemployment will also be smaller, at any given level of demand, if there is a better *cultural* accommodation to the needs of the industrial system. There will then be a smaller core of functional illiterates who cannot be used at all. And there will be a larger number not only to fill the vacancies calling for higher qualification but also with the added mobility between occupations and regions that goes with education.[14] Modern unemployment is not only aggregate (in the sense that it results from a shortage of demand) and structural but also cultural.

It may be noted that unemployment, as a simple statistical concept, now has little relevance in the industrial system. This system requires a progressive accommodation of educated manpower to its needs. If this accommodation is imperfect, there will be a shortage of workers for specialized tasks. And there will, at the same time, be unemployment. Both measure the failure in the accommodation. Depending on the qualitative nature of the failure, the unemployed will consist of those who are unemployable because of insufficient education, or those who are occupationally or geographically immobile because of absence of education, or those who have a skill or speciality for which there is no demand and which, for reasons unrelated to education, they cannot exchange for one that is wanted. Or unemployment may have a quite different cause. It may be the result of an insufficiency of aggregate demand which reflects yet another accommodation of society to the needs of the industrial system. Simple statistics of unemployment reveal, it will be evident, almost nothing about the nature of the failure of accommodation at any given time. The crude steel capacity

14. In recent years, in much of western Europe unemployment has been consistently a smaller proportion of the labour force than in the United States. Something is to be attributed to a more persistent pressure of demand and to relatively larger employment opportunities outside the industrial system. But national educational standards and, in consequence, a more homogeneously qualified labour force have certainly been contributing factors. Foreign workers of lesser educational qualifications have been added to the domestic labour force, but it has been possible for countries such as Germany, France and Switzerland to take these in the numbers needed and leave the unemployment associated with such lower qualification behind in Spain, Turkey or southern Italy.

of a country was once a rather good indication of its ability to build railroads and meet its other needs for steel. It now tells nothing of the ability to provide special steels for the skin of supersonic aircraft or for similar uses. Technology has made the crude totals far less meaningful. One must now know the nature of the accommodation to the more refined, more specialized and constantly changing requirements for the metal. A surplus of steel could be combined with a severe shortage. So it is with labour. Here too one must look beyond the totals to the accommodation to educationally more refined, more specialized and constantly changing requirements. Here also totals have slight meaning. And here, as with steel, technology is one of the things that has made them so.

VI

Much may be learned of the character of any society from its social conflicts and passions. When capital was the key to economic success, social conflict was between the rich and the poor. Money made the difference; possession or non-possession justified contempt for, or resentment of, those oppositely situated. Sociology, economics, political science and fiction celebrated the war between the two sides of the tracks and the relation of the mansion on the hill to the tenement below.

In recent times education has become the difference that divides. All who have educational advantage, as with the moneyed of an earlier day, are reminded of their *noblesse oblige* and also of the advantages of reticence. They should help those who are less fortunate; they must avoid reflecting aloud on their advantage in knowledge. But this doesn't serve to paper over the conflict. It is visible in almost every community.

Thus the city with a high rate of accommodation to the requirements of the industrial system, i.e. a good educational system and a well-qualified working force, will attract industry and have a strong aspect of well-being. It will be the natural Canaan of the more energetic among those who were born in less favoured communities. This explains the modern migration from the South, Southwest and border states to California, the upper Middle West and the eastern seaboard. Many of these migrants will be unqualified for employment in the industrial system. They thus contribute heavily to welfare and unemployment rolls in the communities to which they have moved. The nature of the opprobrium to which they are subject is indicated by the appellations that are applied to them – they are hillbillies, Okies or jungle-bunnies. It is not that they are poorer but that they are culturally inferior. It is such groups, not the working proletariat, that now react in resentment and violence to their subordination.

Politics also reflects the new division. In the United States suspicion or resentment is no longer directed to the capitalists or the merely rich. It is the intellectuals who are eyed with misgiving and alarm. This should surprise no one. Nor should it be a matter for surprise when semi-literate millionaires turn up leading or financing the ignorant in struggle against the intellectually privileged and content. This reflects the relevant class distinction in our time.

A further consequence of the new pattern of employment and unemployment is that full employment, though it remains an important test of successful performance of the economic system, can be approached only against increasing resistance. For, as noted, while the unemployed are reduced in number, they come to consist more and more of those, primarily the uneducated, who are unemployable in the industrial system. The counterpart of this resistant core is a growing number of vacancies for highly qualified workers and a strong bargaining position for those who are employed. This leads to the final source of instability in the industrial system and to yet a further resort to the state. This we now examine.

Chapter 22

THE CONTROL OF THE
WAGE-PRICE SPIRAL

MEN of conservative temperament have long suspected that
one thing leads to another. The effect of the regulation of
aggregate demand on public wage and price policy admirably
validates their suspicion.

The state regulates aggregate demand by providing a volume
of purchasing power sufficient to employ the available labour
force. A low level of unemployment is a recognized test of the
success of the economy and of the proficiency of those who
guide it. And this, as the last chapter has shown, is not easily
achieved. The notion of employment and unemployment has
little meaning in the industrial system. What is involved is a
complex fitting of highly diverse qualifications to highly diverse
needs. For those with the least educational qualification, there
is comparatively little need. Only a very high level of aggregate
demand will bring them into employment, if they can be employed at all, and by that time there will be great shortages of
manpower in the higher levels of qualification.

At any reasonably high level of demand, prices and wages in
the industrial system are inherently unstable. This is certainly
so when demand is strong enough to begin enrolling the hard
core of more or less unemployable unemployed. Then wages
and prices press each other up in a continuing spiral. It is
convenient, in describing this spiral, to break into it at the
point where wages act on prices. But it is a continuous process
and no causal significance should be attached to wage increases
merely because they are the starting point.

II

When unemployment is small, the bargaining position of
unions is, in general, strong. Members can face a strike with the

assurance that they cannot be replaced. As a more practical matter they know that they will be inflicting the maximum loss of business on the employer and that after the strike is over they will promptly be recalled to work.

Employers, on their side, will deem it wise under such circumstances to grant increases in wages. The strong demand ensures that the added costs of the higher wages can be passed along to the consumer or other buyer. By the time unemployment is reduced to the hard-core categories, there will usually be a shortage of some classes of production workers.[1] Higher wages will seem to be a way of holding or recruiting manpower. Collective bargaining ordinarily embraces a substantial part of the industry. This means that all or most firms are affected by the wage increase at the same time. All will thus be led to increase prices at the same time. This, together with the strong demand, eases or erases the fear that the control over prices so essential for planning will be jeopardized because some firm will not go along.

The rise of the mature corporation has added significantly to the likelihood of the spiral. The entrepreneurial corporation was presumed to maximize the profits that were allowed to it by the current state of demand. And this, we may agree, was its tendency. If the profits had previously been at a maximum and prices were then at the level that yielded this maximum, wage increases could not be passed on in the form of higher prices. One cannot improve on the most. If wage increases could not be passed on, they would have to be paid for out of earnings. And in the nature of the entrepreneurial enterprise these earnings accrued in substantial measure to the entrepreneur. Again there is the special poignancy of paying when the individual has himself to pay. The entrepreneur had reason to resist. If he did yield, the wage increase did not necessarily increase prices, since, to repeat, these were already set to yield the maximum profit.

In the mature corporation the technostructure sets prices

1. To be distinguished from the unfilled positions in the higher levels of qualification in the technostructure.

not where they maximize profits but where they best contribute to the security of the technostructure and to the growth of the firm. This means with rare exceptions that it has latitude to increase revenues by increasing prices. Accordingly, it can pass wage increases along. It will be led to do so because a strike, implying contingencies and uncertainties beyond the control of the technostructure, is always a threat to its security. Labour conflict also cultivates attitudes that are hostile to identification and thus damaging to the motivational system. And, finally, the technostructure with which the decision on wages resides, does not itself have to pay.

The circle can now be completed. Price increases become cost increases for customers – either other industries or ultimate consumers. In either case, eventually or immediately, they raise living costs and thus become an inducement to another round of wage demands. Given regulation of demand with the goal of providing full employment, and in the absence of other steps, this spiral of wage and price increases is an organic feature of the industrial system.[2, 3]

It also accords solidly with experience. That the modern large firm has the option of passing on wage increases is taken for granted. If demand and employment are high, no one ever asks whether the steel, automobile or aluminium industry can raise their prices following the conclusion of a new collective

2. In recent years there has been a formidable dispute between economists as to whether demand pulls up prices, or costs, especially wages, push them up. Much polemical blood has also been spilled on the issue. Again something more than scientific verity is involved. If demand is the activating factor, then unemployment could be minimized and inflation could be controlled by precise regulation of demand. No questions of price and wage control arise. But if wages shove up prices and the higher prices lead to new wage demands, the plausible course is to control one or both. The cost-push thesis is also inconsistent with the doctrine of maximization, for, as noted, if a firm can respond to a wage increase by raising prices and increasing its net revenues (some rather remote theoretical contingencies apart) it could have done so before the wage increase. It did not, so it was not maximizing its revenues prior to the wage increase.

In fact, within the industrial system, as just indicated, both strong bargaining contract, but only whether they will need or choose to do so.[4] Between 1947 and 1960 there was no year in which wholesale prices of durable consumer goods as well as those of finished capital goods did not rise. Both categories are closely identified with the industrial system. The increase in the price of consumer durables during these thirteen years was about 25 per cent; for capital goods it was about 40 per cent. In agriculture and non-durable consumer goods, which are wholly or partially outside the industrial system, the price increase was much smaller and much less persistent. Price behaviour in the industrial system strongly coloured attitudes toward prices as a whole. 'The domestic economic policy of the United States during the last years of the 1950s [was] dominated by the fear of inflation.'[5]

III

The seemingly obvious remedy for the wage-price spiral is to regulate prices and wages by public authority. In World War II and the Korean War in the United States, demand pressed strongly the capacity of the labour force as well as that of the

---

demand and the push of costs are factors in the instability of prices at or near full employment. For a further and competent discussion of these relationships, see William G. Bowen, 'Wage Behavior and the Cost-Inflation Problem' in *Labor and the National Economy*, edited by the same author (New York: Norton, 1965). An important study, affirming the cost-push thesis, to which I am much indebted is Sidney Weintraub's *Some Aspects of Wage Theory and Policy* (New York: Chilton Books, 1963).

3. It is not necessarily characteristic of the economy outside the industrial system. In agriculture, professional and other services, imported products and some raw materials, the push of wages is likely to be unimportant. Prices rise primarily in response to strong demand. Some of the past debate between economists over the comparative importance of cost-push and demand-pull inflation has been the result of different men looking at different parts of the economy.

4. This is a choice which nearly all economists concede but which cannot be reconciled in any practical way with the doctrine of profit maximization.

5. Charles L. Schultze, 'Creeping Inflation – Causes and Consequences,' *Business Horizons*, Summer 1960, University of Indiana. Dr Schultze,

industrial plant. Apart from the exceptional strength of this pressure, especially in World War II, there was nothing unique about the wartime situation. Economic institutions and behaviour are not drastically altered either by declared or undeclared war. During both conflicts the wage-price spiral was successfully contained by controls. In the two years of 1941 and 1942 in the United States, the wholesale price index of industrial products rose a little more than 7 points. In the following three years, with greatly increased demand and virtual full employment, but with controls in effect, the index increased only 2·4 points. Price increases for machinery, chemicals and metal products, all closely identified with the industrial system, were even less. Between 1950 and 1951, after the outbreak of the Korean War, the wholesale index of capital goods showed prices rising by 7 points; that of consumer durables rose by 5 points. The following year, after wage and price controls were imposed, each index rose by only about one point.

This experience was not, however, greatly influential. It was assumed that war had, somehow, established new conditions as well as new imperatives. These made the experience irrelevant for peacetime. All groups influentially concerned also had a strong traditional resistance to controls. On few questions, indeed, have employers, unions and professional economists been

───────────

at this writing Director of the Budget, has argued that a contributing cause of inflation during this time was unusually sharp changes in demand. These exerted an upward pull on prices in industries where the demand was increasing; and since prices rise more easily than they fall there was no compensating reduction in areas of declining demand. At the same time union demands are increased by the favourable earnings in the areas of expansion and the demands are readily conceded. This exaggerates the spiral. Cf. *Recent Inflation in the United States*, Study Paper No. 1, Joint Economic Committee, Congress of the United States, Study of Employment, Growth and Price Levels (September 1959). Also, W. G. Bowen and S. H. Masters, 'Shifts in the Composition of Demand and the Inflation Problem,' *The American Economic Review*, Vol. LIV, No. 6 (December 1964). It will be evident that this explanation is an elaboration rather than a contradiction of the explanation offered above. Inflation occurs when demand is strong and the effect of strong demand is exaggerated by shifts in demand.

more united in ideology than in opposition to price and wage regulation.

Employers had always reacted to controls in the tradition of the entrepreneurial firm. Price control could only be for the purpose of reducing profits. Public interference with wages might be a way of reinforcing the demands of the unions. But perhaps also it might seem to be a threat to the autonomy of the technostructure. And, more generally, the mystique of freedom, embracing but presumably going beyond the freedom to make money, strongly defended the principle of free markets.

Unions had also long reacted adversely. This was a legacy of their experience with the entrepreneurial firm. That firm had a strong interest in resisting union demands. It had privileged access to newspapers, public opinion and the state. Any wage regulation, other than that establishing minimum wages, would be, it was felt, for the purpose of keeping wages down. To be dependent even on a friendly government was to lose capacity for independent action to press rightful demands.

For economists, as will be sufficiently evident, a massive intellectual vested interest was involved. As noted, nearly all teaching and technical discourse assumed markets with unfettered prices in which producers sought to maximize their return. To admit of the need for price or wage control was to destroy the determinacy of this system and the associated theoretical apparatus. Instead of revealing to students by precise and rational diagrams the prices that would maximize profits for a producer, it would be necessary to consider what price a bureaucrat might believe consistent with wage and price stability. Economics would be reduced to the level of political science. Truth has its obligations to dignity.

Besides it would not work. Here we encounter again the commitment to avarice. Only the soft-minded could suppose that government, by regulation, could thwart the primal instinct for self-enrichment.

In consequence, professional economists had accepted the inevitability of inflation at full employment or had simply evaded the issue with whatever grace they could command.

'Most economists would, in normal peacetime, favour controlling inflation by ... fiscal and monetary policies rather than by simply legislating price ceilings.' 'It would be nice if we could insist upon having complete price stability and maximal employment and growth ... it may be that citizens of a modern mixed economy can find no shelters in which they can live with full security and compromise.'[6]

IV

Yet, paradoxically, all associated with the industrial system also benefit substantially from restraints on prices and wages. What is opposed in principle is desirable in practice. Uncontrolled price and cost increases are much less dangerous to the security of the technostructure than uncontrolled price reductions such as might result from price competition or be forced by a severe shrinkage of aggregate demand. Given the strong demand that induces the price and cost increases in the first place, it is possible to offset cost increases by raising prices. It is not at all easy to offset falling prices by reducing wages or other costs. Nevertheless, planning is greatly facilitated if prices and costs are stable. Inflationary price and cost increases, moving unpredictably through the system, make long-term contracts impossible and everywhere introduce an unwelcome element of randomness and error. Price stability also facilitates the management of demand. Prices being given, the way is open to persuade the customer on other points. If prices are changing, he may respond in his purchase to these. This response is unpredictable, which is to say it interferes with effective management.

If wages are rising, increases in compensation for white-collar employees and in the technostructure will also be required. This will be at a time when there are unfilled positions. There will be some resulting danger of unsettling the salary structure and inducing competition for scarce talent. Another

6. Paul A. Samuelson, *Economics*, Sixth Edition (New York: McGraw, 1964), pp. 386, 792.

random element thus enters and interferes with planning. The mature corporation and its technostructure therefore have good reasons for wishing to avoid the wage-price spiral. And to accept restraint, since it applies to both costs and wages, is not necessarily to sacrifice earnings. Should there be sacrifice, as always in the mature corporation, it is not suffered by those who agree to it.

Thus, once again economic development shows a remarkable degree of internal consistency. The industrial system must, by its nature, be subject to external restraint on its prices. As the mature corporation evolves it can accept and even welcome such restraint.

Restraint is useful in practice also to the unions. The spiral requires that they invest much of their energies in keeping abreast of price increases. Only a small and unpredictable portion of a pay rise brings higher real income. The rest compensates for price increases. Thus with uncontrolled wages and prices, the union has a large and essentially unproductive task of merely keeping even. For the rank and file the effect is even worse. Gains are won as the result of lengthy and elaborate collective bargaining. If only for demonstration purposes there will be an occasional strike. And then these gains evaporate as prices rise. The whole process has an unpleasant aspect of legerdemain. 'It makes no sense to have the boss put a nickel in wages in your pocket with one hand and take out a dime in prices with the other.'[7]

Outside of the industrial system, the spiral also has adverse effects. And these sectors of the economy are important in forming public attitudes. Here are farmers, civil servants, the self-employed and the employees of small enterprises. Within the industrial system, as wages force up prices and prices force up wages, those who receive these payments remain automatically abreast. A passenger in even a very fast automobile is reasonably certain of keeping up with it. A man

7. A. H. Raskin, 'The Squeeze of the Unions,' *The Atlantic Monthly*, April 1961. Reprinted in Bowen, op. cit., p. 8. He was commenting on a common attitude of steel workers.

running alongside is not so well situated. The insiders are protected against loss of real income; the outsiders are not. More generally the individual who gets added income, as a result of a general inflationary movement, attributes it not to larger economic causes but to his own virtue and diligence. The higher prices that take it away he attributes to bad public policy. Finally, there are many categories of income recipients – municipal employees, hospital and library and like workers, pensioners of all kinds – whose incomes do not rise appreciably. Their complaint is even more acute.

Economic discussion in the fifties was not only dominated by the problem of inflation but also by efforts to shift the blame. The corporation blamed the excessive wage demands of the unions. The unions blamed the avaricious and monopolistic prices of the corporation.[8] Democrats blamed the Republican administration and Republicans the previous Democratic administration and the Congress. Some saw the spiral as a communist plot to debauch the currency, and the Reverend Gerald L. K. Smith thoughtfully blamed the Jews.

In fact, the wage-price spiral is the functional counterpart of unemployment. The latter occurs when there is insufficient demand; the spiral operates when there is too much and also, unfortunately, when there is just enough. Both unemployment and inflation are taken by the public to be indications of failure. Here the economists re-enter. Whatever their predilections, they cannot escape public attitudes. These will no more allow excuses for inflation than for unemployment. And since the system is unstable at full employment, there is no alternative to control. However regretted, it is inescapable. This even the most ardent defenders of the market have discovered when they have arrived in Washington to take a position with the Council of Economic Advisers or otherwise experience the chilling realities of responsibility. For the duration of their service, the notion of maintaining full employment without interference with markets has to be put aside. Only when they are safely back in the universities again can it be gratefully exhumed.

8. See the discussion by Schultze, op. cit.

The New Industrial State

V

Since all the relevant groups affirm the importance of free markets in principle, while needing control in practice, the solution has been to impose control in practice while affirming the commitment to free markets in principle. This semantic triumph has been aided by long-standing recognition that what is not permissible in principle is often necessary in practice.

It has also been aided by the technological dynamic of the industrial system. This, with its associated use of capital, ensures a progressive increase in output per worker, although in varying amounts from industry to industry. These productivity gains allow, in turn, for annual wage increases without either higher prices or reduced earnings. Given a reasonably affluent wage level – an exemption from the pressures of physical need – workers may be more content to accept a moderate wage increase with stable prices than a larger one with the prospect of partial loss from rising living costs. Since the corporation is not experiencing rising costs, it can accept stable prices as its part of the bargain. All that remains is for the state to give a clear initiative in this regulation.

This initiative was, perhaps, the most important innovation in economic policy of the administration of President John F. Kennedy. In the earliest days of the administration, it was agreed among those concerned with economic policy that some special mechanism for restraint would be required were there to be a close approach to full employment. Generalized pleas to unions and employers for restraint had been sufficiently tried; in the absence of definition, all parties identified restraint with their normal behaviour. Accordingly, in September of 1961 the United Steel Workers, then engaged in contract negotiations with the steel companies, were asked by President Kennedy to hold their demands within what could be granted from productivity gains. And the steel companies were asked to keep their prices stable. The policy and the standards for its application were then detailed the following January in the annual Economic Report. 'The general guide for non-inflationary wage behaviour is that the rate of increase in wage rates (including fringe benefits) in each industry be equal to the trend rate of over-all productivity increases.'[9] In April 1962, after negotiating a wage contract generally consistent with these standards, the steel companies, led by the United States Steel Corporation, announced an increase in steel prices averaging six dollars a ton. Strong government pressure, strongly adverse public and business opinion and some historic Presidential invective brought a recision of the increases. Thereafter for several years the wage guideposts, as they came to be called, and the counterpart price behaviour were a reasonably accepted feature of government policy. Wage negotiations were closely consistent with the guidelines. Prices of manufactured goods were stable.

VI

Nevertheless, of the various adaptations of government policy to the planning of the industrial system, the control of wages and prices is on the least secure footing. Partly this is because the divorce of ideology from action has so far excluded any deliberate effort to devise a fully effective system of control. On occasions of public ceremony, businessmen and numerous union leaders must still proclaim their commitment to the free market. And likewise economists. It is hard to turn from these liturgical exercises to a consideration of practical measures for ensuring that the guideposts will be observed. In the thirties, although the commitment of economists to the canons of sound finance was still strong, a minority accepted the implications of the Keynesian system and proceeded to work out its application to practical fiscal policy. Though radical this was not wholly disreputable. To work on methods of wage and price control is not reputable. Only after a scholar is in public office is the ban lifted. And then he is careful to speak not of control but (as frequently here) of restraint. The amenability of the corporations and unions to control – ideology to the contrary

9. *Economic Report of the President*, January 1962.

– means that it need not be very strong. But it is hard to take purely hortatory enforcement very seriously. 'These guideposts . . . do not have the force of law; the scowls by the President . . . cannot solve the dilemmas of full employment and price stability.'[10]

This lack of ideological sanction also leaves the danger that someone will appear in a position of responsibility for whom the liturgy of the free market is a guide to action. He will insist that there be no interference with wages and prices. Otherwise the gods of free enterprise will be not appeased. Then it will have to be learned anew that, given the imperatives of demand regulation and full employment, there will be inflation.[11]

Finally there is a serious danger – one that is evident as this is written in 1966 – that wage and price restraints will be asked to accomplish more than they are capable of doing. In a sense they do not prevent inflation. Rather they keep the wage and price spiral from producing inflationary increases in prices – increases in prices over a large range of products and unrelated to any expansion in output – when demand is at levels sufficient to provide full or nearly full employment. But demand must not be greatly in excess of this amount. If it is too high, price increases outside the industrial system, competition to fill vacancies, payments for early or preferential deliveries and the feeling of unions that they should share in high profits will act to break down the restraints. The proper remedy is

10. Samuelson, op. cit., p. 792.

11. This tendency to divorce ideology from practical action, with the danger that innocent but devout believers will be guided by the ideology, is a more general affliction. Thus our relations with the Soviet Union are presumed, by ideology, to be marked by total conflict – the climactic confrontation between socialism and free enterprise. In fact, they have been characterized by practical accommodation on a great many matters – in Berlin, in resisting the proliferation of nuclear weapons, in awareness of the danger of war by accident, in preventing nuclear fallout, in the U.N. and in a considerable range of scientific and cultural development. In 1964 in the campaign of Senator Goldwater the policy fell into the hands of those who were guided by the liturgy of conflict rather than by the reality of accommodation.

higher taxes or reduced government spending to cut down on the demand. These are painful actions. The regulation of demand is politically asymmetrical; expansion is far easier than contraction. Accordingly a failure of wage and price restraints in face of excessive aggregate demand also remains a danger to this accommodation to industrial planning.

VII

Yet, while there may be difficulties, and interim failures or retreats are possible and indeed probable, a system of wage and price restraint is inevitable in the industrial system. As noted, neither inflation nor unemployment are acceptable alternatives.[12] No other advanced industrial community, socialist, non-socialist or ideologically hostile to socialism, has found it possible to dispense with such regulation. The United States, the most developed of the industrial communities, will not be an exception.

The necessity for control arises in the apparatus of industrial planning. This planning, we have seen, replaces prices that are established by the market with prices that are established by the firm. The firm, in tacit collaboration with the other firms in the industry, has wholly sufficient power to set and maintain minimum prices. Although in Europe cartels can seek the support of the courts for this purpose, this recourse is not essential. And the firm goes on to exercise control over what is purchased at these prices. Given this management of demand for the individual product together with an effective regulation of aggregate demand, the minimum prices so set are secure. There is no serious danger that they will be broken down by competition or a failure of demand.

This price control accords protection, however, only against price reduction. It does not embrace the unions and hence

12. I once considered it possible that, by adequate compensation, a volume of unemployment consistent with stable prices could be made socially and politically tolerable. Cf. *The Affluent Society*, pp. 298–307. This I now doubt.

does not provide any protection against concessions to them and concurrent price increases. And the remedy is beyond the scope of the individual firm. It knows that others will forswear price reductions that are disastrous for all. But it cannot count on others to resist wage increases and to forgo resultant price increases, for these, however inconvenient for planning and the economy at large, are not disastrous. The market having been abandoned in favour of planning of prices and demand, there is no hope that it will supply this last missing element of restraint. All that remains is the state. So, in the end, there is no alternative to having the state complete the structure of planning.

With minimum prices established by the firms, demand that is managed by them for specific products, demand that is managed in the aggregate by the state and maximum levels established by the state for wages and prices, the planning structure of the industrial system is effectively complete. All that remains is to ensure that everyone, at all times, refer to it as an unplanned or market system.

In this connexion, it is worth noting, the weakness of the present machinery for enforcing maximum prices will not, in the end, be a handicap. The entrepreneurial enterprise was subordinate to and regulated by the market. Being under the dominance of the market, it had substantial independence from the state. The power of the state to control its behaviour was, accordingly, a most important question. The enterprise was free to bring to bear formidable powers of obstruction and resistance. The mature corporation, as part of a comprehensive structure of planning, has no similar independence. It identifies itself with social goals, and adapts these to its needs. It cannot easily fight that with which it is so associated. More specifically, if the state is effectively to manage demand, the public sector of the economy, as we have seen, must be relatively large. That means that the state is an important customer, and it is especially needed in developing advanced technology which would otherwise be beyond the scope of industrial planning. Under these circumstances the independence of the mature corporation is further circumscribed. It is deeply dependent on the state. It does not accordingly have the luxury of defiance. It may go far in adapting the goals of the state to its needs. But it cannot, any more than a department of government itself, pursue objectives at odds with those of the state. In numerous ways the state can deny it vital needs. And since other firms are identified with social goals and these reflect adaptation, they will tend to consider the resistance antisocial and the sanctions justified.[13] There is no chance, on this issue, of a solid front by mature corporations against the state.

13. Efforts by the steel industry – U.S. Steel in 1962 and Bethlehem in 1966 – to break through current price restraints are a case in point. These efforts were a reflection of older entrepreneurial attitudes. The government on both occasions threatened use of its power as a customer – though it is less in the case of steel than in many industries. Both public and a good deal of business opinion condemned the actions as antisocial or, at a minimum, showing a poor sense of public relations. On the latter, see Richard Austin Smith, *Corporations in Crisis* (New York: Doubleday, 1963), pp. 157 et. seq.

Chapter 23

THE INDUSTRIAL SYSTEM AND THE UNION I

> This change is taking place at a time when the public still
> thinks of trade unions as Goliaths of power. SOLOMON
> BARKIN[1]

FOR most of their brief history in the United States, trade
unions have been embattled. Employers have usually wished
they did not exist. The wish has often been strengthened by
belief. These desires and convictions have led regularly to
resistance suitably supported by scholarly argument. The latter
has always been available. One of the small but rewarding
vocations of a free society is the provision of needed conclusions, properly supported by statistics and moral indignation,
for those in a position to pay.

Quite commonly arguments of this genre have led to the
conclusion that, with industrial progress and enlightenment,
unions have lost their function. Class conflict is the nostalgia
of the antique revolutionary. Unions exist only because they
have fastened themselves on the back of the worker and, like
the Old Man of the Sea, cannot be dismounted. Impressionable
employers, captivated by such arguments, have on occasion
held out the hand of friendship to their men only to have it
enthusiastically bitten.

Against this background, a conclusion that unions have a
drastically reduced function in the industrial system will be
received by many with scepticism. Another man has fallen
victim to nonsense. The measure of a scholar is not how he
reacts to evidence but how well he resists tendentious propaganda.

Yet, as this is written, unions within the industrial system

1. 'The Decline of the Labor Movement,' in *The Corporation Take-
over*, Andrew Hacker, ed. (New York: Harper, 1964), p. 263.

have long since ceased to expand and have, indeed, lost ground. In almost any view they are less militant in attitude and less powerful in politics than in earlier times. Industrial relations have become markedly more peaceful as collective bargaining has come to be accepted by the modern large industrial enterprise. Unions and their leaders are widely accepted and on occasion accorded a measure of applause for sound social behaviour both by employers and the community at large. All this suggests some change.

The present analysis foretells further such change and leads to the conclusion that it has durable significance. The loss of union membership is not a temporary setback pending the organization of white-collar employees and engineers but the earlier stages of a permanent decline. The increasingly conciliatory character of modern industrial relations, especially in the larger corporation, has come about not because labour leaders and vice presidents in charge of labour relations have entered upon an era of pacific enlightenment, the operative agent being the rise of industrial statesmanship and the somewhat delayed triumph of Judeo-Christian ethics and the golden rule. It has come about because interests that were once radically opposed are now much more nearly in harmony. Behaviour is not better; it is merely that interests are concordant. Were interests still opposed, labour relations would still be characterized by argument and invective, accented on occasion by clubs, stones, and low-yield explosives. The unquestioned expertise of the modern industrial relations man would not appreciably ease the passion.

II

All of the changes here examined – the shift in power from ownership and the entrepreneur to the technostructure, technological advance, the regulation of markets and aggregate demand, and the imperatives of price and wage regulation – have had an effect on the position of the union. In every case they have subtracted from its role.

The employee was linked to the entrepreneurial firm by pecuniary motivation. There was an unquestioned conflict in pecuniary interest between the employee and employer. As indicated in the last chapter, an increase in labour costs,[2] when the firm was already maximizing profits, could only reduce profits. These profits, or a substantial share of them, accrued to the entrepreneur. And his interest in pecuniary return, since among other things it rewarded the capital he supplied or commanded, was also strong.

The union, in these circumstances, had the power, unavailable to the individual worker, of forcing the employer to accept the higher costs and reduced profits, by threatening the even greater cost and profit reduction of a strike. It follows that the employer had every reason to resist the union and regret its existence. And the worker had equal reason for wanting it. The resistance of the employer might keep the union from gaining a foothold. But its importance to the worker was equally a factor in giving it strength. Additionally, the man who sided with the employer was abetting the income of another man instead of his own. If he was rewarded he was a fink and if not he was a fool. In either case any tendency he might have to identify himself with the goals of the employer could be regarded with contempt and be, by the union, so characterized.

In the United States the classic last-ditch battles against the unions – those of Ford, Ernest Weir, Thomas Girdler and Sewell Avery – were all waged by entrepreneurs. All these were in industries in which mature corporations led the way in surrender.

The first goal of the technostructure is its own security. Profits, provided that they are above the minimum necessary

2. That is to say if wages go up independently of any increase in productivity. As a concession to technical precision, it should perhaps be noted that with certain market structures and demand and cost functions, longer-run adjustments may occur which pass along the costs. These do not impair the present case which is that there is an immediate conflict of pecuniary interest.

for security, are secondary to growth. Labour relations, naturally enough, are conducted in accordance with the goals of the technostructure.

This means that the technostructure may readily trade profits for protection against such an undirected event with such an unpredictable outcome as a strike. Once again there is the important fact that those who make the decision during union negotiations do not themselves have to pay.

But no reduction in profits may be required from yielding to the union. Since the mature firm does not maximize profits, it can maintain income by increasing its prices. The wage settlement, since it affects all or most firms in the industry, provides all with a common signal to consider such action. Its effect on growth will, of course, be considered. But since this will be the same for all firms in the industry, and since the regulation of aggregate demand keeps the latter at a high level, price increases will often seem allowable.

No absolute rule can be laid down on the reaction of the technostructure to a union demand. It will depend on the existing level of prices and earnings, the effectiveness of the management of demand for the products or product, the importance of wage costs and other factors. But in general the mature corporation in the pursuit of its own goals will accede far more readily than the entrepreneurial enterprise to the demands of the union, and accordingly, is much less averse to its existence. It may even pay something for what is called a good employer image. These tendencies, far more than Christian revelation, explain the harmony that increasingly characterizes the labour relations of the mature corporation, to the pride of all concerned.

But while the task of the union is much easier, the union is also much less essential for the worker. What the technostructure gives to the union, it can also give without a union or to avoid having a union. At a minimum the union shrinks in stature. A fighting lawyer is a figure of great majesty before a hanging judge. His stature is less before one who places everyone on probation.

III

It has long been a minor tenet of trade union doctrine that all employers are essentially alike. All seek their own best gain. All, accordingly, are inimical to the interest of the worker. Thus any worker who identifies his interest with that of his boss is making a mistake. The vehemence with which this doctrine has been enunciated in modern times may indicate uneasiness as to the truth of the proposition in the case of the mature corporation. Such teaching was not so necessary in the age of the Homestead massacre and the Pullman strike. In any case it is not true.

As compared with the entrepreneurial firm, not only is there a much less flat opposition of interest between workers in the mature corporation and those who have the power of decision on matters relating to wages and other conditions of employment, but identification is part of the established and accepted system of motivation. And, although identification is most important in the technostructure, its existence there serves to make it a more general tendency. Loyalty to the firm will often be part of the general mood. This is adverse to the union. Additionally, in the earlier stages of industrial technology – in the early steel mills or on the early automobile assembly lines – hard, repetitive and tedious work acted as a barrier to identification. Among machinists, toolmakers, steam fitters and other skilled workers there was the sense of common interest arising from a shared skill. As machinery replaces both repetitive and drudging work and eliminates skilled occupations, it lowers these barriers to identification. This increases the difficulties of organization and thus adds to the problems of the union.

But much more important, modern technology opens the way for a massive shift from workers who are within the reach of unions to those who are not. Both the capital resources and the goals of the technostructure of the mature corporation strongly facilitate and encourage such a shift.

This tendency has already been briefly observed.[3] In its

3. Chapter 21.

planning, the technostructure seeks to minimize the number of contingencies that are beyond its control. Labour costs and supply are significantly of this character and more so when there is a union. To substitute capital, in the form of machinery, the supply and cost of which are wholly or largely under control, for labour which is not and which can strike, is an admirable bargain. It is worth the sacrifice of some earnings. It is also adverse to the union for that is the purpose.[4]

The substitution, as earlier noticed, has been proceeding rapidly. In the eighteen years from 1947 to 1965, white-collar workers in the United States – professional, managerial, office and sales workers – increased by 9·6 million. In these years blue-collar workers – craftsmen, operatives, and labourers, farmers and miners apart – decreased by 4 million. By 1965 there were nearly 8 million more white- than blue-collar workers – 44·5 million as compared with 36·7 million. During these years the number of professional and technical workers, the category most characteristic of the technostructure, approximately doubled.[5] No other group had increased so rapidly. In industries strongly typical of the industrial system the change has been much more dramatic. Between 1947 and 1965 the number of white-collar workers increased from 16·4 to 25·6 per cent of employed workers in manufacturing. In the primary

---

4. We have here another example of the way the industrial system accommodates belief to its convenience. It has been the lurking conviction of quite a few unions that technical change is an instrument adverse to their interests and thus to be resisted. This attitude has been uniformly deplored as wrong and regressive and no more fitting of civilized advocacy than sodomy, self-flagellation and the refusal to use soap. All right-thinking people should accept machines and participate in the general fruits of progress. In fact, the instinct of the unions was sound. And, from the point of view of those immediately involved, the tactic of resistance may also have been sound. Over a longer period, of course, the resisting unions have been outflanked by competitive change – as the anthracite miners were outflanked by oil and the railroad brotherhood by automobiles, trucks and planes.

5. *Manpower Report of the President and a Report on Manpower Requirements, Resources, Utilization, and Training*, United States Department of Labor, March 1966, p. 165.

metal industries the increase was from 12·9 to 18·3 per cent; in fabricated metal products from 16·5 to 22·6 per cent; in transportation equipment (automotive and aircraft) it was from 18·5 to 28·7 per cent; in electrical equipment it was from 21·7 to 31·5 per cent.[6]

White-collar workers have rarely been susceptible to organization in the United States and, with the rise of the technostructure, they are almost certainly less so. In the entrepreneurial corporation a visible line divided the bosses – those whose position depended on ownership or their ability to produce profits for the owners – from clerks, bookkeepers, timekeepers, secretaries, salesmen and others who were purely employees. In the mature corporation this line disappears. Decision is divorced from ownership; the location of decision moves in the direction of the body of white-collar workers. Distinctions between those who make decisions and those who carry them out, and between employer and employee, are obscured by the technicians, scientists, market analysts, computer programmers, industrial stylists and other specialists who do, or are, both. A continuum thus exists between the centre of the technostructure and the more routine white-collar workers on the fringe. At some point, power or the chance for moving towards the centre becomes negligible. But it is no longer possible to recognize that point.

In consequence, white-collar workers identify themselves with the technostructure from which they are not visibly distinct. A survey of such workers in 1957 showed that more than three-quarters regarded themselves as being more closely associated with management than with production workers.[7] As a

6. Ibid., p. 201. There is strong indication that these trends will continue. The National Commission on Technology, Automation and Economic Progress (as noted) estimates that white-collar workers, including professional and technical workers, will be 48 per cent of the labour force in 1975.

7. A. A. Blum, 'Prospects for Organization of White Collar Workers,' U.S. Department of Labor, *Monthly Labor Review*, Vol. 87, No. 2 (February 1964).

result, they have remained unorganized. For them, 'Persuasion, pressure, and manipulation [and bureaucratic gamesmanship] ... take the place of the face-to-face combat of an earlier age.'[8]

IV

Finally, both high employment resulting from the regulation of aggregate demand and comparative affluence reduce the dependence of the individual worker on the union. Once again we see the interconnected character of change. If unemployment is endemic and incomes are close to the minimum required for physical survival, men are held to their jobs by the threat of physical suffering. In these circumstances the union greatly enhances the liberty of the worker. The worker cannot walk off the job by himself. But he knows that if things become intolerable he can walk off with all of the others. Shared privation is easier to bear than individual privation. And a union may have strike pay or a soup kitchen to mitigate, however slightly, the hardship involved.

Both high employment and high income are solvents for the sense of compulsion and thus are substitutes for the union. If employment is high, there will be alternative jobs. Accordingly, a man can quit. It is the high employment, not the union, that rescues him from his slavish dependence on the job he holds. In the United States, as in Britain, Canada and elsewhere, the regulation of aggregate demand to ensure high employment was strongly pressed by the unions. It was the accommodation of the state to the needs of the industrial system that the labour movement most sought. It was the thing most designed to make unions less needed.[9]

8. Clark Kerr, John T. Dunlop, Frederick Harbison and Charles A. Myers, *Industrialism and Industrial Man* (Cambridge: Harvard University Press, 1960), p. 292.

9. The role of unemployment in according a firm control by employers over the labour force was strongly stressed by Marx. 'The industrial reserve army [i.e. the unemployed], during the periods of stagnation and average prosperity, weighs down the active labour-army; during the periods of over-production and paroxysm, it holds its pretensions in

High income also lessens the danger of fear of physical privation. Thus it accords the worker liberty that he once obtained from the union. And, therefore, it too weakens dependence on the union. However, the relation of income to the need and willingness to work in the industrial system is a complex and much misunderstood matter. A digression is necessary here to explain it.

V

The natural tendency of man, as manifested in primitive societies, is almost certainly to work until a given consumption is achieved. Then he relaxes, engages in sport, hunting, orgiastic or propitiating ceremonies or other forms of physical enjoyment or spiritual betterment. This tendency for primitive man to achieve contentment has been the despair of those who regard themselves as agents of civilization and remains so to this day. What is called economic development consists in no small part in devising strategies to overcome the tendency of men to place limits on their objectives as regards income and thus on their efforts. Commodities involving physical and progressive addiction were long considered especially useful in this regard; this explains the great esteem that attached, in the early stages of modern civilization, to tobacco, alcohol, coca and opium, a value that they have not entirely lost in the

---

check. Relative surplus-population is therefore the pivot upon which the law of demand and supply of labour works. It confines the field of action of this law within the limits absolutely convenient ... to the domination of capital.' Marx was equally insistent on the intolerable effects (from the viewpoint of the capitalist) of full employment (*Capital*, Chapter XXV, The Modern Library Edition, p. 701). One imagines that Marx would have regarded a full employment policy, if successfully pursued over any length of time, as having radical implications for his system, the class struggle and the laws of capitalist accumulation. His followers, until comparatively recently, were unwilling to attach such significance to the policy. Keynesian economics was long dismissed as a superficial effort to prop up capitalism which did not affect the fundamental position of the worker.

present day. However, goods which by their novelty appeal to vanity or to emulative or competitive adornment or display are now considered more legitimate. Also, though need for food and shelter, especially in benign climates, is rather readily satisfied, the pressures of emulation and competition in adornment and display have no clear terminal point. Until recent times, California farmers and labour contractors encouraged their Filipino workers to invest heavily in clothing. The pressure of debt, and the pressure on each to emulate the most extravagant, quickly converted these happy and easygoing people into a modern and reliable work force. In all underdeveloped countries, the effort inspired by the introduction of modern consumer goods – cosmetics, motor scooters, transistor radios, canned food, bicycles, phonograph records, movies, American cigarettes – is recognized to be of the highest importance in the strategy of development.

In the advanced industrial countries, the creation of wants, and therewith the need to work, is a matter of considerable sophistication, but the principles are the same. It is also a task of great importance. In 1939 the real income of employed workers in the United States was very nearly the highest on record and it was then the highest of any country in the world. In the next quarter-century it doubled. Had the 1939 income been a terminal objective, work effort would have been cut in half in the ensuing twenty-five years. In fact, there was a slight increase in weekly hours actually worked. This was a remarkable achievement.

It was accomplished partly by the now well-understood ability of the industrial system to adapt belief to its needs. To increase income and consumption is held to be socially and morally sound. Leisure is something to be regarded with misgiving, especially in lower income brackets. Accordingly, a reduction in the standard work week must always be considered dubious social policy inducing moral or spiritual weakness.

Economists, performing one of their now well-recognized functions, have accorded important canonical reinforcement to these beliefs. They have made the rate of increase in the production of goods the prime test of social achievement. To substitute leisure for work is, thus, to be antisocial. Economic theory has long insisted on the homogeneity and insatiability of wants. There is no proof that an expensive woman obtains the same satisfaction from yet another gown as does a hungry man from a hamburger. But there is no proof that she does not. Since it cannot be proven that she does not, her desire, it is held, must be accorded equal standing with that of a poor man for meat. Doctoral aspirants in economics still risk failure in many places if they assert otherwise. If all wants are of equally good standing, it follows that the moral and social obligation to work to fill them remains undiminished in power no matter how much is produced.[10] Corporate executives with an overly acute sense of persecution have sometimes supposed that economists, in the ideas they advance, are their enemies. In fact, the economics profession is strongly in the service of the beliefs they most need. It would, *prima facie*, be plausible to set a limit on the national product that a nation requires. The test of economic achievement would then be how rapidly it could reduce the number of hours of toil that are needed to meet this requirement. Were economists to advocate this goal, with the revolutionary effects that it would have on the industrial system, there would be grounds for complaint. None have been so uncooperative.

However, the more immediate device for ensuring that there is no terminal objective as regards income is advertising and the related arts of salesmanship. Here we have yet another of the interlocking developments which so admirably serve the industrial system. Advertising and salesmanship – the management of consumer demand – are vital for planning in the industrial system. At the same time, the wants so created ensure the services of the worker. Ideally, his wants are kept slightly in excess of his income. Compelling inducements are then provided for him to go into debt. The pressure of the resulting debt adds to his reliability as a worker.

10. I have dealt with the underlying theory in *The Affluent Society* (Boston: Houghton, 1958), Chapters X, XI.

It is held, of course, that wants are not contrived. They are deeply organic in the human situation. Their satisfaction is not only a source of rich reward to those served but the highest secular function of the society. Even to hold this process up for examination is to invite the suggestion that one is ascetic, unworldly, determinedly impractical and disposed to substitute his own odd and esoteric values for the lustier instincts of the masses. Yet one cannot have it both ways. If wants are inherent, they need not be contrived. But few producers of consumer goods would care to leave the purchase of their products to the spontaneous and hence unmanaged responses of the public. Nor, on reflection, would they have much confidence in the reliability of their labour force in the absence of pressure to purchase the next car or to meet the payments on the last.[11]

It is now time to return to the union.

11. Professional advertising men, who, as earlier noted, have wished for a substantial social justification for their services, have frequently argued that without their efforts to stimulate wants men would not work and the economy would falter. Economists, almost without exception, have dismissed this as the special pleading of an economically unlearned and conscience-ridden community. In fact, the advertising men have a good case. It has been rejected by economists because to admit that advertising promotes wants is to concede that the goods would be un-wanted in the absence of such persuasion. This casts doubt on the pivotal contentions that wants are homogeneous and insatiable and that the volume of production measures the success of the society. One cannot give equal status with bread to what must be contrived by advertising and one cannot measure the success of an economy by its ability to keep up with Madison Avenue. Again these are matters which I have dealt with at more length in *The Affluent Society*.

Chapter 24

THE INDUSTRIAL SYSTEM AND THE
UNION II: THE MINISTERIAL UNION

THE industrial system, it seems clear, is unfavourable to the union. Power passes to the technostructure and this lessens the conflict of interest between employer and employee which gave the union much of its reason for existence. Capital and technology allow the firm to substitute white-collar workers and machines that cannot be organized for blue-collar workers that can. The regulation of aggregate demand, the resulting high level of employment together with the general increase in well-being all, on balance, make the union less necessary or less powerful or both. The conclusion seems inevitable. The union belongs to a particular stage in the development of the industrial system. When that stage passes so does the union in anything like its original position of power. And, as an added touch of paradox, things for which the unions fought vigorously – the regulation of aggregate demand to ensure full employment and higher real income for members – have contributed to their decline.

Yet it would be premature to write off the union entirely. Numerous organizations – the Fishmongers and the Cordwainers in the City of London, the House Un-American Activities Committee in Washington – regularly survive their function. Once a union is in being there is nothing in continuing its existence – the collection or deduction of dues, the enrolment of newly hired members, the holding of conventions and the designation of officers – that is nearly so difficult as bringing it to an end. And while the industrial system undermines old functions, it does not eliminate them entirely, and it does add some new ones. Finally, not all unions are within the industrial system and those outside have a better prospect. The overall effect of the rise of the industrial system is greatly to reduce the union as a social force. But it will not disappear or become entirely unimportant.

II

The trend in union strength is clearly adverse. After 1957, total union membership in the United States began to fall and in the next five years, although the number of workers in non-agricultural employment increased by more than four million, the number enrolled in unions fell by 1·7 million. (Unions had an estimated 16·6 million members in 1956 and 14·9 million members in 1962.) The decline was especially severe in manufacturing, and within manufacturing the unions suffering the most severe losses were the Automobile Workers and the Steelworkers. Both are in industries strongly characteristic of the industrial system.[1] Between 1957 and 1962, the proportion of the non-agricultural labour force belonging to unions fell from 31·4 per cent to 26·7 per cent. In the years following 1962, large gains in employment brought a modest rise in union membership but the proportion of all workers belonging to unions continued to decline.[2]

As observed in the last chapter, white-collar workers including technical and professional workers are a rapidly expanding proportion of the labour force – they were 17·6 per cent of the labour force in 1900 and 44·5 per cent in 1965.[3] Only about

1. Data are from Leo Troy, 'Trade Union Membership, 1897–1962,' *The Review of Economics and Statistics*, Vol. XLVII, No. 1 (February 1965). The estimates from this study are somewhat lower than those of the Bureau of Labor Statistics which, however, show a similar decline. A third union which suffered a major decline in membership was the United Mine Workers. These were years of rapid consolidation and mechanization of bituminous coal production – in brief, of movement toward the industrial system. I do not suggest, of course, that all changes in union membership are explained by this one factor.

2. Through 1964, the last year for which figures are available as this is written.

3. The distribution in 1965 was white-collar workers 44·5 per cent; blue-collar workers 36·7 per cent; service workers 12·9 per cent; and farm workers 5·9 per cent. *Manpower Report of the President and a*

12 per cent of all white-collar workers belong to unions and in manufacturing the proportion is only about 5 per cent.

Nor is the white-collar worker the only problem. Production workers in areas of advanced technology – computer and data-processing industries, instrumentation, telemetry, specified electronics, and the like – are not easily organized. If the number of production workers is large and the firm has closely related branches that have unions, the new workers are often added to the existing unions without difficulty. In isolated branches or otherwise unorganized firms, or where the proportion of engineers and technicians is high, the unions do not make headway.[4, 5] The workers, in effect, become an extension of the technostructure and evidently so see themselves.

III

However, there are opposing trends. In the early stages of industrialization the working force was, as previously noted, a homogeneous mass. Members could be paid and treated alike

Report on Manpower Requirements, Resources, Utilization, and Training, United States Department of Labor, March 1966, p. 165.

4. I am indebted to my admirably informed colleague, Professor John T. Dunlop, for guidance on these observations. For a confirming view, see Solomon Barkin, 'The Decline of the Labor Movement,' in *The Corporation Takeover,* Andrew Hacker, ed. (New York: Harper, 1964), pp. 223–45.

5. The most significant recent increase in union membership of white-collar workers has been among government employees. Here, in contrast with the mature corporation, there has been no shift in the focus of control over wages and working conditions towards the worker. These remain with legislative bodies. Accordingly, it is at least possible that the white-collar public employee feels himself more removed from his employer, in sharper pecuniary conflict with him as a taxpayer and, in consequence, less inclined to identify himself with his goals than does the white-collar worker in the industrial system. However, this is speculative. A more relaxed attitude, legal and otherwise, to union membership by public employees has also contributed. And the pay of steel workers and coal-miners who retain employment frequently much exceeds that of teachers, policemen, welfare workers, nurses and civil servants in the same communities. Organization provides the best hope for equality.

or, at most, they fell into a few simple classifications. The modern working force, by contrast, is highly differentiated. The rules that regulate pay, other benefits, seniority and conditions of promotion and retirement for the various classes of workers are voluminous. Any unilateral application of such rules would, however meticulous, seem arbitrary or unjust to some. By helping to frame the rules and by participating in their administration through the grievance machinery, the union serves invaluably to mitigate the feeling that such systems or their administration are arbitrary or unjust. It is a measure of the importance of this function that, where the union does not exist, good management practice calls for the development of some substitute. In helping to prevent discontent and, therewith, a sense of alienation, the union also removes barriers to identification – barriers which once contributed to its own power.

Also, while some unions have resisted technological change, others have greatly helped it by aiding the accommodation to change. They have helped to arrange a trade of higher pay, a shorter week, severance pay or other provision for those sacrificed for smaller employment. And they have persuaded their members to accept the bargain. The industrial system attaches great importance to such help. The union leader who provides it is accorded its highest encomium, that of labour statesman.[6]

In the Soviet-type economies, the union has long had an ambiguous and somewhat unsettled role. As the historic voice of the worker in the class struggle, it had to exist and be nurtured. But unions could not be accorded any role which was inconsistent with the full identification of their members with the goals of the firm by which they were employed. In the end their functions have been much the same as those just mentioned. Along with educational and welfare activities,

---

6. John L. Lewis, once when fighting for wage and welfare improvement considered an inimical figure in American industrial relations, was eventually accorded this title for his undeviating support of mechanization of coal-mining.

which are also of some importance in some American and Western European unions, the Soviet unions serve as a channel of communications between the firm and its workers and a way of according the latter a voice in the framing of rules and in their administration.[7]

IV

However, in the non-Soviet systems the union renders a further service; it is an important factor in planning and, therewith, in the relations of the industrial system with the state.

We have already noticed that the unions assumed the principal role in winning approval of the policy of regulating aggregate demand. Though commonly billed as having the objective of providing full employment, this policy is also essential for the planning of the industrial system. Unions furthermore have a potentially important role in stabilizing demand for particular products procured by the state. Such procurement, that for defence needs in particular, cannot be claimed as something that serves the needs of the firm. It must be regarded strictly as an outgrowth of broad public policy. So, in seeking contracts, the technostructure cannot publicly plead the pressure of its own convenience, necessity or earnings. But it can with more decency plead the adverse effect of contract termination, or failure to win renewal, or denial of a new contract on its workers or the community. Here the union can be a valuable seconding voice. Such cooperation between unions and technostructure is by no means complete; in all legislative matters there is a good deal of traditional hostility to overcome.

The much more important service of the union to planning

7. David Granick, *The Red Executive* (New York: Doubleday, 1954), pp. 219 et seq. Also Emily Clark Brown, 'The Local Union in Soviet Industry: Its Relations with Members, Party and Management,' *Industrial and Labor Relations Review*, Vol. 13, No. 2 (January 1960), pp. 209 et seq.

is to standardize wage costs between different industrial firms and to ensure that changes in wages will occur at approximately the same time. This greatly assists price control by the industry. And it also greatly facilitates the public regulation of prices and wages. Both services are far more important than is commonly recognized.

Specifically, if there is an industry-wide union, one of its tasks will be to ensure that rates of pay will be more or less the same for the same kinds of work. This is done in the name of fairness and equity but it means too that no firm can reduce prices because of lower wage rates and none will be impelled to seek higher prices because its rates of pay are higher. Price-setting and maintenance where there are a number of firms are thus facilitated. So is planning.

Rates will also change when the labour contract for the industry expires. This change will affect all firms at approximately the same time and by approximately the same amount. All accordingly have a common signal to adjust their prices; the same change is called for by all. So wage adjustment and related changes, which might otherwise be a threat to minimum price setting in the industry, cease to be a serious problem.

At the same time the union contract brings wage levels within the purview of the state. The situation here is akin to that of diplomacy. It may be difficult to do business with a strong government such as that of the Soviet Union. But when business is done, something is accomplished. This is not the case where, as with the Congo, Laos or South Viet Nam, the writ of the government runs only to the airport. There is no way of enforcing that to which governments agree. Similarly wage control may be difficult with a union. The latter may resist energetically the terms. But it also brings workers within the ambit of control.

The union negotiates a bargain that is binding on all of its members. If this bargain can be influenced by the state then the level of wages is subject to influence – or control. And since collective bargaining contracts are for some period of time – a period that, in yet another accommodation to the industrial system, is tending to become longer – the number of occasions when the state must intervene is kept down to a practical number. In between, the contract acts as a ceiling on wage payments. Were wage bargains struck by individuals or for a vast number of small categories of workers, and were they of indeterminate duration, control and surveillance would be impossible.[8]

V

The union renders a yet further service. The commonplace strategy of wage and price stabilization is to hold wage increases within the amounts that can be paid from gains in productivity. The amount of the productivity gain – the increase in output per worker – only becomes known over time. And it differs for different firms. The period of the contract allows time for knowledge of the gains in productivity to accumulate and for calculation as to what increase can be afforded without prejudice to price stability. The union, since it bargains for an industry-wide membership, settles not for what the individual firm can afford, which would mean different wage rates for different firms, which would be an impossible complication, but for what all can afford as an average. This is an invaluable simplification.

The union does not render these services to wage and price stabilization deliberately or even willingly. It has no choice. Should it refuse to conform to a broad strategy of stabilization, the firms with which it has contracts would, in turn, raise their prices. If an appreciable number of unions get wage advances greater than justified by gains in productivity, then all must be accorded them. Responding price increases will then be general. And part or all of the gains from wage increases will be lost in price increases. The union will have opposed public authority, and perhaps risked popular displeasure, for gains that its own members will recognize to be transitory. This alternative

8. Rather more in the United States than in Europe where employers sometimes go beyond contract levels to attract workers.

may, on occasion, be tried. But it is not an attractive alternative. Nor is it one that strengthens the union.

In fact the industrial system has now largely encompassed the labour movement. It has dissolved some of its most important functions; it has greatly narrowed its area of action; and it has bent its residual operations very largely to its own needs. Since World War II, the acceptance of the union by the industrial firm and the emergence thereafter of an era of comparatively peaceful industrial relations have been hailed as the final triumph of trade unionism. On closer examination it is seen to reveal many of the features of Jonah's triumph over the whale.

Such then is the present stage in the journey on from the Tolpuddle Martyrs.

Chapter 25

THE EDUCATIONAL AND
SCIENTIFIC ESTATE

As the trade unions retreat, more or less permanently, into the shadows, a rapidly growing body of educators and research scientists emerges. This group connects at the edges with scientists and engineers within the technostructure and with civil servants, journalists, writers and artists outside. Most directly nurtured by the industrial system are the educators and scientists in the schools, colleges, universities and research institutions. They stand in relation to the industrial system much as did the banking and financial community to the earlier stages of industrial development. Then capital was decisive, and a vast network of banks, savings banks, insurance companies, brokerage houses and investment bankers came into existence to mobilize savings and thus to meet the need. In the mature corporation the decisive factor of production, as we have seen, is the supply of qualified talent. A similar complex of educational institutions has similarly come into being to supply this need. And the values and attitudes of the society have been appropriately altered to reinforce the change. When savings and capital were decisive, thrift was the most applauded of social virtues. It mattered not that most of the population lived and died in abysmal illiteracy and ignorance. As qualified manpower has become important, thrift, as a virtue, has acquired overtones of antiquity and even eccentricity. Education, instead, has now the greatest solemnity of social purpose.

The educational and scientific estate,[1] like the financial com-

1. There is no good term for this large group which is associated with education and scientific research apart from that undertaken by the technostructure. In political discourse they are grouped with writers and poets and referred to either as intellectuals or eggheads. The first term is too restrictive in its connotation and if not too restrictive, too pre-

munity before it, acquires prestige from the productive agent that it supplies. Potentially, at least, this is also a source of power. Likewise, and even more than the financial community, it acquires a position within the apparatus of government. The nature of this educational and scientific estate, the sources of its influence and its relation to the technostructure and the state are the next subject for consideration.

II

The parallel between the financial community and the educational and scientific estate cannot be carried too far. Both owe (or owed) their prestige and influence to their association with the decisive factor of production. But the power of the financial community was that of the hand that holds the spigot. It could turn the supply of capital for a user off or on. Appearances in connexion with the use of this power, it should be noted, are untrustworthy. Power must always be exercised with appropriate gravity of demeanour. If a man must be subject to the authority of another, he can at least ask that it not be an occasion for glee. Financial transactions – a new issue of stock or debentures, the provision of a new line of credit – are still occasions for solemn ritual even though the transactions are not greatly more complex than the purchase of a typewriter, and alternatives are readily available. This is a carry-over from the days when power was involved. Much of the ceremony that surrounds the largely ministerial functions of a central bank is of the same order.[2] None of this should be allowed to obscure the reality which is that the power has passed.[3]

tentious. The second is insufficiently solemn. One should coin a new term only as a last resort; we have a great many words already and new ones always afflict the ears. Accordingly, I have appropriated and somewhat altered the usage of my friend Professor Don K. Price who speaks of the scientific community (including that part employed by industry and the government) as The Scientific Estate. I am much indebted to his valuable book by this title (Cambridge: Harvard University Press, 1965).

2. The insistence in the United States that the central bank should, nominally at least, be independent of the Federal executive reflects a

The educational and scientific estate has no control over the supply of talent similar to that of the banker over access to savings. It can to some slight extent influence its people on their choice of employment and this is not an insignificant sanction. But most of its influence follows from its rapidly increasing numbers with consequent political implication; from its privileged access to scientific innovation; and on its nearly unique role in social innovation. These are the sources of influence to be examined.

Until well along in the present century the educational community in the United States was very small and concerned largely with elementary education. This has changed explosively in recent times. College and university teachers, who numbered 24,000 in 1900 and 49,000 in 1920 will total 480,000 by the end of this decade. This is a twentyfold increase in seventy years. Only 238,000 students were enrolled in all colleges and universities in 1900 as compared with 3,377,000 in 1959 and a prospective 6,700,000 in 1969. Only 669,000 were in high school grades in 1900 as compared with 9,271,000 in 1959 and a prospective 14,600,000 in 1969.[4] In the early industrial system only a modest number were needed with advanced technical or other skills. Colleges and universities were principally required to train men for the learned professions – medicine, law, the church, veterinary medicine and the like – or to supply the very exiguous cultural adornment thought appropriate to the offspring of the well-to-do.

Apart from their numerical insignificance, educators in the earlier stages of industrial development – in the United States

_____

similar nostalgia. It is a reminder of the days when the central bank could facilitate or prevent borrowing by the government and thus control its policies on taxation and expenditure.

3. Specifically, by way of reminder, that power depends on the absence of alternatives and the fact that when capital is abundant and the firm has internal sources of savings, it has such alternatives.

4. Figures are from the Office of Education, Department of Health, Education and Welfare. Total educational expenditures, which were approximately $275 million, in current dollars, in 1900, are estimated to reach $42·5 billion in 1970.

until well into this century – were also, economically, an inferior caste. Funds for financing higher education in private colleges and universities came from the well-to-do either in the form of charitable gifts or as tuition paid on behalf of their offspring. It was naturally assumed that here as elsewhere provision of money accorded right of proprietorship. This should be exercised by the men most accustomed to wielding such authority, namely the business entrepreneurs. 'The modern civilized community is reluctant to trust its serious interests to others than men of pecuniary substance, who have proved their fitness for the direction of academic affairs by acquiring, or by otherwise being possessed of, considerable wealth.'[5] The principle, having been accepted for private institutions, was applied to public colleges and universities as well. These also, since attendance involved both expense and ability to defer earning a living, were enclaves for individuals of much better than average income.

The doctrine of financial paramountcy – of the ultimate power of those who paid the bills – was not fully accepted by the academic community. In principle, and on occasion even in practice, educators asserted their right to speak their minds and even to criticize those who paid their salaries. This tendency was associated with a sharp conflict of goals. The entrepreneur had a straightforward pecuniary measure of success. A man was judged by what he made. But the application of any such measure in the academic community would have either conceded mass failure, given the modest pay, or have been immoderately expensive. So while educators on occasion admitted inferiority, and more often simply assumed it, many also professed the goals that they held to be intellectually more demanding or aesthetically more refined than the pecuniary preoccupations of the entrepreneur. This was ill received. As a result, suspicion and dislike, leading recurrently to minor conflict between the business and academic communities, was

5. Thorstein Veblen, *The Higher Learning in America*. A memorandum on the conduct of universities by businessmen (Stanford: Academic Reprints, 1954), pp. 67–8.

until recent times an established feature of the American academic scene.[6, 7]

This conflict was aggravated by the role of the colleges and universities as a principal source of social innovation in the United States. While they have great power in carrying or resisting legislation, business firms, unions and those professionally concerned with politics in the United States are not socially inventive. On the contrary they are, in this respect, comparatively sterile. Some ideas for social change come from unattached reformers and the bureaucracy. But their most important source for many years has been the academic community.

In the early stages of industrialization, most of these suggestions were for the purpose of making industrial development more equitable, humane or just. The need for such reform was always far more evident to the professors than to those who saw themselves as their natural masters. The latter had to look on while proposals for limiting monopoly power, regulating prices or rates of natural monopolies, encouraging and protecting unions, making taxes more progressive, supporting the

---

6. The tension created by this relationship extended into the universities and colleges themselves. College presidents and other administrative officials were obliged by necessity or conviction to defend the value system of their boards of trustees and the larger business community. In doing so they frequently aroused the mistrust or contempt of the faculty. An even more interesting case is that of the business school or faculty of business administration. In virtually all universities of academic merit, its professors were until fairly recent times accorded a second-class citizenship. The allegedly unsubstantial character of the subject matter was partial cause. But the professor of business administration was also required by his position to accept and even avow the goals of the business entrepreneur but without receiving his emoluments. Thus he had the worst of all worlds – the comparative indigence of the academic community but without its pretension to superior goals.

7. The alienation of the artist and unattached intellectual from the business community had similar sources. Business imposed a pecuniary valuation on this work. In a community in which the educational and cultural standards were accommodated to the requirements of the early industrial system, the standards of taste were not high. Also, the market for new cultural wares, even of modest sophistication, could be very

bargaining position of farmers, limiting the exploitation of natural resources, regulating conditions of employment, and, on occasion, for abolishing private entrepreneurship, emanated from the colleges and universities and were defended as an exercise of academic freedom. Nor did these reforms remain an academic matter. Many had a tendency to be taken up.

Without question, inconvenient views were often muted by discretion or suppressed. Academic expression was accommodated to 'the views and prepossessions prevalent among the respectable, conservative middle class; with a more particular regard to that more select body of substantial citizens who have the disposal of accumulated wealth'.[8] But this is not the whole story. A very large amount of legislation or policy regarded as highly inimical by the entrepreneurial enterprise received its initial impetus from the academic community. Laws against monopoly, regulating access to the capital markets, in support of a wide range of welfare measures, in support of progressive taxation owed much to such origins.

During the years of burgeoning industrial development, the academic community – indigent, subordinate and weak – has invariably been pictured by historians in its relation to business as the aggrieved party. On the record this is not so certain. In consequence of its capacity for social invention, it may well have given more than it received. This has been obscured partly by the fact that members of the academic community have written the history, no minor source of power in itself, and also by the different ways in which influence manifests itself. Pecuniary power expresses itself in highly unsubtle form; it offers financial reward for conformity or threatens financial damage for dissent. Proposals for reform, by contrast, begin

thin. So the pecuniary value placed on the work of the artist or intellectual was low. They accordingly ascribed their own value to their work and dismissed that of the businessman as inherently bogus, vulgar or naïve. These adjectives were synonymous with bourgeois taste. On this, see the discussion of Seymour Martin Lipset in *Political Man* (New York: Doubleday, 1960), pp. 318 et seq.

8. Veblen, op. cit., p. 194.

as seemingly eccentric and implausible suggestions. Gradually they gain adherents; in time they emerge as grave needs; and then they become fundamental human rights. It is not so easy to attribute power to those who set this process in motion.

The power that is associated with capacity for social innovation is important for what follows. For the moment, it is sufficient that it once provided a very good reason for conflict between the entrepreneurial enterprise and the academic community.[9]

III

With the rise of the technostructure, relations between those associated with economic enterprise and the educational and scientific estate undergo a radical transformation. There is no longer an abrupt conflict in motivation. Like the educational and scientific estate, the technostructure is no longer exclusively, or perhaps even primarily, responsive to pecuniary motivation. Both see themselves as identified with social goals, or with organizations serving social purposes. And both, it may be assumed, seek to adapt social goals to their own. If there is difference it is not in the motivational system but in the goals.

At this stage, the educational and scientific estate is no longer small; on the contrary, it is very large. It is no longer dependent on private income and wealth for its support; most of its sustenance is provided by the state. Private influence is weakened in an important further respect. The entrepreneur

9. We have here explanation of the seemingly neurotic preoccupation of conservative organizations and individuals in the United States with education and especially with the ideas held and taught in the universities. Such groups reflect entrepreneurial attitudes; they are strongly applauded by the independent oil man or real estate operator, and disdained by the self-respecting member of the technostructure. And the complainants are not wrong in believing both that the colleges and universities are influential and that they have been the source of the ideas that have brought about their decline. Accordingly, their reaction, however discomfiting, is not without cause. Academic people should be philosophical. They cannot, as on occasion in the past, hope to combine influence for their ideas with immunity from attack.

combined a strong proprietary instinct with owned wealth. The members of the technostructure, though they may be generously rewarded by salary and capital gains, are unlikely to have any similar amount of wealth at their disposal. Owners – those known to the modern academic money-raiser as the old rich – do. And the alternative to the use of such wealth for education is often an only moderately lower loss through taxation. But being divorced from influence in the corporation, these men no longer reflect its attitudes in any reliable way. And they are considerably less likely than the erstwhile entrepreneur to expect to exercise influence as the result of the support they accord. They have learned from their experience with corporate ownership that wealth does not accord such power of intervention.

Meanwhile the technostructure has become deeply dependent on the educational and scientific estate for its supply of trained manpower. It needs also to maintain a close relation with the scientific sector of this estate to ensure that it is safely abreast of scientific and technological innovation. And, unlike the entrepreneurial corporation, the mature corporation is much less troubled by the social inventiveness of the educational and scientific estate. The costs of reform legislation – improvements in medical care, guaranteed incomes for the poor, regeneration of slums – can be passed forward to customers or back to stockholders. The burden of interpreting or abiding by regulation is absorbed by lawyers, accountants, industrial relations specialists and other parts of the corporate bureaucracy. By contrast, the entrepreneur paid for – and the smaller one struggled with – the regulation by himself. The burden of regulation like that of taxation is appreciably lessened by having it fall on someone else.[10]

10. The resistance of the doctors to Federal measures for improved medical care is at least partly so explained. '. . . the practitioner of medicine is a member of the shrinking body of American entrepreneurs. Most doctors continue to "run their own businesses" and are understandably opposed to interference with their economic affairs. . . .' 'Why Are Doctors Out of Step?' by Louis Lasagna, *The New Republic*, 2 January 1965.

Also, it must be borne in mind that two important recent measures of social innovation – the regulation of aggregate demand and the stabilization of price and wages – are both important for planning and thus for the success of the techno-structure. The latter, we have seen, is not indifferent to its own interest.

Further – and perhaps a lesser matter – social innovation no longer has overtones of revolution, and the academic, like the large intellectual, community no longer engages in disquieting conversation on revolutions. This too is the result of the intricate web of change which we are here unravelling. The revolution, as delineated by Marx, assumed the progressive immiserization of the working class. Instead of the expected impoverishment there has been increasing affluence. Marxists no longer deny this or convincingly suggest that worker well-being is illusory or transitory. The revolution was to be catalysed by the capitalist crisis – the apocalyptic depression which would bring an already attenuated structure down in ruins. But the industrial system has, as an integral requirement, an arrangement for regulating aggregate demand which, while permitting it to plan, gives promise of preventing or mitigating depression. So the danger of an apocalyptic crisis seems more remote. The trade union, militantly expressing the power of the worker, was to be the cutting edge of the revolution. But the industrial system mellows and even absorbs the union. Most important perhaps, of all, the revolution has occurred in some countries. And there the lineaments of industrialization – planning, large producing organizations, the resulting discipline, the measures of success by economic growth – no longer seem as different as they did in the fears and hopes of a half century ago. Everything on which the revolution seemed to depend, and even the revolution itself, has disintegrated. Not even academic disputation can easily survive such erosion.

As might be expected, the new dependence of the technostructure on the educational and scientific estate is reflected in the relation between the two. The business executive no longer sits on the college board as a source of worldly knowledge and guardian against social heresy. Rather it is because he is accorded a traditional obeisance. And his presence provides him with an opportunity to maintain closer liaison with sources of talent or to keep more closely abreast of scientific and technological innovation. While the corporation president has become increasingly a traditional or ceremonial figure in his association with education, the modern scholar of science, mathematics, information systems or communications theory is ever more in demand to guide the mature corporation through its besetting problems of science, technology and computerization. The name of a famous banker on a board of directors once advertised to the world that the corporation had access to the full capital resources of the economy. Now, the name of a scientist or, at a minimum, a college president is displayed, along with those of former Air Force generals, to show that the firm is attuned to the very latest in technological advance.

In social matters we customarily attribute to improving intelligence or virtue or better manners what, in fact, is brought by circumstance. In the context of the earlier difference in motivation and goals between the academic community and the entrepreneurial firm, the more articulate and dedicated entrepreneurs recurrently denounced professors for long-haired radicalism, impractical idealism, irrelevant theorizing, suborning attacks on the constitution and the rights of private property, and for failing to support individual freedom which, in context, meant, in the main, freedom to make money. This now only rarely happens. The member of the technostructure finds little in university discussion that so arouses him. And if he were to express such sentiments he would promptly be warned by more circumspect colleagues that he was making life unnecessarily difficult for those who visit campuses to recruit talent and that he risked having his more distinguished academic consultants take their knowledge and their possible secrets to some less vocal leadership.

v

The question remains as to how closely the educational and scientific estate, which owes its modern expansion and eminence to the requirements of the industrial system, will identify itself with the goals of the latter. No generalization is possible, for the educational and scientific estate is not homogenous. We have seen that economics, as a discipline, has extensively and rather subtly accommodated itself to the goals of the industrial system. Conclusions which are not serviceable to these goals – which minimize the role of the market and profit maximization, accord importance to the effect of advertising on and cast doubt on consumer sovereignty or the approved sequence, or look candidly on the close association of the mature corporation with the state – have an aspect of heresy. The same tendencies can doubtless be expected elsewhere. The chemist who devotes a substantial share of his time to Du Pont or Monsanto can be expected to identify himself with the goals of these corporations. He may also have some adaptive effect on university goals – his department may come to measure its success less by the quality of its teaching and research than by the number of its commercial and governmental contracts, the size of its physical plant and the growth in its personnel and payroll. Economic growth is here a goal. At the same time numerous other scholarly disciplines – the classics, humanities, some of the social sciences – are largely unaffected by this new relation with the technostructure. They will retain and (observing the prosperity and perquisites of their scientific colleagues) avow with increasing vehemence the older goals of the academy. They will criticize their scientific colleagues for doing excessively purposive research, for no longer having a primary obligation to knowledge and its transmission and, implicitly, for abandoning the vow of academic poverty. The scientists will reply with hurt protestations of the immunity of their virtue to pecuniary corruption and the need for someone to pay the bills. This is already a familiar discussion in nearly all larger universities.

VI

But there remain more general sources of conflict between the educational and scientific estate and the technostructure. One is the management of individual behaviour.

In the absence of a clear view of the nature of this conflict, much of the dispute centres not on its ultimate causes but on the techniques of management. Management requires extensive access to means of communication – newspapers, billboards, radio and especially television. To ensure attention these media must be raucous and dissonant. It is also of the utmost importance that this effort convey an impression, however mere-tricious, of the importance of the goods being sold. The market for soap can only be managed if the attention of consumers is captured for what, otherwise, is a rather incidental artifact. Accordingly, the smell of soap, the texture of its suds, the whiteness of textiles treated thereby and the resulting esteem and prestige in the neighbourhood are held to be of highest moment. Housewives are imagined to discuss such matters with an intensity otherwise reserved for unwanted pregnancy and nuclear war. Similarly with cigarettes, laxatives, pain-killers, beer, automobiles, dentrifices, packaged foods and all other significant consumer products.

The educational and scientific estate and the larger intellectual community tend to view this effort with disdain. The technostructure, sensing this but aware also of the vital importance of the management of demand, reacts defensively and with earnest protestations of its importance for the health and survival of the economic system. Its case is closer to the truth than is commonly imagined.

Thus the paradox. The economy for its success requires organized public bamboozlement. At the same time it nurtures

297

a growing class which feels itself superior to such bamboozlement and deplores it as intellectually corrupt. The sub-culture which requires such obfuscation for its existence can only be regarded with disdain. That culture responds with a sense of hurt and guilt and the indignation which comes from the knowledge that its needs sustain and nourish its academic critics.

This conflict, in one form or another, is inevitable with planning. That requires that the needs of the producing mechanism take precedence over the freely expressed will of the individual. This will always invite the disaffection of the individual. In the Soviet-type economies the resentment is expressed against the state and the heavy and visible apparatus by which it exercises control over the individual. Under non-Soviet planning it is expressed against the techniques and instruments – advertising and the mass communications which carry it – by which the individual is managed. Curiously in neither society does the attack centre on the planning which is the deeper cause.

VII

Finally, there is potential competition and conflict between the educational and scientific estate and the technostructure growing out of their respective relations to the state. The member of the technostructure is strongly inhibited in his political role. He cannot divest himself of the organization which gives him being. And he cannot carry it with him into political life. On the other hand, he wields great public influence as, in effect, an extended arm of the bureaucracy.

The educational and scientific estate is not inhibited politically by the ties of organization. It is also growing rapidly in numbers. It still lacks a sense of its own identity. It has also sat for many years under the shadow of entrepreneurial power. A seemingly respectable measure of cynicism as well as a residual Marxism join in deprecating any political power not founded firmly on the possession of money. Yet it is possible that the educational and scientific estate requires only a strongly creative political hand to become a decisive instrument of political power. This could, in turn, threaten established associations between the bureaucracy and the technostructure, for they, in a fashion not different from the management of demand for consumer products, require a substantial measure of popular illusion. I now turn to these matters.

Chapter 26

THE INDUSTRIAL SYSTEM
AND THE STATE I

QUALIFIED manpower is decisive for the success of the industrial system. The education on which it depends is provided mostly in the public sector of the economy. By contrast, capital, which was once decisive, comes mostly from the private economy. The market for the most advanced technology and that which best allows of planning is also in the public sector. Much scientific and technical innovation comes from, or is sponsored by, the state or by publicly supported universities and research institutions. The state regulates the aggregate demand for the products of the industrial system. This is indispensable for its planning. And, still discreetly and with infirmity of intent, somewhat in the manner of a conservative cleric viewing an erotic statue, the state provides the wage and price regulation without which prices in the industrial system are unstable. Clearly the modern organized economy was designed with a perverse hand. For how, otherwise, could so many needs seeming so inescapable conspire to make a system which still rejoices in the name of free enterprise in truth be so dependent on government?

The industrial system, in fact, is inextricably associated with the state. In notable respects the mature corporation is an arm of the state. And the state, in important matters, is an instrument of the industrial system. This runs strongly counter to the accepted doctrine. That assumes and affirms a clear line between government and private business enterprise. The position of this line – what is given to the state and what is accorded to private enterprise – tells whether the society is socialist or non-socialist. Nothing is so important. Any union between public and private organization is held, by liberal and conservative alike, to be deviant sin. To the liberal it means that public power has been captured for private advantage and profit. To the conservative it means that high private prerogative has been lost to the state. In fact, the line between public and private authority in the industrial system is indistinct and in large measure imaginary, and the abhorrent association of public and private organizations is normal. When this is perceived, the central trends in American economic and political life become clear. On few matters is an effort to free the mind more rewarding.

The relationship between the technostructure and the state is very different from that between the state and the entrepreneurial enterprise. This difference is our point of departure.

II

The relationship between the state and the entrepreneurial corporation was, like all of the other relationships of this entity, principally pecuniary. It was also unstable with a tendency to be a zero sum game. The corporation might be strong. Then it would be independent of public restraint. It might even use public power to enhance its own revenues. Or the state might be strong in which case it curbed the private power, and therewith the profits, of the entrepreneur. If extremely powerful, the state would move to socialize such enterprise. Weakness on one side would be exploited by the other. Constant and reciprocal vigilance would be necessary to prevent domination of the state by business or of business by the state.

Such was the common view of the relationship between the entrepreneurial corporation and the state. The balance in this relationship is assumed to have altered over time. Seventy-five years ago, in the United States, it was believed the corporation was naturally the paramount power. Business control of the state was the thing to fear. Men of subtle mind agreed with Marx that the state would come to be the executive committee of capitalist enterprise. With the passage of time, however, fear of business domination receded while fear of state domination increased. The corporation was once the octopus. This became the image of government. Where entrepreneurs had once gathered in the Senate to consider the needs of their class, they now gathered in convention to deplore the intentions of Washington. Golf, once an opportunity for consolidating power over some aspect of the life of the community, became an occasion for collective complaint about bureaucrats. Both the earlier and later fears reflect the circumstances of the entrepreneurial corporation. Though both continue to influence contemporary attitudes, neither reflects the modern reality.

As noted, the relationship of the entrepreneurial corporation to the state, in accordance with the principle of consistency, was primarily a pecuniary one. The state had much to offer that was of pecuniary advantage and, through taxation and regulation, it could do much to deny revenues to the corporation. The entrepreneurial corporation, in turn, had much with which to pay for what it wanted. And it had few legal or other barriers to doing so.

Thus the state, through the tariff, could accord the entrepreneur protection from foreign competition; it also had railroad, power or other public utility franchises to grant; it possessed land, mineral rights, forests and other natural resources for private exploitation; it could offer exemption or mitigation of taxes; and it could provide moral or armed support in managing refractory workers. As a further and important point, these and other benefits could all be given or withheld in response to relatively simple decision.

The entrepreneurial enterprise had, in turn, the ability to deploy financial resources for political ends that reflected its advantage. The entrepreneur unites in his own person the right to receive and dispose of the revenues of the enterprise. So revenues are at his command for purchase of votes, legislators or legislative action. If he is subject to some legal constraint in the expenditure of corporate funds for political purposes, he can transfer them, as dividends, to himself and his associates and spend from a privy purse. The public benefits so purchased accrue to the entrepreneur. This, along with the commitment to pecuniary motivation, meant that the entrepreneurial corporation had every incentive to spend for political advantage. The financial resources of the corporation could be fully deployed for political purposes and that by the men who derived personal advantage from doing so.

In a society where economic activity is subject strongly to pecuniary motivation, such motivation will seem normal in the relations between business firms and the state. It will be assumed that public officials will be responsive to opportunity for pecuniary gain. Nor will this seem totally iniquitous. Where the society approves and applauds moneymaking as the highest social purpose, public servants will often think it appropriate that they sell themselves or their decisions for what they are worth to the buyers.

In the heyday of the entrepreneurial corporation this occurred. The company town and the company-dominated state – California of the Southern Pacific, Montana of Anaconda, Pennsylvania of the steel and coal companies, Michigan of the automobile companies – were familiar features of the industrial landscape. It was assumed that Congressmen and Senators would be the spokesmen, paid or otherwise, of the industrial firms of their states or districts. From those so financed or controlled, the entrepreneurial corporation got much of what it wanted. The control was not absolute but it was sufficiently extensive to justify belief in corporate domination as a normal fact of life.

To this day, the independent entrepreneur – the highway contractor, insurance firm, real estate operator, loan shark – is the most important source of political funds and the principal remaining exponent of purchased influence. Those who have won major distinction in this general area in modern times have all been independent entrepreneurs. Texas oil operators, almost alone among modern businessmen, are able to obtain implicit obedience from their state's Congressional delegation.

While the entrepreneurial corporation had resources with which to purchase pecuniary opportunity from the state, it was also independent of the state. Its revenues were made in the market. Thence came its instructions. Had it need to fight the state, the battle might cost it money but it would not be mortal.

III

In time, as noted, the fear that the corporation would dominate the state was matched and replaced by the fear that the state would dominate business. This change occurred especially in the thirties. There were two causes: the rise of the trade union and the response of the state to the new needs of the industrial system.

The Great Depression gave a strong impetus to the trade union movement. By destroying his alternatives and thus increasing the element of compulsion in his attachment to his job, the depression arrested any tendency for the worker to identify himself with the goals of his employer. And it made the union more important to the worker. He needed its support against pressures for wage reduction. As his alternatives dwindled the union compensated for his weakness and countered his sense of compulsion. As they grew in membership in this favourable environment, the unions became a factor in politics; as their role was adversary within the corporation so it was adversary in their influence on the state. What the unions lacked in financial resources they compensated for in voting power. They found an ally in the emerging educational and scientific[1] estate with its long-standing alienation from the entrepreneurial corporation. This, with some support from the farmers, was the heart of the Roosevelt coalition. It was easy for business enterprise to imagine that it was about to pass under the political authority of a state permanently dominated by the unions and the 'intellectuals'.

At the same time the entrepreneurial corporation was giving way steadily to the mature corporation and to control by the technostructure. In their study of the 200 largest non-financial

1. Still rather more educational in this period than scientific.

corporations in 1930, Berle and Means found that, by then, 44 per cent of the firms by numbers and 58 per cent by wealth were effectively controlled by their management.[2]

For direct political action the technostructure is far more circumscribed than the entrepreneur. This is a matter of prime importance. The members of the technostructure do not themselves receive the revenues of the corporation. An early gesture, designed to limit the political advantage of the business enterprise resulting from its wealth, prohibited the use of corporate funds for political purposes. This did not greatly hurt the entrepreneur; he could, as noted, transfer the funds to his own account as dividends and spend with impunity. But this the technostructure cannot do; it does not get the dividends.

Nor does it have the same incentive to do so. Bribery of public officials, purchase of the electorate or promiscuous use of financial power to influence public decision (e.g. the threat to discharge workers or close a plant) are not especially prestigious activities. They often result in unpleasant publicity; there is risk in all bribery that the practitioner's hand will slip and that he will be publicly pilloried by all who have not received his subvention and by the more adaptable of those who have. These risks were often worthwhile for the entrepreneur; the mantle of the sanguinary industrial pirate can be worn with some comfort if the wearer receives the loot. But it is not something one does on a salary.

The technostructure is also handicapped in its political activity by its collegial character. Political leadership, persuasion and action are activities of individuals; they are not readily undertaken by men who are accustomed to operating as a group. The mature corporation is run by committees. But

2. That is to say, the Board of Directors was selected by the management rather than by the stockholders and, in turn, selected the management. Adolf Berle and Gardiner Means, *The Modern Corporation and Private Property* (New York: Macmillan, 1934), p. 94. In effective control of important decisions, as discussed in Chapter 8, the erosion of the power of the owners had, unquestionably, gone much farther.

the suborning of a legislature or even the persuasion of an electorate is accomplished, on the whole, by men working as individuals.

This point cannot be carried too far. The technostructure has ready access to communications media – press, television, radio – and thus to political influence. In mature corporations which have particular need for favourable political action – the alcoholic beverage industry has in the past been an example – executives pay themselves salaries which provide a margin for political purposes. Much minor bribery is still used by mature corporations to buy needed action or inaction from state legislatures. And ample funds are available for persuasive lobbying, as distinct from the older forms of direct purchase of legislators or votes. Nevertheless the conclusion stands. The technostructure of the mature corporation is far less able to deploy financial resources for political purposes than was the entrepreneurial corporation, has less incentive to do so and, in consequence of its group character, is far less effective in direct political action.

The opposition to the rising power of the state in the thirties, like opposition to the rising power of the unions, was led not by the mature corporations but by the surviving entrepreneurs. The names of Ernest Weir, Thomas Girdler, Henry Ford, the du Ponts and Sewell Avery are associated with this resistance. General Motors, General Electric, U.S. Steel and other mature corporations were much more inclined to accept such innovations as NRA, to be somewhat more philosophical about Roosevelt and otherwise to accommodate themselves to the New Deal.

IV

Nor is this all. We have seen that much government activity has a very different effect on the entrepreneurial corporation as compared with the mature corporation. What is damaging to the first is benign for the second. This began to be evident in the thirties and became increasingly so thereafter. The striking case was the regulation of aggregate demand. Such regulation, we have sufficiently seen, is essential for the effective planning of the industrial system and, accordingly, for the security and success of the technostructure. A large public sector, supported by a progressive tax structure and with such added offsets to declining income as unemployment insurance, is not welcome in itself. But it is the fulcrum of the regulatory apparatus. Members of the technostructure do not themselves have to pay the corporation income tax which is a central part of this machinery. It falls on the stockholders or, given the control of prices, can be passed along to customers. Social security taxes and associated record-keeping are, for the technostructure, merely administrative problems to be solved.

The entrepreneurial corporation, by contrast, had less need for the regulation of aggregate demand, and its owners stood much more of the cost. Being in an earlier stage of development, it did less planning. So it was less troubled by fluctuations in demand. The entrepreneur was answerable to himself for a failure in earnings; however disagreeable, it did not necessarily threaten his survival. He had less organization to protect. Meanwhile since he sought, in principle, to maximize earnings, higher corporation taxes came out of that maximum and with incidence on himself. Similarly with his share of social security taxes. And similarly with administrative costs and annoyances.

Other accommodation by the state to the needs of the industrial system also had a contrasting effect. The entrepreneurial corporation, again as a result of its lower level of development, had less need for the trained personnel that the state provided. Its technology being more primitive, it had less to gain from public underwriting of research and markets. Unions, the subject of state encouragement and support, perform, we have just seen, a ministerial and communications role for the mature corporation; for the entrepreneurial corporation their purpose remained the winning of a larger share of the profits. Restraints on prices which for the mature corporation helped ensure wage and price stability could be a way of reducing returns for the entrepreneur.

It would be a mistake to paint this contrast in unduly sharp tones. The tendency nonetheless is unmistakable. What seemed, at first glance, to be a damaging accession of power by the state was damaging principally to the entrepreneurial corporation. For the mature corporation it was not. Rather, it reflected the accommodation of the state to its needs.

From the thirties on, the fear of government by business seemed to be a uniform and permanent feature of the American political landscape. 'Opposition to government is more than disaffection from the policies of a particular party or administration. The [American business] creed contains a generalized distrust and scorn of politicians and bureaucrats, whatever the party and whatever the politics they advocate and execute.'[3]

But appearances are deceiving. Until comparatively recent times the tone and attitude of business in these matters were set by the entrepreneurs. Being without the political inhibition of organization, they were most outspoken. Unlike members of the technostructure they also had grievances. The members of the technostructure said nothing or they echoed the complaints of the entrepreneurs about government for this was the conventional wisdom of the businessman. Or they reacted only to their need for autonomy on internal decisions. The staffs of the business organizations continued, under inertial guidance, to recite the liturgy of entrepreneurial complaint. Entrepreneurs did not see that the accommodation of the state to the needs of the mature corporation was a substantial source of their discomfort. They did not see that they were, in effect, the victims of a passive conspiracy between other businessmen and the state.

3. Francis X. Sutton, Seymour E. Harris, Carl Kaysen and James Tobin, *The American Business Creed* (Cambridge: Harvard University Press, 1956).

v

The threads may now be drawn together. Business in its relations with the state is anything but homogeneous. Once, in the day of the entrepreneur and the entrepreneurial corporation, it was so. And it was also transcendent in its direct political power – its power over votes and legislators. The mature corporation does not exercise similar power. But it has won an accommodation by the state to its needs that is highly favourable. And this accommodation has not been nearly so favourable to the surviving entrepreneurs. Their position in relation to the state has been substantially weakened. While they seemed to have the general support of all business they, in fact, did not.[4] The mature corporations were all the time seeking many of the things the entrepreneurs most opposed.

It will be evident that at this stage there is a certain puzzle in the political position of the mature corporation. As we have seen, its capacity for, and incentive to, direct political action – management of the electorate, control of legislatures, procurement of legislation – is much less than that of its entrepreneurial antecedents. But, at the same time, the trend of public policy has been highly favourable to its needs. If this is accidental it reflects from the point of view of the mature corporation one of the happiest conjunctions of circumstance in history. But to explain anything of this importance in the closely interlocked system we are here examining as an accident would be odd. And it is nothing of the kind. As the

4. In 1964, the independent entrepreneurs, large and small, were mostly for Senator Goldwater. His domestic programme – shrinkage of the Federal government, less reliance on progressive taxes, aversion to social security – was consistent with their interest. It was not consistent with the interest of the technostructure and it is noteworthy that this group shifted in large numbers to the Democratic Party. On the changing political alignments of businessmen in this election as indicated by campaign contributions, see Herbert E. Alexander and Harold B. Meyers, 'The Switch in Campaign Giving', *Fortune*, November 1965.

industrial system in general, and the mature corporation in particular, have lost direct political power, they have acquired other methods of influencing social action of far, far greater significance. These explain the benign tendencies, from their viewpoint, of the state.

Chapter 27

THE INDUSTRIAL SYSTEM
AND THE STATE II

... power in the N.A.M. used to center [on the presidents
of] ... the middle-sized companies.... Most of them are
gone now; they have been replaced by representatives of the
major corporations whose biggest customer is government,
which, as the biggest customer, has a claim to be if not
always, at least often enough, right. MURRAY KEMPTON,
The New Republic, 18 December 1965.

The N.A.S.A. administrator ... stated that a government
agency could not contract out the entire management of
a new technology such as space systems. It must have
competence to specify the tasks it wants industry to perform.
MURRAY L. WEIDENBAUM, *Challenge, The Magazine
of Economic Affairs*, May/June 1966.

THE entrepreneurial firm had a pecuniary relationship with
society. The market transmitted to the entrepreneur the instructions of the consumer in the only language that the
market can employ – namely the offer of more or less revenue
for more or less product. His relationship with his employees
was predominantly pecuniary; they served him not for love or
duty but for money. The governing factor in his relationship
to the state was the same; the principle of consistency holds as
always. He sought to influence the state in order to enhance
his pecuniary return. The state obtained his services when
needed by paying for them. It used its tax and regulatory
powers to influence his behaviour and regulate his income. As
in relations between entrepreneur and employees, that between
entrepreneur and state regularly involved conflict over the
amount of the return. This conflict minimized or excluded
identification by the entrepreneurial corporation with the goals
of the state. It especially did as the balance in this relationship
swung from control of the state by the entrepreneur to a substantial fear of the reverse.

311

We have seen that the technostructure of the mature corporation neither deploys the resources nor has the incentive for purchase of political power. At the same time it has become much more dependent on the state. The entrepreneurial corporation, from public resources to favourable tariffs to tax concessions, had much to get from the state. And from adverse regulation and higher taxation it had considerable to lose. But, apart from the provision of law and order which on occasion it supplied to itself, it was not deeply dependent on the government. The mature corporation by contrast depends on the state for trained manpower, the regulation of aggregate demand, for stability in wages and prices. All are essential to the planning with which it replaces the market. The state, through military and other technical procurement, underwrites the corporation's largest capital commitments in its area of most advanced technology. The mature corporation cannot buy political power. Yet, obviously, it would seem to require it.

Its influence on the state is, in fact, much greater than that of the entrepreneurial corporation. Those who look for it usually look in the wrong place. Given the past pre-eminence of pecuniary relationships, they naturally look for these. They look for legislators who are in the pay of corporations and for public officials who are responsive to financial blandishment. They delve for five-per-centers and lobbyists who dispense alcohol, mink, vicuña, freezers, hospitality in Nassau and New York hotel suites and the attention of far more vivid and adaptable young women than the public servant encounters of an evening in Falls Church. The best discovery of all is of a traditionalist who carries money in a black bag. These last are rare but every year one or more exponents of one or another of the techniques of bribery is discovered and drummed out of the company of respectable men, often with the help of those who, until recently, had thought well of such resourcefulness. These victims are the archaic survivors of an earlier era and methodology. Their public destruction for minor peculation – it rarely amounts to the price of the most insignificant modern weapon – is a purification rite. Minor sin is washed away in an orgiastic burst of indignation. Iniquitous influence is thus extirpated from government. It may well be to the advantage of the industrial system that simple men should continue to suppose that influence is exerted on the state principally by such means.

II

Members of the technostructure, we have seen, identify themselves with its goals because they find these goals superior to their own and because there is a chance of adapting them to their own. The relationship of the technostructure of the mature corporation to the state is the same. The state is strongly concerned with the stability of the economy. And with its expansion or growth. And with education. And with technical and scientific advance. And, most notably, with the national defence. These are *the* national goals; they are sufficiently trite so that one has a reassuring sense of the obvious in articulating them. All have their counterpart in the needs and goals of the technostructure. It requires stability in demand for its planning. Growth brings promotion and prestige. It requires trained manpower. It needs government underwriting of research and development. Military and other technical procurement support its most developed form of planning. At each point the government has goals with which the technostructure can identify itself. Or, plausibly, these goals reflect adaptation of public goals to the goals of the technostructure. As the individual serves the technostructure in response to a complex system of motivation in which identification and adaptation are extremely important, so the same motivation is reflected in the relations of the mature corporation to the state. Again we find the principle of consistency rendering faithful service. Therein lies the influence of the mature corporation – an influence which makes purely pecuniary relationships pallid by comparison.

Let us now give these abstractions specific form – and put them to test.

III

The practical manifestation of this process is to be seen most clearly in defence procurement. With the $60 billion it spends for this purpose each year (as this is written) the Department of Defense supports, as noted, the most highly developed planning in the industrial system. It provides contracts of long duration, calling for large investment of capital in areas of advanced technology. There is no risk of price fluctuations. There is full protection against any change in requirements, i.e., any change in demand. Should a contract be cancelled the firm is protected on the investment it has made. For no other products can the technostructure plan with such certainty and assurance. Given the inevitability of planning, there is much attraction in circumstances where it can be done so well.

This leads the technostructure to identify itself closely with the goals of the armed services and, not infrequently, with the specific goals of the particular service, Army, Navy or Air Force, which it most intimately serves. Simple association, as in the case of individual and organization, supports this tendency. In consequence the technostructure comes to see the same urgency in weapons development, the same security in technical pre-eminence, the same requirement for a particular weapons system, the same advantage in an enlarged mission for (say) the Air Force or Navy, as does the particular service itself. Its members develop the same commitment to these goals as do officers of the services.

This relationship accords parallel opportunity for adaptation. The need to combine the work of diverse specialists and technicians means that the development of (say) a new weapons system requires organization. This the technostructure, and frequently it alone, can provide. So the armed services are deeply dependent on their supplying corporations for technical development. And, in practice, numerous other tasks requiring the resources of organization – the planning of logistics systems, planning and development of base facilities, even on occasion the definitions of the missions of a particular service or one of its branches – are contracted out to supplying corporations.

In its rapid climb during the fifties, the Air Force fostered a growing band of private companies which took over a substantial part of regular military operations, including maintaining aircraft, firing rockets, building and maintaining launching sites, organizing and directing other contractors, and making major public decisions. . . . The Air Force's success over her sister services . . . established the magic formula that all federal agencies soon imitated.[1]

A firm that is developing a new generation of fighter aircraft is in an admirable position to influence the design and equipment of the plane. It can have something to say on the mission for which it is adapted, the numbers of planes required, their deployment, and, by implication, on the choice of the enemy toward which it is directed. This will reflect the firm's own views, and, *pari passu*, its own needs. If the firm has been accorded a more explicit planning function, it helps to establish assumptions as to probable enemies, points of probable attack, the nature of the resulting hostilities and the other factors on which defence procurement depends. In conjunction with other such planning, including, of course, that of public agencies, it helps to establish the official view of defence requirements and therewith of some part of the foreign policy. These will be a broad reflection of the firm's own goals; it would be eccentric to expect otherwise.

This influence is not absolute. In the autumn of 1962, the Department of Defense cancelled plans for further development of the Skybolt, a missile of disturbingly erratic behaviour designed for launching in flight from a manned bomber. If successful, it would have ensured, in turn, a further demand for manned bombers, a weapon which otherwise would be obsolescent. In advertising and other forms of persuasion, the

1. H. L. Nieburg, *In the Name of Science* (Chicago: Quadrangle Books, 1966), pp. 188, 189. This study, which appeared after this book had been substantially completed, provides admirably detailed documentation on the relation of government and technostructure as here outlined. Cf. particularly Chapters X and XI.

putative manufacturer made a strong case for the eventual technical proficiency of Skybolt and its importance in the defensive strategy of the United States. It failed. But the failure was not in this last rather desperate effort but in the earlier inability to have it incorporated, without particular public discussion, in the general catalogue of military needs. This would have been the normal manifestation of influence.

IV

Not only are identification and adaptation important for influencing decisions by the technostructure on weapons procurement, they are very nearly the only source of such influence.

We have seen that the head of the modern corporation cannot order up a new civilian product in response to a major exercise of imagination. The toaster will be recalled. It must emerge from the teams of scientists, engineers, designers, production experts, market researchers and sales executives. That is why power has shifted to, and into, the technostructure. For the same reason the modern business firm cannot buy defence decisions favourable to itself. There is, to speak loosely, no decision available for purchase. There is, instead, a process of decision-making in which many people participate over a long period of time. Some are members of the technostructure, some of the public agency. From this process come decisions on the feasibility, need for and design of an anti-missile system, a new transport aircraft or a new warhead of unparalleled destructive power. By then familiarity with the design and other requirements, including possession of the requisite technical knowledge and experience, will have gone far to decide who gets the contract. A new contender, entering at this point, would have little chance. There is influence only if there has been this prior and intimate and long-continued participation.

This was not always so. When the army contracted for mules, blankets, shoes or muskets, an open-handed lobbyist or a determined legislator could have influence on the award. Only a simple, single decision was required; to control the decision, or the man who made it, was to control the outcome. To this day the Congress retains a certain voice on whether army bases, arsenals, ships' repair facilities and other relatively uncomplicated installations of an earlier period are to be used or abandoned. It has at best limited and more often no voice at all in the decision to proceed with or abandon a weapons system, a nuclear propulsion system or a space vehicle or as to who the manufacturer will be. These decisions are taken by teams and committees and then passed for review through a hierarchy of teams and committees. Participation in this process is again the key to power. Even a superior Secretary of Defense is deeply subordinate to this group decision-making, and the usual one is utterly so.

V

In the nature of the market, one organization or enterprise sells to another and the boundaries between the two are sharp. This same delineation characterizes the private firm selling (say) powdered milk to the Department of Agriculture. But when planning replaces the market, and identification and adaptation supplement pecuniary compensation, matters are very different. No sharp line separates government from the private firm; the line becomes very indistinct and even imaginary. Each organization is important to the other, members are intermingled in daily work; each organization comes to accept the other's goals; each adapts the goals of the other to its own. Each organization, accordingly, is an extension of the other. The large aerospace contractor is related to the Air Force by ties that, however different superficially, are in their substance the same as those that relate the Air Force to the United States government. Shared goals are the decisive link in each case.

This notion is rather fiercely resisted. Tradition, derived from the antecedent separation of government and its suppliers

317

by the market, defends a sharp separation of public from private activity. Socialism is not an evocative word in the United States. The myth of separation helps to suppress any suggestion that the mature corporation in its public business is, in principle, a part of a larger public bureaucracy. It also helps the technostructure defend its autonomy – and protect itself from a good deal of awkward supervision. Government interference on rates of pay, expense accounts, plant location, executive nepotism and patronage and numerous other matters of public or political interest can be minimized (though not wholly resisted) on the grounds that this is a *private* operation. Expenditure of public funds by a public agency is governed by a stern ethic. Attitudes toward nominally private firms, even when spending public funds, are considerably more relaxed. Only those who wish to be fooled will, however, ignore the reality which is that the modern motivational system blurs the line into irrelevance.

Although the firm is related to the procurement agencies by shared goals, the result of identification and adaptation, these do not, of course, exclude pecuniary compensation and motivation. As we have seen in Chapter 11, a motivational system that combines identification and adaptation with pecuniary reward is internally consistent and self-reinforcing. But as pay fails to explain the relationship of a general or a Pentagon official to his job, so pecuniary motivation fails equally to explain the relationship of the mature corporation to the procurement agencies. To suppose that the modern weapons-maker offers his wares to the government only for pay and profit, as did the vintage maker of muskets, has an overtone of hardy, muscular intelligence which appeals to the social radical including the Marxist. But so to believe is to see almost nothing of the modern reality of industrial power.

Nor, of course, is this power exercised only in relation to the Department of Defense. The National Space Agency, the Atomic Energy Commission, the Federal Aviation Agency and other public bodies all underwrite industrial planning with long-term contracts involving large capital outlays and advanced technology. There are few mature corporations which do not have this relationship with the modern state.

VI

Identification and adaptation cannot ordinarily be reconciled with political hostility to the state or any particular party or administration. As noted, the entrepreneurial corporation did not have an intimate and continuing dependence on the state; its fortunes in respect of the state were affected by individual and discreet actions – the award of a contract, sale of public lands, imposition of a tax or tariff, passage of a regulation – which it could influence as such without worrying excessively about the general political environment. But the mature corporation has a continuing and intimate relationship for which doors must always be open and access to public officials always be easy and without tension. Adverse political action or even hostile oratory lessens this ease of access. Men arriving with their briefcases for the day's meetings in Washington or at Wright Field cannot have the added burden of explaining the testimony of a company president who has just attacked the government and all its minions hip and thigh.

But this is not a mere matter of expediency. Identification is a psychological phenomenon. If it is operative, there can be no mental or moral barriers to accepting the goals of the state. Such will be the consequence of political polemics and conflict. To denounce Democrats as destroyers of business and liberal Republicans as conscious agents of communism is to proclaim one's alienation from their goals. For the technostructure it means rejecting the identification and therewith the adaptation which are the source of its power. This, obviously, makes no sense.

We have here a guide to the political tendencies of the modern large corporation. Increasingly it will be passive rather than active in politics. It will eschew any strong identification with a political party – as the entrepreneur is identified with the Republican Party. It will not speak out on partisan issues.

To some extent, perhaps, it will take on the political colouration of whatever party is in office.

All of this is by way of protecting a much stronger and more
vital position of influence as an extension of the arm of the
bureaucracy. In this role the corporation can participate in
the decisions that count. It can help shape the highly technical
choices which, in turn, govern the demand for its own military
and other products. It will have access to the decisions on
military strategy which establish the need for such products.
And it will help to shape the current beliefs or assumptions on
foreign policy. These, obviously, are a far more important
power. It is the difference between the formal grandeur of
the legislative hearing and the shirt-sleeved rooms with black-
boards and tables heavy with data, drawings and tapes where
the important decisions, bit by bit, are actually made. The
technostructure selects its theatre of influence with discrimination and intelligence.

VII

Industrial planning, we have seen, requires the control of
prices and the management of the consumer. As a result, instruction passes not alone from the sovereign consumer to the
producer; it proceeds also from the producer to the consumer
in accordance with the needs of the technostructure. This is
the revised sequence. The revised sequence operates also in
the field of public procurement.

Those who, for purposes of rebuttal, would wish to find
that I had argued that all public spending is an accommodation to the needs of the modern corporation will be disap-
pointed. The influence of the industrial firm on military
procurement is singularly a matter where those who reach
inconvenient conclusions are impelled to make themselves
vulnerable by overstatement. They are then destroyed by those
who say that, since they do not value exact truth, they do not
value truth. I seek to be less obliging. I argue only for a complex two-way flow of influence. That, however, has deep
consequences for public action to which I will later return.

Chapter 28

A FURTHER SUMMARY

THE principal topography of the individual system is now in view. Most will think it a formidable sight. Few will minimize the complexity of its probable social effect; the only man who must surely be wrong about the industrial system is the one who essays a simple judgement upon it.

The system produces goods and renders services in vast and increasing volume. There are many poor people left in the industrial countries, and notably in the United States. The fact that they are not the central theme of this treatise should not be taken as proof either of ignorance of their existence or indifference to their fate. But the poor, by any applicable tests, are outside the industrial system. They are those who have not been drawn into its service or who cannot qualify. And not only has the industrial system – its boundaries as here defined are to be kept in mind – eliminated poverty for those who have been drawn into its embrace but it has also greatly reduced the burden of manual toil. Only those who have never experienced hard and tedious labour, one imagines, can be wholly indifferent to its elimination.

Once it was imagined that the economic system provided man with the artifacts by which he has anciently surrounded himself in response to his original and sovereign desires. This source of economic motivation is still celebrated in the formal liturgy of the system. But, as we have sufficiently seen, the system, if it accommodates to man's wants, also and increasingly accommodates men to its needs. And it must. This latter accommodation is no trivial exercise in salesmanship. It is deeply organic. High technology and heavy capital use cannot be subordinate to the ebb and flow of market demand. They require planning; it is the essence of planning that public behaviour be made predictable – that it be subject to control.

And from this control flow further important consequences. It ensures that men and numerous women will work with undiminished effort however great their supply of goods. And it helps ensure that the society will measure its accomplishment by its annual increase in production. Nothing would be more discomfiting for economic discipline than were men to establish goals for themselves and on reaching them say, 'I've got what I need. That is all for this week.' Not by accident is such behaviour thought irresponsible and feckless. It would mean that increased output would no longer have high social urgency. Enough would be enough. The achievement of the society could then no longer be measured by the annual increase in Gross National Product. And if increased production ceased to be of prime importance, the needs of the industrial system would no longer be accorded automatic priority. The required readjustment in social attitudes would be appalling.

The management to which we are subject is not onerous. It works not on the body but on the mind. It first wins acquiescence or belief; action is in response to this mental conditioning and thus devoid of any sense of compulsion. It is not that we are required to have a newly configured automobile or a novel reverse-action laxative; it is because we believe that we must have them. It is open to anyone who can resist belief to contract out of this control. But we are no less managed because we are not physically compelled. On the contrary, though this is poorly understood, physical compulsion would have a far lower order of efficiency.

II

The industrial system has brought its supply of capital, and in substantial measure also its labour supply, within its control, and thus within the ambit of its planning. And it has extended its influence deeply into the state. Those policies of the state that are vital for the industrial system – regulation of aggregate demand, maintenance of the large public (if preferably technical) sector on which this regulation depends, underwriting of advanced technology and provision of an increasing volume of trained and educated manpower – are believed to be of the highest social urgency. This belief accords with the needs of the system. And the influence of the technostructure of the mature firm extends to shaping the demand for its particular product or range of products. Individual members of the technostructure identify themselves with the design, development and production of items purchased by the government as the technostructure identifies itself with the social goal (say) of an effective national defence. And the members of the technostructure adapt design, development or need for items procured by the government to what accords with their own goals. These goals reflect, inevitably, the needs of the technostructure and of its planning.

Paralleling these changes, partly as a result and partly as a cause, has been a profound shift in the locus of economic and political power. The financier and the union leader are dwindling influences in the society. They are honoured more for their past eminence than for their present power. The technostructure exercises much less direct political power than did the antecedent entrepreneur. But that is because it has far more influence as an arm of the bureaucracy and in its influence on the larger climate of belief. The scientific, technical, organizational and planning needs of the technostructure have brought into being a large educational and scientific estate. And, while the commitment of the culture, under the tutelage of the industrial system, to a single-minded preoccupation with the production of goods is strong, it is not complete. Rising income also nurtures a further artistic and intellectual community outside of the industrial system.

III

Such in briefest sketch are the principal results of this pilgrimage. Two questions inevitably follow: Where does it take us? How should it be guided?

Neither question is, in fact, as important as those already

considered, and, one hopes, resolved. Agreeable as it is to know where one is proceeding, it is far more important to know where one has arrived. And while there will always be resistance to accepting what has come to exist – a resistance nurtured by nostalgia, vested interest in painfully acquired error which is thus understandably precious, and the omnipresent need to sustain belief in what is convenient as distinct from what is real – one has, where the present is concerned, appellate rights in two great courts, namely the internal consistency of the ideas and their coherence with what can be seen. It will perhaps be agreed that these have rendered good service here. When one turns to the future, these guides are lost. There are wise and foolish predictions but the difference between them is not so clear.

There are also difficulties in talking, at the same time, about what will happen and what should happen. Marx must on occasion have wondered, if revolution were inevitable, as he proclaimed, why it required the passionate and unrelenting advocacy which he accorded it. Should baleful tendencies be predicted when one hopes that popular understanding will bring the reaction that reverses them? No one who believes in ideas and their advocacy can ever persuade himself that they are uninfluential. Nor are they. And those who deal in ideas, if they are wise, will welcome attack. Only a peaceful passage should dismay them for it proves that the ideas do not affect anyone very much. I have hopes that popular understanding will reverse some of the less agreeable tendencies of the industrial system and invalidate, therewith, the predictions that proceed from these tendencies. And I am not without hope for the controversy that attests the importance of such change.

IV

There is another reason why, whatever the inconvenience, the future must be faced. Although those who presume to loftier, scientific attitudes regularly deplore it, the Anglo-American tradition in economic discourse is strongly normative. The test of whether a diagnostician is to be taken seriously or not is his response to the question: 'Well, what would *you* do?' I have been primarily concerned to tell what the industrial system is like. But to do this and no more would be to persuade most people that the description was not terribly useful.

Moreover, some problems of no small importance have been suggested by the preceding discussion. There is, for example, the prime role of technology in the industrial system and its peculiar association with weapons of unimaginable ferocity and destructiveness. How are we to be saved from these? There is also the question of the individual in this system – a system that requires, both in production and consumption, that individuality be suppressed. Given our commitment to the sovereignty and sanctity of the person, by what means, if at all, is human personality to be saved? Obviously there are dimensions of life, those of art for example, which the industrial system does not serve. One is led to inquire whether education remains education when it is chained too tightly to the wheel of the industrial system. And there is the relation of the industrial system to intellectual expression and political pluralism. This requires a special word.

V

For most of man's history, as philosophers of such diverse views as Marx and Alfred Marshall have agreed, political interest and conflict have originated in economic interest and economic conflict. And so it has been in the United States. Our politics have been the expression, in various conflicts and coalitions, of debtor and creditor interests, domestic and export interests, urban and rural interests, consumer and producer interests and, notably and classically, of the interests of the capitalist entrepreneur and the industrial working class.

To a remarkable extent, as we have seen, the industrial system embraces and absorbs these class interests. It does so partly by minimizing the reality of conflict and partly by exploiting the resulting malleability of attitude to win control of belief. The goals of the industrial system, in this process, become the goals of all who are associated with it and thus, by slight extension, the goals of the society itself.

In the past, criticism and introspection concerning the economic system and its goals have been both allowed and induced by the conflict in economic interest and the resulting political division. The capitalist entrepreneur or the labour leader has rarely been a source of penetrating criticism of himself or his own goals. But, with his spokesmen, sympathizers, captive scholars and sycophants he has been a good deal less restrained in discussing those with whom he has been economically at war. And much scholarship has also flourished in the interstices of this conflict. When its conclusions were unfavourable to one side they had the implicit protection of the other.

The question arises whether the industrial system, in absorbing economic conflict, ends all examination of social goals. Do its techniques of control – its management of market behaviour and its identification with and adaptation of social goals – serve also to minimize social introspection? In brief, is the industrial system monolithic by nature? And also very bland? To what extent does a society draw strength from pluralism of economic interests which, in turn, sustains pluralism of political discussion and social thought?

An interesting and widely remarked political phenomenon of recent years has been an ill-defined discontent, especially among students and intellectuals, with the accepted and approved modalities of social thought. These, whether espoused by professed liberals or conservatives, are held to be the views of 'The Establishment'. Not inappropriately, the rejection extends not only to the economic, social and political views of the Establishment but also to its clothing, conventional housing and even to the soap, depilatory apparatus and other goods, the production of which is the sanctioned measure of success. All these are eschewed by the dissidents in a highly visible manner. Is this the natural line of dissent in a society in which the previous lines of conflict have been subsumed? To this range of questions, but in a much less definitive mood than in the last chapters, I now turn.

I begin in the next chapter with some of the near-term consequences and needs of the industrial system. Thereafter I look at more distant horizons. But let me repeat once more that, on the whole, I am less interested in telling where the industrial system is going than in providing the materials for consideration of where it has arrived.

Chapter 29

THE INDUSTRIAL SYSTEM
AND THE COLD WAR

Every man, woman, and child lives under a nuclear sword of Damocles hanging by the slenderest of threads, capable of being cut at any moment by accident or miscalculation or by madness. JOHN F. KENNEDY, while President.

ALMOST everyone who wins a positive score in an intelligence test recognizes that the selling of goods – the management of demand for particular products – requires well-considered mendacity. Most goods perform commonplace functions – they suppress hunger, serve alcohol or nicotine addiction, move people gradually through heavy traffic, move waste products more rapidly through the intestinal tract or assist in removing filth. Little or nothing of importance can truthfully be said about the way a product performs these routine functions. Flat lies as to their performances are generally impermissible. But a surrogate for the truth, in which minor or even imaginary qualities confer great benefits, is essential.

It is hard to compromise on the advantages of rigorous candour but it may be, as a practical matter, that this contrivance does little direct damage. As noted, only in a comparatively affluent country are people open to persuasion on how they spend their money. Being affluent, it does not greatly matter how they spend it. Meretricious argument, if it influences unimportant decision, is evidently undamaging. And, more important, the case is recognized, subjectively, as being meretricious. That is because modern man is exposed to a large volume of information of varying degrees of unreliability. In response he establishes a system of discounts which he applies to various sources almost without thought. Information from a friend or neighbour, in the absence of a specific reputation for falsehood, is assumed to be reliable. Similarly that from a teacher or a scientist on his subject, and that from a physician, prognoses of the effects of overeating, alcohol and tobacco and diagnoses of cancer apart. Historians, as distinct from official historians and autobiographers, are assumed to tell the truth. So are most journalists. For pundits and preachers on the probability of doom there is a very heavy discount, as there is for politicians discussing moral integrity, peace and disarmament. The discount becomes nearly total for all forms of advertising. The merest child watching television dismisses the health and status-giving claims of a breakfast cereal as 'a commercial'. Conceivably, for non-lethal products, the government should not presume to insist on truth in advertising. People might assume success and then fail to apply the automatic discount which is their present more comprehensive protection.

Failure to win belief does not impair the effectiveness of the management of demand for consumer products. Management involves the creation of a compelling image of the product in the mind of the consumer. To this he responds more or less automatically under circumstances where the purchase does not merit a great deal of thought. For building this image, palpable fantasy may be more valuable than circumstantial evidence.

II

Fantasy and image-building also play an important role in the relationship between the industrial system and the state. By contriving an appropriate image of the position, prospects, problems or dangers of the state the industrial system can ensure a reaction favourable to its needs. If the image is one of a country lagging in technological development in a world where that is a prime test of national success, it can ensure investment in scientific research and technological development. If the image is of a nation beset by enemies, there will be responding investment in weapons. If it is one of a state in which liberty is threatened by controls, there will be resistance to regulation of various kinds.

However, the process of building these images is a good deal less obvious than that by which the demands of the consumer are created. In consequence, belief is a good deal deeper. A measure of amiable cynicism is associated with the management of demand for cigarettes or soap; not all involved will imagine that their use provides a formula for a long, happy or infinitely inoffensive life. More often, perhaps, there is professional pride in a measure of workmanlike bamboozlement. Only the oratory of the advertising industry is firmly grounded in sincerity. But the images of the state, in contrast, are taken very seriously. The men who contrive, or in the more frequent case perpetuate them, do so with the utmost seriousness. They persuade themselves. They see the result not as the image of reality but as the reality. To suggest that it is imagery is to be irresponsible, eccentric or, conceivably, subversive. As a result, though in public affairs as well as in private affairs, and for the same reasons, we are subject to contrivance that serves the industrial system, it takes a far greater effort of mind to see imagery as imagery and contrivance as contrivance in the field of public affairs. But since, for that reason, the normal discounts do not operate, it is much more important that they be identified.

III

The industrial system requires, we have seen, a large public sector for the stabilization of aggregate demand. And the system's planning, we have seen, reaches its highest state of development in conjunction with modern military procurement. The latter is supported by large sums of money. These are easily obtained by a process that is routine; it would require far more effort by a President to reduce military spending by twenty per cent than to increase it by a like amount. To hold at a given level or, better, to allow modest increases from year to year, is the easiest of all.[1] It is necessary, however, that there be an image of the world which justifies or rationalizes the military expenditures that the arrangement requires.

For nearly twenty years as this is written, the requisite image has been that of the Cold War. That this image owes its existence only to the needs of the industrial system is not suggested for a second. The revolutionary and national aspirations of the Soviets, and more recently of the Chinese, and the compulsive vigour of their assertion, were the undoubted historical source. But history must be separated from result. (We may also ignore for the moment the purposes the Cold War serves in the communist countries.)

In its more simplistic outline in the last twenty years, the relation of the Cold War to the needs of the industrial system has been remarkably close. It is a relentless, implacable, permanent, but ultimately benign, struggle with the world communist movement as led by the Soviet Union. It is occasioned by the difference in economic systems from which, primarily, are derived differences in individual liberty.[2] The latter contrast is stark and unshackled. The highly organized and planned system of the Soviets requires the subordination of the individual to the goals of the state. He is constrained in

1. '... an established tradition ... holds that a bill to spend billions of dollars for the machinery of war must be rushed through the House and the Senate in a matter of hours, while a treaty to advance the cause of peace, or a program to help the undeveloped nations ... guarantee the rights of all our citizens, or ... to advance the interests of the poor must be scrutinized and debated and amended and thrashed over for weeks and perhaps months.' Senator Gaylord Nelson, U.S. Senate, February 1964. Quoted by Julius Duscha, *Arms, Money and Politics* (New York: Ives Washburn, 1965), p. 2.

2. 'The Soviet leadership is irrevocably committed to the achievement of the ultimate Communist objective, which is annihilation of the capitalist system and establishment of Communist dictatorship over all the nations of the world.... Any pacts and agreements with the Soviets can be expected to be as meaningless and one-sided in the future as they have been in the past. ... The Soviets endeavor to attain their ends without getting involved in a nuclear war, even if they were certain of winning it.' Thomas S. Power, General, U.S.A.F. Ret., *Design for Survival* (New York: Coward, 1964), pp. 43–4.

his expression to a spectrum of acceptable belief. No such constraint by organization or planning is required by the western system of free enterprise.

Both systems must be evangelistic. Communism, tactical concessions and coexistence notwithstanding, is committed to ultimate and universal dominance. But no man who believes in liberty can accept a world that is forever half slave and half free.

The incompatibility of the systems, and the associated evangelism, lead directly to military competition. The Soviets would impose their system by force if they could; a strong deterrent prevents this and sustains faith in the ultimate and necessary triumph of liberty. In the main, this competition is technological – its decisive feature is the competitive development of weapons and weapons systems and related defences.

This competition is not unlimited; it proceeds within generous but real limits of cost. But although it is deemed somewhat reckless to say so, the competition is ultimately benign. That is because, if the competition is energetically pursued, it tends to a stalemate – neither side can destroy the other without suffering unacceptable damage itself. And, both being rational, the showdown is avoided. Disarmament is regarded as a serious threat to a balanced prospect for reciprocal destruction. For, since ambitions are unrelenting and good faith lacking, there is danger of being tricked by negotiations into concessions which would allow the other side to destroy with impunity. The competition is held to be safer, so, although it is discussed, few associated with these matters take seriously the possibility of disarmament. Rather, the discussion is an act of obeisance. It makes clear that the arms competition is being undertaken in lieu of successful disarmament instead of for its own sake.

All features of this competition are closely congruent with need. Since the aspirations of the communists are implacable, there is no danger that momentary accommodation or easing of tension will lead to a reduction in outlays. It can only be tactical or a trick. The ruling passion will always be 'how to get on with their world revolution'.[3] In an orthodox conflict the arrival of peace abruptly removes the support for further outlays. A war without fighting neatly obviates the danger that fighting will stop. By its nature a technological competition is never resolved. Safety depends on keeping innovations at a high level – although not at the highest possible level, for there are some things that are simply too expensive. Obsolescence in a technological competition is a nearly perfect substitute for battlefield attrition. Formal agreement to arrest the competition is excluded by the belief that it is more dangerous than the competition. Once war involved the conscription of a large mass of low-wage participants on whom the dangers and discomforts of the battlefield fell with particular weight. In consequence it encountered, although by no means universally, the opposition of the working masses. The Cold War arouses no such antipathy. Nor has the modern union energy to spare for what would seem to be a purely intellectual reaction against immediate interest. So the unions, too, find the Cold War image generally agreeable.

Even a calculation that the competition may, at some point, lead to total destruction of all life is not a definitive objection. Liberty, not material well-being, is involved. This is an ultimate value that cannot be compromised in the face of any threat. 'I am confident that the vast majority of the American people would passionately reject ... ignominious defeatism and, instead, proclaim: "Rather dead than Red!" '[4] Thus the competition is protected from even the most adverse estimates of its outcome.

The power of the Cold War image in the United States has not been constant. In the decade of the fifties it reached something of a zenith. The then Secretary of State, John Foster Dulles, saw its acceptance not only as an exercise in social belief but as a test of religious ardour and moral stamina. Nor

3. Secretary of State Dean Rusk, 'Address before American Political Science Association,' Washington, D.C., September 1965.

4. Power, op. cit., p. 69.

was acceptance entirely voluntary. Congressional committees, other public investigatory bodies, personnel security boards and private magistrates in the motion picture and communications industries reasoned that if the struggle for liberty were so important it should be obligatory. Dissent or even insufficient zeal could lead to loss of employment, other economic sanction or social ostracism. These circumstances were highly favourable to the weapons competition. It proceeded with vigour and even abandon. Numerous weapons systems, some emerging from the services and some from firms individually identified with a service, were put into simultaneous and overlapping development. To the competition with the Soviets was added the further zest of competition between the sponsoring services. Identification and adaptation were facilitated by drawing officials of the Defense Department for short terms of duty – the average during much of the decade was less than a year – from the industrial technostructure. Secretaries of Defense, during this period, refrained from interfering with subordinate decision-making and, indeed, were principally functional in their public relations. That the weapons competition, and the image of international relations on which it depended, originated partly in the industrial system was recognized with remarkable explicitness by President Eisenhower. He noted just before leaving office that the 'conjunction of an immense military establishment and a large arms industry' was something new in the American experience and urged that the nation 'guard against the acquisition of unwarranted influence, whether sought or unsought, by the military industrial complex. The potential for the disastrous rise of misplaced power exists and will persist ... we should take nothing for granted.'

IV

The problem is what not to take for granted – and how. The industrial system helps win belief for the image of implacable conflict (with associated features) that justifies its need. Belief being won, the arms competition seems normal, natural and inevitable as do the actions based upon it. Dissent seems eccentric and irresponsible. Herein is the power of a system that depends on persuasion rather than on compelled support.

Yet, on examination, much of what is believed turns out to be fanciful. The reality in the case of the United States and the Soviet Union is of two large industrial nations. Both, it has been amply shown, can achieve success by their very similar economic tests of success at the same time. Theirs is anything but implacable conflict, anything but a zero sum game as it is actually being played.

There is a large and unquestioned difference in the two systems in the role of politicians, writers, artists and scientists. None may minimize the difference made by the First Amendment. But it is less clear that the contrast in the systems of economic management is so great. Both systems are subject to the imperatives of industrialization. This for both means planning. And while each uses different techniques for dealing with the individual who contracts out of the planning, planning in all cases means setting aside the market mechanism in favour of the control of prices and individual economic behaviour. Both countries, quite clearly, solicit belief for what serves the goals of the industrial mechanism. Instead of contrast leading to implacable conflict, a more evident economic tendency is convergence.

The notion that the arms competition is ultimately benign likewise has small foundation. There is no inconsiderable chance of accident. There is always a chance that some day some true believer will react to the liturgy of conflict and provoke the ultimate conflict.

That the risks of agreed disarmament are greater than those of a continuing and unresolved weapons competition is also unproven. It is not clear why agreements can be negotiated in good faith with the communists on all subjects except disarmament. To eliminate civilized life for all time in response to a short-run calculation that liberty might otherwise be endangered is also irrational. And those who would make such a decision are themselves strongly subordinate to a system of belief. They are not free men.

It is extremely important in itself to know that our imagery is, in part, derived from the needs of the industrial system. This leads to introspection and scrutiny that would not, otherwise, be forthcoming. For the same reason it helps us to know that part of our view of the world and of its politics originates not in our minds but in the needs of the industrial system.

But two other steps are also necessary. One is to ensure that sceptical scrutiny of official belief is an important political function. The other is to meet the technological and planning needs of the industrial system by ways that are less mortal than the weapons competition.

v

In the past, imagery favourable to the entrepreneur was assured of close scrutiny because of the opposed pecuniary interest of the trade unions. If the entrepreneur sought to impose on the society in which enterprise was promoted by a tax system which fell resoundingly on the poor, the unions could be counted upon to come up with a countering doctrine. There is no hope that they will serve a similar function in relation to the images of foreign policy. For, apart from their general enfeeblement, their needs on these matters are far too closely aligned with those of the technostructure.

The principal hope for such scrutiny, in conjunction with the political power to make it effective, lies with the educational and scientific estate. In the past, this community has been ambiguous as regards the imagery of the industrial system. In economics, on such matters as the control of the firm by the market or the origin of wants with the sovereign individual, its tendency, we have seen, has been to underwrite the needed beliefs of the industrial system. On larger questions of foreign policy, this tendency has been less clear. In the early years of the Cold War, there was a fairly full acceptance of its tenets. And for very good reason. Stalinist oppression, later to be affirmed by the Soviets themselves, was no contrivance. It was highly objective. So was the overt attack in Korea. In their wake university specialists in Cold War strategy, and the associated arms competition, proliferated. Doctrines of deterrence, war games, coalition architecture and economic warfare became fashionable subjects for university research, reflection and instruction. At the highest levels of sophistication, scholars calculated the acceptable levels of loss in the event of nuclear war and weighed the comparative disadvantages of forty or eighty million casualties. University centres for the study of international relations, which had once concerned themselves with peace, became preoccupied with the Cold War. Close relations were maintained with the services; a small aristocracy of scholars did periodic duty with R.A.N.D. Scientists and engineers had similar association with the services or defence firms. It was easy to imagine that the educational and scientific estate would come to have much the same relation, by identification and adaptation, to the state in these matters as the technostructure itself. Any hope of a different view of the imagery by which all alike were sustained would be lost.

On the whole, it has not happened. The larger educational and scientific estate has not been strongly receptive to the Cold War imagery. Its mood has on the whole been one of growing scepticism. And the Cold War specialists within the scholarly community have become an increasingly alienated group. The price of an intimate and committed association with official war planning has often been some slight suspicion of scholarly rectitude.

There are a number of reasons for this. The scientists have been peculiarly situated to see the dangers of the weapons competition including the possibilities of conflict by accident. It was they, not the university specialists on international relations or the professional diplomats, who instituted the steps leading to the partial test ban. They have similarly led on other discussions with the Soviets [5] on weapons control and disarmament. There had been general and growing suspicion of the doctrine of implacable conflict based on a bilateral confrontation of good and evil. The educational and scientific estate has also been open to evidence on the growing pluralism of the communist world with its adverse effect on the doctrine of monolithic and hostile conspiracy. There would appear to have been a similar response to liberalizing trends in the communist world with the accompanying implication that the approprate policy is not one of conflict but of patience. Finally, the educational and scientific estate has been open to the view that communist protestations in behalf of a policy of peaceful coexistence may not be a trick but could reflect a disinterest in nuclear annihilation.

In the present decade there has been a recurrent conflict between the university community and the intellectuals on the one hand and the State Department and foreign policy establishment on the other. The image of a unified conspiracy as manifested in the Cold War imagery requires an automatic reaction to any communist initiative. Otherwise, after exploiting one opportunity, it will be encouraged to proceed to the next. This has been deeply questioned by the educational and scientific estate. It is, on the whole, an encouraging development.

As the educational and scientific estate grows in numbers and self-confidence; and as it comes to realize that foreign policy is based on an imagery that derives in part from the needs of the industrial system; and as it realizes further that this tendency is organic; and as it sees that the only corrective is its own scrutiny and involvement and that this involvement is not a matter of choice but an obligation imposed by its position in the economic and political structure, we can reasonably expect it to be more effective. Nothing in our time is more important.

5. Soviet scientists, perhaps similarly motivated, seem to have assumed similar leadership.

VI

In the field of international relations, especially since the onset of the Cold War, high public officials have invariably been more diligent in instructing other governments than their own. Though often cautious and deferential in their relations with the Congress, Secretaries of State have been bold and forthright in informing the Soviets of their error. The late John Foster Dulles rarely missed an opportunity to advise the Russians on the merits of liberty and the rule of law and the sanctity of freedom of speech. He was more reserved as regards Senator Joseph McCarthy although the latter, on frequent occasions, attacked freedom of expression and due process and did not omit to concern himself with Mr Dulles's own Department. Mr Dean Rusk, a circumspect man in dealing with domestic critics, especially those who might charge undue liberalism in relations with China, has shown contrasting boldness in telling the communist powers of their shortcomings. Indeed, it may be laid down as a rule of foreign relations that the lower the probability that advice will be taken, the more firmly it will be proffered. Our officials are more circumspect in advising the Congress of its error than in admonishing the British. They are much more cautious in telling the British what to do than the French. They are least inhibited in instructing the Soviets and the Chinese, and it is rare that the leaders of either of the latter two countries will encounter a State Department speech which fails to inform them of their faults and point the way to improvement. The tendency of Soviet and Chinese leaders in instructing the United States is the same. The action in response to this advice is slight but does not discourage it.

No progress can be made in reducing the commitment to the Cold War without concurrent action of the Soviet Union.[6]

6. In the mystique of the Cold War, the Chinese are playing an increasingly important role and their behaviour is highly favourable to the image of enduring conflict. However, it is not yet practical to argue that China is scientifically and technologically a serious competitor to the United States in the weapons competition.

On this it is well to be completely clear. Still there is merit in departing from the rules and addressing advice in this matter to the United States. It is the country that one can advise with effect as distinct from immunity. It is also richer than the Soviet Union, has greater scientific and technological resources and tends, in consequence, to be the pace-setter in the weapons competition. If we understand that we are subject to the imagery of the industrial system in these matters, and seek to act in accordance not with the image but with the reality of our situation, then it may be possible to make a bargain with the Soviets. It may also prove impossible. We do not know for sure to what images the Soviets are subject. We may wisely assume that, as in other matters, there are parallel tendencies here and that the weapons competition has an organic role in Soviet society. Yet it remains that the Cold War has elements of a self-fulfilling prophecy for it has cultivated the reciprocal mistrust which it assumes. Only if we understand our situation is there a chance that matters will improve.

It is also extremely important that we be aware of what, given the needs of the industrial system, can be made to happen most easily. Escape from the weapons competition, with its attendant dangers, should follow the path of least rather than of maximum resistance. In the past we have proposed Calvinist solutions and made no progress. We shall do better with Catholic solutions which, if less satisfying to the Calvinist soul, could serve to keep it longer in this world.

VII

In the conventional view, as earlier noted, we could escape our commitment to the weapons competition without insuperable economic difficulty. We would need to offset the decline in arms expenditure by increasing other public outlays or by cutting taxes or by both, and we would need to help those affected retrain, re-educate and relocate themselves. These would be formidable but feasible undertakings. And without minimizing the required action, the orthodox discussion of

340

disarmament almost invariably concludes by saying how welcome would be this challenging task. This pious expression of hope is also partly liturgical. Given the remarkable destructiveness of modern weapons, it is necessary to assure ourselves that we are not dependent on their production. Any other view of the economy is unsettling.[7] Additionally, the ancient Marxian contention, still reflected in some modern Soviet propaganda, holds that a capitalist economy suffers from an inherently limited market. Arms expenditure, like imperialism, is one of the necessary correctives. No circumspect scholar wishes to have it said that he has served, wittingly or unwittingly, the purposes of communist propaganda. Indeed, one of the more cautious tenets of Cold War behaviour was that no scholar should do so. So grave was this conflict that embarrassing truth should be constrained for *raison d'état*.

There is, in fact, nothing to the Marxian contention. The market is not limited as Marx held; the management of aggregate demand, a possibility which he did not foresee, can be served by different types of public spending. And it has now been amply shown that, by such management, the size of the market can be increased as employment or other considerations require.[8] Arms expenditures have no unique value for increasing aggregate demand.

But the orthodox statement of the problem of disarmament, as the present analysis also amply shows, is deficient in two other respects. One cannot replace the spending for armament with private outlays for consumption and investment, such as would be encouraged by a massive reduction in taxes. The regulation of aggregate demand requires that the public sector of the economy be large. It must be so if personal

7. For a very good but generally orthodox view of the task, see *Report of the Committee on the Economic Impact of Defense Disarmament*, July 1965. This report does urge, very sensibly, that the government replace defence expenditures with increased support for scientific and technological development.

8. The point is now conceded at least by the younger generation of Soviet economists.

income and corporation taxes are to be large enough to have their indispensable stabilizing effect.

And while all expenditures, whether for arms or old age pensions or air pollution, add to demand, not all play the same role in underwriting technology. Military spending, we have seen, is highly serviceable in this regard. It also pays for innovation that may be useful for civilian production.[9] Risks that would otherwise be unacceptable can be assumed in the civilian economy if they are protected by the much more nearly riskless weapons economy. General Dynamics was helped to survive its disastrous misadventure on jet air transports earlier mentioned,[10] and the Studebaker Corporation was able to survive the loss of its automobile business [11] because of a large (and in the case of Studebaker) expanding participation in military procurement. These advantages of the weapons competition to the industrial system could not easily be sacrificed by the industrial system. A simple increase in consumer spending resulting from tax reduction or in public spending for housing or pensions would be no substitute. A drastic reduction in weapons competition following a general release from the commitment to the Cold War would be sharply in conflict with the needs of the industrial system.[12]

But these needs do not have to be met by weapons. Anything that is roughly equivalent in scale and technical com-

9. Although it is increasingly the view of scientists and engineers that the civilian applications of military research and development are rather limited. 'Of the total [present research and development] effort, overwhelmingly oriented to defense, relatively little is directed toward the creation of new consumer products, or to improve machines to make the products, or to improve processes to make the machines.' Secretary of Commerce Luther Hodges. Quoted by Don K. Price in *The Scientific Estate* (Cambridge: Harvard University Press, 1965), p. 40.

10. Richard Austin Smith, *Corporations in Crisis* (New York: Doubleday, 1963), pp. 63 et seq.

11. The effect of military orders in saving the company is described by Duscha, op. cit., p. 16.

12. The latter, we may be reminded once more, would not react with open advocacy of the Cold War. But in conjunction with the services, the industrial system is the source of attitudes and estimates on disarmament

plexity will serve. Thus, could the image of the conflict with the Soviet Union be shifted from weapons competition to more general scientific and engineering competition, this would be equally satisfactory provided always that the costs are sufficiently great.

VIII

It is the nature of competition that the rewards of winning need not be examined. To excel, or to hope to excel, is sufficient to justify the contest, and this is equally the case for football, chess, sexual prowess, money-making or scientific achievement. A scientific and engineering competition in any field is thus quite as capable of enlisting the serious energies of man as a weapons competition. And akin to an athletic competition, while it is capable of generating a substantial amount of reciprocal ill will, it could be much more benign as to pollution of atmosphere, possibility of accident, and ultimate outcome than a weapons competition.

It is also clear that we have already come some distance along this path in our relations with the Soviet Union. The competition in space exploration is largely – although not totally – devoid of military implication. It has shown that it can arouse the competitive passions of both countries. It is devoid of danger of accident except to the passengers. And, as compared with earlier competition in trans-oceanic aviation, this is small. In relation to the needs of the industrial system, the space competition is nearly ideal. It requires very high spending on complex and sophisticated technology. It underwrites the same highly developed planning as does the weapons competition and, hence, is an admirable substitute for it.

---

action and its effects. The relevant estimates would show the impact on technical development, on parallel Soviet development, probable evasion, eventual Soviet reaction and, in sum, on national security. These estimates will be the working materials of those who make policy on disarmament as well as of the White House, Bureau of the Budget and the Congress. Far more effectively than any open advocacy, they will reflect the needs of the industrial system.

The imagery of the industrial system strongly supports the space race. It is held to be of the utmost importance to the international prestige of the United States that its vehicles be first to the moon, the other parts of the solar system and the less convenient reaches of the universe.

There has been some tendency to question the validity of this imagery. Why is it uniquely important that the United States be first to Saturn? Is it likely that the imperialist prospect will be especially rewarding. Is not the area of cultivable land likely to be small? Are there not better uses for the resources so employed? There is no rational answer to these questions as there is none to a query as to why negotiated disarmament is inherently more dangerous than a continuance of the weapons competition. Truth in both instances is subordinate to need and the needed belief. But this does not affect the value of the space competition in meeting the needs of the industrial system in a comparatively harmless instead of in an extremely dangerous competition. A similar case can be made for competitive underwriting of the widest area of general scientific research; in high speed land and air communications; in exploring the ocean floor and the regions below the earth's crust; in altering climate for better or worse; and much more.

The industrial system has not become identified with the weapons competition by preference or because it is inherently bloody. Rather, this has been the area where the largest amount of money to support planning was available with the fewest questions asked. And since armies and cannon have always been in the public sector, government underwriting in this area had the fewest overtones of socialism. But the space race shows that underwriting outside the area of weaponry is equally acceptable.

The path to salvation for the two great industrial systems is now clear. Whether it will be followed is less certain. There must be agreement on arresting and eliminating the competition in lethal technology. On this, survival of both the industrial and the non-industrial populations of the world plausibly depends. It is of prime importance to this effort that it be realized how much of past action has been based not on reality but on imagery and the sources of the latter. Nor may it be supposed that this imagery is confined to one side. Discussion of disarmament must now result in action. It can no longer serve, as now, as the surrogate for action.

But agreement will be much less painful if competition continues and is encouraged and widened in non-lethal spheres. This competition is not a luxury; it serves an organic need of the industrial system as now constituted. And it does not culminate in explosions of immeasurable effect.

Chapter 30

THE FURTHER DIMENSIONS

... for the first time since his creation man will be faced
with his ... permanent problem – how to use his freedom
from pressing economic cares, how to occupy the leisure,
which science and compound interest will have won for him,
to live wisely and agreeably and well. JOHN MAYNARD
KEYNES, *Essays in Persuasion.*

We should not fall prey to the beautification extremists who
have no sense of economic reality. FRED L. HARTLEY,
President of the Union Oil Company.

THE industrial system identifies itself with the goals of society.
And it adapts these to its needs. The adaptation would not be
so successful were those who comprise society aware of it
– did they know, in effect, how they are guided. It is the genius
of the industrial system that it makes the goals that reflect its
needs – efficient production of goods, a steady expansion in
their output, a steady expansion in their consumption, a
powerful preference for goods over leisure, an unqualified
commitment to technological change, autonomy for the technostructure, an adequate supply of trained and educated
manpower – coordinate with social virtue and human enlightenment. These goals are not thought to be derived from our
environment. They are assumed to be original with human
personality. To believe this is to hold a sensibly material view
of mankind. To question it is to risk a reputation for eccentricity or asceticism.

Or so it has been. Few things are so appealing as reflection
on the novelty or originality of one's own position. In recent
times there has, in fact, been a persistent questioning of conventional economic and social goals. Economic values have
been especially questioned. Alienation has been evident among
youth. It has manifested itself in rejection of conventional

346

attitudes on work, career, clothing, and foreign policy. But this unease is not confined to youth. It has been widespread in the educational and scientific estate. And it has invaded, even, the great philanthropic foundations where it has led to grants to groups duly constituted to re-examine the purposes of the society. Such re-examination has invariably led to a strong affirmation of the goals that serve the needs of the industrial system.[1]

These pages have shown, one trusts, the considerable social and economic foundation for our unease. They also make clear the nature of the forces by which we have been captured. What, now, are the mechanics of emancipation?

The most important step has already been accomplished by the diligent and responsive reader. For knowledge of the forces by which one is constrained is the first step towards freedom. But another is to have clearly in view the dimensions of life which the industrial system, by its nature, does not or cannot serve and which, because of its disabilities, it will tend to minimize.

A further step, no less important, is to identify a mechanism which will assert and promote the neglected dimensions of life against the powerful adaptive motivation of the industrial system. In less formidable language, there must be some political force for accomplishing what the industrial system ignores and, indeed, holds to be unimportant. I come to this in later chapters.

1. Cf. *Prospects for America, The Rockefeller Panel Reports* (New York: Doubleday, 1961), and *Goals for Americans.* The Report of the President's Commission on National Goals (New York: Prentice-Hall, 1960).

The last mentioned provides a superbly conventional list. 'The economy should grow at the maximum rate consistent with primary dependence upon free enterprise ... Technological change should be promoted and encouraged as a powerful force for advancing our economy ... The development of the individual and the nation demand that education at every level in every discipline be strengthened ... Communist aggression and subversion ... threaten all that we seek to do both at home and abroad ... Disarmament should be our ultimate goal.' pp. 3–20.

The industrial system generally ignores or holds unimportant those services of the state which are not closely related to the system's needs. National defence, support to research and technological development, such collateral needs of industrial growth as highways and air traffic management are not neglected. Nor is education. With the passage of time, support for education reflects not alone the needs of the industrial system but also the increasing political power of the educational and scientific estate. Educators, in pursuit of political interest, differ from others only in the impression of exceptional purity of motive which they are able to convey.

Services of the state that are not directly related to the needs of the industrial system are much less favoured. Two factors operate here. Services that are unneeded by the industrial system and which, unavoidably, the state must render, suffer from a negative discrimination. Soap and dentifrices are accorded importance by the industrial system by the advertising by which it manages demand. Public clinics, which may do more for health, are the beneficiaries of no similar promotion. They suffer accordingly. Still other activities of the state are inimical to the industrial system, or to the goals it avows and the priorities it enjoys. They encounter the active opposition of the industrial system. Both cases require brief examination.

Such services of the state as the care of the ill, aged and physically or mentally infirm, the provision of health services in general, the provision of parks and recreation areas, the removal of rubbish, the provision of agreeable public structures, assistance to the impoverished and many other services are not of particular importance to the industrial system. And they are in competition for funds with the wants that result from the aggressive management of the consumer by the industrial system. In consequence, hospitals do badly in competition for resources with automobiles. Expenditures for parks for outdoor play do poorly in competition with those for chromatic television. And so forth.

And belief is extensively, although imperfectly, accommodated to this discrimination. Private virtue consists in producing more for more money. Public virtue still lies, on the whole, not with the politician who proposes to accomplish more for the same expenditure, but with the one who proposes to do more for less. And the voice of the man who wishes government to do less for less is still heard. By especially accommodating philosophers it is still held that the state should minimize its services. Otherwise, it abridges the right of the individual to decide his purchases for himself.

Doctrine thus supports organic tendency to create a natural imbalance between the goods produced and the services supplied by the industrial system and those which are supplied by the state and which do not serve the needs of the industrial system. But these are matters on which I have written elsewhere and at length.[2] With no views is it so pleasant to agree in detail as with one's own. But the temptation must be put down.

I turn now from the negative discrimination against public services to the much stronger opposition that arises from the association of the state with goals that are alien or inimical to the industrial system.

III

Beyond the area of goods and services, however supplied, and the demand for them, however contrived, is the further world of aesthetic experience. This is served not by factories or engineers but, in one manifestation or other, by artists. Enjoyment of the experience owes something to preparation; no more than the response to a lighter, smoother, blended whisky is it original in the soul of man.

The aesthetic experience was once a very large part of life – unimaginably large, given the values of the industrial system. The traveller from the United States or the industrial cities of

2. In *The Affluent Society*.

Europe or Japan goes each summer to visit the remnants of pre-industrial civilizations. That is because Athens, Florence, Venice, Seville, Agra, Kyoto and Samarkand, though they were infinitely poor by the standards of modern Nagoya, Düsseldorf, Dagenham, Flint or Magnitogorsk, included, as part of life, a much wider aesthetic perspective. No city of the post-industrial era is, in consequence, of remotely comparable artistic interest. Indeed, no traveller of predominantly artistic interest ever visits an industrial city and he visits very few of any kind which owe their distinction to architecture and urban design postdating the publication of Adam Smith's *Wealth of Nations* in 1776.

One of the terms of disapprobation in the industrial system is aesthete. This is because aesthetic achievement is beyond the reach of the industrial system and, in substantial measure, in conflict with it. There would be little need to stress the conflict were it not part of the litany of the industrial system that none exists.

The conflict derives partly from a conflict in goals and partly because aesthetic goals are beyond the reach of the techno-structure, which is to say that it cannot identify itself with them. So, if they are strongly asserted, they will be viewed as a constraint.

Thus, in an obvious case, if aesthetic goals are strongly asserted, this will affect the location of industrial plants. These will be placed not where they are most efficient but where they are least offensive. Their mode of operation, including the odours they dispense into the atmosphere and the wastes they deposit into streams, lakes and subsoil, will also be controlled. This means higher cost, smaller output or both. Questions would be asked about products – about the shape, number and construction of automobiles that is consistent with a pleasant urban aspect or an agreeably neutral air.

Such constraints would be inconvenient. Social thought in the industrial system does not allow of inquiry as to whether increased or more efficient production of a particular product is a good thing. It is, *per se*, a good thing.

Aesthetic goals contest the claims of power lines over landscape, of power development over natural streams or national parks, of highways over urban open spaces, strip mining over virgin mountainsides, shopping centres over antique squares and high-speed air travel over tranquillity below. Many of these claims to industrial priority have, in fact, been contested. The contests are seen, however, as episodic and accidental rather than organic, and the burden of proof remains heavily upon those who assert the aesthetic priority. If economic advantage – the effect on output, income and cost – is clear, it will usually be decisive. Aesthetic considerations must usually prove that they yield economic advantage in the long run.

Were aesthetic goals accorded priority, their assertion would be normal and there would be a presumption that industrial efficiency would be subordinate to them. This too would be inconvenient.

To assert aesthetic goals is also to interfere seriously with the management of the consumer. This, in many of its manifestations, requires dissonance – a jarring of the aesthetic sensibilities. An advertising billboard that blends gracefully into the landscape is of little value; it must be in sharp contrast with surroundings. This jarring effect then becomes competitive. The same principles of planned dissonance are even more spectacularly in evidence in the radio and television commercial. They also characterize the design or packaging of numerous industrial products. And an effort is made to bring this dissonance within the ambit of social goals. It is defended interestingly by the contention that it 'gives the consumer what he wants'. If he did not approve, he would not respond. A man who comes to a full stop because he is hit over the head with an axe proves similarly by his response that it was what he was yearning for.

IV

The industrial system has a yet further and more fundamental conflict with the aesthetic dimension. The industrial system, as we have sufficiently seen, depends urgently on organization.

Fragments of information, each associated with a person, are combined to produce a result which is far beyond the capacity of any one of the constituent individuals. But while this is a procedure which lends itself admirably to technological development and to the less inspired levels of scientific research, it does not lend itself to art. Artists do not come in teams. The greatest industrial achievement, myth to the contrary, emerges from committees. But not the greatest painting, sculpture or music. The artist may be more of a social being than the legend holds. It is noticeable that he regularly eschews, in practice, the cruel isolation which, as a deeply creative being, he is supposed to suffer in principle. His flocking and nesting tendencies are no less convivial than those of accountants, engineers and high executives. But he does, in his work, enfold the whole of his task within himself. He cannot work on or with a team. We have here a principal explanation of why the high technical and productive achievements of the industrial system are so regularly combined with banal or even offensive design.

The aesthetic dimension being beyond the ready reach of the industrial system, members of that system are led naturally to assert its unimportance. Juveniles who do not like Latin, economists who do not like mathematics and men who do not like women manifest precisely the same tendency.

But this is not all. Cultivation of the aesthetic dimension accords a new and important role to the state and one to which, by virtue of its handicaps, the industrial system is unrelated. Part of this role has already been implied. Where there is a conflict between industrial and aesthetic priorities, it is the state which must assert aesthetic priority against the industrial need. Only the state can defend the landscape against power lines, advertisers, lumbermen, coal miners, and, on frequent occasions, its own highwaymen. Only it can rule that some patterns of consumption – the automobile in the downtown areas of the modern city is a prominent possibility – are inconsistent with aesthetic goals. The state alone can protect radio and television from contrived dissonance – or provide alternatives that are exempt. And were aesthetic priority asserted, the state would be required to come to its defence not, as now, episodically and in response to some exceptional outrage of aesthetic sensibilities. It would have to do so normally and naturally as the defender of goals in which aesthetic considerations were consistently important. Such goals, it must be added, will not occasionally but usually be achieved at some cost to industrial expansion – to economic growth. That one must pause to affirm that beauty is worth the sacrifice of some increase in the Gross National Product shows how effectively our beliefs have been accommodated to the needs of the industrial system.

v

But the role of the state on the aesthetic dimension is not merely protective; it is also affirmative. While art is an expression of individual personality, important branches of the arts can only flourish within a framework of order. This must be provided by the state. Specifically, painting, sculpture and music, although not within the ambit of the industrial system, do reasonably well on the patronage that it provides. There is need for instruction in appreciation and enjoyment. (In keeping with the ethos of the system this is considered a much inferior employment of educational funds to their devotion to science, mathematics and engineering.) But, while there is much that the state can do by way of encouragement here, its role is not decisive.

In the case of architecture and urban and environmental design, its role is decisive. Art is one manifestation of order. And it is the first casualty of disorder. Florence, Seville, Bloomsbury and Georgetown are beautiful because each part is in orderly relation to the whole. The modern commercial highway, the sprawling fringe of any city, the route into town from any airport is hideous because no part is related to a larger design. This order is rarely if ever achieved permissively; it must always be imposed by the state or by social pressure.

Good architecture is also mostly meaningless unless it is within a consistent framework. The Taj Mahal would lose much of its queenly elegance if surrounded by modern service stations. This has been the fate of quite a few distinguished modern buildings. Nineteenth-century Paris owes its excellence not to the brilliance of the individual buildings but to the consistency of the overall design.

Further, there is much architecture of which the state must always be the patron. It is the natural source of distinguished buildings, interesting monuments, agreeable gardens and fountains, long vistas, imposing squares, soaring towers and rich façades. Only as nations have become very rich and the industrial system has made economic growth identical with life, have we ceased to suppose that such patronage is a fit function of government. Quite commonly it is said that it cannot be afforded.

VI

It would be foolish to insist that government in the United States – whether of cities, states, or the Federal government – is a good custodian of aesthetic goals. Politicians may well have a special penchant for banality. Those who do not urge it out of personal preference will think it necessary as a concession to the popular taste. Although the world owes a greater debt to public architecture than to private, it owes more to the taste of talented despots – Shah Jahan, Cosimo and Lorenzo, Peter the Great, Louis XIV – than to democrats. It is part of the case against public sponsorship of aesthetic goals by modern democratic governments that they will be strongly biased in favour of what is bad.

This cannot be denied. It is only that for asserting aesthetic priorities and providing the essential framework for artistic effort there is no alternative to the state. Those who say that in consequence of its shortcomings the state must forgo all concern for art thereby reject aesthetic priority. They become advocates of environmental disorder.

For even when the state exercises artistically imperfect con-

354

trol over environment, the result will be better than when there is none at all. In the late twenties and early thirties the planners and architects of Washington, DC swept clear an area between Pennsylvania and Constitution Avenues to build a vast block of buildings called the Federal Triangle. The Triangle is unimaginative, derivative and pretentious. Artists rightly condemned it. But it is far better than the cabbage patch of buildings it replaced. In its general cohesiveness it has come to be admired in comparison with those parts of the city where no similar effort was ever made.

And the state can be expected to do better in support of the aesthetic dimension in the future than in the modern past. For this will be recognized as a high public responsibility. What is done as an afterthought is rarely done well. Something better can be expected when a task is seen to be central, not marginal, to life. It is worth hoping that the educational and scientific estate, as it grows in power, will encourage and enforce more exacting aesthetic standards. Nothing would more justify its intrusion on public life.

VII

For many years, politicians completing a term of office and seeking another have taken, as the measure of their deservedness, whether their constituency is more prosperous than when they began. If it is, and larceny has not been palpable, they consider themselves to have a good claim for re-election. It is a test which it has been hard for even the most negligible statesman to fail. All, the intelligent and stupid, diligent and idle, have been swept along on a current of increased output that, in the usual case, owed nothing whatever to their efforts.

The aesthetic dimension introduces a new and much stronger test. It means that mayors completing a term at city hall, governors at the state capital, Presidents in the White House, Prime Ministers at 10 Downing Street will be asked whether they have left their city, state or country more beautiful than before. This test will not be so easy. Few if any in this century would have passed. The fact of universal failure is another reason for insisting on the unimportance of the aesthetic dimension. No one likes an examination which he surely flunks. But far more than the test of production, which is far too easy, the test of aesthetic achievement is the one that, one day, the progressive community will apply.

Chapter 31

THE PLANNING LACUNAE

THE genius of the industrial system lies in its organized use of capital and technology. This is made possible, as we have duly seen, by extensively replacing the market with planning. The notable accomplishments of the industrial system are all the result of such planning: there would be no flights to the moon and not many to Los Angeles were market incentives relied upon to bring into existence the required vehicles. The same is true of other services, amenities and artifacts of the industrial system from telephone communications to Chevrolets to dentifrices. In all cases there are careful projections of output; careful control of prices; careful steps to see that the projections of output are validated in the greatest possible measure by consumer response; and careful steps to see that the things needed for production – labour, components, machinery – are available in the requisite amounts at the anticipated prices at the right time. To leave these matters to the market would be regarded, by those principally involved, as the equivalent of leaving them to chance.

Yet, as we have seen, the myth of the system is quite different. That holds, and a large, expensive though not universally successful educational effort teaches, that all credit belongs to the market which is a force of transcendent power. It alone motivates and regulates performance. There are agnostics who do not place their trust in God. But a deeper faith reposes trust in the market. The community that does so cannot go wrong.

There is an inherent implausibility about this faith – apart from the impossibility of reconciling it with the practice of the industrial system. In all other aspects of business organization, profoundly rational and determinist attitudes rule. As little as possible is left to faith and hope. But then at the ultimate and decisive point, where the great and important decisions are made on what and how much and at what price things are to be produced, there is assumed to be abdication to the impersonal magic of the market. This is improbable as well as wrong. But it still solicits belief.

One consequence is a great deal of physical discomfort. The industrial system performs its tasks with competence. That is why it seeks to make the competent production of goods the only social purpose and the sole test of social performance. But for a variety of reasons the industrial system does not perform all necessary tasks. Since there is a presumption that the industrial system functions in response to the market, rather than through its instruments for planning supply and demand, it is naturally assumed that the market will also work its unplanned wonders where the writ of the industrial system does not run.

In quite a large area outside the industrial system – the world of the small retail entrepreneur, repairman, independent craftsman, barber, market gardener, bookmaker – the market does work adequately or well. The inferior performance of such services or their absence is one of the notable features of the fully planned economies of Eastern Europe. However there are also products and services, some of them of the highest convenience or necessity, which cannot be called into being by the market. The society recognizes the failure of the market in these areas. But since the market is assumed generally to be a success, the planning in these areas of failure is conceived to be abnormal. It is approached half-heartedly and with a sense of being unfaithful to principle. Nor are all of the requisites of effective planning identified and provided. In consequence, these tasks are badly performed to the general public's discomfort, or worse. Were it recognized that they require planning, and in the context of a largely planned economy have been left unplanned, there would be no hesitation or apology in the use of all the necessary instruments for planning. Performance would be much better.

These abstractions may now be fleshed out with specific examples.

II

The clearest case is urban and interurban surface transportation of people. This, it is clear in retrospect, required that there be one corporation, that is to say one planning instrument, covering the cities of an entire region including the lines between. The local systems would then have been developed in relation to the inter-city and inter-regional system with joint use of rights-of-way, terminals and other facilities as appropriate. The prospective growth of the entire system would have been projected in a systematic and orderly way together with the investment requirements in the various parts and at various stages. A planning unit of such scope and power would have been largely independent of local influences and pressures in setting fares. Prices, in other words, would have been wholly or largely under its planning control. It could have held its own with the automobile industry and the airlines in managing, i.e., promoting, the demand for its services. It could have held its own with the automobile industry and the highway users in getting requisite public underwriting of its facilities – were costs and risks too great for it to carry, it could have pleaded military necessity as did the automobile industry and highway users in the case of the interstate highway system. Pleading further the doctrine of military necessity, it could have sought state underwriting of technical development. This would have placed it more nearly on a parity with the airlines which, in the last thirty years, have had many billions of dollars of subsidy in the form of military development of aircraft (ultimately usable as passenger vehicles) and in the development and installation of navigational facilities. The planning unit, assuming success, would have had internal sources of capital from earnings. This would have exempted it from petty interference by local governments or other sources of funds. It would have been able to make its own decisions on growth and technical innovation and would have tended to measure its success by its virtuosity in this regard. Its size and capacity for technical change, including automation, would have given it leverage in dealing with unions. Not least important, such a unit would have had a developed technostructure in which group decision would have replaced the vagaries of individual competence.

None of this has happened. Local transit systems developed under public and private auspices and subject to local political influences and regulation. The railroads, under a different system of regulation, followed their own rather special pattern of development.[1] Each part provided a fraction of the total services of moving people locally and regionally; none, in consequence, could plan the entire service. None had appreciable authority over prices, use of service, capital supply or labour supply. None had a developed technostructure. In an industry which required planning, none of the requisites of planned performance were available. It is not surprising that the results have been singularly bad.

III

Although no parallels are exact, it is interesting to contemplate the different development of telephone service. This makes use of an old form of electronic communication. As in the case of the railroads and urban transit, alternative technology has been massively subsidized by the Federal government for military purposes. But in the telephone industry one giant

---

1. Most American railroads have had a pattern of development different from that of the firms of similar size in the industrial system. There is no similarly developed technostructure; for most of their history there has been no similar technical dynamic; there has been no similar capacity for taking control of prices, demand for the services, labour and capital supply and the other requisites of successful planning. Regulation, prohibitions on mergers and diversification of activities and a tradition of routine, highly ritualized management of low technical aspiration and competence have all been factors. In Japan, France, Canada and other countries where there has been one national system or one or two dominant systems, the industry has had greater control over the requisites of its planning and its comparative performance and survival value have been much better.

corporation had planning authority coordinate with the whole task. It embraced both local and long-distance service. It had resources for competitive technical development and also for seeking government underwriting of such development where, as is usually the case, this could be justified by military application. The scale of A. T. & T. accorded it substantial authority over rates; it could enter actively on the management of the demand for its services; it had control over its capital supply; size combined with technological advance have enabled it to plan its labour requirements, keep them within the prospective supply and maintain authority over its labour force.

Had local telephone service been provided by one or more companies in each city, town and hamlet; had all these rates been subject to local regulation and influence; had long-distance service been supplied by numerous separate companies, only loosely coordinated with the local service; had there been little or no research or technical development anywhere in the system; had the local units been strongly dependent on external authority – municipal government or local banks – for capital; and had there been no planned provision for labour supply or substitute technology, it seems unlikely that telephonic communications could have survived in any very useful form.[2] That they flourished, none can doubt, is owing not to a mindless response to a free market but to the subordination of the market at all points to comprehensive planning.

In recent years, by support to technical development in interurban transit and diverse subsidies to local transit systems, steps have been taken to offset the patent incompetence of past performance in the field of surface transportation. This action has been typical of the half-hearted planning which assumes that such action is the exception rather than the rule. The plausible course, reflecting the rule, would be to constitute one

2. As a partial demonstration of the point, it has been suggested that, in the absence of automatic transmission of calls, it would require approximately the entire female working force of the country to handle current traffic.

autonomous company with ample capital to take over all mass surface movement of people in the United States (say) east of the Appalachians. This would have running rights over the railroads and full control over other facilities. It would have a wide latitude in setting rates and promoting use. Massive technological innovation would be encouraged and subsidized and urgent defence need would of course be invoked. It is entirely possible, by such a step, that urban and inter-urban movement of people might continue to be possible.

IV

Urban and inter-urban transit is one of the most visible and dramatic of the planning lacunae. It is not the most important. The most painful consequences from assuming the competence of the market are in urban and suburban housing, commercial and other real property development.

In the slums, it has long been recognized, there is no socially useful market response. Rents, because of demand for space, tend to be at the highest level the traffic will bear. Being at the maximum, they will be no higher if the property is replaced, improved or even decently maintained. The most profitable course is to minimize outlay and, where possible, to pack more people in.

Commercial urban development is responsive to the market. But it is also responsive to the greatest opportunity for gain for the individual owner. This will frequently be inconsistent with the best economic opportunity for the community – a profitable slaughterhouse will have a more than offsetting effect on the earnings of an adjacent shopping centre or the rents of an adjacent housing development. And the best commercial opportunity, in the manner of the vertical greenhouses on modern Manhattan, will often be either aesthetically inferior or offensive. Only as an act of charity will space be left for pedestrians.

The suburban residential market response is also frequently perverse. Nothing can be sold so cheaply as a house that is unprovided with sewerage, trash collection, police protection and schools. An isolated house without such amenities transgresses only upon itself. A community of such houses is incestuously offensive. The contemporary classic is the strip town which is by way of connecting all urban centres in the United States. This is the pattern of development which the market encourages.

These shortcomings are recognized. Again, however, they are assumed to be isolated failures of the market. In consequence, the corrective is the patchwork planning provided by weakly financed housing authorities of limited power and autonomy; housing and building codes which seek to enforce less profitable, but socially more desirable, behaviour; zoning regulations which seek to deny to the owners of land what seems to them their normal right to the best return; and subsidies to offset the financial advantages of bad use and promote redevelopment. Or, as also happens, nothing is done and the adverse consequences are suffered in the belief or hope that market responses, however bad in the present, will eventually become benign.

The remedy is a two-fold one. The first step is to minimize or neutralize the adverse market influences. The second is to develop a planning authority of adequate power. Only strong and comprehensive planning will redeem and make livable the modern city and its surroundings.

Since the focus of market forces is the return to, and capital gains from, land, this solution means that there must be public land acquisition wherever market influences are palpably adverse. Planning, which under urban and metropolitan administration will never be strong, will not then have to contend in each decision with the resistances of the market. Those with a vested interest in bad land use are unlikely to welcome such a remedy. But, in the end, there will prove to be no other.

The proper instrument for urban and related land acquisition and administration is a strong planning, housing and development authority. And, no less than for the manufacture of automobiles or the colonization of the moon, it will require the scale, financial autonomy, control over prices, and opportunity to develop a technostructure which are the requisites of effective planning.

The remedy also carries a price. Only liberal Republicans on first coming to office imagine that there can be social gain with no cost. Although money is important, as elsewhere in the industrial system, power and organization are even more important. And, as elsewhere, individuals will have to surrender to the goals of organization. It is thus that planning, like the industrial system in general, accomplishes its tasks. The horse-breeder and buggy-maker were far less subject to organization than the General Motors man. They were also far less successful in imposing their values on their customers. But they were less efficient in moving people about. The wretched freedoms of the slums are the counterpart of the individualism of the buggy-maker.

v

Viewing the whole economy in purely technical terms, no natural superiority can be assumed either for the market or for planning. In some places market responses still serve. Over a very large area such responses cannot be relied upon; the market must give way to more or less comprehensive planning of demand and supply. Here, if the industrial system does not plan, performance will be poor and perhaps appalling. The conservation of natural resources, the development of outdoor recreation, forestry in the eastern United States, are all further examples. The error is in basing action on generalization. There is no natural presumption in favour of the market; given the growth of the industrial system the presumption is, if anything, the reverse. And to rely on the market where planning is required is to invite a nasty mess.

Chapter 32

OF TOIL

> Don't mourn for me, friends, don't
>   weep for me never,
> For I'm going to do nothing forever
>   and ever.
>
> *Traditional epitaph
> of an English charwoman.*

THE industrial system has long held out one rather striking promise to its participants. This is the eventual opportunity for a great deal more leisure. The work week and the work year will be radically reduced. There will be much more free time. Over the last quarter-century, a reputation for cerebration beyond the reach of run-of-the-mill minds has been most easily achieved by speculation on how, when this day comes, men will employ what is invariably called their newfound leisure. It is agreed that the question deserves the most careful study. There are dangers of abuse. Over the last quarter-century, as this is written, the average work week in industry has increased moderately. The standard work week has declined but this has been more than offset by increased demand for overtime work and the companion willingness to supply it.[1] During this period average weekly earnings, adjusted for price increases, have nearly doubled. On the evidence, one must conclude that, as their incomes rise, men will work longer hours and seek less leisure.

The notion of a new era of greatly expanded leisure is, in fact, a conventional conversation piece. Nor will it serve much longer to convey an impression of social vision. The tendency of the industrial system is not in this direction.

1. In 1941 the average work week in manufacturing was 40·6 hours; in 1965 it was 41·1 hours and rising. *Economic Report of the President,* 1966.

Specifically, in the early stages of the industrial system, toil was dreary, repetitive and physically painful. It was also very long. Severe prison sentences featured the inclusion of hard labour. Heaven was a place, above all, of eternal rest. Until curbed by the enlightened intervention of (among others) Warren Gamaliel Harding, the steel industry in the United States worked a twelve-hour day and an eighty-four-hour week. There were no holidays; in the steel towns all days were alike. When the shift changed, a man worked twice around the clock; as a reward, in return, he had twenty-four hours off a fortnight later. The management of wants was still in its infancy and the steelworker – without radio or television and often illiterate – was well beyond its reach. As important therefore as making more money, and perhaps more important, was to make it with fewer hours of this hideous toil. Men worked to meet a minimum – to make a living. Few non-workers have been able since to suppose that progressive reduction in hours can be other than a prime goal of the working stiff.

Outside of the industrial system, as in the cotton and vegetable fields, work can still be hard and tedious. But within the industrial system, though always with exceptions, work is unlikely to be painful and it may be pleasant. And the worker has now been brought within the fully deployed power of modern demand management. He too is subject to the revised sequence. So, where his precursor in the steel towns worked to make a living, he works to satisfy his constantly expanded wants. The result is obvious. With more pleasant work and expanded wants, a man is somewhat more likely to choose more work than more leisure.

As one moves into and up through the technostructure, men increasingly exercise the option of more work and more income. And some pride themselves on an unlimited and competitive commitment to toil – one that, regularly, outruns even the most imaginative possibilities for the acquisition and use of goods and services.

Of Toil

It follows that to argue for less work and more leisure, as a natural goal of industrial man, is to misread the character of the industrial system. There is no intrinsic reason why work must be more unpleasant than non-work. Presiding over the console that regulates the movements of billets through a steel mill may be as pleasant as sojourning with a connubial fish-wife. To urge more leisure is a feckless exercise so long as the industrial system has the capacity to persuade its people that goods are more important. Men will value leisure over work only as they find the uses of leisure more interesting or rewarding than those of work, or as they win emancipation from the management of their wants, or both. Leisure is not wanted *per se* but only as these prerequisites are provided.

The two ends – the cultivation of interests that are an attractive alternative to work and the greater or less emancipation from demand management – are both, it is reasonable to assume, the result of education. Men of substantial mental accomplishment have not usually lacked interesting ways of employing their time apart from toil. And it seems likely that they will be somewhat less susceptible to the management of demand. The ethos of the educational and scientific estate is illuminating in this connexion. Especially in its higher orders, the academic community ostentatiously resists demand management and insists on extensive exemption from formal commitment to toil. Excessive attention to goods is considered *gauche*; an elderly automobile, casual and shabby clothing, undistinguished furniture, self-designed entertainment, unluxurious travel, the absence of a television receiver and even functionally clothed women are sources of distinction. Academic prestige is associated with a minimum of formal teaching and other academic obligations. Long vacations, sabbatical years and further leaves of absence are established rights. All are assumed to enable the individual to cultivate interests not served by his formal hours of toil. As the capitalist of an earlier era thought himself entitled to the homage of the community by natural and even divine right, so the aforementioned privileges are regarded by the academic community as appropriately unique to itself. Only men whose minds are tooled to similarly fine response could require such protection from routine – and use it well. This may not be so. More likely, it is merely one of the fringe benefits of education and opportunity.

Most people will believe that the greatest possible emancipation of the individual from the management to which he is subject, the considerable cost to the industrial system by its own standards notwithstanding, is a worthy objective. And it follows that the greatest chance for achieving such emancipation lies with education. This requires, in turn, that the educational and scientific estate have a clear view both of its powers and its responsibilities. I come to these matters in the next two chapters. Additionally, and as a quite practical matter, there is need for a much larger range of options for the individual person in the industrial system. This will allow those who are able to emancipate themselves to do so. This opportunity for choice between toil and its alternatives, not leisure *per se*, is the immediate need. It is something that could engage the residual energies of the trade unions.

III

Few things are more fully adapted to the convenience and the values of the industrial system than the arrangements to which the labour force is subject. It is assumed that all men should work a standard number of hours a week. Those who wish may, by overtime or moonlighting, work more; none may work less. Negotiation is ordinarily for increased income or its equivalent. If more leisure – for example, paid vacations – is sought it is obtained in equal amount for all alike. The ethos of the industrial system is evident at all points. A basic minimum of toil is required from all. All have a normal preference for money. All have the same desire and capacity for leisure. All should be treated alike.

None of this is necessary. The employed person should be accorded a much wider set of options than at present as between work and goods on the one hand and leisure on the other. The way should be open for the individual who wishes to satisfy his needs for food, clothing and simple houseroom with ten or twenty hours of labour a week to do so. We should look with interest and hopefully with admiration on inventive use of the remaining time.

But the options should not be confined to the work week. This is a poor unit around which to organize the effective use of leisure time; it has long been a perquisite of high social, educational or financial position that life – holidays, travel, tasks – is planned in terms of months or years. All individuals, in return for a lower annual pay, should have the option of several months' paid vacation. And all should similarly have the option of extended leaves of absence. The employees exercising these options would not be favoured in compensation per hour worked. What they are offered is the opportunity of choosing absence and exemption from toil in various forms as an alternative to earnings. There would be some inconvenience. But to fail to allow such choice – to be guided by the belief that everyone should work a standard week and year – is to make the needs of the industrial system, not the opportunity of the individual to fashion his own existence, the ruling social concern. Men who speak much of liberty should allow and even encourage it.

IV

In the United States as in other industrial countries, the natural objects of social concern are the wage worker, and subject to local circumstance, Negroes, small farmers, the mentally deficient, the aged and the endemically indigent. Others are thought able to look after themselves. While businessmen and the rich occasionally appeal for compassion, it is usually with reference to some specific act of public oppression such as a tax. And they often argue that the ultimate incidence of their affliction is on some manual toiler for whom they suffer as a surrogate. The scholar who devotes himself to the woes of the well-to-do has been thought by the captious to have a special concern for the hand that feeds him or which might.

Yet it could be that the industrial system, and its ethos, impose the greatest burden on its leaders – on those who are at the centre of the technostructure. This is not because they subordinate their personality to organization; that is inherent and could be remedied only by dispensing with the industrial system. And, in any case, the surrender is voluntary; it occurs because men find the goals of organization superior to their own.[2]

But the technostructure has compulsions that are in addition to the demands of organization. And, far more than for the workers, these shape the lives of its members or those of the inner circles. It begins with education. Success in the technostructure calls for mastery of one or more of the arts associated with planning, technology or organization or the management of demand. In some of its scientific and technological branches this study has considerable intrinsic interest. But it seems likely that in a culture where education was pursued for its own sake, few men would study personnel management, media analysis, market research or costs and quality control.

In the inner circles of the technostructure the commitment of mental energy and moral purpose must, for all practical purposes, be total. The purposes of the industrial system being identical with all life, those so serving it must make it identical with life. The blue-collar worker who supplies forty hours of service each week is morally acceptable. For a senior executive to set any such limits on his efforts is morally deficient. He must have recreation. He cannot be indifferent to juvenile delinquency, cancer, drug addiction, heart disease, or civic growth. But all of this must, generally speaking, be in support of his primary business function.

And the outcome is not attractive. Having been measured through his lifetime by the single-mindedness with which he subordinates all normal tastes and enjoyments to the needs of

2. Chapter 11.

the corporation, he is then at the age of sixty-five firmly retired. This is essential. In an occupation which depends on group activity and oral interchange, no one is so feared as the putatively senile. Uncontrolled and undirected talk must be guarded against at all costs. The habit of total commitment having been fully established, he has now nothing to do – or only what is obvious make-work. Having become wholly habituated to group activity, he is now alone. It is not a beautifully sculptured arrangement. Millions since the dawn of man have led a less inspired existence but never on comparable income.

Ultimately one of the problems of the industrial system may be in reproducing the technostructure. And there may already be signs of difficulty. Once the schools of business, the most general training ground for the technostructure, were among the most prestigious branches of American higher education. They are so no longer. Some, with the caution of those who do not wish admission of a fact to reinforce a trend, report a serious decline in the quality of their applicants. The best schools have ceased to expect to recruit the best students. And good students, when asked about business, are increasingly adverse. They hold it to be excessively disciplined, damaging to individuality, not worth the high pay, or dull.[3]

We reach an interesting if speculative result. Emancipation could be the salvation of the industrial system. Its discipline will be worse but only thus will it attract people who are sufficiently good.

3. These are impressions drawn primarily from discussion with faculty and students at Harvard. It is a common impression that in Middle-western universities and colleges the prestige of business continues to be higher.

Chapter 33

EDUCATION AND EMANCIPATION

BOTH the basic tendency of the industrial system and the thrust of needed policy are now clear. As an organic characteristic of its operation, the industrial system reaches out comprehensively to win the belief that validates its planning and which wins acceptance of its goals. Therewith it ensures the success of the organization on which it so greatly depends. There is, most will think, an uncomfortably collectivist and monolithic aspect to this. The countering action is what helps the individual escape this subordination. The requirements are twofold: The first is comprehension and scepticism which ensures that there will be systematic questioning of the beliefs impressed by the industrial system. The second is a political pluralism which voices the ideas and goals of those who, intellectually speaking, choose to contract out of the industrial system.

For this emancipation, education – higher education in particular – is obviously strategic. It is, among other things, an apparatus for affecting belief and inducing more critical belief. The industrial system, by making trained and educated manpower the decisive factor of production, requires a highly developed educational system. If the educational system serves generally the beliefs of the industrial system, the influence and monolithic character of the latter will be enhanced. By the same token, should it be superior to and independent of the industrial system, it can be the necessary force for scepticism, emancipation and pluralism.

Modern higher education is, of course, extensively accommodated to the needs of the industrial system. The schools and colleges of business administration, mentioned in the last chapter, are preparatory academies for the technostructure. The great prestige of the pure and applied sciences and mathematics in modern times, and the support accorded them, reflect the needs of the technostructure. The ample sums available for research and related graduate training in these areas reflect specific adaptation to such need, whereas the lesser prestige and lesser support for the arts and humanities suggest their inferior role. No modern university administration would insist, in fact as distinct from speech, that the study of the theatre, fine arts or *Beowulf* had the same claim to funds in the same amounts as an electronic accelerator or a computer centre. Such is the influence of the industrial system.

This influence has not gone unchallenged. Too complete an orientation to the needs of the industrial system is resisted, at least in the more mature and self-confident educational communities. The business and engineering schools are valued for their reassuring aspect of utility as are the scientists and mathematicians for their association with pregnant and often alarming change. But the service of the university to the aesthetic, cultural and intellectual enjoyments of the individual is still asserted. Indeed, such assertion comprises, by a wide margin, the largest part of the ceremonial literature of modern higher education. No university president is inaugurated, few speak, only rarely is a commencement address given, no anniversary is celebrated, and no great educator is retired without a reference to the continuing importance of liberal education for its own sake. In part this reflects the paucity of non-controversial topics available to men of high reputation for wisdom but slight specific information. It reflects also the deep conviction of the modern college president that any unsatisfactory educational tendency can be exorcised by sufficiently solemn oratory. To transfer actual funds from engineering to fine arts would be more difficult. Yet even the oratory, however vacuous, suggests the problem. The industrial system has induced an enormous expansion in education. This can only be welcomed. But unless its tendencies are clearly foreseen and strongly resisted, it will place a preclusive emphasis on education that most serves the needs, but least questions the goals, of that system.

The New Industrial State

II

The proper course of action is clear. The college and university community must retain paramount authority for the education it provides and for the research it undertakes. The needs of the industrial system must always be secondary to the cultivation of general understanding and perception. Similarly, support for research and scholarship must be in accordance with some natural distribution of human curiosity and competence. It will be urged that this is a counsel of perfection. It is, and it suggests how readily we assume that education and research must be subordinate to the needs of the industrial system. But they need not be subordinate if it is realized that the educator is a figure of power in this context. He is the source of the factor of production on which industrial success depends; he must realize this and exert his power, not on behalf of the industrial system but on behalf of the entire human personality.

The first, and very practical, step is for educational institutions to regain control of their own budgets. For many years this control has been undergoing steady erosion. Funds are accepted from the Federal government and, in lesser measure, directly from industrial firms, for research, for teaching and for scholarships for specified purposes or areas. The funds reflect the areas of industrial need. In effect, it means that the industrial system, acting on its own behalf or through the agency of the Federal government, has by-passed the university administration to adapt education to its requirements. The nineteenth-century entrepreneur who, from his position on the university board, intervened to suppress heresy and insist on proper respect for Christian principles and acquisitive capitalism, exercised only the most trivial influence as compared with the power thus deployed. It is a measure of its subtlety, and of that of the standard college president, that the latter, declaiming on his commitment to academic freedom, is often unaware of how much of it he has himself surrendered.

If individual university disciplines are directly subsidized by the state or the business enterprise and continue to have and expand contractual relationships with these sources of funds, the result is nearly certain. Not only will the subjects so favoured have a distorted growth in response to the needs of the system but those involved will tend to identify themselves increasingly with the goals of the contracting agencies and enterprises. They will not be immune to tendencies here analysed; they will come more or less fully into the orbit of the industrial system. The university will become a shell with which they have only a residential association. If, however, universities can regain and retain power in the distribution of their resources not only is there chance that these will be allocated in accordance with humane and intellectual, as opposed to industrial, need, but moreover the identification of the constituent members will be with the corporate entity of the university and with its goals. Both the possibility of this, and its importance, the present analysis sufficiently shows.

III

In the distribution of educational resources it ought to be the rule that the student preparing for a career in personnel management, television advertising or computer programming as a servant of the industrial system, will find the requisite educational facilities and have access to the needed financial support. Concern for a remunerative career will ensure an adequate number of applicants. But the individual whose concern is with poetry or painting and but slightly with his financial prospects will have equal opportunity including equal chance for a scholarship. Similarly with provision for research and scholarly effort. The price that the industrial system must pay for the education of *its* people and the conduct of *its* research is the support of general enlightenment.

To support and encourage those concerned with aesthetic and intellectual experience is to support the requisite scrutiny of the industrial system and to sustain the requisite pluralism. The cultivation of these attitudes and interests is by no means a hopeless or even difficult task. The young have a reassuring tendency to take a fresh view of life. Education that accords with the needs of the industrial system does not have a natural aspect of interest, plausibility or importance. Much of it is dull. The learning that enables an individual to participate effectively in the development of the monogramming toaster described heretofore does not have an intrinsic air of social urgency. Nor does preparation for the manufacture of automobiles in a world gorged with vehicles, or of a more potently and precisely destructive missile in a world which has already arranged extensively for its own incineration. Against this, education that serves purely intellectual and aesthetic interests, and encourages the resulting detachment from the goals of the industrial system, is by no means unattractive.

Commitment to these alternative goals, and the associated questioning and pluralism, will also characterize the larger intellectual and artistic community. But the commitment can be directly cultivated only by the proper educational policy. This is a matter about which no serious educator can be indifferent, for to be indifferent is to give passive support to a preclusive role for the goals of the industrial system. Though these serve the industrial system well, they do so by diminishing the aesthetic and intellectual dimensions of life. To this no one who takes himself seriously as a teacher or as an intellectual can consent. And the industrial system also constructs images of public and foreign policy which, though they serve admirably the needs of the industrial system, could if unchallenged be mortal for civilization.

IV

These changes, important though they are, will not come easily to American education. For one thing, next only to businessmen, educators have acquired the habit of lecturing each other on their social responsibilities and as a necessary counterpart, since reaction to this flood of adjuration would be impossible, of ignoring it. The first inclination of most educators will be to dismiss these pages as another hortatory exercise. It can only be hoped that reflection will lead to a more useful response.

Additionally, American colleges and universities were long fed on the crumbs from the rich man's plate or accorded public funds only after genuinely important matters such as roads, the courts, public hygiene, jails and insane asylums were provided for. They were frequently watched for heresy by the entrepreneur or his appointed agents. Many maintained their independence less by courage than guile, although one must not minimize the astonishing intransigence of those whose vanity lies not in wealth or power but in the right to think. All college and university administrations and many professors developed habits of extreme obsequiousness where money was concerned. Many scholars persuaded themselves, in one way or another, that they had no political or public responsibilities of any kind. Some came to believe that, as scholars, they were required to eschew all public responsibility.

Educators have yet to realize how deeply the industrial system is dependent upon them. That public and private funds are supplied in comparative abundance as a result of this dependence still evokes surprise. After living so long on charity, the habits of obsequiousness continue. That the purposes of the university should be strongly asserted, even where money is at stake, still seems a trifle irresponsible.

Such attitudes of mind are both out of date and dangerous. Colleges and universities can serve the needs of the technostructure and reinforce the goals of the industrial system. They can train the people and cultivate the attitudes which ensure technological advance, allow of effective planning and ensure acquiescence in the management of consumer and public demand. And they can affirm the policy images, including those on foreign policy, that the latter requires. This is the line of least resistance; it will be the consequence of a purely passive response by educators to the development of the industrial system. It will be the consequence of the orthodox view by the educator of his role. Or colleges and universities can strongly assert the values and goals of educated men – those that serve not the production of goods and associated planning but the intellectual and artistic development of man. It is hard to believe there is a choice.

The educational and scientific estate has the power to exercise its option. It holds the critical cards. For in committing itself to technology, planning and organization, the industrial system has made itself deeply dependent on the manpower which these require. The banker, in the days when capital was decisive, was not unaware of his bargaining power. The educator should not be more innocent today.

The growth and influence of college and university communities are in response to the needs of the industrial system. But this does not necessarily create a primary obligation to the needs of the industrial system. Gratitude and debt do not exist as between social institutions. The only reality is the right social purpose.

v

There can be little doubt that higher education, which has been most extensively and expensively accommodated to the needs of the industrial system, is the point where effort must be concentrated. Secondary and primary education have been less accommodated and lend themselves less to accommodation to the needs of the industrial system and to its beliefs. Adolescents, accordingly, emerge in comparatively malleable condition. Here too there is benefit and safety in recognizing how our social belief, and what is taught or assumed, tends to reflect the needs of the industrial system. But, *prima facie* at least, no dangers or correctives seem urgent. As compared with the pressures of the earlier industrialism, there can only be satisfaction at the influence which the industrial system exerts for improved primary and secondary education.

The industrial system has little direct power over channels of written communication. Much of this reflects approved belief. But this fact is the result of indoctrination, persuasion or absence of persuasively argued alternatives rather than of repression. The dissenter to the industrial system has little problem in expressing his dissent. If nothing else, the fact that most instruments of literary communication – newspapers, magazines, book publishers – must be manned by intellectuals ensures that the goals of the intellectuals will be respected. This also accounts, one imagines, for a good part of the leverage exercised by intellectuals on behalf of more liberal expression in the Soviet Union and the Eastern European states.[1]

Those who complain that they have been censored in the United States usually turn out, on examination, to have had nothing much to say.

In one area the industrial system is uniquely powerful, although less in the propagation of ideas than in general mental conditioning. This is radio and especially television broadcasting. As we have seen, these are essential for effective management of demand and thus for industrial planning. The process by which this management is accomplished, the iterated and re-iterated emphasis on the real and assumed virtues of goods, is powerful propaganda for the values and goals of the system. It reaches to all cultural levels. In the United States there is no satisfactory non-commercial alternative.

It would be good if there were. The desideratum is not educational radio and television but radio and television offering a wide range of enjoyment which is not committed by its nature to the service of the industrial system. As this goes to press it is being urged that revenues accruing to government-financed innovation in electronic communication, specifically from the communications satellite, be used to finance a non-commercial television system. This demand is a response to a genuine need, the solid foundations of which will now be clear.

1. And elsewhere. A year or two ago I gave a lecture in Spain. It argued the utilitarian as well as the intellectual values of academic and political freedom, made a strong case for unions and urged the benign character of popular and democratic pressure on the state. I was told that I would get extensive press coverage for, in the absence of specific censorship instructions, reporters and editors would exploit their natural libertarian bias. So it was.

379

Chapter 34

THE POLITICAL LEAD

ONLY the innocent reformer and the obtuse conservative imagine the state to be an instrument of change apart from the interests and aspirations of those who comprise it. The interests or needs of the industrial system are advanced with subtlety and power. Since they are made to seem coordinate with the purposes of society, government action serving the needs of the industrial system has a strong aspect of social purpose. And, as we have seen, the line between the industrial system and the state becomes increasingly artificial and indistinct. The technostructure of the large corporation tends to become an extension of those parts of the Federal bureaucracy – notably the armed services, N.A.S.A., A.E.C. and other agencies concerned with technological development – on which it most depends. It identifies itself with the purposes of the agency and adapts these to its needs.

The last chapters have told something of what we must do if we are to have a safer and more durable as well as a more eclectic, agreeable and intellectually and aesthetically progressive society. Some of the needs, notably a safer basis for underwriting technology and an understanding between industrial societies on this point, are obviously important for the survival of the industrial system as well as of all other organizations requiring the continued use of human beings. Other steps – the expansion of public services that are not sponsored by the industrial system, the assertion of the aesthetic dimension of life, widened choice as between income and leisure, the emancipation of education – require that the monopoly of the industrial system on social purpose be broken. This will not, one imagines, be welcomed by all members of the industrial system. They will see, correctly, that it is designed to reduce the role of the latter in life. But it is not inconsistent with the continued existence of that system. As the next chapter suggests, that will be decided by other circumstances.

Still, none of these changes can be brought about save by some agency that is powerfully determined to get them. What is this agency?

II

The needed changes, including those in the images by which military and foreign policy are shaped, all involve the sensibilities and concerns of the mind. Their natural, although by no means exclusive, interest therefore is to those who are called intellectuals. The largest number of intellectuals with an occupational identification are those in the educational and scientific estate. It is to the educational and scientific estate, accordingly, that we must turn for the requisite political initiative. The initiative cannot come from the industrial system, although support can be recruited from individuals therein. Nor will it come from the trade unions. Apart from their declining numbers and power, they are under no particular compulsion to question the goals of the industrial system or the tendency to make all social purpose identical with those goals.

This is written at a time of much rather incoherent and unfocused dissent by younger people. Much of this dissent reflects a dissatisfaction with the goals so self-confidently asserted by the industrial system and its spokesmen. It will be highly responsive to leadership. It will be unfocused and ineffective until this leadership is supplied.

In a study of this sort, one must ration carefully one's generalizations concerning the fate of man. No currency is so quickly devalued. Those one would least trust to decide man's fate are invariably the first to pronounce upon it. Yet it is safe to say that the future of what is called modern society depends on how willingly and effectively the intellectual community in general, and the educational and scientific estate in particular, assume responsibilities for political action and leadership.

For this they have numerous advantages. There is a tradition, limited but significant, of their political involvement in the United States as well as elsewhere. The intellectual, as he is loosely described, is a commonplace figure in American politics. The professional politician with his florid speech, unvalidated self-confidence, ineffable affability, skill at evading issues and undemanding mind is more highly regarded by journalists and novelists to whom he gives a rewarding sense of superiority. Both regularly give credence to the professional's estimate of the ineptitude of the intellectual in politics. Withal, it is the intellectual, or at least the man who is intelligently committed to social purpose, who survives. At the moment when political pundits are according him the greatest praise for his acuity, the accomplished professional is usually going down to well-merited defeat.

Unlike members of the technostructure, the educational and scientific estate is not handicapped in political action by being accustomed to function only as part of an organization. It gains power in a socially complex society from its capacity for social invention. And while its power must rest on its ability to attract the support of attached and unattached individuals, in the future its numbers will command respect. In several states as this is written – Michigan, Wisconsin, Minnesota, California – the educational and scientific estate has a strong hold on the state and local organization of the Democratic Party. And the university and college community has been expressing itself with special insistence on issues of foreign policy. Although bureaucratic and military attitudes have not been perceptibly affected, political leadership has not been indifferent. One of the indices of the growing power of the educational and scientific estate has been the reaction which its intervention on foreign policy has provoked. Like the middle class a century ago and the unions a generation back, it has been regularly advised that it should eschew such interference and confine itself rigorously to its proper tasks. It is perhaps sensed that numerous of our present images of foreign policy and national security are vulnerable to competent scrutiny.

Finally, since World War II, scientists have emerged as an independent force, especially where science impinges on foreign policy. As earlier observed, the nuclear test ban treaty of 1963 would not have been achieved except by the initiative of the scientific community. General public and political awareness of the dangers of nuclear conflict, the desirability of *détente* with the Soviet Union and the technical possibilities for disarmament owes a great deal to the scientific community. It owes very little to the military, diplomatic and industrial community.

III

The educational and scientific estate, with its allies in the larger intellectual community, has formidable difficulties to overcome. Like any new political force it lacks self-confidence. This includes a lack of confidence in its own objectives. There is wide scepticism in the educational and scientific estate about the images that underlie the arms race. The ethos of the industrial system – its measurement of success by its capacity to increase production in response to wants of its own creation – evokes scepticism. There would be considerable agreement on the need to assert the other dimensions of life and on the use of social authority on their behalf. It would not be difficult to arouse support for wider options in regard to work and leisure or an educational system more strongly oriented to aesthetic and intellectual values, as distinct from the vocational needs of the industrial system. But not all will believe that there is any chance of persuading the larger national community of their importance, or even that the educational and scientific estate has any responsibility in the matter. It still has a strong tendency to surrender to the goals of the industrial system before the battle is joined.

There are also dangers in the lead that is assumed, more or less as a right, by economists in these matters. Not all economists accept the goals of the industrial system; professional concern with the discipline encourages speculation on the origins and sanctity of conventional belief. That our beliefs are extensively accommodated to the needs of the industrial system will not seem improbable to many economists. They will not be resistant to the present argument.

But the economic stereotypes – the production models that lend themselves to assembly-line instruction – insist on the approved sequence. And doubtless, for reasons of sunk costs and convenience, they will continue to do so. Their defenders will hold that wants are original with the individual; that the success of the society is measured by the amount that it supplies to satisfy these wants; that this test, so convenient for the industrial system, is the only sensible one to apply. These beliefs are inherent in man's nature and the result of no social conditioning of any kind. Other goals being unimportant and other beliefs being frivolous, they hardly call for political effort.

In recent years it has often appeared to those outside the discipline that the economists were in heavy conflict with the industrial system. This especially concerned regulation of aggregate demand. The economists proposed more spending by the state for a wide variety of things; they advocated tax reduction and deliberate deficits. Businessmen recoiled in alarm. To the rest of the educational and scientific estate the economists seemed thus to be the defenders of the broader social purposes of employment and expansion against the smaller, more parochial objectives of their business critics. This is an illusion. The economists were partly at odds with the entrepreneurs who, unlike the technostructure, were not major beneficiaries of these policies. Their general capacity for social innovation had put them somewhat in advance of the technostructure in the policies they urged. And they differed on methods and on the vigour with which the goals of full employment and growth should be pursued. But these differences, and the associated polemics, did not involve goals as such. There has been full agreement on the preclusive importance of high and expanding production and, therewith, high employment. To the extent that the rest of the educational and scientific estate surrendered responsibility for social purpose to the economists, they accepted the goals of the industrial system.

Were economic goals of central importance, economists, always assuming competence, would be a safe guide to social action. As economic goals have diminished in relative importance, they have become, progressively, a less safe guide. Allowing for numerous exceptions, they will be prone to identify economic goals with all of life. They are not, accordingly, the best proponents of the public, aesthetic and intellectual priorities on which the quality and safety of life increasingly depend. They are, in the main, the natural allies of the industrial system.[1]

IV

Finally, both the educational and scientific estate and the intellectual community are handicapped by the belief that their role is professionally passive – that it is to feel and think but not to act. Righteousness, as well as convenience, defends this passivity. Politics is not the business of the intellectual or the artist. Nor of the educator nor of the scientist. Theirs is the purer domain of the spirit and the mind. This can only be sullied by concern for practical affairs. In the last milli-second before the ultimate nuclear fusion, a scientist will be heard to observe that the issue of nuclear control and military security is really one for politicians and their military and diplomatic advisers. And as the last horizon is lost behind the smoke, gas, neon lights and detritus of the industrial civilization, men of self-confessed artistic sensitivity will be heard to observe that, unfortunately, none of this is the business of the true artist. In fact, no intellectual, no artist, no educator, no scientist can allow himself the convenience of doubting his responsibility. For the goals that are now important there are no other saviours. In a scientifically exacting world scientists must assume responsibility for the consequences of science and technology. For custody of the aesthetic dimension of life there is

1. Again I refer the reader, the dubious one in particular, to the Addendum following the next chapter.

no substitute for the artist. The individual member of the educational and scientific estate may wish to avoid responsibility; but he cannot justify it by the claim of higher commitment.

In the earlier stages of economic development, when the academic community was a small, weak and partially decorative appendage of the industrial society, it was natural that many should see their best role as being seen and not heard. Commanding power lay with the entrepreneur. It made sense not to affront it. If a righteous commitment to science or art could be adduced as the justification for this discretion, it was ideal – the equivalent of a priestly indulgence for cowardice. Those who would suffer from a more active role by the educational and scientific estate, as it grows in numbers and power, will naturally hope that it will continue to find such reasons for abstaining from political concern. And they will applaud as saintly persons those who do.

The educational and scientific estate, like the intellectual community in general, has tended also to be diverted by the surrogates for political action. Writing, lecturing and even determined conversation bulk large in this regard. They are the tools of the intellectual's trade; since they are what he possesses he must, like an air force general contemplating the use of bombers to prevent men from walking through a jungle, assume that they are of value. He ends either by persuading those who are already persuaded or he sharpens disagreement on the small neat points that are so cherished in academic debate and so damaging to political effectiveness. Nearly all of the matters here urged – redirection of the weapons competition, social control of environment, a wider range of choice by the individual, emancipation of education – require some form of political action. Political action requires that legislators be persuaded or replaced by those who do not need persuasion. There is no alternative to having effective friends of these ideas occupy the relative elective and appointive public offices and to having them held firmly to their duty by a watchful and determined constituency.

But in other respects the prospect for such political action is better. The educational and scientific estate, and the associated intellectual community, are – as repeatedly noted – growing rapidly to a formidable size. And this occurs, as also noted, at a time when there is a strong tendency to question established goals. In both foreign and domestic economic policy there is suspicion of what is believed, not inaccurately, to be the unexamined or automatic position of what has come to be called the Establishment. Such attitudes await the political lead here urged.

This questioning of goals comes because a long current of liberal reform has now run its course. In the past liberals have been economic liberals; reform has meant economic reform. The goals of this reform have been reproduced in hundreds of platforms, speeches, and manifestos. Production must rise; income must rise; distribution of income must improve; unemployment must fall. This, for decades, has been the platform of the liberal reformer; not even the Ten Commandments are as familiar and certainly they are far from being as well realized. Except as he may stress more equitable distribution of income, the reformer's goals are identical with those of the industrial system. Except as he concerns himself specifically with the poor he has become the political voice of the industrial system. It is an effortless role; no loud controversy is involved, there are no unseemly quarrels, no one need be persuaded. It is merely necessary to stand modestly at attention and take a bow as the Gross National Product goes up again, perhaps by a record amount. Reformers who so spend their time are, in effect, unemployed. And it cannot be doubted that many realize that this is their case.

Progress on the present agenda will be much less measurable than that which associates all progress with percentage increases in Gross National Product or percentage levels of unemployment. It is because the goals of the industrial system are so narrow that they lend themselves to precise statistical assessment. But life is meant to be complex. There will be dispute over the definition of success. And there will be considerable controversy over both the legitimacy of the alternative goals and the means of achieving them – over aesthetically motivated control of environment, for example. There will be opposition from both entrenched interest and inert intellect. And there will be need to persuade. In short, there are tasks here, once more, that are worthy of a reformer's mettle.

Chapter 35

THE FUTURE OF THE INDUSTRIAL SYSTEM

IN the latter part of the last century and the early decades of this, no subject was more discussed than the future of capitalism. Economists, men of unspecific wisdom, Chautauqua lecturers, editorial writers, knowledgeable ecclesiastics and socialists contributed their personal revelation. It was taken for granted that the economic system was in a state of development and in time would transform itself into something hopefully better but certainly different. Socialists drew strength from the belief that theirs was the plausible next stage in a natural process of change.

The future of the industrial system, by contrast, is not discussed. The prospect for agriculture is subject to debate – it is assumed to be in course of change. So are the chances for survival for the small entrepreneur or the private medical practitioner. But General Motors, General Electric and U.S. Steel are viewed as an ultimate achievement. One does not wonder where one is going if one is already there.

Yet to suppose that the industrial system is a terminal phenomenon is, *per se*, implausible. It is itself the product, in the last sixty years, of a vast and autonomous transformation. During this time the scale of the individual corporation has grown enormously. The entrepreneurial corporation has declined. The technostructure has developed, removed itself from control by the stockholders and acquired its own internal sources of capital. There has been a large change in its relations with the workers and a yet larger one in its relations with the state. It would be strange were such a manifestation of social dynamics to be now at an end. So to suggest is to deny one of the philosophical tenets of the system itself, one that is solemnly articulated on all occasions of business ritual – conventions, stockholders' meetings, board meetings, executive committee meetings, management development conferences, budget conferences, product review meetings, senior officer retreats and dealer relation workshops. It is that change is the law of economic life.

The future of the industrial system is not discussed partly because of the power it exercises over belief. It has succeeded, tacitly, in excluding the notion that it is a transitory, which would be to say that it is a somewhat imperfect, phenomenon. More important, perhaps, to consider the future would be to fix attention on where it has already arrived. Among the least enchanting words in the business lexicon are planning, government control, state support and socialism. To consider the likelihood of these in the future would be to bring home the appalling extent to which they are already a fact. And it would not be ignored that these grievous things have arrived, at a minimum with the acquiescence and, at a maximum, on the demand, of the system itself.

II

Such reflection on the future would also emphasize the convergent tendencies of industrial societies, however different their popular or ideological billing; the convergence being to a roughly similar design for organization and planning. A word in review may be worthwhile. Convergence begins with modern large-scale production, with heavy requirements of capital, sophisticated technology and, as a prime consequence, elaborate organization. These require control of prices and, so far as possible, of what is bought at those prices. This is to say that planning must replace the market. In the Soviet-type economies, the control of prices is a function of the state. The management of demand (eased by the knowledge that their people will mostly want what Americans and Western Europeans already have) is partly by according preference to the alert and early-rising who are first to the store; partly, as in the case of houseroom, by direct allocation to the recipient; and partly, as in the case of automobiles, by making patience (as well as political position or need) a test of eligibility. With us this management is accomplished less formally by the corporations, their advertising agencies, salesmen, dealers and retailers. But these, obviously, are differences in method rather than purpose. Large-scale industrialism requires, in both cases, that the market and consumer sovereignty be extensively superseded.

Large-scale organization also requires autonomy. The intrusion of an external and uninformed will is damaging. In the non-Soviet systems this means excluding the capitalist from effective power. But the same imperative operates in the socialist economy. There the business firm seeks to minimize or exclude control by the bureaucracy. To gain autonomy for the enterprise is what, in substantial measure, the modern communist theoretician calls reform. Nothing in our time is more interesting than that the erstwhile capitalist corporation and the erstwhile communist firm should, under the imperatives of organization, come together as oligarchies of their own members. Ideology is not the relevant force. Large and complex organizations can use diverse knowledge and talent and thus function effectively only if under their own authority. This, it must be stressed once more, is not autonomy that subordinates a firm to the market. It is autonomy that allows the firm authority over its planning.

The industrial system has no inherent capacity for regulating total demand – for ensuring a supply of purchasing power sufficient to acquire what it produces. So it relies on the state for this. At full employment there is no mechanism for holding prices and wages stable. This stabilization too is a function of the state. The Soviet-type systems also make a careful calculation of the income that is being provided in relation to the value of the goods available for purchase. Stabilization of wages and prices in general is, of course, a natural consequence of fixing individual prices and wage rates.

Finally, the industrial system must rely on the state for trained and educated manpower, now the decisive factor of production. So it also is under socialist industrialism. A decade ago, following the flight of the first sputnik, there was great and fashionable concern in the United States for scientific and technical education. Many argued that the Soviet system, with its higher priority for state functions, among which education is prominent, had a natural advantage in this regard.

Thus convergence between the two ostensibly different industrial systems occurs at all fundamental points. This is an exceedingly fortunate thing. In time, and perhaps in less time than may be imagined, it will dispose of the notion of inevitable conflict based on irreconcilable difference. This will not be soon agreed. Marx did not foresee the convergence and he is accorded, with suitable interpretation, the remarkable, even supernatural, power of foreseeing all. Those who speak for the unbridgeable gulf that divides the free world from the communist world and free enterprise from communism are protected by an equally ecclesiastical faith that whatever the evolution of free enterprise may be, it cannot conceivably come to resemble socialism. But these positions can survive the evidence only for a time. Only the most committed ideologist or the most fervent propagandist can stand firm against the feeling that an increasing number of people regard him as obsolete. Vanity is a great force for intellectual modernization.

To recognize that industrial systems are convergent in their development will, one imagines, help toward agreement on the common dangers in the weapons competition, on ending it or shifting it to more benign areas. Perhaps nothing casts more light on the future of the industrial system than this, for it implies, in contrast with the present images, that it could have a future.

III

Given the deep dependence of the industrial system on the state and the nature of its motivational relationship to the state, i.e., its identification with public goals and the adaptation of these to its needs, the industrial system will not long be regarded as something apart from government. Rather it will increasingly be seen as part of a much larger complex which embraces both the industrial system and the state. Private enterprise was anciently so characterized because it was subordinate to the market and those in command derived their power from ownership of private property. The modern corporation is no longer subordinate to the market; those who run it no longer depend on property ownership for their authority. They must have autonomy within a framework of goals. But this fully allows them to work in association with the bureaucracy and, indeed, to perform for the bureaucracy tasks that it cannot do, or cannot do as well, for itself. In consequence, so we have seen, for tasks of technical sophistication, there is a close fusion of the industrial system with the state. Members of the technostructure work closely with their public counterparts not only in the development and manufacture of products but in advising them of their needs. Were it not so celebrated in ideology, it would long since have been agreed that the line that now divides public from so-called private organization in military procurement, space exploration and atomic energy is so indistinct as to be nearly imperceptible. Men move easily across the line. On retirement, admirals and generals, as well as high civil servants, go more or less automatically to the more closely associated industries. One experienced observer has already called these firms the 'semi-nationalized' branch of the economy.[1] It has been noted, 'the Market mechanism [is replaced by] . . . the administrative mechanism. For the profit share of private entrepreneurs, it substitutes the fixed fee, a payment in lieu of profits foregone. And for the independent private business unit, it substitutes the integrated hierarchical structure of an organization composed of an agency . . . and its contractors.'[2]

The foregoing refers to firms which sell most of their output

1. Murray L. Weidenbaum, 'The Defense-Space Complex: Impact on Whom?' *Challenge. The Magazine of Economic Affairs*, April 1956. Professor Weidenbaum is a former employee of Boeing.

2. From a study by Richard Tybout, *Government Contracting in Atomic Energy* (Ann Arbor: University of Michigan Press, 1956), p. 175. Professor Tybout is referring especially to cost-plus-fixed-fee contracts.

to the government – to Boeing which (at this writing) sells 65 per cent of its output to the government; General Dynamics which sells a like percentage; Raytheon which sells 70 per cent; Lockheed which sells 81 per cent; and Republic Aviation which sells 100 per cent.[3] But firms which have a smaller proportion of sales to the government are more dependent on it for the regulation of aggregate demand and not much less so for the stabilization of wages and prices, the underwriting of especially expensive technology and the supply of trained and educated manpower.

So comprehensive a relationship cannot be denied or ignored indefinitely. Increasingly it will be recognized that the mature corporation, as it develops, becomes part of the larger administrative complex associated with the state. In time the line between the two will disappear. Men will look back in amusement at the pretence that once caused people to refer to General Dynamics and North American Aviation and A. T. & T. as *private* business.

Though this recognition will not be universally welcomed, it will be healthy. There is always a presumption in social matters in favour of reality as opposed to myth. The autonomy of the technostructure is, to repeat yet again, a functional necessity of the industrial system. But the goals this autonomy serves allow some range of choice. If the mature corporation is recognized to be part of the penumbra of the state, it will be more strongly in the service of social goals. It cannot plead its inherently private character or its subordination to the market as cover for the pursuit of different goals of particular interest to itself. The public has an unquestioned tendency to pursue goals that reflect its own interest and convenience and to adapt social objective thereto. But it cannot plead this as a superior right. There may well be danger in this association of public and economic power. But it is less if it is recognized.

Other changes can be imagined. As the public character of the mature corporation comes to be recognized, attention will

3. Data from Michael D. Reagan, *Politics, Economics and the General Welfare* (Chicago: Scott, Foresman and Company, 1965), p. 113.

doubtless focus on the position of the stockholder in this corporation. This is anomalous. He is a passive and functionless figure, remarkable only in his capacity to share, without effort or even without appreciable risk, in the gains from the growth by which the technostructure measures its success. No grant of feudal privilege has ever equalled, for effortless return, that of the grandparent who bought and endowed his descendants with a thousand shares of General Motors or General Electric. The beneficiaries of this foresight have become and remain rich by no exercise of effort or intelligence beyond the decision to do nothing, embracing as it did the decision not to sell. But these matters need not be pursued here. Questions of equity and social justice as between the fortuitously rich have their own special expertise.

IV

Most of the individual developments which are leading, if the harshest term may be employed, to the socialization of the mature corporation will be conceded, even by men of the most conservative disposition. The control by the mature corporation over its prices, its influence on consumer behaviour, the euthanasia of stockholder power, the regulation by the state of aggregate demand, the effort to stabilize prices and wages, the role of publicly supported research and development, the role of military, space and related procurement, the influence of the firm on these government activities and the modern role of education are, more or less, accepted facts of life.

What is avoided is reflection on the consequences of putting them all together, of seeing them as a system. But it cannot be supposed that the principal beams and buttresses of the industrial system have all been changed and that the structure remains as before. If the parts have changed, so then has the whole. If this associates the mature corporation inextricably with the state, the fact cannot be exorcised by a simple refusal to add.

It will be urged, of course, that the industrial system is not the whole economy. Apart from the world of General Motors,

Standard Oil, Ford, General Electric, U.S. Steel, Chrysler, Texaco, Gulf, Western Electric and Du Pont is that of the independent retailer, the farmer, the shoe repairman, the bookmaker, narcotics peddler, pizza merchant and that of the car and dog laundry. Here prices are not controlled. Here the consumer is sovereign. Here pecuniary motivation is unimpaired. Here technology is simple and there is no research or development to make it otherwise. Here there are no government contracts; independence from the state is a reality. None of these entrepreneurs patrol the precincts of the Massachusetts Institute of Technology in search of talent. The existence of all this I concede. And this part of the economic system is not insignificant. It is not, however, the part of the economy with which this book has been concerned. It has been concerned with the world of the large corporation. This too is important; and it is more deeply characteristic of the modern industrial scene than the dog laundry or the small manufacturer with a large idea. One should always cherish one's critics and protect them where possible from foolish error. The tendency of the mature corporation in the industrial system to become part of the administrative complex of the state ought not to be refuted by appeal to contrary tendencies outside the industrial system.

Some who dislike the notion that the industrial system merges into the state in its development will be tempted to assault not the tendency but those who adumbrate it. This, it must be urged, is not in keeping with contemporary ethics and manners. Once the bearers of bad tidings were hanged, disembowelled or made subject to some other equally sanguinary mistreatment. Now such reaction is regarded as lacking in delicacy. A doctor can inform even the most petulant client that he has terminal cancer without fear of adverse physical consequences. The aide who must advise a politician that a new poll shows him to be held in all but universal distaste need exercise only decent tact. Those who find unappealing the present intelligence are urged to exercise similar restraint. They should also be aware of the causes. It is part of the vanity of modern man that he can decide the character of his economic system. His area of decision is, in fact, exceedingly small. He could, conceivably, decide whether or not he wishes to have a high level of industrialization. Thereafter the imperatives of organization, technology and planning operate similarly, and we have seen to a broadly similar result, on all societies. Given the decision to have modern industry, much of what happens is inevitable and the same.

V

The two questions most asked about an economic system are whether it serves man's physical needs and whether it is consistent with his liberty. There is little doubt as to the ability of the industrial system to serve man's needs. As we have seen, it is able to manage them only because it serves them abundantly. It requires a mechanism for making men want what it provides. But this mechanism would not work – wants would not be subject to manipulation – had not these wants been dulled by sufficiency.[4]

The prospects for liberty involve far more interesting questions. It has always been imagined, especially by conservatives, that to associate all, or a large part, of economic activity with the state is to endanger freedom. The individual and his preferences, in one way or another, will be sacrificed to the needs and conveniences of the apparatus created ostensibly to serve him. As the industrial system evolves into a penumbra of the state, the question of its relation to liberty thus arises in urgent form. In recent years, in the Soviet-type economies, there has been an ill-concealed conflict between the state and the intellectuals. In essence, this has been a conflict between those for whom the needs of the government, including above all its needs as economic planner and producer of goods, are preeminent and those who assert the high but inconvenient claims

4. As indicated in Chapter 21 (and as I have urged at length on other occasions), it excludes the unqualified and the unfortunate from its beneficence.

of uninhibited intellectual and artistic expression. Is this a warning?

The instinct which warns of dangers in this association of economic and public power is sound. It comes close to being the subject of this book. But conservatives have looked in the wrong direction for the danger. They have feared that the state might reach out and destroy the vigorous, money-making entrepreneur. They have not noticed that, all the while, the successors to the entrepreneur were uniting themselves ever more closely with the state and rejoicing in the result. They were also, and with enthusiasm, accepting abridgement of their freedom. Part of this is implicit in the subordination of individual personality to the needs of organization. Some of it is in the exact pattern of the classical business expectation. The president of Republic Aviation is not much more likely in public to speak critically, or even candidly, of the Air Force than is the head of a Soviet *combinat* of the ministry to which he reports. No modern head of the Ford Motor Company will ever react with the same pristine vigour to the presumed foolishness of Washington as did its founder. No head of Montgomery Ward will ever again breathe defiance of a President as did Sewell Avery. Manners may be involved. But it would also be conceded that 'too much is at stake'.

The problem, however, is not the freedom of the businessman. Business orators have spoken much about freedom in the past. But it can be laid down as a rule that those who speak most of liberty are least inclined to use it. The high executive who speaks fulsomely of personal freedom carefully submits his speeches on the subject for review and elimination of controversial words, phrases and ideas, as befits a good organization man. The general who tells his troops, and the world, that they are in the forefront of the fight for freedom is a man who has always submitted happily to army discipline. The high State Department official, who adverts feelingly to the values of the free world extravagantly admires the orthodoxy of his own views.

The danger to liberty lies in the subordination of belief to the needs of the industrial system. In this the state and the industrial system will be partners. This threat has already been assessed, as also the means for minimizing it.

VI

If we continue to believe that the goals of the industrial system – the expansion of output, the companion increase in consumption, technological advance, the public images that sustain it – are coordinate with life, then all of our lives will be in the service of these goals. What is consistent with these ends we shall have or be allowed; all else will be off limits. Our wants will be managed in accordance with the needs of the industrial system; the policies of the state will be subject to similar influence; education will be adapted to industrial need; the disciplines required by the industrial system will be the conventional morality of the community. All other goals will be made to seem precious, unimportant or antisocial. We will be bound to the ends of the industrial system. The state will add its moral, and perhaps some of its legal, power to their enforcement. What will eventuate, on the whole, will be the benign servitude of the household retainer who is taught to love her mistress and see her interests as her own, and not the compelled servitude of the field hand. But it will not be freedom.

If, on the other hand, the industrial system is only a part, and relatively a diminishing part, of life, there is much less occasion for concern. Aesthetic goals will have pride of place; those who serve them will not be subject to the goals of the industrial system; the industrial system itself will be subordinate to the claims of these dimensions of life. Intellectual preparation will be for its own sake and not for the better service to the industrial system. Men will not be entrapped by the belief that apart from the goals of the industrial system – apart from the production of goods and income by progressively more advanced technical methods – there is nothing important in life.

The foregoing being so, we may, over time, come to see the

industrial system in fitting light as an essentially technical arrangement for providing convenient goods and services in adequate volume. Those who rise through its bureaucracy will so see themselves. And the public consequences will be in keeping, for if economic goals are the only goals of the society it is natural that the industrial system should dominate the state and the state should serve its ends. If other goals are strongly asserted, the industrial system will fall into its place as a detached and autonomous arm of the state, but responsive to the larger purposes of the society.

We have seen wherein the chance for salvation lies. The industrial system, in contrast with its economic antecedents, is intellectually demanding. It brings into existence, to serve its intellectual and scientific needs, the community that, hopefully, will reject its monopoly of social purpose.

AN ADDENDUM ON ECONOMIC
METHOD AND THE NATURE
OF SOCIAL ARGUMENT

It has generally held true that the accredited learned class and the seminaries of the higher learning have looked askance at all innovation. THORSTEIN VEBLEN, *The Theory of the Leisure Class.*

It is not, in general, my instinct to avoid controversy or criticism. Those who seek to do so have, not infrequently, reconciled themselves to irrelevance. But it is probably unwise to invite criticism that assumes innocence when, in fact, one is writing after what may well have been excessively solemn deliberation. Economics, like other disciplines, has its canons by which behaviour is judged. These, in general, call for careful specialization on particular issues; for having one person deal with one subject at a time; for according a very high priority to economic judgements; and, on the whole, for being suspicious of change. All of these canons have been violated in the preceding pages. Some professional wrath may be contained and some will certainly be understood if this is known to be highly deliberate and if the reasons for not worshipping at these accepted altars are adumbrated. Let me deal first with specialization.

Economists, on the whole, think well of what they do themselves and much less well of what their professional colleagues do. If a scholar probes deeply into a small section of the subject, he is fairly certain to mistrust, as superficial, the man who ranges more widely. The latter, in turn, will think the specialist lacking in vision or what is called reach. By knowing ever more about ever less, he will seem to risk becoming quite ignorant. Those who are mathematically inclined see others as in retreat from rigour. The others think those who manipulate symbols impractical. The statisticians believe those who prove points deductively to be dangerously intuitive. But, by their colleagues, those who are controlled by numbers are often thought unduly cautious or even dull. It is exceedingly fortunate for the psychic health of the profession that inadequacy lies so uniformly with others. The situation in the other social sciences is said to be equally satisfactory.

This book has not, it will be agreed, been confined to narrow points. But I have singularly little quarrel with those who so restrict themselves. I have drawn on their work, quantitative and qualitative, at every stage; I could not have written without their prior efforts. So I have nothing but admiration and gratitude for the patient and sceptical men who get deeply into questions, and I am available to support their application to the Ford Foundation however minute the matter to be explored. I expect them to judge sternly the way their material has been used in this book.

But we must remind ourselves that specialization is a scientific convenience, not a scientific virtue. It allows, among other things, the use of a wider spectrum of talent. A quarter of a century ago, at the University of California, there were specialists not on economic theory, not on price theory, not on agricultural prices, not on fruit prices but on prune prices and citrus prices. These were not great men but they did useful work and were highly respected by the prune growers and citrus cooperatives. They would have been less useful if exposed to more cosmic questions or even diversified to artichokes. Specialization also permits an indispensable division of scientific labour and allows for the development of subcultures of scholarship in which participants are known to each other, communicate readily, and from cooperation, competition, criticism and scholarly recrimination deepen their knowledge of their own subject matter. But, at least in the social sciences, specialization is also a source of error. The world to its discredit does not divide neatly along the lines that separate the specialists. These lines were drawn in the first instance by deans, department chairmen or academic committees. They were meant to provide guidance in appointing professors, establishing courses and supporting research. Excellent though the architects were, they cannot be credited with a uniquely valid view of the segments into which society naturally divides itself. And if they could there would still be danger that the specialist, in concentrating on his specialty, would deny himself knowledge that could only be had from outside.

In economics, economic theory – the subject which deals with the way prices, output and incomes for individuals, firms and the economy at large are decided – is one area of specialization. The corporation is another. Decision theory – how decisions are reached in complex organizations – is yet another and more modern field. For many years those who specialize on the problems of the corporation have been much concerned with the way control in the large firm has been passing without recourse from stockholders to the hired management. The latter, as sufficiently noted in this study, selects itself and its successors as an autonomous and self-perpetuating oligarchy. Reasons in the past have been sought by the specialists in their own area of concern – in the control of proxy machinery by management, in failure to keep stockholders informed, in the practice of holding annual meetings in obscure New Jersey hamlets where none but the most intrepid stockholder would penetrate. Remedy has been sought (with no visible effect on the way corporations are controlled) in these same areas, i.e., within the field of corporate practice. We have seen that a highly plausible reason for the shift in control of the corporations is the declining importance of capital in relation to trained manpower, and the increasing complexity of decision-making in the modern corporation. There is less power gained from having supplied capital; there are fewer decisions on which the stockholder can hope to intervene. Those who make decisions have greatly increased bargaining power. But questions concerning the supply of capital and labour belong to the economic theorist, and the problems of decision-making belong to the specialist on decision theory. In general their knowledge has not been brought to bear on the changing constitution of the corporation.[1]

1. To make error reciprocal, the economic theorists have assumed (and most still do) that the men who ran the business received the profits.

Thus to deal with the larger matrix of change is to complement and very possibly to illuminate the work of the specialist on his own specialty. Since it does not follow that the work on smaller points is any less necessary, the conclusion that emerges seems clear. In economics, and social sciences generally, one may justly distinguish between competent and incompetent work. As between kinds of work, judgement, save as it may be necessary to support the self-esteem of the man who is praising his own line, is less wise.

II

According to the experience of all but the most accomplished jugglers, it is easier to keep one ball in the air than many. To deal simultaneously, or even in close sequence, with all of the interrelated changes which have shaped the industrial system and the modern organized economy, is more difficult than to deal with one change or a few. The problem of exposition is especially taxing. All who write on economic matters must decide how much of the burden of exposition to shoulder themselves and how much of the task they should leave to the reader. Justice requires, no doubt, that much be left to the reader. Writing is hard enough work without having to make it comprehensible, and scholarship endorses a division of labour between those who write and those who read.

I have, on occasion, found the problem of exposition more taxing than that of analysis. And doubtless the reader has found passages that he has considered worthy of his mettle. But it has not been my purpose to test it. There are few, if any, useful ideas in economics that cannot be expressed in clear English. Obscurity rarely if ever denotes complexity of subject matter; it never denotes superior scholarship. It usually signifies either inability to write clear English or – and more commonly – muddled or incomplete thought.

All specialists in corporation matters knew the managers to be recipients (in the main) of salaried income and to be normally quite independent of those who own the enterprise and receive the profits. But theirs was a different field.

Addendum on Economic Method

And though to deal with change comprehensively is a source of difficulty, it is also a great simplification. In real life change in one place does beget change in other places, and the latter changes react on the first and elsewhere. Accordingly, to deal with the complex of change is to deal with the world as it is. A change in one place alerts one to likely change elsewhere. In searching for causes, one has before him the companion changes that are the most likely causes.

Also, since one is dealing with things as they are, one can check conclusions for their consistency with what exists or seems to exist. The reader of these pages will have seen, I venture to think, how usefully this test can be employed. To see change comprehensively, or as much so as may be possible, is also to be prepared for what otherwise may seem odd. The unwashed and unlettered men who came out of the fens and down from the north to Runnymede in 1215 derived their power from their control of land. The Great Charter, accordingly, is mostly concerned with the just and unjust liabilities of the landed. The protection it was subsequently to accord to the liberties of the landless was foreseen, if at all, only by the philosophical, if any. To King John this intrusion of landed power upon divine right seemed arbitrary, impertinent and uncouth, and of highly questionable legitimacy. It greatly justified him in his intention not to honour his signature.

In the last century capital became more important than land. Power associated itself with this. To the older ruling classes the new capitalists again seemed obtrusive, uncivilized and of questionable legitimacy.

In recent times, through the agency of the union, substantial economic power accrued to labour. Political power once again went with it. Union exercise of political power seemed of highly questionable legitimacy. Labour leaders were widely advised to leave politics alone.

In yet more recent times, complex technology and highly developed organization have become important for economic success. One would expect power to pass to those who are skilled in guiding or serving organization. One would also expect the sources of such specialized manpower to win prestige and authority. One would also be prepared to learn that this new exercise of power appeared to many to be impertinent and obtrusive and of questionable legitimacy.

The legitimacy of the non-owning management of the modern corporation has been deeply questioned. The displacement of the owning stockholder has been viewed with alarm. So have the growing power and assertiveness of the universities which supply this manpower. Faculty members and students have played a significant, and in some cases strategic, role in civil rights legislation, educational policy, and, most important, in foreign policy where they have ended, one hopes decisively, a long habit of acquiescence in whatever was officially proclaimed to be the policy of the United States. Their political role is important in some states. By professional politicians with a comfortable identification with business and labour, and by the traditional archons of the foreign policy, this academic intrusion has seemed impertinent and irregular and a highly illegitimate use of scholarly energy. All concerned have been strongly advised to confine themselves to the campus.

To view the new power of the managers or the more assertive role of the universities in isolation from other change is to see almost nothing of their significance. They are minor eddies in the pattern of life, the sort of thing that attracts attention for a season. But viewed in the whole context of change, as part of a new and further transfer of power to organization and to those who supply it with talent, it becomes a development of durable importance, as this book has duly urged.

III

The advantages of dealing comprehensively with change are considerable. Those of dealing with change that extends beyond economics are also great and, with passage of time, become more so. That is because with improvement in popular well-being, economics becomes progressively more inadequate as a basis for social judgement and as a guide to public policy. This too calls for a brief comment.

If people are hungry, ill-clad, unsheltered or diseased, nothing is so important as to remedy their condition. Higher income is the basic remedy; their problem is thus an economic problem. It will be time to worry about leisure, contemplation, the appreciation of beauty and the other higher purposes of life when everyone has had a decent meal. Even personal liberty is best defended and spiritual salvation best pursued on a full stomach. In a poor society, economics is not all of life but, as a practical matter, it is most of it.

With high income, questions beyond the reach of economics obtrude. These require consideration of how much beauty should be sacrificed for increased output. Or how many civilized values in order that goods can be more effectively sold – for no experience suggests that sober and quiet truth is as valuable for this purpose as meretricious and raucous violence. Or how extensively should education be accommodated to the needs of production as opposed to the needs of enlightenment? Or how much discipline should be enforced on men to ensure greater output? Or how much military risk should be run to win new technology? Or how completely should the individual subordinate his personality to the organization which was created to supply his wants?

That these questions, or some of them, are important has long been conceded by economists; textbooks, teachers and economists in high office regularly warn that economic judgements are not the total judgement on life. This warning having been given, economics is then, routinely, made the final test of public policy. The rate of increase in income and output in National Income and Gross National Product, together with the amount of unemployment, remains the all but exclusive measure of social achievement. This is the modern morality. St Peter is assumed to ask applicants only what they have done to increase the G.N.P.

There are good reasons for this insistence on the totality of economic goals. It arrests what otherwise would be a disconcerting obsolescence in the profession of economics. For so long as social achievement is coterminous with economic performance, economists are the highest arbiters of social policy. Otherwise not. Theirs is an eminence not to be sacrificed casually.

There is a further advantage in economic goals. The quality of life is subjective and disputable. Cultural and aesthetic progress cannot easily be measured. Who can say for sure what arrangements best allow for the development of individual personality? Who can be certain what advances the total of human happiness? Who can guess how much clean air or uncluttered highways are enjoyed? Gross National Product and the level of unemployment, on the other hand, are objective and measurable. To many it will always seem better to have measurable progress toward the wrong goals than unmeasurable and hence uncertain progress toward the right ones. But this would hardly have served the purposes of this book.

IV

The supremacy of economic goals is also vital for the division of labour within the field of economics. For specialization is only possible if the specialists are united by a common and accepted goal. As matters now stand a man can work on the economics of the textile, steel or chemical industry or he can concern himself with agriculture, labour or transportation and be secure in the knowledge that if a course of policy makes possible a larger output with given resources it is socially sound. Were it open to a man working on textile, steel or chemicals to conclude that social virtue lay on the side of smaller production of these things with more relaxed conditions of toil or less air or water pollution, there would be chaos. He would have, however gently, to be retired. The situation of a labour economist who concluded that too many men were already at work producing things of marginal, sub-marginal or carcinomatous significance would be sadly similar. That of a specialist on fiscal policy who urged a particular tax because he sought a lower rate of growth, more sharing of work and a larger amount of leisure would be the most difficult of all. A serious, as distinct from a purely oral, concern for larger social goals would have an exceedingly disturbing effect on economics as it is professionally practised.

Some adverse reaction can even now be detected. The espousal of non-economic goals has an aspect of menace from which the professionally sensitive automatically recoil. They dismiss such extra-economic concerns as 'soft', which is to say that they are professionally sub-standard.

Yet professional convenience and vested interest are not the safest guides in social thought. The questions that are beyond the reach of economics – the beauty, dignity, pleasure and durability of life – may be inconvenient but they are important.

V

In a book that has much to do with change, it is perhaps particularly useful to say a word about the economist's reaction to change. It tends to be conservative and this is true not only of the few who call themselves conservatives but of quite a number who unhesitantly describe themselves as liberals.

The reasons trace to the twofold character of change in economics. In the physical sciences – chemistry, physics, biology – change is associated only with discovery, with the improving state of knowledge. The matter being studied does not change. In economics, as in the other social sciences, there is change both in the state of knowledge and in what is being studied. There is improvement in the knowledge of the way prices are established. There is also change in the *way* prices are established. This will happen as the small proprietorship with no control of its market gives way to the giant corporation which has such control, or as both make way for government price-fixing.

Economists are not inherently resistant to novelty but they react very differently to the two types of change. New knowledge or new interpretations of existing knowledge are much welcomed. Changes in the underlying institutions are much more slowly assimilated.

Thus at any time in the last fifty years a new view of wage determination in competitive markets would have been quickly taken up. Some were. But the existence of the trade union was for a long time unrecognized in the theory of wages. Although the labour economist took unions for granted, the more prestigious economic theorist continued to assume 'an absence of impediments' in the labour market.[2] Similarly the theory of the firm, and how it maximizes its revenue in the market, has undergone endless refinement in recent decades. This theory assumes that the man who maximizes the revenue gets that revenue or a compelling share. So he does on a Wisconsin dairy farm. But this is not so in the modern large corporation where the management is on a salary and the beneficiaries are stockholders whom the managers have never seen. Although the large corporation, like the union, is far from new, it has never been really assimilated into the main body of economics.[3]

Extensive government procurement in areas of high technology; extensive government intervention on wages and prices; widespread affluence, with its evident effect on the economic problem that it partly solves, have still to work their passage into the main body of economic theory.

Conservatism in these matters is not without justification. The fringes of economic discussion have long been afflicted by aborted revolutions or ones that turned out to be inconsequential. The demonetization of silver, the N.R.A. codes, the effects of minimum wage legislation, court decisions bringing oligopoly within the ambit of the Sherman Act, the passage and

2. E.g., F. H. Knight, 'Wages and Labor Union Action in the Light of Economic Analysis,' in *The Public Stake in Union Power*, P. D. Bradley, ed. (Charlottesville: University of Virginia Press, 1959).

3. 'The functioning of the corporate system has not to date been adequately explained, or, if certain explanations are accepted as adequate, it seems difficult to justify.' Edward S. Mason in *The Corporation in Modern Society*, Edward S. Mason, ed. (Cambridge: Harvard University Press, 1959), p. 4. The author is the acknowledged dean of authorities on the modern corporation.

amendment of the Taft-Hartley Act were all such nine-day wonders. In the end they changed little. This has caused economists to take a conservative view of institutional change.

But economists also resist consequential and durable change because it seems more scientific to do so. Physics, chemistry, geology and biology are indubitably sciences; they are mounted on an unchanging subject matter. If economics is to be equally scientific, it presumably should have a similarly stable platform. If this does not exist, it can be assumed. To accept underlying change is to be dubiously respectful of the scientific aspirations of economics. To deny that it has relevance is to assume a much better scientific posture.

These attitudes also accord well with vested interest. Knowledge for the intellectual is what skill is for the artisan and capital for the businessman. In all, the instinct is to fear obsolescence. But the intellectual is in a far better position to resist obsolescence than the craftsman or businessman. The machine that replaces the craftsman is wholly tangible. His only line of resistance is overt – a strike or a sledgehammer to smash the thing. Both encounter social disfavour. The out-of-date machine of the businessman is equally objective. His modes of recourse – to regulate or suppress innovation – are equally reprehensible. But the intellectual can deny that there has been any change. The factors making for his alleged obsolescence, he can insist, are the figment of an undisciplined imagination. He can be a Luddite without violence and indeed without knowing it. It would be surprising indeed were such opportunity to be unexploited.

For a book which is concerned with change and its consequences, it is obviously desirable that the reader and the critic be disposed to accept both the fact and the importance of change. Thus this argument.

But one is aided by the fact that the change here examined is not unobtrusive. The work of modern science and technology is highly visible. It will be assumed by most that it must have its effects on economic organization and social behaviour. The great corporation is not easily concealed. Not many will imagine that the social impact of General Motors – on employees, markets, customers and the state – is the same as that of the Wisconsin dairy farm. The state is clearly a vastly greater force in economic affairs than it was fifty years ago. That science, technology and organization have placed new demands on educational institutions or that they have changed the balance of power as between capital and organization will not seem improbable.

Indeed many will agree that the burden of proof is on those who aver that these changes have left conclusions concerning economic life unchanged. And that, precisely, is where I wish to have that burden placed.

INDEX

Abrams, Frank, 133

Accepted sequence, 216, 217, 220–23

Adaptation: as motivation, 139, 144, 146, 152, 167–9; and compulsion, 140, 141; and identification, 142, 143; in the mature corporation, 162–3, 164; and political hostility, 319

Adelman, M. A., 39n., 42n., 84n.

Advertising, 208, 209–12, 215; TV and radio, 213; of job opportunities, 244n.; and the creation of wants, 276–7; intellectual community's disdain of, 297; truth in, 328–9, 330

Aesthetic experience, 349–50

Aesthetic goals: and the industrial system, 349–52; and the state, 352–6

Affluent Society, The, 9, 10, 11, 207n., 263n., 276n., 349n.

Agriculture: and prices, 40–41, 195n.–196n.

Air India, 111n.

Air pollution, 30

Airlines, 99n.–100n., 111n.

Airplanes: World War I, 29; World War II, 29; development of, 36–7, 314–15

Aldrich, Winthrop W., 87–8

Alexander, Herbert E., 309n.

Allis-Chalmers, 197

American Industry: Structure, Conduct, Performance, Caves, 12

American Telephone and Telegraph Company, 156, 361, 394

Antitrust laws, 189–202

Archbold, John D., 97n.

Architecture, 354–5

Armada, Spanish, 29

Artists, 352

Arts, state patronage of, 353–4

Associated Gas and Electric, 125

Atlantic and Pacific Tea Company, 91

Atomic Energy Commission, 318, 380

'Automation', ambiguity of, 240n.

Automobiles, 22–8

Autonomy: threats to, 89–91; in Great Britain, 107–9; in Ceylon, 109–11; in India, 109–11; in Soviet firms, 112–16; and the technostructure, 167, 173–7, 229–30; and the industrial system, 391

Avery, Sewell, 99, 268, 306, 398

Bain, Joe S., 85n.

Baldwin I, King of Jersalem, 60

Barkin, Solomon, 266, 280n.

Barlow, Robin, 145n.

Barnard, Chester I., 137n.

Barton, Bruce, 133

Baumol, William J., 132 and n., 174n., 177n.

Bennett, Harry, 98

Berg, Elliot J., 110n.

Berle, Adolf, 88n., 126n., 127, 305

413

Index

Bethlehem Steel Corporation, 93, 265n.
Bevan, Aneurin, 108
Blum, A. A., 272n.
Boeing Aircraft, 394
Bowen, William G., 245n., 254n., 255n., 258n.
Bradley, P. D., 410n.
Brazer, Harvey E., 145n.
Breech, Ernest, 99
Bribery, political, 305–6, 312–13
Bristol-Myers, 203
Brown, Emily Clark, 282n.
Bundy, McGeorge, 9
Business: stereotyped hierarchy of, 74–5; lack of prestige, 371
Business cycle, 15
Business schools, 371, 372–3

California, University of, 402
California Institute of Technology, 136, 153
Capital: required by advanced technology, 16, 17, 25; savings as source of, 44–8; and obtaining talent, 66
Carnegie Corporation, 10
Carnegie Institute of Technology, 138n.
Caves, Richard, 12
Celler-Kefauver Anti-merger Act, 189
Central bank, 287n.
Ceylon, 109–11
Chamberlain, Joseph, 64
Cheit, Earl F., 101n., 120n., 193n.
Chrysler Corporation, 128n.
Clayton Act, 189
Cleveland, H. van B., 150n.
Cold War: military competition during, 331–6; and the educational and scientific estate, 335–9; and advice of public officials, 338–40
Colleges and universities:

enrolment, 288; funds for, 289; as source of social innovation, 289–91; and control of their budgets, 374–5; and the industrial system, 374, 376–8. *See also* Educational and scientific estate
Committees: versus individuals, 69, 75; exchange and testing of information through, 72
Communist Party, 113. *See also* Cold War *and* Soviet Union
Compulsion: as motivation, 137, 146; and pecuniary compensation, 139–40, 141–2; and land, 146; in Soviet Union, 149–51; in the U.S., 151–2
Conformance, 138n.
Connor, John T., 58n., 103n.
Consolidation, industrial, 96–7
Consumer sovereignty, 216
Consumption: emphasis on, 47; and maximization of satisfaction, 217–20
Continental Trading Company, 87
Contracts, elimination of market uncertainty through, 40–41
Convergence, industrial societies and, 390–93
Coolidge, Calvin, 126
Corporations: growth of, 13–14; and corporate saving, 17; and the industrial system, 21; polyglot, 37; legal image of 81–2; kinds of, 82–3; large modern, 83–6; vulnerability to external intervention, 86–9; and retained earnings, 90; profits of, 91; influence of owners on, 91; small, 94–5; adaptability of, 94–6; and personal enrichment of managers, 125–6; declared purposes of, 132–4; goals of, 135–6, 154, 161–2, 165–7; and

Index

Corporations – *cont.*
motivation toward common
goals, 137–45; motivation in,
153–4; and regulation of
aggregate demand, 228. *See also
next two entries*

Corporations, entrepreneurial,
100; and wage-price spiral,
252–3; and unions, 268; and
the state, 301–9, 318–19. *See also*
Entrepreneur

Corporations, mature, 100;
motivation in, 155–64; and
price control, 194; and
wage-price spiral, 251–4; and
the state, 264–5, 311–12, 312–14,
318–19; political position of,
309–10; developing socialization
of, 393, 394–7

Council of Economic Advisers, 259

Couzens, James, 26–7

Crosland, C. A. R., 108n., 109n.

Crusades, the, 60

Curtis Publishing Company, 90

Decision-making: modern
industrial, 70–72; group, 72–6,
86; in market control, 75–8;
damaged by external
interference, 77–9; individual
versus group, 91–2

Defence: national, 14;
expenditures for, 232–3, 235–7;
procurement, 314–17, 317–19;
image-making and, 329–31,
334–6, 341–3

Defense, Department of, 314, 315,
317, 318, 334

Demand: stabilization of, 17;
management of, 205–7, 212–13;
and advertising, 208–12, 214–15;
and TV and radio, 213;
management of, and individual's
satisfaction, 221–3; aggregate,
regulation of, 224–37

Democratic Party, 382

Depression: and savings, 52, 227;
and union, 304

Devons, Ely, 114n.

Disarmament, 332, 335–6;
problem of, 340–42; necessity
for, 344–5

Dissonance, planned, 351

Dodge Brothers, 25, 26

Dorfman, Robert, 12, 130n., 186n.,
188n., 189n., 209n.

Dougall, Herbert E., 82n.

Downie, Jack, 132 and n.

Drake, Sir Francis, 29

Drucker, Peter, 98n.

Dudintsev, Vladimir, 114

Duesenberry, James S., 47n.

Dulles, John Foster, 333, 339

Dunlop, John T., 12, 280n.

Du Pont family, 91, 156, 306

Duscha, Julius, 331n., 342n.

Earnings: retained, 49, 225; and
management, 49; and
technostructure autonomy,
89–90, 173–5; as
technostructure goal, 181–3

Eastern Airlines, 91, 100n.

Economists, 401–2; and profit
maximization, 128–33; and
pecuniary motivation, 153; and
price control, 256–7; and goals
of the industrial system, 383–5;
and reaction to change, 408–12

Edsel (automobile), 23n., 211n.

Education: higher, expansion in,
15; labour force and, 239–44,
246–9; as the difference that
divides, 249–50; and
conservatives, 292n.; and worker
emancipation, 367–8, 369–71,
372; influence of industrial
system on, 372–5, 376–9;
alternative goals for, 375–6. *See
also next two entries*

Index

Educational and scientific estate:
power of, 287–8; and the
technostructure, 292–8; political
role, 298–9; and scrutiny of
Cold War imagery, 335–9; and
influence on educational goals,
368, 378; and responsibility for
political action and leadership,
381–3, 385–7; lack of confidence
of, 383–4

Educators: numbers of, 288; as
inferior caste, 289; and social
innovation, 290–91, 293–4

Eisenhower, Dwight D., 101,
334

Elk Hills transaction, 87

Elliott, Osborn, 100n., 103n.

Elliott, William Y., 150n.

Employment: 1951–64, 241–2;
full, 250. *See also*
Unemployment

Entrepreneur: replacement of,
79–80; role in consolidation,
96–8; as leader, 101, 102–3;
burden of taxes on, 230; and
battles with unions, 268–9;
educators' attitudes toward,
289–90, 291–2; and purchased
influence, 302–4; and fear of
the state, 306, 307–9, 311–12.
See also Corporations,
entrepreneurial

'Establishment, The', 325–7, 387

Executives: job security of, 102;
sustained by organization, 105;
salaries of, 123–4; motivations
of, 144–5; identification with
organization, 160–61. *See also*
Management

Fall, Albert B., 87

Federal Aviation Agency, 318

Federal Securities Act, 127

Federal Trade Commission Act,
189

Federal Triangle, Washington,
DC, 355

Fermi, Enrico, 75

Firestone family, 91

Fish, Lounsbury S., 69n.

Fisher, Franklin M., 209n., 216n.

Flagler, H. M., 97n.

Ford, Henry, 14, 25, 26, 98, 99,
101, 268, 306

Ford family, 14, 91

Ford Motor Company, 14, 26–7,
84, 98–9, 123n.; employment
and assets, 22–3; cars, 22–3, 24,
25, 26, 27–8, 211n.

Foreign policy, academic
community and, 338, 382–3

Fortune, quoted, 203

Friedman, Milton, 120n.

Friend, Irwin, 46n.

Gardner, John, 10

Gary, Elbert, 96n.

General Dynamics Corporation,
14, 36, 342, 394

General Electric Company, 36, 81,
130, 197, 306, 389

General Motors Corporation, 14,
16, 38–40, 81, 82, 84, 85, 98, 103,
130, 306, 389

Germany, slave workers in, 148–9

Gideonse, Harry D., 150n.

Girdler, Thomas, 268, 306

Goal(s): hierarchy of, 167;
corporate growth as, 177–83;
re-examination of, 347, 387;
of industrial system, 346,
399–400; aesthetic, 349–56;
economic, 407–9

Godfrey of Bouillon, 60

Goldwater, Barry, 262n., 309n.

Goodman, Paul, 216

Gordon, R. A., 69, 88, 123n.,
129n., 164n., 174n.

Government: *see* State, the

Grace, J. Peter, 100n.

Granick, David, 114n., 115, 282n.
Gray, Horace M., 42n.
Great Britain, 179; limited socialism in, 107–8
Great Charter, 405
Griliches, Zvi, 209n., 216n.
Groves, Major General Leslie R., 75
Growth, corporate: as goal, 177–83
Guthmann, Harry G., 82n.

Hacker, Andrew, 210n., 266n., 280n.
Hansen, Alvin, 228n.
Harbison, Frederick, 245n., 273n.
Harding, Warren G., 366
Harris, Seymour, 100n., 223n., 228n., 308n.
Hartley, Fred L., 346
Hindustan Machine Tool Company, 111n.
Hodges, Luther, 342n.
Hofstadter, Richarl, 193n.
Holden, Paul E., 69n.
Homer, Arthur B., 93
Housing, 362–4
Hughes, Howard, 37n., 99n.
Hughes Aircraft, 153
Humphreys, Colonel E. A., 87
Hungary, 49
Huntington, Collis P., 64

Identification: as motivation, 138–9, 144–5, 146, 152; and compulsion, 140; and adaptation, 142–3; of production workers, 157, 270–71; within the technostructure, 159–61, 163–4; consistency in, 167–8; and white-collar workers, 272–3; and political hostility, 319
Image-building: by the state, 329–31; and the Cold War, 331–6; and the space race, 343–4

Income objectives, 274–7
India, 14, 52, 61, 109–11
Individual(s): versus the organization, 69–70, 75; eminence sustained by the organization, 103–4; power of, and accepted sequence, 220–23
Industrial system: defined, 21; re-examination of goals of, 346–8; state services ignored by, 348–9; and aesthetic goals, 349–56; work and non-work under, 365–71; and education, 372–9; convergence between differing kinds of, 390–93; changing relationship to state, 392–5, 397–9; goals, 399–400
Inflation, 52, 256–7, 258–9, 262–3
Ingersoll-Rand, 197
Innovation, technical, 180–81
Insull, Samuel, 125
Intellectuals, 381, 382. *See also* Educational and scientific estate
Interest rate, 51
Investment, savings and, 225–7

Jet Propulsion Laboratory, 153
Johnson, G. C., 231n.
Johnson, Grace, 11

Kaysen, Carl, 12, 39n., 58n., 84n., 100n., 132, 175n., 190n., 209n., 216n., 223n., 308n.
Kefauver, Estes, 93
Kempton, Murray, quoted, 311
Kennedy, John F., 10, 76n., 260, 328
Kerr, Clark, 273n.
Keynes, John Maynard, 12, 52–3, 66, 228, 346; *General Theory*, 12, 52–3
Keynesian Revolution, 14, 17–18, 228–9n.
Khrushchev, Nikita, 150
Killingsworth, Charles C., 245n.

Index

Klein, Burton H., 149n.

Knight, F. H., 410n.

Korean War, wage-price spiral in, 254–5

Kreuger, Ivar, 126

Kuh, Edwin, 200n., 226n.

Labour, notion of division of, 23–4n.

Labour force: 19th century, 62; changes in, 238–9; effect of mechanization on, 241; white-collar versus blue-collar, 271–3, 279–80. *See also* Manpower

Land ownership, and power, 60–63, 65

Larner, R. J., 88n.

Lasagna, Louis, 293n.

Latin America, 53, 135

Leisure, 275–6, 365–6; versus work, 367–8

Levitt, Theodore, 121n., 134n.

Lewis, Ben W., 121n.

Lewis, John L., 281n.

Liberty: and the Cold War, 333; the economic system and, 396–9

Lipset, Seymour Martin, 291n.

Lockheed Aircraft, 153, 394

Loew's, 90

London School of Economics, 109

Los Alamos Laboratory, 75

Louis XIV, 354

McCann-Erickson, 209

McCarthy, Joseph, 339

McElroy, Neil H., 103

McNamara, Robert, 22n.

Macroeconomics, 188n.

Magna Carta, 405

Malcolmson, Alexander, 26

Malthus, Thomas, 56, 62

Management: power of, 58–9, 66–8; defined, 80; and profit maximization, 122–9. *See also* Executives

Manpower: specialized, 26, 27, 66, 70–72; need for educationally qualified, 239–44, 246–9; and mechanization, 241; early requirements for, 242–3. *See also* Labour force

March, James G., 138n., 159

Market(s): organization control of, 17–18; strategies for dealing with uncertainty in, 36–7, 47–8; control of, 38–41; and government intervention, 40–41; management of, 71–2; and group decision-making, 75–8; and the small firm, 94–5; and planning, 118–19; and price-making, 185–93; conflict of principle and practice in, 259–62; versus planning, 357–64

Marris, Robin, 35n., 129n., 132, 175n., 177n.

Marshall, Alfred, 56, 325

Marx, Karl, 294, 301, 324, 325, 341, 392; ideas on unemployment, 34, 273–4n.; on power, 57–8, 59; on capital, 147

Mason, Edward S., 12, 39n., 58n., 59n., 108n., 121n., 175n., 410n.

Masters, S. H., 255n.

Mattingly, Garrett, 29n.

Means, Gardiner, 88n., 126n., 305

Mechanization, labour force and, 241

Medici, Cosimo and Lorenzo, 354

Meyer, John R., 12, 200n., 226n.

Microeconomics, 188n.

Military procurement: see Defence

Mill, J. S., 56

Monopoly: and market power, 39n.; and prices, 185–93

Montgomery Ward, 99

Moon landing, 29–30. *See also* Space race
Moore, Wilbert E., 48n., 124n.
Morgan, James N., 145n.
Morgan, John Pierpont, 64, 96
Motivation, organizational, 137–9; relation between forces, 139–45; in the mature corporation, 155–64; paradox of, 177; of workers and unions, 269–70. *See also* Adaptation, Compulsion, Identification, *and* Pecuniary compensation
Murphy, Walter T., 22n.
Mustang (automobile), 22, 26, 28
Myers, Charles A., 273n.
Myers, Harold B., 309n.

National Recovery Administration (N.R.A.), 306, 410
National Resources Planning Board, 32
National (Aeronautics and) Space Agency (NASA), 153, 318, 380
Negroes, unemployment among, 246
Nelson, Gaylord, 331n.
Nelson, Lord Horatio, 29
Nelson, Ralph L., 331n.
Nevins, Allan, 22n., 28n., 97n.
New York Central Railroad, 90
Newcomer, Mabel, 88n., 123n., 164n.
Nieburg, H.L., 315n.
North American Aviation, 394
Norway, 14
Nuclear Test Ban Treaty of 1963, 337, 383

Ogilvy, Benson and Mather, 209
Oligopoly: price-making under, 185–93; and advertising, 209
Organization: versus the individual, 104–5; most famous definition of, 137

Output, expansion and contraction of, 177–8
Oxford University, 109

Pakistan, 53
Palmer, A.M.F., 108n.
Payne, Oliver H., 97n.
Pecuniary compensation: as motivation, 136, 137, 146, 147–8, 152–4, 167–8; and compulsion, 139–40, 141–2, 143; paradox of, 144–5; stockholders and, 156; and production workers, 157–8
Perkins, James, 10
Persuasion, growth in apparatus of, 15. *See also* Advertising
Peter the Great, 354
Peter the Hermit, 60
Peterson, Shorey, 130n., 178n.
Philip II, King of Spain, 28
Pigou, A.C., 12
Planning: necessity for, 27; ideological overtones of, 32–3; in the market economy, 33–6; and industrial size, 41–3; versus the market, 357–8; and transportation, 359–60, 361–2; and telephone service, 360–61; and urban development, 362–3
Poland, 14, 49
Power: and the factors of production, 55–62, 64–6; in 19th-century England, 64; contrasting impression of, 64–5; shift of, 66–8; group, 72–80; modern corporate, 133–4; in the technostructure, 173–4
Power, General Thomas S., 331n., 333n.
Pratt, Charles, 97n.
Price, Don K., 287n., 342n.
Price(s): control, 38–40, 194–8, 254–7; and profit maximization, 120; stable, 198–200; changing of, 199–200; imperfection in

Index

Price(s) – *cont.*
control of, 203–4; and
management of demand, 204–5;
benefits of, 257–9
Procter and Gamble, 103
Production: relation between
factors of, 55–6; increased, as
goal, 169–70, 176–9
Profit maximization, 120–23; and
management, 123–9; and
economic theory, 128–32; and
corporation, 133–4; and
declared purposes of
pecuniary compensation, 136;
as goal, 176–9
Public Policies Toward Business,
Wilcox, 12
Public services, negative
discrimination against, 348–9
Public Utility Holding Company
Act of 1935, 127

Radio, 213, 279
Railroads, 90, 360
RAND, 337
Raskin, A.H., 258n.
Raytheon Corporation, 394
Reagan, Michael D., 394n.
Recession: prevention of, 53;
effect on personal savings, 227
Religion and land, 60–61
Republic Aviation, 394
Revised sequence, 217–20
Ricardo, David, 56, 62, 63
Rickenbacker, Eddie, 100n.
Ripley, William Z., 126
Rockefeller, John D., 14, 87, 88,
96, 97n., 183
Rockefeller, John D., Jr, 88
Rogers, H. H., 97n.
Rose, Billy, 156
Rostow, Eugene V., 121n., 133n.
Runciman, Steven, 60n.
Rusk, Dean, 333n., 339
Russia, *see* Soviet Union

Safeway, 91
Salaries, executive, 122–4
Samuelson, Paul A., 12, 55n.,
130n., 188n., 209n., 216, 218n.,
220n., 228n., 235n., 257n., 262n.
Satisfaction, maximization of,
217–20
Sauckel, Fritz, 149n.
Savings: for capital formation,
44–6; personal and business in
1965, 46; volume determined by
government, 49–50; industrial,
49, 51–2; problem of
management and use of, 52–3;
and planning, 52–4; paradox
of, 66; personal, 53; effect of
Great Depression on, 225–6, 227
Say, Jean Baptiste, 226; Law of
Markets, 224
Schlesinger, Arthur M., Jr, 11–12
Schor, Stanley, 46n.
Schultze, Charles L., 254–5n.
Schumpeter, Joseph A., 79n.
Scientists: emergence of, as
independent force, 383;
responsibility of, 385–6
Sears, Roebuck, 37, 91
Securities and Exchange
Commission, 127
Seligman, Ben B., 97n., 240n.
Sequence: accepted, 216, 217–18,
220–23; revised, 217–20
Shah Jahan, 354
Sherman Act, 189, 410
Silberman, Charles E., 240n.
Simon, Herbert A., 137n., 138,
159
Skybolt missile, 315–16
Slavery, 140, 141–2, 146–7; in
Germany, 149
Smith, Adam, 24n., 56, 62, 63n.,
142, 148n.; *Wealth of Nations*,
350
Smith, Rev. Gerald L. K., 259
Smith, Hubert L., 69n.

Index

Smith, Richard Austin, 37n., 265n., 342n.

Smyth, Henry De Wolf, 75n.

Socony-Vacuum Company, 38

Sohio, 38

Sorbonne, 109

Sorenson, Charles E., 98

Soviet Union: autonomy in, 112–16; compulsion in, 149–51; price control in, 196; and the Cold War, 311–2, 335–6, 338, 339–40, 342–3; and the space race, 343

Space race, 14, 343–4

Spain, 29

Specialists, coordination of, 27

Specialization, economics and, 401–4, 408

Speer, Albert, 149n.

Standard Oil Company, 14

Standard Oil of Indiana, 87

Standard Oil of New Jersey, 81, 84, 97n., 130

Starr, John, 88n.

State, the: economic activity of, 14–15; elimination of market uncertainty by, 40–41; and savings, 49, 51–2; and technostructure autonomy, 176–7; spending and aggregate demand, 230–33; relation between technostructure and, 300–308; and the mature corporation, 312, 313, 318–19; image-building as tool of, 329–31, 334–6; and the industrial system, 348–9, 392–5, 397–9; and the aesthetic dimension, 351–6; funds for education, 374–5

Steel industry: suits against, 198; price restraints in, 260, 265n.; work week, 366

Stewart, Colonel Robert W., 87, 88

Stigler, George J., 120n., 204n.

Stockholders, power of, 58–9, 86–9, 92–3; profit maximization for, 122–3; and corporation goals, 156–7

Studebaker Company, 98, 342

Sutton, Francis X., 100n., 223n., 308n.

Sweden, 14

Taft-Hartley Act, 411

Talent, specialized coordination of, 27, 66, 70–72

Taxes: personal and corporate income, 230, 232; corporation income, 307

Teapot Dome transaction, 87

Technology: large capital requirements for, 16, 17, 25; and expansive business organization, 16; and the modern state, 17; underwriting of, 19, 170; as the application of organized knowledge, 23; consequences of, 24–8; problem-solving as feature of, 29–30; as enemy of the market, 43; and need for specialized talent, 66, 70–71; virtuosity in, 180–81, 182

Technostructure: defined, 80; and corporations, 86, 90–91; protected from outside interference, 89–90; threats to autonomy of, 90–91; power of, 106; goals of, 118–19; and profit maximization, 122–3; autonomy in, 172–7; and price control, 194–202; and unions, 269–70, 271; and the educational and scientific estate, 292–9; and the state, 300–308; and the armed services, 314–17, 318–19; problem of reproducing, 371

Telephone service, 360–61

Television, 213, 379
Thompson J. Walter, Agency, 209
Thornton, Charles 'Tex', 100n.
Tobin, James, 100n., 223n., 308n.
Toynbee, Arnold J., quoted, 106
Trade Unions: *see* Unions
Transportation, urban and interurban surface, 359–60, 361
Troy, Leo, 279n.
Turner, Donald F., 190n.
TWA (Trans World Airlines), 99n.
Tybout, Richard, 393n.

Unemployment: and educational qualifications, 244–5, 251; among racial minorities, 246; and industrial change, 246; in western Europe, 248n.; and inflation, 258–9
Unions: decline of, 15, 266–7, 267–74, 278–9; membership in, 15, 279; power of, 65n., 251–2; and white-collar workers, 279–80; and accommodation to technological change, 281; in Soviet countries, 281–2; as factor in planning, 282–4; and wage and price stabilization, 284; given impetus by Great Depression, 304
United Automobile Workers, 279
United Mine Workers, 279n.
U.S. Department of Commerce: pamphlet on capitalism, 20, 49n., 59n., 187n.; on efficient pricing, 187
U.S. Department of Defense, 314, 315, 317, 318, 334
U.S. Department of State, 339
United States Steel Corporation, 40, 91, 96, 185, 261, 265n., 306, 389
United Steel Workers, 260, 279
Universities: *see* Colleges and universities
Urban development, need for planning in, 362–4

Van Sweringen, M. J., 126
Van Sweringen, O. P., 126
Veblen, Thorstein, 289n., 291n., 401
Vertical integration, 37–8, 41
Victory, ship, 29

Wage guideposts, 261
Wants, creation of, 274–7
Water pollution, 30
Weapons competition, economic importance of, 340–45. *See also* Defence
Weidenbaum, Murray L., 311, 393n.
Weintraub, Sidney, 254n.
Weir, Ernest, 268, 306
Werner, M. R., 88n.
Westinghouse, 197
Wheeling Steel, 37–8n., 90
Whitehead, Alfred North, quoted, 117
Whitney, Richard, 122
Whyte, William H., Jr, 160n., 161n.
Wiener, Norbert, quoted, 238
Wiggin, Albert H., 126
Wilcox, Clair, 12
Williams, Andrea, 11
Work week, 365
Workers, white-collar, 270–73. 278–80. *See also* Labour force *and* Manpower
World War, Second, wage-price spiral in, 254